Leslie A. Adelson
Cosmic Miniatures and the Future Sense

Interdisciplinary German Cultural Studies

Edited by
Irene Kacandes

Volume 22

Leslie A. Adelson

Cosmic Miniatures and the Future Sense

―

Alexander Kluge's 21st-Century Literary Experiments
in German Culture and Narrative Form

DE GRUYTER

ISBN 978-3-11-061108-3
e-ISBN (PDF) 978-3-11-052564-9
e-ISBN (EPUB) 978-3-11-052432-1
ISSN 1861-8030

Library of Congress Cataloging-in-Publication Data
A CIP catalog record for this book has been applied for at the Library of Congress.

Bibliographic information published by the Deutsche Nationalbibliothek
The Deutsche Nationalbibliothek lists this publication in the Deutsche Nationalbibliografie;
detailed bibliographic data are available on the Internet at http://dnb.dnb.de.

© 2018 Walter de Gruyter GmbH, Berlin/Boston
This volume is text- and page-identical with the hardback published in 2017.
Cover image: Saturn © oorka/iStock/thinkstock
Printing and binding: CPI books GmbH, Leck

♾ Printed on acid-free paper
Printed in Germany

www.degruyter.com

dedicated to

Alexander Kluge, for his fierce and tender brilliance

and

Larry E. Bieri, for hope beyond words

Acknowledgements

This book is about entangled and interpenetrating scales of cosmic, global, and more concentrated proportions. The writing of it has benefited in ways both large and small from the manifold kindnesses of many colleagues, friends, students, relatives, strangers, assistants, and other helping spirits along the way. I am first and foremost beholden to members of the Cornell University community, past and present, who continue to inspire me on a daily basis, whether they know it or not: Gerard Aching, Esra Akcan, Andrea Bachner, Anindita Banerjee, David Bathrick, Erik Born, Jonathan Boyarin, Susan Buck-Morss, Cierra Rae Cain, Holly Case, Andrew Chignell, Ellie Choi, Duane Corpis, Iftikhar Dadi, Brett de Bary, Naminata Diabate, Ramez Elias, Grant Farred, Magnus Fiskesjö, Paul Fleming, Nicole Giannella, Peter Gilgen, Werner Goehner, Travis Gosa, Sandra Greene, Arthur Groos, Bonnie Buettner Groos, Sabine Haenni, Brían Hanrahan, Salah Hassan, Peter Uwe Hohendahl, Isabel Hull, Murad Idris, Karen Jaime, Michael Jones-Correa, Rayna Kalas, Peter Katzenstein, Michelle Kosch, Dominick LaCapra, Gunhild Lischke, Fouad Makki, Kya Mangrum, Grit Matthias, Barry Maxwell, Brent McBride, Patrizia McBride, Natalie Melas, Christian Metz, Mostafa Minawi, Hirokazu Miyazaki, Viranjini Munasinghe, Sarah Murray, Lorenzo Perillo, Olga Petrova, Christopher Pexa, Ekaterina Pirozhenko, Hunter R. Rawlings III, Carina Ray, Diana Reese, Annette Richards, Jolene Rickard, Camille Robcis, Neil Saccamano, Naoki Sakai, Elissa Sampson, Anette Schwarz, Suman Seth, Samantha Sheppard, Elke Siegel, Tanvi Solanki, Hortense Spillers, Michael Steinberg, Enzo Traverso, Danielle Terrazas Williams, Amy Villarejo, Geoffrey Waite, Kizer Walker, Sunn Shelley Wong, David Yearsley, Samantha Zacher, and Miriam Zubal. I am deeply grateful to them all, as I am to the graduate students and research assistants who have encouraged and facilitated the completion of this project in intellectual as well as practical ways for a much longer stretch than I care to recall. Johannes Wankhammer, Jamie Trnka, Katrina Nousek, Matthias Müller, Carl Gelderloos, and Josh Dittrich merit my special thanks for herculean labors over time. To all those distinguished colleagues from whom I have learned so much, Ingrid Oesterle and Günter Oesterle among them, over years of rigorous and pleasurable exchange with the Department of German Literature at the Humboldt University of Berlin and the Graduate Centre for the Study of Culture at the Justus-Liebig-University of Giessen, I am likewise deeply grateful. To Manuela Gerlof, editorial director with De Gruyter Publishers, Irene Kacandes, The Dartmouth Professor of German Studies and Comparative Literature and book series editor for Interdisciplinary German Cultural Studies, and Stella Diedrich, project editor with De Gruyter Publishers, I owe thanks without end for the utter professionalism and warm graciousness with which they have welcomed my work, and for giving this book a home in print.

To Alexander Kluge, whose story "Plugging Up a Child's Brain" started me on the path to contemplating the role of counterfactual hope in his work and my life when I first encountered this short text in 1977, I owe a debt that can never be repaid. I hope he knows how much his incomparable dedication to the conjoined causes of survival and happiness has meant and continues to mean to so many. Andrew Bowie, who wrote one of the earliest and most incisive dissertations anywhere on Kluge's radical approach to historical narrative, generously allowed me to sit in his kitchen and spend hours poring over the only extant copy of his thesis one day in 1988. Steve Giles, who introduced me to both W.G. Sebald and Andrew Bowie that spring, has remained an attentive, attuned, and valued friend and interlocutor ever since. The bond of friendship I share with Holger Iburg, who gave me my cherished copy of Kluge's early work on "realistic method" early on, is strengthened by our shared love of laughing and thinking with this polymath of European modernity. Holger Iburg also introduced me to Torsten Meiffert, who in many ways opened my eyes to Walter Benjamin as well. Andreas Huyssen and Michael Jennings in different ways have each brought exceptional generosity, encouragement, and insight to our respective exchanges, and for their inspiring work and friendship too I am profoundly thankful. Within the ever-widening circle of Kluge enthusiasts I am above all indebted to Devin Fore, Christopher Pavsek, Rainer Stollmann, and Richard Langston for the sheer big-heartedness, keen intelligence, and capacious erudition of their critical engagement with my research. Richard Langston was additionally kind enough to share many materials with me that I would not have been otherwise able to obtain. A longstanding probing dialogue with Devin Fore has heartened me at crucial junctures and delighted me at every turn. To all those responsive listeners and careful readers, known to me and not, who have fortified my work with the fruits of their own, in Ithaca and elsewhere, I am bound beyond measure. Alan Beyerchen, Claudia Brodsky, Nahum Chandler, Devin Fore, Heinz Gubler, Christopher Pexa, Christine Rinderknecht, and Johannes Türk hold very special places on that very special list.

I am fortunate to have many friends and family members who would still love me even if I had never finished writing this book but who share my gladness in completion. On both counts I thank each and every one of them. To Eric, Keiko, Hikari, Ray, and Tiara Mabuchi I wish to express my gratitude for bringing so much unexpected joy into my life. May it return to them a thousandfold. As Alexander Kluge is fond of reminding us: no one writes books alone. I alone am responsible for any flaws in this one. Anything within these pages that proves worth the reader's while has been made possible by my alchemical friendship with the ever-luminous Christine Rinderknecht and by the sustaining magic of my beloved husband, Larry E. Bieri, who is my lodestar.

The first section of Part One of *Cosmic Miniatures and the Future Sense* originally appeared in article form as "Horizons of Hope: Alexander Kluge's Cosmic Miniatures and Walter Benjamin" in *Gegenwartsliteratur: Ein germanistisches Jahrbuch* (2014): 203–225. It appears here with the kind permission of both Stauffenburg Press under the direction of Brigitte Narr in Tübingen and Paul Michael Lützeler, Editor-in-Chief of *Gegenwartsliteratur*. Approximately half of an earlier journal article, "The Future of Futurity: Alexander Kluge and Yoko Tawada," which was originally published in *The Germanic Review* 86.3 (2011): 153–184, appears with slight modifications in *Cosmic Miniatures and the Future Sense* with express permission of the Taylor & Francis Group, an Informa business.

Contents

Introduction: Hope in Time —— 1

Part One
Cosmic Miniatures and Critical Horizons: Exercising the Future Sense —— 30
1   Heliotropic Horizons with and beyond Benjamin —— 30
2   Heliotropic Narrative with and beyond Adorno —— 50
    2.1 Something Missing and Counterfactual Hope —— 50
    2.2 Gap Aesthetics and "Ways Out" —— 71
    2.3 Utopian Longing and Narrative Orientation —— 86
    2.4 Adorno's "Heliotrope" and Oscillating Perspective —— 95
    2.5 Kluge's Flawed Beauty and Unnatural Narration —— 110
    2.6 Kluge's Future Narrative: "Saturday in Utopia" —— 125
3   Extraterrestrial Speculations with and beyond Kant —— 147

Part Two
Global Miniatures and Marxist Horizons: Conjunctions in Narrative Time —— 166
1   Permanent Revolution —— 166
2   Global Connectivity —— 179
3   Revolutionary Subjectivity —— 187
4   Counter-Catastrophic Futurity —— 191

Part Three
German Miniatures and Perspectival Horizons: Recalibrating Historical Voice —— 198
1   Persons One Can Lose and Those One Can Gain —— 198
2   The Six-Year-Old within Me, the Starry Sky above Me, and Narrative Voice —— 201
3   Long Arcs of Cosmic Formation and the Narrative Trajectory of First-Person Pronouns —— 205
4   Werner Scholem and the Life Writing of the Future Sense —— 217
5   Making Time: *Zeit-Zeugen*, Holocaust History, and Co-Operative Voice —— 231

Postscript: Futurity as Fairy Tale? From *Flaschenpost* to *Nachricht* and More —— 247

Works Cited —— 252

Alphabetical List of Kluge Titles Discussed, in German and English —— 281

Index of Persons —— 284

Index of Works —— 291

Index of Terms —— 297

Introduction: Hope in Time

Above and below are two vectors of spatial orientation that have played a formative role in literary and cinematic works by Alexander Kluge since the early 1960s, after efforts by Theodor W. Adorno to secure a film internship for the young lawyer in the 1950s had resulted in Kluge crafting what would later become his first published stories in the cafeteria for Fritz Lang's film crew during the Berlin production of *The Tiger of Eschnapur*.[1] Kluge's dovetailing of strategies "from above" [*Strategie von oben*] and "from below" [*Strategie von unten*] is most strikingly, famously, and explicitly evident in his storied rendition of the Allied bombing of his German hometown of Halberstadt shortly before World War II ended in Europe. Embedded in his designated "new stories" of 1977 on the untimeliness of time and again in his remixed "chronicle of feelings" in 2000, "Der Luftangriff auf Halberstadt am 8. April 1945" ["The Attack by Air on Halberstadt on April 8, 1945"] configures the militarized rain of deadly bombs from above and desultory civilian efforts on the ground below—and even "below ground"

---

1 See Rainer Lewandowski, who notes that Kluge was allowed "to watch" (9). Kluge's stories were first published as *Lebensläufe* in 1962 and appeared in Leila Vennewitz's translation as both *Attendance List for a Funeral* (1966) and *Case Histories* (1988). Lewandowski also mentions Lang's second talking film with Indian motifs, *Das indische Grabmal* (*The Indian Tomb*) in this connection; in the United States the "tiger" film was distributed as *Journey to the Lost City*. For slightly longer accounts of Kluge's internship experience or his limited connection to Lang, see Detlev Claussen (172–173) and Tara Forrest (*The Politics of Imagination* 131–132). On Adorno's interest in Kluge, whom Claussen calls "one of his most talented pupils" (172), see also Stefan Müller-Doohm's Adorno biography (619–621). Müller-Doohm dates the beginning of the personal friendship between Adorno and Kluge to 1962 (938), though Kluge dates his acquaintance with Adorno to 1956 (*Personen und Reden* ["Persons and Speeches"] 70). Citing a much later conversation between Kluge and Gertrud Koch, Klaus Scherpe suggests that Adorno had recommended Kluge to Lang in order to dissuade Kluge from pursuing his interests in film (316). In a 1988 interview with Stuart Liebman, however, Kluge indicates that Adorno may have recommended him to Lang in order to dissuade him from wanting to write "any books" (36). For incisive remarks on Adorno and Kluge's intellectual influences on each other in the 1960s (especially in relation to cinema, writing, subjectivity, society, and montage), see Miriam Hansen ("Introduction to Adorno: 'Transparencies on Film' [1966]"). Hansen attributes the dropping of Adorno's "defenses against film as a mass media and [his willingness to] consider the possibility of an alternative cinematic practice" in the context of New German Cinema, at least in significant part, to modernist elements in Kluge's "own literary activities [as] the mediating element for Kluge's practices in film" (194). See also Miriam Hansen, "Alexander Kluge: Crossings between Film, Literature, Critical Theory." Unless otherwise attributed, all English translations of German source texts cited in *Cosmic Miniatures* are my own.

DOI 10.1515/9783110525649-001

[*unterirdisch*]—to escape almost certain destruction.² For W.G. Sebald, the expatriate German novelist whose oeuvre is riddled with the melancholic aftermath of Nazi genocide and European colonialism, garnering him an extensive transnational readership since his own untimely death in 2001, Kluge's fictionalized account of the Allied raid on Halberstadt is one of only a handful of attempts in postwar German literature to address the catastrophic "devastation suffered by the cities of Germany" in the violence waged from the air (1; see 60–68 for Sebald's extended commentary on Kluge). Sebald's overall indictment of "the inability of a whole generation of German authors to describe what they had seen and to render it accessible to our memory" [*die Unfähigkeit einer ganzen Generation von deutschen Autoren, das, was sie gesehen hatten, aufzuzeichnen und einzubringen in unser Gedächtnis*] is pointedly situated for Sebald in a much larger field of "always looking and looking away at the same time" in reference to what transpired between 1930 and 1950 in the name of Germany (*On the Natural History of Destruction* ix–x; *Luftkrieg und Literatur* 6–7).³ The exceptional role that he ascribes to Kluge in this landscape of ostensible literary failure is the attempted "anticipation of a future"—even in the midst of acute danger—that could be predicated on something other than fear and repression (*On the Natural History of Destruction* 63–64). A view "from a vantage point above the destruction" (67) is key to what Sebald imagines Kluge's perspective as a writer to be, and yet for Sebald, even Kluge's laudable attempts at hope must fail because the destruction of German cities in World War II was too systematically

---

2 For the most extensive historical analysis to date of the European air war conducted by Allied forces, see Richard Overy. Rainer Stollmann notes the "persistent effect" that the "shock" of the Halberstadt bombing for the thirteen-year-old Kluge (including destruction of the family home) seems to have had for Kluge's life and work (*Alexander Kluge zur Einführung* 139). The "Luftangriff" text can be found in several variations: Kluge, *Neue Geschichten* ["New Stories/New Histories"] 33–106; Kluge, *Chronik der Gefühle* ["Chronicle of Feelings"], Vol. 2, 27–82; and the freestanding *Der Luftangriff auf Halberstadt am 8. April 1945* (2008), which also contains seventeen new pieces pertaining to the air war as well as a relevant excerpt from W.G. Sebald's *Luftkrieg und Literatur* (1999), which appeared in 2003 in English as *On the Natural History of Destruction*. A modified English version of Kluge's text appeared as "The Air Raid on Halberstadt, 8 April 1945" in *Semiotext(e)* in 1982. See also *Air Raid*, which is the freestanding English translation by Martin Chalmers of the German publication from 2008. Sebald refers to Kluge's text as published in 1977.

3 Here I deviate from Anthea Bell's translation, which renders Sebald's "einzubringen in unser Gedächtnis" (7) as "to convey it to our minds" (x). Sebald uses the years "1930 to 1950" in his preface (ix) rather than naming specific phenomena such as the Third Reich, the Holocaust, or military occupation, for example. Sebald's writings overall have been widely noted for the author's profound and even pervasive engagement with the Holocaust (see for example Julia Hell, "Eyes Wide Shut").

planned and executed to allow for anything else (64). Sebald's portrait of Kluge in *On the Natural History of Destruction* overtly aligns the latter's gaze with the visual perspective on catastrophe that Walter Benjamin ascribed to the angel of history as the Nazis were laying ruin to Europe, but the story that Sebald tells of Kluge as a writer in effect casts him as a tragic hero, doomed to fail when even his extraordinary capabilities misjudge and are eclipsed by the sheer and "systematic" magnitude of disaster. This book offers a different story of Kluge's storytelling projects at the crossroads of hope and destruction, and the tale that will unfold here draws its breath from relations between the very large and the very small that are easily overlooked whether one prefers to stress the warp of destruction or the woof of hope in his prose. Yet I shall argue that these other relations of scale and perspective—cosmic, global, and German—are key to unlocking what operatively binds the strands of hope and destruction together in narrative form for Kluge's newer literary miniatures as 21st-century experiments, not in space but in time.[4]

Like Sebald albeit to different ends, Fredric Jameson, one of the leading literary theorists in the Anglophone world, turns to Kluge's writing about World War II in Europe to probe crucial relations between war and representation by literary means. For Jameson, who focuses on three German texts in the main—Kluge's "Luftangriff auf Halberstadt" as published in 2000, his much earlier work on the strategically decisive battle of Stalingrad in 1943 (*Schlachtbeschreibung* [*The Battle*], 1964), and Hans Jakob Christoffel von Grimmelshausen's rambunctious account of the Thirty Years' War (*Der abentheuerliche Simplicissimus Teutsch* [*The Adventures of Simplicissimus*], 1668)—war poses a heightened "narratological problem" and a particular "challenge to anthropomorphic representation" because it relies on both social abstraction and "sensory immediacy" in ways that essentially privilege scene over character and action ("War and Representation," *The Antinomies of Realism* 232–258, here 232 and 239).[5] To Jameson's mind, this renders war "ultimately unrepresentable" (233) and Kluge and Grimmelshausen's texts "virtually non-narrative" (251–252), for war is one extreme example of historical experience "designating an impossible collective totality,

---

4 As Part Three will show, this also applies to Kluge's stories about the destruction of the Holocaust.
5 For his discussion of "scene," Jameson draws significantly from Kenneth Burke. Here Jameson tends to speak of anthropomorphism and abstraction as opposing schemes of representation. For a conceptual approach that highlights their entwinement in the historical avant-garde, see Devin Fore, *Realism After Modernism*. In another section of *Antinomies of Realism* Jameson discusses a different Kluge story on mass death in terms of "realism after affect" (187–192).

a manifold of consciousnesses as unimaginable as it is real" (257).⁶ Where Sebald raged against what he saw as a catastrophic failure of German literary culture in the wake of catastrophic death and destruction, Jameson—who briefly cites Sebald and may well be thinking through a structural problematic of war and representation with him—articulates an aporia of one form of social life that necessarily resists narration by literary means. One could take this to mean both that the aporia he describes cannot be rendered with the tools of literary narration and that the resistance to narration he outlines is effected by literary means that may themselves be narrative to greater or lesser degrees. For our purposes, Jameson is especially helpful because he correctly identifies Kluge's "differentiation of a strategy from below and a strategy from above" as "the formal secret" underwriting the work on Halberstadt and furthermore underscores that no strategic perspective in Kluge's writing on the air war can be grasped in terms of merely subjective points of view (for example, points of view that we might otherwise associate with discrete individual characters such as pilots and bombers on the planes or civilians on the ground) (255–256).⁷

This introductory sketch of a recurring deictic motif in both Kluge's body of work and the international scholarship it has generated helps set the stage for what follows, however, precisely because the book at hand will diverge from Sebald and Jameson's configuration of hope and destruction in Kluge's writing in a number of consequential ways. First, a less remarked but nonetheless foundational cosmic aspect of Kluge's constellation of threat to life and hope for surviv-

---

6 Jameson continues: "War is one among such collective realities, which exceed representation fully as much as they do conceptualization, and yet which ceaselessly tempts and exasperates narrative ambitions, conventional and experimental alike" (257). Matteo Galli, who like Jameson focuses on Kluge's 1964 book about the Battle of Stalingrad, argues by contrast that "Kluge's hermeneutic categories can still be considered valid, also for interpretation of following wars" (313).

7 Jameson explicitly rejects the classification of "picaresque novel" for *Simplicissimus* because it is "episodic in the extreme," an extraordinarily generative "machine for generic production" and "non-teleological proliferation of generic exercises" (249). His account implies a rejection as well of the sorts of bird's eye views and frog's perspectives that often inform discussions of the picaresque. Jameson's insights into the nexus of war and representation must also be understood in relation to Andrew Bowie's early insights into Kluge's poetic critique of the West German postwar culture of *Vergangenheitsbewältigung* (usually understood as critical efforts to come to terms with the Nazi past). For Bowie, Kluge's literary interest in abstract forms of social life rejects literary efforts in the 1950s and beyond to convey historical experience with recourse to anthropomorphism and phenomenology ("New Histories"). When Kluge was awarded the city of Frankfurt's Adorno Prize in 2009, Friedrich Kittler observed in his laudatio that Kluge's work cannot be understood in terms of "'memory culture'" [*Gedächtniskultur*] ("'Alles steuert der Blitz'" 14).

al may apply to the circumstances of war but is by no means confined to them and is relevant to many more ordinary circumstances as well. Second, the interplay of perspectives to unfold here does not revolve around relations above, below, and on the ground so much as it does around lived relations to something outside the earthly realm. In German one might say that this is neither *überirdisch* (transcendental) nor *unterirdisch* (subterranean) but *außerirdisch* (extraterrestrial). Several of Kluge's "new stories"—a form of writing he has been cultivating for decades—literally feature invisible extraterrestrials for example. One group of them in 2006 even takes a tour of the White House in a miniature that will be discussed in Part One. Where do they come from, and what narrative work are these unseen but imagined figures doing in Kluge's prose? The German literary critic Karsten Witte may have captured a key piece of this larger puzzle best when he wrote in 1990 of a quickening of "science fiction with social fiction" in Kluge's "peculiar form of a fictional documentary style." For Witte, this also entails something that we might translate as off-planet [*Weltentrücktes*].[8] How do strategies from "above" in this sense—reconfigured as strategies of hope—manifest in strategies from "below" in the miniscule details of Kluge's quirky prose? How does something not of this world enter into the story scenes of his making, where threats to life are everywhere and world-making—generally considered a staple feature of literary narrative and science fiction alike—is constantly undone?

When Kluge interviewed Yoko Tawada in 1993 as a featured guest for one of his so-called cultural windows in the German landscape of television broadcasting, the critical theorist *extraordinaire* repeatedly asked this multilingual author to provide literal translations for poetic phrases she had crafted in German or Japanese and to explain in German what things such as ghosts, books, metaphors, mirrors, and moons mean in Japanese culture (Kluge and Tawada). Out of the blue these surprisingly predictable requests for literal and cultural translation are punctuated by more elaborate, speculative, and excited questions from Kluge of a far less ordinary sort. "And are there sometimes also extraterrestrials," he asks, "that come into our world and take on a body other than their own?" [*Und gibt es manchmal auch Außerirdische, die auf unsere Welt kommen und auch einen fremden Leib annehmen?*] Here the interviewer invites his guest

---

8 The word "Weltentrücktes" literally means something at a distance from this world. With regard to the relationship between science fiction and what he in his German text calls "Social Fiction," Witte uses the reflexive verb "sich verquicken," which means to blend or combine with each other (369–370). In this sense it is a false but apt cognate in this connection for the English "quicken," which means to "[g]ive or restore life" or to "animate," according to the Oxford English Dictionary.

to ponder where such an extraterrestrial might be located. "Where would he be? Would he be on your skin or really deep inside?" [*Wo wäre der? Wäre der auf der Haut oder ganz tief im Inneren?*] In that interview setting Kluge's questions about extraterrestrials might conceivably be prompted by Tawada's remark that she as a foreigner had eaten and drunk Europe but not yet "arrived" in it. Nonetheless, there is quite a leap from her figuration of ingestion and internalization to Kluge's sudden focus on extraterrestrials, which alters the rhythm and intensity of the exchange.

One might say the same of the many extraterrestrials that appear—or rather, figure without actually appearing, since they are invoked but rarely described—in Kluge's large-scale literary output since 2000. This applies in the qualitative sense that the intensity accruing to Kluge's invisible extraterrestrials can be understood in light of what Erich Kleinschmidt analyzes as an emergent "figure of thought" in the European Enlightenment, albeit in Kluge's case without any attendant attachment to linear progress in time. As Kleinschmidt puts it for the Enlightenment's configuration of intensity as a kind of perceptual and cognitive threshold: "Intensity is always an excess, but also a vagueness with regard to a border value" [*Intensität ist immer ein Überschuss, aber auch eine Unschärfe im Bezug auf einen Grenzwert*] (13).[9] The intensification of Kluge's recourse to unseen but imagined extraterrestrials applies in a vague quantitative sense as well. The two massive volumes of "Chronicle of Feelings," which were published by Suhrkamp in 2000 and include mainly re-publications of the prolific author's earlier work, each contain only one piece explicitly featuring extraterrestrials. The one devoted to Heraclitus, Friedrich Hölderlin, and quantum physicists in Siberia is called "Weltzeit" ["World Time"] and differentiates the living sensorium for time on planet Earth from that embodied in extraterrestrials. According to this text, the former knows only "eight elementary times" [*acht elementare Zeiten*], while extraterrestrials have "23 elementary structures of time, a primary number" [*23 elementare Zeitstrukturen, eine Primzahl*] ("Chronicle" I, 485).[10]

---

9 Kleinschmidt speaks of intensity as a form of "modulation oriented to thresholds" (13) and ties this especially to the conceptualization of progress in Schiller's "Über naïve und sentimentalische Dichtung" (9, 76–77). For a rigorous account of Walter Benjamin's critique of Enlightenment models of "intensity" that are predicated on linguistic, philosophical, and mathematical precepts of continuous progress, see Werner Hamacher, who elaborates how Benjamin conceives intensity in the field of translation in relationship to "the rupture of the continuum" instead (234).

10 The narrative voice in "World Time" speaks as "we quantum physicists of Siberia" [*wir Quantenphysiker Sibiriens*] (486) and specifies that only seven of the eight earthly times "grant life" [*Leben gestatten*] (485). The piece featuring extraterrestrials in Vol. 2 of "Chronicle of Feelings"

Since 2000, explicit and varied references to extraterrestrials—all relevant to Kluge's constant tinkering with differential temporalities—have proliferated along with the author's new book publications.[11] This applies especially to *Tür an Tür mit einem anderen Leben* ["Door to Door with an Other Life"] (2006) and *Die Lücke, die der Teufel läßt: Im Umfeld des neuen Jahrhunderts* ["The Gap the Devil Leaves Us: In the Surroundings of the New Century"] (2003) but also to lesser degrees to *Geschichten vom Kino* [*Cinema Stories*] (2007), *Das fünfte Buch* ["The Fifth Book"] (2012), *"Wer ein Wort des Trostes spricht, ist ein Verräter": 48 Geschichten für Fritz Bauer* ["'Whoever speaks a word of consolation is a traitor': 48 Stories for Fritz Bauer"] (2013), *Kongs große Stunde* ["Kong's Great Hour"] (2015), and more.[12] One story from "The Gap the Devil Leaves Us" titled

---

is situated in relation to the Cold War and titled "Begegnung mit dem Unbekannten" ["Encounter with the Unknown"] (967–971).

[11] Awarded numerous prestigious prizes in several fields—including Germany's coveted Kleist and Büchner prizes for literature in 1985 and 2003 respectively, the German Film Academy's award for a lifetime of accomplishment in 2008, Frankfurt's Adorno Prize in 2009, and Düsseldorf's Heinrich Heine Prize in 2014, just to name a few—Kluge is widely reported to consider his books his "major work" [*Hauptwerk*]. The figure of books becomes, for Kluge, "the last desperate barricade of subjectivity" [*die letzte Wagenburg der Subjektivität*] ("The Gap the Devil Leaves Us" 7) against the falseness of reality and the writers of books the "guardians" of differential temporalities ("Wächter der Differenz").

[12] Of the longer story collections listed here, only *Die Lücke, die der Teufel läßt: Im Umfeld des neuen Jahrhunderts* has as yet appeared in English translation as a book, the title for which translators Martin Chalmers and Michael Hulse render as *The Devil's Blind Spot: Tales from the New Century*. *The Devil's Blind Spot* includes only selected stories from Kluge's *Lücke*. (Some additional stories from *Lücke* appear in English translation by Kurt Beals under the heading "At the 2003 International Security Conference" in Tara Forrest's anthology, *Alexander Kluge: Raw Materials for the Imagination* [291–301]). I will hereafter reference *Die Lücke, die der Teufel läßt* as "The Gap the Devil Leaves Us," with the book title appearing in quotation marks and with page references to the German publication unless otherwise indicated. *Tür an Tür mit einem anderen Leben*, for which no English translation as yet exists, will be similarly referenced as "Door to Door with an Other Life." All other Kluge titles will be provided in both German and English at first mention and subsequently provided in English only except in specific instances when reference to the German publication is necessary for discussion of content omitted from published translations. Textual material as such will be provided in both languages. Texts featuring extraterrestrials in "The Gap the Devil Leaves Us" include "'Grausam wie ein Mongole'" ["'Cruel As a Mongolian'"] (102–104), "Kot von Außerirdischen" ["Extraterrestrials' Shit"] (225), "Die Mondkräfte und der Endsieg" ["Lunar Forces and Ultimate Victory"] (292–293), "Schwarzer Tropfen/Bailyscher Tropfen" ["Black Drop/Baily's Beads"] (360), "Intelligenz zweiten Grades" ["Second-Order Intelligence"] (366–368), and "Einen Ausweg muß es geben" ["There Has to Be A Way Out"] (755–758). Texts featuring extraterrestrials in the story collection "Door to Door with an Other Life" include "Snowball-Earth," "Besuch im Weißen Haus" ["Visitors in the White House"], "Außerirdische unterwegs" ["Extraterrestrials on the Move"]—all

"Die blaue Gefahr" ["The Blue Peril"] references Walter Benjamin's own reference in the Arcades Project to Maurice Renard's 1912 work of science fiction in French (*Le péril bleu*), but here Kluge uses the phrase "visitors from a foreign star" [*Besucher von einem fremden Stern*, 863] rather than a variant of the German word for extraterrestrials [*Außerirdische*].[13] This variation in phrasing suggests that there might be considerably more allusions to extraterrestrials and their dimensional effects in both space and time in Kluge's body of work than the mere quantification of off-planet nouns and adjectives for "extraterrestrial" would allow. Yet even if we could locate all the allusions to extraterrestrials and outer space in Kluge's literary fictions alone—just as Kluge asked Tawada to locate where an extraterrestrial might be if one did come to Earth—we must still travel in time to ascertain what narrative functions accrue to them.

The Theory of the Novel, penned by Georg Lukács in the early years of World War I, gives us a powerful poetic image of "transcendental homelessness" that pivots on modernity's alienated relationship to "the starry sky" [*Sternenhimmel*], which in turn marks, for Lukács, an absolute historical difference between the moderns and the ancients (29, 41). Yet despite their shared if also divergent interests in Marxist thought and practice at different junctures in the history of the 20th century, Kluge's own work on alienation, freedom, and form hardly allows for any presumption of radical historical difference in this or any other sense.

---

parts of a larger subsection titled "Wir Glückskinder der Ersten Globalisierung" ["We Fortunate Children of the First Globalization"] (29–40)—"Mentalesisch" ["Mentalese"] (114–115), and "Hybride Formen des Zirkus" ["Hybrid Forms of the Circus"] (457–458). One of the relevant passages in *Geschichten vom Kino* that is not included in *Cinema Stories* refers back to the extraterrestrials touring the White House in "Door to Door with an Other Life." This passage explains that they go undetected by the President, "because, in a dimension far below an atom, i.e. in Planck-length, they arrived from far outside" [*weil sie in einer Dimension weit unterhalb eines Atoms, d.h. in Planck-Länge, von weit draußen ankamen*] (317). In "The Gap the Devil Leaves Us" a different story is titled "Der Teufel im Weißen Haus" ["The Devil in the White House"] (903–905). Some but not all of these stories appear in Chalmers and Hulse's translation in *The Devil's Blind Spot*, including one rendered as "Intelligence of the Second Degree" (297–300).

13 Among the early sketches for his Arcades Project Benjamin invokes the Renard book to address what he calls a "reorientation in space" in his study of the arcades (*The Arcades Project* 828). The Eiland and McLaughlin translation renders Benjamin's original phrasing "Bewohner eines fremden Sterns" as "inhabitants of a distant planet" (828). Kluge's phrasing gives us "visitors" [*Besucher*] rather than "inhabitants" [*Bewohner*]. The published English translation of Kluge's story "The Blue Peril" uses "visitors from a distant planet" (*The Devil's Blind Spot*, 296), whereby Chalmers and Hulse are faithful to both Kluge's use of "Besucher" and Eiland and McLaughlin's use of "distant planet." However, all four translators deviate from Benjamin and Kluge's combined use of "fremd" and "Stern," which gives us a star rather than a planet and one that is arguably foreign or strange rather than distant.

As is frequently remarked, Kluge's myriad projects revolve around his ongoing commitment to disjunctive temporalities that could resist the unilinear and oppressive temporal order that capitalist modernity seems to demand.[14] Accepting the prestigious Kleist Prize for German literature in 1985 (all the more prestigious because it was the first prize that the Heinrich von Kleist Society bestowed since the Nazis had risen to power in Germany in 1933), Kluge himself characterized writers as "guardians of the last left-over bits of [...] the grammar of time," that is to say, "guardians of the difference" between past, present, and future ("'Wächter der Differenz'" 26, 37).[15] His commitment to disjunctive temporalities must thus also be understood as an ongoing investment in differential temporalities, in the sense that temporal differences among past, present, and future are always and variously entangled in time, which is to say, also conjunctive and not merely disjunctive alone. We should therefore not be entirely surprised when even Kluge's literary miniature featuring other-worldly visitors wandering through the White House conjoins a Kantian motif of the "power of judgment" [*Urteilskraft*] to Kluge's figuration of these unseen extraterrestrials. They are the ones striving for the power of judgment though, we read, and they fail in this instance because their perceptual universe and ours do not converge. "Unrecognized and without cognition they traversed the Oval Office" [*Unerkannt und ohne Kenntnis durchfuhren sie das Oval Office*] ("Door to Door with an Other Life" 31).

---

[14] Richard Langston thus speaks of a kind of desirable and necessary "usefulness of anachronistic media" for Kluge, since Kluge's cultivation of useful anachronisms upholds "the differences between different orders of time at work within everyday experience" that capitalist media would otherwise "collapse" (*Visions of Violence* 195). Langston's analysis of Kluge's multimedial oeuvre in relation to post-fascist avant-garde arts in Germany additionally speaks of "time travel" in the sense of "traveling backward through Kluge's oeuvre, from his beginnings in television in 1988 to the debut of his Stalingrad novel in 1964" (201). According to Langston, "[l]iterature is for Kluge the preeminent time machine, for what it tells always requires less than the time it spends smoldering in the reader's head" (200), and the labor of fantasy in Kluge's work must generally be understood as "a time machine that travels into the past and future" from the present (220–221). My own comments on the importance of traveling in time rather than space to understand the narrative function of Kluge's extraterrestrials and other cosmic motifs in his 21st-century prose will focus on new approaches to futurity instead. On Kluge in relationship to the "temporal imperialism" of capitalist modernity, see also Christopher Pavsek (*The Utopia of Film* 172–173). Commenting in related veins on Kluge's 20th-century critical work in visual media, Peter Lutze once characterized Kluge as "the last modernist."

[15] In this same speech Kluge likens the responsibilities of writers to those of physicists in the age of "star wars" initiatives. Horrified by a television advertisement that aimed at children by downplaying the danger of such wars, Kluge resorts to English to describe the misleading image of a rainbow acting as a protective shield: "And there are bouncing the rockets" (34).

Kluge's invisible but imagined extraterrestrials—figurations that are crucial but largely lacking in physical qualities that could be described—can and must be understood in a larger field of cosmic motifs that underwrite but do not overdetermine his literary writing for the 21st century.[16] This field also includes stars, suns, moons, planets, virtually the entire history of astrophysics, related optical technologies, and more. The significance of this larger field for Kluge's creative reconfiguration of contemporary relations between the starry sky above, earthly hopes below against all odds of destruction, narrative forms of futurity, and the German tradition of critical theory will be the subject of Part One on Kluge's cosmic miniatures and the horizons they engender. At the present juncture though it behooves us to recall that our traveling extraterrestrials figure as objects of narrative speculation without serving a Kantian project of systematic cognition. Kant too gave considerable thought to extraterrestrials in his seminal articulation of modern philosophy in the European tradition, and as Peter Szendy details in *Kant in the Land of Extraterrestrials: Cosmopolitical Philosofictions*, extraterrestrials were also for Kant "impossible" to render fully present (48, 78).[17] This does not prevent Szendy from observing that Kant sometimes describes "Martians and Venusians with a level of detail that made them almost palpable" (5), but it is the "almost" or "as if" quality of what Szendy calls Kant's "philosofictive" reflections on cosmopolitanism that makes Kant's extraterrestrials—in Szendy's extensive analysis—the virtual keystone in the overarching structure of the philosopher's 18th-century oeuvre (57–58).

Building on but also exceeding previous scholarship by Steven J. Dick (*The Plurality of Worlds: The Extraterrestrial Life Debate from Democritus to Kant*), Michael J. Crowe (*The Extraterrestrial Life Debate, 1750–1900*), and Geoffrey Bennington (*Frontières kantiennes*), Szendy illuminates Kant's multifaceted contributions to "a long-standing philosophical tradition interested in extraterrestrial life" (5) from three new perspectives. The first, to which I have just alluded and about which I shall say more shortly, concerns the indispensable structural function that Szendy ascribes to Kant's extraterrestrials in Kant's various accounts of

---

[16] Adjectives are largely but not altogether lacking in reference to extraterrestrials. One story does describe them as "highly intelligent" ("Visitors in the White House," "Door to Door with an Other Life" 30), while one voice in another wonders whether an interlocutor in speculative dialogue could imagine extraterrestrials that would be "like insects" [*insektenartig*] and "merciless" [*erbarmungslos*] ("'Grausam wie ein Mongole'," "The Gap the Devil Leaves Us" 103).

[17] See also Martin Schönfeld's briefer commentary on how Kant's "conjectures that there may well be extraterrestrial life" pertain to Kant's larger field of reflections on natural science, including astronomy, and moral philosophy alike (30). Schönfeld also discusses Kant's three treatises in 1756 on the catastrophic earthquake of 1755 in Lisbon (38–39).

human anthropology, disinterested judgment, and universal reason, from Kant's *Universal Natural History and Theory of the Heavens* in 1755 through to the *Critique of the Power of Judgment* in 1790 and *The Conflict of the Faculties* and *Anthropology from a Pragmatic Point of View* in 1798. Second, Szendy faults philosophy from the 19th century on for ceding its interest in the starry heavens to science, and he therefore focuses philosophical interest on cosmic relations anew in order to challenge what he considers a widespread "anthropogeocentrism" in Western philosophy since Hegel (5). Third, he poses this challenge as especially necessary now given geopolitical contestations, legal debates, and exploratory ventures into the cosmos that have only intensified since the Sputnik era. Indicting a kind of "astral Realpolitik" (16) that he sees proliferating since the end of the cold war in particular, Szendy understands 21st-century "globalization" (33) as a field of tension between highly politicized efforts to control access to the cosmos and even pre-occupy outer space (16), on the one hand, and often misleading claims that such efforts proceed in the interests of "humanity," on the other (16 – 17).[18] Effacement of the political in the name of the human is a concern that Szendy shares with Carl Schmitt writing in the wake of World War II, and for this reason Szendy devotes a full chapter of his book on Kant in relation to extraterrestrials in the service of peace and justice to Schmitt in relation to "star wars" (9 – 44; see also 6). Citing Schmitt's observation of 1962 that we "'need to think of a nomos of the cosmos'" (19; Schmitt, "El orden del mundo" 24)—that is to say, in Schmittian terms of a spatially manifest politics of exploitive appropriation, division, and production—Szendy nonetheless seems to favor Kant's cosmic philosophy of reason even as he faults Kant and Schmitt alike for remaining too earth-bound in their critical orientations.[19] For

---

[18] A scholarly journal has recently been devoted to this field under the title *Astropolitics: The International Journal of Space Politics and Policy.* One related subfield that Szendy does not mention is the inchoate academic field of "astrosociology." See for example Simone Caroti, "Defining Astrosociology from a Science Fiction Perspective."

[19] Szendy provides his own translation for "nomos of the cosmos" from Schmitt's Spanish essay on the new "world order" of the day. Division, appropriation, and production serve as three primary categories of analysis in Schmitt's major publication of 1950, *The Nomos of the Earth*, on which Szendy mainly relies for his own analysis in his chapter titled "Star Wars." Schmitt writes in *Nomos:* "'In every stage of life, in every economic order, in every period of legal history until now, things have been appropriated, distributed, and produced. Prior to every legal, economic, and social order are these elementary questions: *Where and how was it appropriated? Where and how was it divided? Where and how was it produced?*'" (327 – 328, as cited by Szendy 20). Szendy also devotes considerable discussion to the importance of the sea as a contrastive foil to land for Schmitt's understanding of the political, including the politics and strategies of war (21 – 26). Szendy is sympathetic to Schmitt's extension of "the triple

Szendy, that which is earthly or telluric "will always be privileged in Schmitt's work" (21), and Kant falls prey in spite of his own cosmic commitments to a "re-earthing gesture" (127; see also 24, 54, and 70).[20] Szendy proposes to undo this gesture precisely by delving even more faithfully into Kant than Kant himself did. This is the sense in which Szendy's account of Kant's extraterrestrials aims to give us both a more robust understanding of Kant's attention to the cosmos, and greater insight into Kant's other-worldly usefulness in thinking cosmopolitanism as a critical alternative to globalization today.[21]

Kant's extraterrestrials are essential for Szendy because they signal without representing a "constantly retreating threshold" (3), an "infinite opening" (3) toward "a radical alterity" (4) on which any cosmopolitanism "worthy of its name" (6) must rely. As Szendy puts it, this is and must be construed as "cosmopolitics just beyond the horizon" (3) inasmuch as Kant defined "us humans, as Earthlings, from the point of view of an exteriority to which we do not have access" (4). If Schmitt speaks in 1978 of *Weltraumnahme* or the "'appropriation of outer space'" marking "the end of politics" and a new world order of unfreedom when there is no space left outside or beyond hegemony (26),[22] Szendy counters this by situating Kant's extraterrestrials at the spatial and conceptual core of any political appeal to human freedom.

> Humanity [...] must be thought from the perspective of its other, from its outside, quite precisely there where this outside has not yet been given a figure or a face, since it is deprived

---

meaning of *nomos* (appropriation, distribution, and productive exploitation) to increasingly abstract or unearthly elements and matters" (23), such as the sea or extraterrestrial space, but he must break with Schmitt because of the latter's insistence on the categorical purity of oppositional concepts (e.g. "*purely terrestrial* war and *purely maritime* war [as] opposed in *Nomos of the Earth*" [25]). For Szendy's articulation of cosmopolitanism to work, he needs a more supple understanding of limit zones that are not limited but infinite, and he derives this understanding from Kant, with occasional assistance from Derrida. See for example Szendy's concluding remarks, where he observes how Derrida's *On Cosmopolitanism and Forgiveness* "seems radically to undermine" (145) the longstanding philosophical foundation of vertical hierarchies in the way that Derrida opens up cosmopolitanism's "condition of possibility yet to come" (146).

20 Szendy sees Kant succumbing to the "repression or denial" of the "possibility of extraterrestrial reason" (as Kant himself has articulated it) when Kant reverts to the "advantage of judgment's humanization or repatriation on earth" (69–70).

21 Szendy does not discuss the vast body of existing scholarship on either cosmopolitanism or globalization. My own review of Szendy's claims aims to provide readers with enough information to appreciate the structure of his argument in its own right, and specifically in relation to my reading of Kluge. I discuss Kluge in relation to globalization in Part Two.

22 I have slightly altered Szendy's translation of Schmitt's "Weltraumnahme," which he renders as "'appropriation of world space'" instead. Szendy is citing here from Schmitt's essay of 1978, "Die legale Weltrevolution."

of all our possible figurations. In short, humanity must be thought on the basis of the *wholly other*, whose radical alterity cannot be localized in a circumscribed outside. (39)

That is to say, paraphrasing Szendy, for Kant in contrast to Schmitt, the cosmic infinity of other possible worlds ensures that there is always an "outside" available—if not accessible—to human thought in the reasoned service of freedom as a regulative idea. This thought hinges on "the *extraterrestrial* comparison" that was for Kant and is for Szendy both necessary and "impossible" (48) in order to rise above what is empirically given and known. If human beings wish to know themselves "as a reasonable species," they may do so only if they imagine themselves oriented "toward the point of view of the wholly other" (55), of which they however can have no direct knowledge or experience. This is why Szendy with Kant characterizes the figure of extraterrestrials as "wholly other" and not merely different in social, cultural, historical, or any other terms.[23] This is also why "the extraterrestrial motif" (71) that Szendy identifies throughout the Kantian corpus marks a threshold "term of comparison" that is at once crucial but also "unpresentable" (47, see also 110).[24] For Kant, "experience contrasts with the far-sightedness of reason which turns toward celestial regions and the cosmos" (Szendy 56).

As Szendy elaborates in reference to *The Conflict of the Faculties*, for example, Kant aligns the "'standpoint'" of reason heliotropically with that of the sun to account for "reason beyond experience" (56). Because this cosmic perspective —of looking back at human life on Earth with an extraterrestrial optic—is both necessary and impossible, as Szendy puts it, "the question of the *as if*, of fiction and fictionality" becomes for Kant "the only possible access to this expanded horizon" (58). Szendy repeatedly remarks the "double movement" of necessity and impossibility that Kant's philosofictions require (see for example 55, 57, 78), and for Szendy, especially now, philosophy in the cause of freedom needs fiction, for it must "*effectively* produce the possibility" of that point of view that reason itself requires (74). Marrying Kant with Schmitt as he does, Szendy

---

[23] This wholly other is "also neither divine nor animal," Szendy explains (69).
[24] Szendy offers distinct and nuanced readings of extraterrestrial motifs—overt and hidden—in a wide range of texts by Kant, including in the later works, where one might not readily expect them. Regarding the late Kant, Szendy observes for example: "The extraterrestrials have disappeared, they've been pushed out of the earthly sublime and had to go back home so that they would not disturb the rigorous demands of the critical isolation of the faculties, to avoid the risk that reason and taste might encroach on each other" (71). Yet as Szendy persuasively details, "the extraterrestrial motif" is in effect crucial to "the question of the universal point of view" that Kant's cosmopolitanism raises (71–72), and "the question of the *point of view* appears omnipresent and is posed pretty much everywhere in Kant's work" (55).

illuminates Kant's extraterrestrials as unearthly but reasonable figures of imaginative orientation to delineate what he calls a *"geopolitics of the sensible"* (79) as a marker of globalization.[25] Given the long history of philosophical speculation about possible life elsewhere in the cosmos, Szendy makes a double Kantian-inflected movement of his own as well. For him, one must say first, speaking philosophically, that extraterrestrials *"will have always already been here"* (40) and yet remain "impossible to find" (112). Second, humans by contrast can aspire to know themselves "only *at the limit* of their infinitely deferred becoming" (78). The philosofictive figuration of extraterrestrial life can be understood here as this limit, or as Szendy puts it: "the nonearthly reasonable being, the *alien* appears as the border and the tangent toward which humanity tends, asymptotically, as a way of finding itself" (78).

As we will have occasion to see, especially in Parts One and Two but also in Part Three, Kluge's speculative fictions of extraterrestrial relations and cosmic perspectives may also be read as threshold figures in many ways that are strikingly compatible with Szendy's account of a contemporary geopolitics of the sensible, and especially with Szendy's reading of "the extraterrestrial motif" in Kant's cosmology. However, there are some significant differences as well. While the Kantian paradigm entails Earthlings contemplating the possibility of other-worldly perspectives on life on Earth (other-worldly eyes looking back at them) and hence a perspectival reciprocity of sorts, Szendy tends to stress the view from elsewhere even though he is adamant and correct in noting that the extraterrestrial perspective in his account is "anything but a mere outside" (127). His tactical emphasis on the view from elsewhere is perhaps most evident in his lively and incisive analyses of several science fiction films, including for example Georges Méliès's *Le Voyage dans la Lune* (1902), Don Siegel's *Invasion of the Body Snatchers* (1956), and Barry Sonnenfeld's *Men in Black* (1997), just to name a few. Associating the pierced eye of the moon in the Méliès film with "the impossible interplanetary effect of the shot and countershot of which Kant also spoke," Szendy strategically foregrounds "intraterrestrial expe-

---

25 Szendy notes that he takes his cue from Hannah Arendt's reading of Kant in *The Human Condition* to "sketch [...] out a pathway from the aesthetic to the political by way of a speculative cosmology" (79). See also n. 9 in Szendy's introduction (155), where Szendy additionally mentions Jacques Rancière's discussion of the *"distribution of the sensible,"* a treatment that Szendy faults for not "clarifying its geopolitical stakes" (155). Szendy repeats his critique of Rancière's account of distributive access to vision and speech about vision in Chapter Three of *Kant in the Land of Extraterrestrials* (118–119), but Szendy does not otherwise engage with Rancière in any detail. Szendy's book includes considerable discussion (peripheral and sustained) of filmic perspective in the visual culture of science fiction.

rience" instead (132). For him, this experience requires "the space that opens within every human or earthling point of view in order to make possible a point of view as such" (132). A tactical emphasis on the view from elsewhere is nonetheless evident when Szendy aligns the pierced eye of the moon with the cinematic screen as pierced "with a gaze sent toward its galactic outside, toward a cosmotheoretical perspective" that is nevertheless "barred to us" (132). Szendy's geopolitics of the sensible thus relies on an extraterrestrial perspective deemed always already to inhere in the structure of modern thought and in the medium of cinematic vision.[26] This is also why Szendy can rely on spatial tropes throughout and still claim that the extraterrestrial perspective he has elaborated is "anything but a mere outside."

One might say that Kluge stresses the other end of the Kantian perspectival spectrum instead, inasmuch as Kluge's extraterrestrials are almost always imagined first and foremost as objects of intense human speculation. This speculative perspective is oriented to "an other life" to be sure, but the emphasis in Kluge's literary miniatures of cosmic dimension is on what his narrative fictions allow rather than what a cosmic perspective would prohibit. In this sense the many speculative dialogues one finds as a recurring form in Kluge's prose may trace their lineage to the *Conversations on the Plurality of Worlds* by Bernard le Bovier de Fontenelle (1686), which Szendy discusses as a "light-hearted" and highly popular precursor to Kant's "formally rigorous philosophical works" of cosmopolitical philosofiction (46). Possibly because of his own concern with popular cultures of science fiction, Szendy also alludes to "invaders come from another world" (6) or "potential invaders from far away at the other end of the universe" (112). One would have to think of any such "invaders" as a cultural complement to the necessary but impossible extraterrestrials in perspectival thought that Szendy characterizes as being "*already here*, at the heart of the perceptible weft, even before it becomes a question of their possible arrival" (112). But it

---

[26] For a different but in some ways resonant account of the way that the relationship between the cinematic medium and modern revolution is configured for Kluge, see Christopher Pavsek's insightful study, *The Utopia of Film: Cinema and Its Futures in Godard, Kluge, and Tahimik*. Pavsek does not address Kluge's extraterrestrial motifs but does claim that Kluge understands his own cinematic project "in classically Kantian terms" (158). Here Pavsek cites at length from Stuart Liebman's interview with Kluge in 1988, in which Kluge recounts how Adorno once read out loud to him from the "Transcendental Logic" section of Kant's *Critique of Pure Reason*. According to Pavsek, cinema for Kluge "mimics the basic structure of human cognition as Kant defines it" (160). Yet Pavsek also argues that "cinema becomes something like a prosthetic sensory organ" in Kluge's utopian filmic approach to montage (162). I shall stress Kluge's literary labors on multiplying dimensions of the sensible and invisible instead, specifically through narrative forms of future-making.

is worth noting that, as far as I have been able to ascertain, Kluge never casts his extraterrestrials as invaders; in his literary miniatures they tend to figure instead as fellow travelers that more often than not go unnoticed and are sometimes even associated with increased rather than decreased chances of human survival. This is the case with our extraterrestrials touring the White House unseen, for example. More to the point however, Kluge's simultaneously present and "unpresentable" extraterrestrials (to borrow Szendy's non-descriptive description of Kant's other-worldly travelers) will emerge in my analysis as threshold figures in narrative perspectives on time. As I shall argue, the cosmic shifts in temporal perspective for which Kluge's narrative miniatures allow are not "infinitely deferred" but experientially accessible in reading Kluge's philosofictive prose. Like Szendy, Kluge too is keenly interested in what we might call, with Szendy, a geopolitics of the sensible. One finds in Kluge's "new stories" of the last several decades for example countless allusions to the macro- and micro-histories and politics of astrophysics alone. Yet Kluge's intensified attention to the matter of the sensible—in time rather than space—will require that we return to Kant, this time paradoxically with the aid of Kant experts who have not yet set their sights on Kant's extraterrestrials as such, in order to discern more clearly how Kluge also diverges from Kant's interest in cosmic dimensions.

Often credited with inaugurating modern thought in Europe, Kant concludes the second of his three mature critiques with telling recourse to the stars. As cited in Paul Guyer's introduction to *The Cambridge Companion to Kant* in 1992, the English translation of the relevant passage from Kant's *Critique of Practical Reason* (1788) reads as follows:

> Two things fill the mind with ever new and increasing admiration and awe, the more often and steadily we reflect upon them: *the starry heavens above me and the moral law within me.* I do not seek or conjecture either of them as if they were veiled obscurities or extravagances beyond the horizon of my vision; I see them before me and connect them immediately with the consciousness of my existence. The first starts at the place that I occupy in the external world of the senses, and extends the connection in which I stand into the limitless magnitude of worlds upon worlds, systems upon systems, as well as into the boundless times of their periodic motion, their beginning and continuation. The second begins with my invisible self, my personality, and displays to me a world that has true infinity, but which can only be detected through the understanding, and with which [...] I know myself to be in not, as in the first case, merely contingent, but universal and necessary connection. The first perspective of a countless multitude of worlds as it were annihilates my importance as an *animal creature*, which must give the matter out of which it has grown back to the planet (a mere speck in the cosmos) after it has been (one knows not how) furnished with life-force for a short time. The second, on the contrary, infinitely elevates my worth, as an *intelligence*, through my personality, in which the moral law reveals to me a life independent of animality and even of the entire world of the senses, at least so far

as may be judged from the purposive determination of my existence through this law, which is not limited to the conditions and boundaries of this life but reaches into the infinite.[27]

This long citation is warranted here, not because Kluge follows Kant exactly or even engages his arguments in any rigorous analytical sense, but because he occasionally mobilizes and alters snippets of the philosopher's corpus by narrative means in order to advance what we might call a poiesis of futurity.[28] We shall see in the analyses to follow that Kluge also works with the critical legacies of other historical figures in similar ways, including major and indispensable German thinkers such as Marx, Benjamin, and Adorno, some of whom even appear now and then as characters in Kluge's social-fiction stories for the 21st century. The vague allusion to Kant we encounter while entertaining "highly intelligent extraterrestrials" in the White House yields to a stronger allusion or citational inversion of a different sort when "Door to Door with an Other Life" concludes with a story titled "Der Sechsjährige in mir und der gestirnte Himmel über mir" ["The Six-Year-Old within Me and the Starry Sky above Me"] (606–607).[29]

As Kant experts elaborate, the philosopher's longstanding interests in the stars above and earthlings below—and scalar as well as perspectival relationships between them—shape his articulation of crucial modern relations between sensible and intelligible worlds of human experience, and between the natural history of the cosmos and the realm and exercise of human freedom oriented to moral law and reason. For Paul Guyer, "unlike rationalists from Descartes to Gottfried Wilhelm Leibniz and Christian Wolff, Kant was not willing to ground human freedom on an alleged rational insight into some objectively perfect world only confusedly grasped by the senses. Instead, Kant ultimately came to see that the validity of both the laws of the starry skies above and the moral law within had to be sought in the legislative power of human intellect itself" (2), and after Kant, "no one could ever again think of either science or morality

---

27 See Guyer, "Introduction: The Starry Heavens and the Moral Law" (1). The German phrasing used by Kant is "der bestirnte Himmel über mir und das moralische Gesetz in mir," which the Pluhar translation of 2002 renders as *"the starry sky above me and the moral law within me"* (Kant, *Critique of Practical Reason* 203). For the German original, see *Kants gesammelte Schriften* V (161–162).
28 Kluge himself stresses poetics above all as a mode of "making" [*Machen*] in his poetics lecture in Frankfurt on 26 June 2012 titled "Die Unabweisbarkeit des Erzählens" ["The Undeniability of Storytelling"] (*Theorie der Erzählung* ["Theory of Storytelling"]).
29 Technically "Door to Door with an Other Life" concludes with several pages of "Nachweise und Hinweise" ["Documentations and References"] and then an initialed word of thanks that itself concludes with the sentence: "One does not write books alone" [*Bücher schreibt man nicht allein*] (631).

as a matter of the passive reception of entirely external truth or reality" (3). While Guyer allows for several changes and even tensions in the development of Kant's philosophical oeuvre over time though—"for all its appearance of systematicity, Kant's thought was in a state of constant evolution throughout his life" (11–12)— Martin Schönfeld ascribes overall coherence and radical significance to Kant's work from beginning to end, which is to say, on scientific and philosophical grounds alike.

For Schönfeld writing in 2012, contemporary discoveries in quantum geometry, string theory, and neuroscience by and large validate Kant's pre-critical writings on "living forces" in nature, dynamic energy fields, astrophysical relations in space and time, winds, weather, and fire. According to Schönfeld:

> Kant did "out-Newton" Newton to the cutting edge of current knowledge. Nature [in Kant's second book, *Universal Natural History and Theory of the Sky* (1755)] streams outward in a wavefront of organization (1.314.1–2), generating worlds (1.314.8), biospheres and sentience (1.317.5–13, 352–3), and finally reason, human and otherwise (1.351–66). Organization is fragile, and spontaneity, pushed far enough, invites chaos. Mature cosmic regions decay, chaos sets in, and entropy follows in the wake of complexity. But entropy provides the very conditions that allow the cosmic pulse to bounce material points back to order. Thus the expanding chaos curdles at its center into order, followed by chaos, by order, by chaos. Like a rising and burning phoenix, nature cycles between life and death (1.312.13). (27)[30]

As Schönfeld tells it, "everything is connected" in Kant's understanding of the cosmos, perfection is "the *telos* of nature" and human reason alike, and the very "makeup of rationality is linked to the constitution of matter" in macro- and micro-dimensions of creation (29, 30).[31] These dimensions are neither divine

---

30 Here Schönfeld cites relevant passages in the standard Akademie edition of *Kants gesammelte Schriften*. One of Kluge's cosmic miniatures not featuring extraterrestrials in "Door to Door with an Other Life" refers to Newton's 1704 treatise on "opticks," cosmic causality, and Enlightenment. Titled "Unsere Vorfahren, die Sterne" ["Our Ancestors, the Stars"], this story ends with a John Donne quotation: "'Prince, subject, father, son, are things forgot,/For every man alone thinks he hath got/TO BE A PHOENIX – –'" (42). Elements of this miniature could thus be read as re-visiting and re-staging Kant's own conversation with Newton. The preface to "Door to Door with an Other Life" also speaks of an inexhaustible "stock of hope" [*Hoffnungsvorrat*] as being "like a phoenix" (7): "No disappointment uses this stock up entirely. Like a phoenix, it comes into being with every new birth, almost undiminished. Always the same type, capable of happiness" [*Keine Enttäuschung braucht diesen Vorrat völlig auf. Wie ein Phönix entsteht er bei jeder Neugeburt, fast ungeschmälert. Stets derselbe glücksfähige Typ*] (7).

31 Schönfeld speaks of Kant's "pre-critical period (1747–1770)," including pathbreaking work of continued scientific relevance on the nature of space, time, evolution, and cosmic formations (1–2, 17–19, 37–38). Here Schönfeld is speaking about Kant's 1749 book, *Thoughts on the*

nor anthropocentric but cosmic. If Guyer underscores the importance of particular operations of human reason for understanding Kant's mature contributions to modern philosophy and moral law, Schönfeld situates even Kant's account of reason in a vaster field of starry skies to celebrate Kant's early and visionary radicalism as a modern scientist.

Focusing on Kant's "figures of speech" as "figures of thought," Predrag Cicovacki strikes a kind of middle ground instead (9 et passim). Among the intellectually generative metaphors he addresses are "Kant's famous Copernican turn" from ontology to epistemology in the preface to the second edition of the *Critique of Pure Reason* (1787; Cicovacki 14) and "the starry heavens above me" from the second critique. Like many other scholars too, Cicovacki notes that Kant's friends had the philosopher's figuration of starry heavens above and moral law within inscribed in stone upon his death. These words marking his gravesite, according to Cicovacki:

> emphasize the two deepest poles of [Kant's] thought: the cosmos, toward which his youthful passion was directed and the moral law, the object of the almost mystical enthusiasm of his old age. In marked contrast to [Plato's] cave allegory, the proper attitude toward these two worlds is not that of "either-or." Unlike Plato before him, or Hegel after him, Kant was convinced that we are citizens of two worlds—worlds that partially overlap, yet cannot be reduced to one. Just as we cannot simply choose one of the antinomical pairs and then abandon the other, we cannot but participate in both worlds; both are genuine, both reveal authentic aspects of our complex and divided nature. This irrevocable dualism does not make it easier but more difficult to find our proper place and role in reality. (13)

Cicovacki ultimately faults Kant for using his Copernican turn to displace the ontological primacy of the object with the epistemological priority of the subject without "allow[ing] for a possibility of an interactive cooperation" between the two that would not necessarily result in "subordination" of one to the other (15). Cicovacki's sustained attention to Kant's rhetoric is instead motivated by Cicovacki's commitment to navigating a constantly changing "interactive cooperation" between subject and object worlds. As he puts it:

> For [Kant], a boundary is something that belongs to both sides of the fence and keeps them in touch and related, however different they might be. For Kant, metaphors are by their nature not only the signpost of boundaries, but also the mediators between what can and what cannot be known. Their role is not only to reveal the edge of the known, but also to create a bridge—however imperfect—to the unknown. (19)

True Estimation of Living Forces, and other works too, e.g. *Universal Natural History and Theory of the Sky* (1755) (24–27 et passim). Schönfeld claims Kant is more radical in his scientific insights than previously realized (2–3) and more radical than Newton (27–28).

When Cicovacki speaks in another section of his essay of Kant's concept of hope as something "unlike an empty wish"—that is to say, "hope as a belief in something that is at least possible"—hope too figures prominently in the ongoing mediation he ascribes to Kant between subjective and objective perspectives, known and unknown worlds, and necessary and possible dimensions of human experience. For Cicovacki, "Kant's hope was that our rational ability and moral conscience would be strong enough to steer us away from the abyss of self-destruction, away from the 'idyllic' peace of the graveyard, and direct us toward the creation of a much better and more just world" (13).

One may certainly regard Kluge's extraterrestrials—as he figures them in narrative though largely non-metaphorical writing "door to door with an other life"—as imperfect and emphatically imprecise sites of mediation between the real and the possible, between the possible and the impossible, between the known and the unknown. And Kluge's entire body of creative and critical work has always been understood as oriented toward hope for human survival and unalienated life in the face of catastrophic destruction associated in the main with cruelty, war, genocide, fascism, dictatorship, and capitalist exploitation of life, labor, and time.[32] Despite shared interests in freedom, history, science, and form from a wide range of large and small perspectives though, and for all their common interests in cosmic dimensions of the starry skies above and human projects of Enlightenment below, Kluge's literary miniatures for the 21st century do not share Kant's thoroughgoing commitments to the rational world of intelligibility, the developmental telos of perfection, or the temporal directionality of progress in its modern European sense.[33] Commenting on Kant's *Groundwork for the Metaphysics of Morals* (1785) as one of his stepping stones toward proving "that human freedom is not just possible but actual," Paul Guyer highlights the specific sort of interaction between sensibility and intelligibility that Kant ascribes to human consciousness, an interaction in which freedom however hinges on Kant's "distinction between sensation and reason" (17). As cited by Guyer, Kant at this point puts it this way:

> A rational being must [...] regard itself as an *intelligence* (therefore not from the side of its lower powers) as belonging to the world of understanding, not of sense; thus it has two standpoints from which it can consider itself and know the laws of the use of its powers,

---

[32] This does not necessarily mean the ubiquitous rhetoric of "redemption" in Kluge scholarship is always justified. For arguments questioning this presumption, see my analysis of Kluge's *Learning Processes with a Deadly Outcome* (Adelson, "Experiment Mars").

[33] Conceptual historian Reinhart Koselleck posits that Kant "may have been the originator of the term *Fortschritt* (progress)" in its modern sense (*Futures Past* 267). For an alternate reading of the temporality of reading Kant's philosophy of history, see Peter Gilgen.

thus of all of its actions, *first*, insofar as it belongs to the world of senses, under natural laws (heteronomy), *second*, as belonging to the intelligible world, under laws which, independent from nature, are not empirical but grounded in reason alone. (4:452). (17)

Even though Guyer then also explains how Kant subsequently modified his account of freedom in the *Critique of Practical Reason*—"Kant's strategy is now not to prove that we are bound by the moral law by offering a theoretical proof that we possess a free will but rather simply to argue that we must possess a free will because of our indubitable recognition that we are in fact bound by the moral law" (18)—the heuristic distinction drawn in 1785 between the sensible and the intelligible nonetheless helps us now to identify an especially important distinction between Kluge and Kant. Giants of innovation at arguably different ends of the historical spectrum of European modernity, both are keenly interested in interactive cooperation—in the service of something construed as human freedom—between subjects of thought and objects of matter. Yet where Kant's concept of autonomous reason favors the realm of intelligible understanding beyond what is empirically perceived, Kluge's creative exercises in unalienated life work in more concentrated fashion (more concentrated than Kant would allow) on the realm of the sensible. As we shall see in Part One, this realm is not confined to empirical reality for either Kluge or Adorno as the critical theorist on whom he most fervently draws. Situated somewhere between epistemological critique and sensual labor, the new "new stories" by Kluge to be discussed in this book are rooted in and indebted to a German critical tradition that begins historically with Kant. Yet as we shall see, they also diverge from this tradition in some significant ways, even as they draw on its long conceptual, citational, and sociopolitical history along the way.

This book argues above all that Kluge's literary experiments for the 21st century use small-scale narrative form to cultivate a new sensorium of time, notably in differential but conjunctive relation to futurity. This will in turn have consequences for our understanding of the cosmic, global, and German horizons of hope and survival in his contemporary but also always disjunctive critical prose. If Kant ascribes "the starry heavens above" to the "external world of the senses," Kluge does the same but then conjoins sensory relations to cosmic horizons to "the six-year-old within me" as well. The rhetoric of a transcendental "moral law" falls away, and the syntactic inversion in Kluge's story title concentrates our attention on something diminutive and close at hand that requires microscopic rather than macroscopic scrutiny. This something is also closely aligned though not at all identical with a voice of narration that would have to be understood in this case as disjunctive and conjunctive too. Made available to non-empirical sense perception in Kluge's prose, this six-year-old within functions as a kind of extraterrestrial figuration in Kluge's narrative writing door to door with an other life, and the social fiction of survival he helps to mediate pivots, not on any classical notion of subjective interiority or cultural memory either but on differential temporalities instead. Despite the spatial coordinates of orientation "above" and "within" that Kluge adapts from Kant (including the figure of orientation itself in Kant's 1786 essay on what it means "to orient oneself in thinking"), the figure of the six-year-old in Kluge's miniature signals in the main a form of temporal estrangement, estrangement that cannot be decoded as alienation. This extraterrestrial within marks a dimensional threshold in time that opens onto hope and destruction in tandem. The "temporalization of utopia" that historian Reinhart Koselleck (*The Practice of Conceptual History* 84–99) has analyzed as a conceptual marker of modern Europe's faith in progress cannot explain this, and neither can a Benjaminian rhetoric of redemption that figures prominently in scholarly accounts of Kluge's work overall. The book at hand thus aims to explain what binds hope and catastrophe together for Kluge in the details of narrative form, in ways that much like Kluge's extraterrestrials in the White House have as yet gone undetected. Developing eyes, ears, and a taste for these off-planet operations in Kluge's literary miniatures will advance, in incremental but non-linear ways, our own cultivation of a future sense in reading his new writing for our dis- and con-junctive times.

This emphasis on the future sense as a long-distance sense organ of temporal perception brought very close in narrative form sets Kluge's storytelling practice—and analyses of the formal role that futurity plays in it—apart from more familiar contemporary scholarly focus on a poetics of knowledge (*Wissenspoetik*), speculative realisms, or what Franco Moretti advances as "distant reading" in the context of quantitative capabilities that digital humanities afford.[34] However, the future sense to be analyzed here as practiced experiments in narrative form must also be teased apart from, even as it stands in abiding relationship to *Eigensinn*, a core concept of Kluge's multimedial oeuvre, including his many theoretical collaborations with Marxist sociologist Oskar Negt. Situated at the cross-

---

[34] For an alternative approach to making Moretti's "distant reading" fruitful for analyzing Kluge's "distant writing," see Gunther Martens. See also Philipp Ekardt's qualitative assessment of Kluge's specifically "digital constellations" and "digital latency" in particular ("Starry Skies and Frozen Lakes"). Although I would disagree with Ekardt's claim that Kluge's "aesthetic commitment to brevity" in film and literature alike rests on "non-narrative order" (107), Ekardt is entirely correct in stressing "correlation" and "conjunction" in Kluge's aesthetic practice rather than "radical break" or "categorical rupture" alone (116). And as Ekardt highlights with regard to Kluge's work in digital media in particular, "[t]he temporal vector of Kluge's work […] is oriented not just towards reconfiguring a relation to the past but also towards the future" (117).

roads of sensibility (with *Sinn* denoting a kind of "sense" rather than "meaning" in this case) and intelligibility, this compound noun is notoriously difficult to translate. The translators of Negt and Kluge's magnum opus *History and Obstinacy* (available since 2014 for the first time in English, in revised form vis-à-vis *Geschichte und Eigensinn* as originally published in 1981) opt for "obstinacy," which accurately connotes a mixture of concentrated affect, intractable will, stubborn mind, and political resistance stemming from some indeterminate but determined thing within or "one's own" [*eigen*].[35] The adjective *eigen* can also mean "peculiar" though, in this instance with critical dialectical notions of "non-identity" attached, and *Eigensinn* can alternately resonate with something akin to either Kantian or Marxian "autonomy" (*History and Obstinacy* 82) or property ownership as well.[36] As Matthew Miller has most recently phrased it, in his discussion of *History and Obstinacy*'s suitability for a global readership and transnational reception (see also Andrew Bowie, "Kluge and Negt 30 Years On"), Negt and Kluge's core concept of *Eigensinn* re-marks the "macropolitical" and "micropolitical" conjunction of (and friction between) capitalist expropriation of the senses, on the one hand, and a sensate "political economy of labor power," on the other ("*Eigensinn* in Transit" 89, 92; on this conjunction see also Christopher Pavsek, "History and Obstinacy" 144–147). By this account, a perceptual "aesthetic economy of *Eigensinn*" fosters "humanity's emancipatory potentials" (Miller 88). As Negt and Kluge themselves put it, *Eigensinn* in political terms denotes "a remainder of obstinacy that is never entirely used up" in

---

35 Christopher Pavsek writes that, for Negt and Kluge, "*obstinacy abides in relationality* itself" ("History and Obstinacy" 153). Miriam Hansen illuminates what she calls the particular "stubborn discourse" of history and storytelling in Kluge's films ("The Stubborn Discourse"). For insights into Kluge's approach to affect as distinguished from emotion in Kluge's use of visual media, see Philipp Ekardt's forthcoming book on Kluge, tentatively titled *Toward Fewer Images*.
36 Christian Schulte compares and contrasts Kluge's work on *Eigensinn* with the "'sense of possibility'" articulated by the Austrian modernist Robert Musil in the novel *Man without Qualities*. According to Schulte, what matters "decisively" for Kluge "is not only that the world is full of a sense of possibility, but that every individual must develop a sense for his own possibilities, i.e. *Eigensinn*" ("Kritische Theorie als Gegenproduktion" 44). Negt and Kluge stress that *Eigensinn* is "[a] fundamental current observable throughout human history. It develops out of a resistance to primitive expropriation. Its elements continually construct themselves anew and grow out of such heterogeneous roots that the type of experience and resistance identified as OBSTINACY cannot be conceptually isolated" (*History and Obstinacy* 390, cited here in Richard Langston and Cyrus Shahan's translation). Kluge's 2015 German version of this glossary entry can be found in his conceptual map, "Landkarte der Begriffe" (21). There he uses a variant of the German verb *eingrenzen*, which yields an obstinacy that "cannot be conceptually isolated" in Langston and Shahan's translation. More precisely in my view, this obstinacy "cannot be conceptually delimited."

social relations, and anything but passive, this obstinacy always entails "orientation and navigation" as forms of labor on social relations themselves (*History and Obstinacy* 395).[37] Yet as Negt and Kluge also underscore, the obstinacy they mean "is not a 'natural' characteristic, but emerges out of destitution" (292). Obstinacy is literally riddled with social life.

For Negt and Kluge, as is well known, this key term is also tied to their seminal reading of one of Kluge's favorite fairy tales, "Das eigensinnige Kind" ["The Stubborn Child"] as recorded by the Brothers Grimm (available in English translation by Jack Zipes). This effectively grounds the concept of *Eigensinn* in a naturalized form of storytelling about unnatural phenomena. Featured in *History and Obstinacy* as "The Obstinate Child" (in Richard Langston's retranslation of the title), this favorite fairy tale is short enough—a miniature of sorts—to be recounted here.

> Once upon a time there was a stubborn child who never did what his mother told him to do. The dear Lord, therefore, did not look kindly upon him and let him become sick. No doctor could cure him, and in a short time, he lay on his deathbed. After he was lowered into his grave and was covered with earth, one of his little arms suddenly emerged and reached up into the air. They pushed it back down and covered the earth with fresh earth, but that did not help. The little arm kept popping out. So the child's mother had to go to the grave herself and smack the little arm with a switch. After she had done that, the arm withdrew, and then, for the first time, the child had peace beneath the earth. (292)[38]

Negt and Kluge derive a conceptual lesson from this: "the discipline experienced by the obstinate child even from beneath the grave is the moral answer to a previously unsuccessful collective expropriation of the senses. Had it been successful, it would not have necessitated persecution that goes to the bone" (292). The

---

[37] As Norbert Bolz put it in 1985, *Eigensinn* is the answer to one of Kluge's primary questions: "Is there a sense to which history bears witness and that can repair the expropriation of the senses?" (47). Bolz suggests that Negt and Kluge's *History and Obstinacy* posits a critical alternative to a Lukácsian focus on "history and class consciousness" (56). For a sampling of additional overviews of Negt and Kluge's deployment of *Eigensinn* (from a range of socio-historical, formal, poststructuralist, Marxist, pedagogical, and medial perspectives), see Jens Birkmeyer, Andrew Bowie ("Geschichte und Eigensinn"), Rudolf Burger, Vinzenz Hoppe and Kaspar Renner, Christian Jäger, Fredric Jameson ("On Negt and Kluge"), Winfried Menninghaus, Christopher Pavsek ("History and Obstinacy"), Marion Pollmanns, Eric Rentschler, Giaco Schiesser, Franz Schuh, and Christian Schulte ("Fernsehen und Eigensinn").

[38] Since the word for child [*Kind*] is grammatically neutral, this child is assigned no gender specificity other than the grammatical neutrum in the German original.

collective devastation that results from such experience "lasts for centuries in society's limbs" (292, translation modified).[39]

Yet as Kluge suggests in a later essay of his own on the alchemical commingling of desire and deprivation in fairy tales, this sort of storytelling is smarter than concepts precisely because "fairy tales 'don't think'" (Kluge, "Glück" 101).[40] This is something that Kluge explains in narrative terms: "Wishes devour bitter facts. That is the principle of narration" (101). "At the same time," he continues: "That which is devoured remains present as a clump in the story, as in an imaginary stomach. The belly wants to be cut open. What comes out is an experiential treasure" (101). The future sense that will be conceptually animated in *Cosmic Miniatures* is one sort of experiential treasure in these combined social and narrative senses of *Eigensinn*. However, scholarly accounts of Kluge's use of *Eigensinn* have tended to stress what is residually resistant to hegemonic appropriation, rather than the phenomenon's productive capacity for future-making, and they have had relatively little to say about the specific properties of literary narrative that generate rather than reflect it.[41] One of Kluge's most

---

39 Langston translates Negt and Kluge's *Glieder* as "ranks" rather than "limbs." Both are correct, but "limbs" underscores a sense of inchoate embodiment that will be important for my discussion of the future sense. Valentin Mertes points out that the Grimm fairy tales coincided more or less chronologically with Hegel's discussion of *Eigensinn* in the context of the master-slave dialectic in *The Phenomenology of Spirit*, where the term connotes a kind of "freedom in unfreedom" (Mertes 126–127).

40 We should take such assertions with a grain of salt though, since—as Devin Fore notes in his editorial introduction to *History and Obstinacy*—"[f]or Negt and Kluge, the complex and artful epistemology of German fairy tales exercises our *Unterscheidungsvermögen*, the faculty of critical distinction, cultivating a sophisticated cognitive framework on a par with today's highly mediatized world" (21). Whatever epistemological exercises fairy tales might enable, for Kluge, thinking should in any event not be considered the only thing they do.

41 Matthew Miller does propose a "reformulation of *Eigensinn* as a specifically literary-aesthetic concept," a reformulation that "concerns its passage from a trope of social theory signifying the behavior of protesting characters (e. g. in the fairytales) to its status as a narrative form designating the ways texts *behave*" (98). Other scholars speak in broader terms of Kluge's work on aesthetic orientation in particular (e. g. Norbert Bolz, "Eigensinn" 40). Miller also speaks of Kluge's literary attention to *Eigensinn* as "mak[ing] time for recipients' *Eigensinn* to unfold responsively" (98). Miller stresses "terra-centric" properties of *Eigensinn* though (90), whereas I shall argue that certain "extraterrestrial" dimensions of Kluge's experimental literary miniatures are key to understanding his use of what I call the future sense. Martin Jay, who analyzes Benjamin's radical approach to "experience without a subject" in relation to literary narrative and the free indirect style of novelistic voice in particular, situates Benjamin's radicality "not in sensation or perception, but in language" ("Experience without a Subject" 148). Kluge arguably uses narrative perspective and voice to work in radical ways on sense perception as such, notably in relation to the dimensional quality of future time.

important interlocutors and muses, Theodor W. Adorno articulated his own conceptual understanding of "obstinacy" or "doggedness" [*Sturheit*] in narrative "reflections from damaged life" in 1945 ("Great and small," *Minima Moralia*, Redmond translation 132 and Jephcott translation 125). For Adorno this obstinacy was no mere residue from the past persisting in the present, but crucially "anachronistic." Gaps as well as bridges in time will prove even more vital for Kluge's 21st-century experiments with the future sense as narrative form and social intervention alike. Above and beyond this, the life-and-death stakes of diminution we encounter in "The Obstinate Child"—the "little death bed" [*Totenbettchen*] and the child's "little arm" [*Ärmchen*] (*Geschichte und Eigensinn* 766) —already alert us to the importance of small details in the larger arc of Kluge's miniaturized storytelling practice: the production of anti-realist hope with real effect in time under ubiquitous conditions of historical catastrophe.

Cosmic Miniatures illuminates how Kluge's experimental use of narrative form incrementally helps to produce the future sense, beyond a mere indexing of hopeful possibility or obstinate resistance. In so doing these experiments convert the time of empirical catastrophe into the temporal dimensionality of what Adorno once called a "future without life's miseries" (*Negative Dialectics* 398). The close readings presented in *Cosmic Miniatures* additionally demonstrate how Kluge's literary miniatures for the 21st century pose significant challenges to conceptual articulations of futurity as form in the contemporary transnational field of narrative studies. In the arena of German-language narrative studies Albrecht Koschorke for example introduces the category of "future fictions" in his magisterial *Wahrheit und Erfindung* [Truth and Invention] (229–230), a book conceived as a "general theory of narrative," as the subtitle indicates. Koschorke differentiates among three subsets of his categorical designation—literary, social, and emphatically modern with a temporal consciousness of futurity as open and therefore "pliable" (230). Koschorke also accounts for subtle variations in ways in which these three heuristic subsets of future fictions navigate relationships between imaginative process and social reality. As the concluding section of Part One in the present study will elaborate, however, the "future fictions" of Koschorke's coinage are ultimately unable to account for what I have dubbed the future sense of Kluge's experimental miniatures, because Koschorke's future fictions are all implicitly predicated on an understanding of futurity as a temporal mode that remains inaccessible to experience. This caveat applies even in the case of Koschorke's sub-category of "social fictions" as social imaginaries in narrative form with real stakes and consequences in social life.

A similar caveat applies to the analytical category of "future narratives" that Christoph Bode and Rainer Dietrich have introduced in the transnational realm of postclassical narratology (*Future Narratives*). For Bode and Dietrich, future narratives entail a structural shift in the organization of narrative form (across a range of literary and other domains) from past events to "nodal" situations instead. By their account, these narrative nodes do not merely "*thematize* openness" but formally allow readers and players "to actually *experience*" the future as "a space of yet unrealized potentiality," a narrative space that readers and players could themselves influence by virtue of the decisions and values they bring to acts of reading and playing (1). Despite their overt emphasis on ways in which future narratives allow those who engage them to experience "situations that fork into different branches," Bode and Dietrich are very clear in insisting that future narratives as they conceive them "preserve the future *as future*" (1). Their phrasing implicitly and essentially invokes a naturalized modern understanding of future time as fundamentally inaccessible to experience (on this point, see especially Koselleck, *Futures Past* 261, and Niklas Luhmann, "The Future Cannot Begin" 131). For reasons that will be argued in greater detail in Part One, the narrative nodes or turning points of temporal conversion in Kluge's cosmic miniatures of future-making under conditions of catastrophe bespeak an anti-realist realism (Kluge, "The Sharpest Ideology: That Reality Appeals to Its Realistic Character") that Bode and Dietrich's otherwise promising narratological concept of "future narratives" cannot help us address.[42] This is

---

[42] For other recent insights into temporal structures of literary narrative in particular (from a range of methodological perspectives and textual materials), see especially Birgit R. Erdle (*Literarische Epistemologie der Zeit*) and Hanna Meretoja (*The Narrative Turn in Fiction and Theory*), neither of whom focuses on futurity. See also the volume edited by Anne Fuchs and Jonathan Long (*Time in German Literature and Culture, 1900–2015*). Hilary P. Dannenberg (*Coincidence and Counterfactuality: Plotting Time and Space in Narrative Fiction*) discusses ways in which readers are allowed to see a fictional world "as one nascent with future possibilities—and thus truly a possible world" (43), but like Bode and Dietrich, she understands the temporal structure of future time in ways that will not apply to Kluge. For additional recent scholarship on literature and futurity, see Benjamin Bühler and Stefan Willer's multiperspectival anthology, *Futurologien*. Amir Eshel explicitly centers his crosscultural approach to literary temporality on his concept of futurity as an ethical imperative and narrative index of possibility (*Futurity: Contemporary Literature and the Quest for the Past*); Eshel's important provocation will be discussed at relevant junctures in analyses to follow. In the German context Daniel Weidner and Stefan Willer focus in more broadly discursive terms on futurity in the form of "prophesy and prognostics" (*Prophetie und Prognostik: Verfügungen über Zukunft in Wissenschaften, Religionen und Künsten*). Willer also writes specifically on the "epistemology of the future" and on tropes of prognosis in German literature since the 18th century ("Zur literarischen Epistemologie der Zeit" and "Vom Nicht-Wissen der Zukunft"). *Futurologien* contains several entries by Willer on the futurity of wishing, strategy, music, and time travel, as well as numerous articles by others on the futurity of ecology, nanotechnology, and more. On German literature and probability, see especially Rüdiger Campe (*The Game of Probability: Literature and Calculation from Pascal to Kleist*).

because Kluge is an inventive and maverick user of utopian, critical, and Marxist traditions alike, and the counterfactual hope that his literary narratives mobilize do make claims to real effect on the experiential status of futurity itself.[43] The future sense that his 21st-century storytelling cultivates is an intangible material product of such social claims and narrative turning points of conversion in time.

The political philosopher Seyla Benhabib once ended her study of the modern foundations of critical theory by invoking utopia that is "no longer utopian, for it is not a mere beyond" (353). That study concludes with Ernst Bloch's 20th-century thoughts on bifurcated trajectories of social thought with aspirations to real effect, one concerned with utopian efforts to secure "'human happiness'" in real time and one stressing "'human dignity'" in theories of natural law (353). Philosophers of various stripes and practitioners of legal systems make cameo appearances throughout Kluge's multimedial oeuvre, including his literary miniatures, as is well known (and as the ensuing analyses here will also show), but Kluge's cosmic experiments in German culture and narrative form are mainly

---

[43] On Ernst Bloch and Walter Benjamin as not utopianists but "users of the utopian tradition," see Barry Maxwell (217–218, 226). For prize-winning reflections on "counterfactuality" and "coincidence" as two overarching strands or "key plots" in the literary history and aesthetic structure of narrative fiction, see Dannenberg, who combines postclassical narratology and cognitive studies to illuminate the fundamentally "interactive history of coincidence and counterfactuality" in an evolving "struggle between forces of narrative convergence and divergence" in early modern, modern, and postmodern literary forms (16). As we shall have occasion to see in Part One, the narrative operations of counterfactual hope and experiential futurity in Kluge's experimental miniatures are also keenly invested in multifaceted tensions between interactive forces of disjunction and conjunction in time as well as form. However, Dannenberg's analytical insights are of limited use in grasping Kluge's narrative experiments with counterfactuality or coincidence, largely because Dannenberg focuses on emplotment, character, and the cognitive sense-making of fictional worlds. By contrast, Kluge's experimental miniatures work in the main on perspective, voice, and "sense" making of an entirely different magnitude. As I shall argue in Part One, a dominant emphasis in Kluge scholarship on "coincidence" or contingency has tended to celebrate other possible story lines without addressing a core conundrum of his radical prose having specifically to do with future time, counterfactual hope, and narrative form. Dannenberg's study may therefore be said to encourage us to consider Kluge's narrative experiments in contemporary German-language literature amidst a broad field of "new techniques and strategies" that in her assessment continue to evolve in the interactive representation of "coincidence and counterfactuality" by narrative means (5). Dannenberg's mapping of a "hierarchy of relations between worlds in counterfactuals and other narrative scenarios that create alternate worlds" might be a useful point of entry for considering Kluge too, to the extent that she allows for an "antirealist" subset in which "the distinction between fact and counterfact" could "become fuzzy or disappear altogether" (120–121). Here too caution is in order though, since her categories are ontologically conceived and in some respects mutually exclusive. This will not hold for Kluge.

concerned with making real those counterfactual opportunities for human happiness that powerfully real histories of human suffering aim to and sometimes do destroy. That making pivots on the future sense as a sense organ of temporal perception, an experiential organ of differential perception that Kluge's intensified investment in experimental storytelling cultivates and exercises for endangered times. *Cosmic Miniatures* therefore aims to demonstrate how Kluge's micrological writing of cosmic proportions both adopts and adapts the German tradition of critical theory for the 21st century (see especially Part One), and in a related vein this study also aims to demonstrate how Kluge's expanded narrative practice of critical theory makes this German tradition more rather than less useful for contemporary consideration of the Anthropocene (see especially Part Two's discussion of Kluge's "global miniatures" of globalization, many of which function in narrative terms as cosmic miniatures too). As Part Three will argue, even the more properly "German" miniatures in Kluge's 21st-century writing must in some ways also be understood paradoxically as "cosmic" and "global" in the critical and revolutionary horizons of temporal orientation they create. Kluge's German miniatures, including the intensified Holocaust stories among them, signal a storytelling investment in the real force of counterfactual hope against competing forces of catastrophe and despair.

Kluge's experimental prose—cosmic, global, and German miniatures alike—makes the real force of such hope accessible to experience with the aid of the future sense, which Kluge's radical storytelling itself engenders by narrative means. Continually reworking the figuration and functions of narrative perspective and historical voice at the same time, as a writer Kluge also challenges narrative theory to reconsider the simultaneously experiential and non-empirical parameters of "unnatural narrative," which even experimental narratologists generally define in terms that ultimately rely on categorical distinctions between what is considered possible in the real world and what is not. For experts Jan Alber, Henrik Skov Nielsen, and Brian Richardson, for example, unnatural narratives "violate common-sense understandings" of perspective, voice, person, and communication, and unnatural narratives "transcend real-world possibility by projecting physically, logically, or humanly impossible scenarios or acts of narration" (Alber, Nielsen, and Richardson 351). Kluge's miniatures certainly violate common-sense understandings of many things, but the narrative practice they entail does not so much "transcend" possibility as transform it in real time by instantiating the future sense as an unnatural organ of temporal perception that also operates as an anti-realist and non-empirical but nonetheless real dimensional phenomenon in time. Oriented to this-worldly and off-worldly horizons at the same time, the future sense is an experiential treasure that Kluge's storytelling gives us in and for our troubled times.

Part One
Cosmic Miniatures and Critical Horizons: Exercising the Future Sense

1 Heliotropic Horizons with and beyond Benjamin

Best known for filmic experimentation in postwar German cinema, broadcasting innovations in television culture, and proletarian social theories of public life, Alexander Kluge has also been a prolific writer of experimental literary prose since the 1960s. One of the most dynamic public intellectuals in Europe today, he has published over five massive volumes of new "new stories" since 2000 alone and in 2012 held the prestigious poetics lectures at the Goethe Universität Frankfurt under the rubric *Theorie der Erzählung* ["Theory of Storytelling"], a lecture series that begins with invocations of critical "orientation in core questions" [*Orientierung in wesentlichen Fragen*] to the sun and the stars ("Das Rumoren der verschluckten Welt" ["Rumblings of the Swallowed World"], 5 June 2012). This polymath of European modernities and German critical culture in the wake of fascism, war, genocide, dictatorship, and now globalization has well documented affinities with the critical theory of Walter Benjamin, notably in relation to Benjamin's reflections on media theory, visual culture, and "the optical unconscious," on the one hand, and on disjunctive temporalities, counter-histories from below, and redemptive vectors of violent pasts, on the other. I take issue with Christoph Zeller's contrary claim that Benjamin's influence on Kluge's creative work has been "overlooked to date," though I agree with Zeller when he notes both that Benjamin plays key roles in Kluge's aesthetics and claims: "A systematic investigation of Benjamin's influence on Kluge remains to be written" (Zeller 122; 126, n. 113).[1] This opening section of Part One will not provide that overarching account but does clarify how some Benjaminian traces operate in Kluge's writing, and how Kluge scholars can overlook these pivotal operations

---

[1] Zeller focuses on the importance for Kluge of Benjamin's concept of allegory and practice of citation as forms of literary montage in relation to catastrophic histories. For a more recent study of the relationship between Benjamin and Kluge in terms of "historical montages" and open textual forms, see Kai Lars Fischer. As Fischer rightly observes: "Alexander Kluge's literary project would be difficult to imagine without Benjamin's *Arcades Project*" (43). Fischer is equally correct when he suggests that reading Kluge can help us learn to read Benjamin differently and that Kluge's creative practice "increasingly" outstrips the concepts scholars have to analyze it (253). On Kluge's adaptations of Benjamin's approach to storytelling, see also Christopher Pavsek, "The Storyteller in the Age of Mechanical Reproduction" (1993).

even when they explicitly or implicitly celebrate Benjamin as Kluge's muse.² In this sense W.G. Sebald merely underscores a larger arc of Kluge scholarship in *On the Natural History of Destruction* (originally published as *Luftkrieg und Literatur*) when he likens Kluge as a writer to Benjamin's angel of history on a backward-looking quest for redemptive futures of possibility against a field of systematic destruction and overwhelming catastrophe (Sebald, *On the Natural History of Destruction* 67).³ Whatever one thinks of these claims, Benjamin's afterlife in contemporary German literature is very much alive in Kluge's growing body of work and in Kluge commentary across the disciplines.

Two dominant trends in this commentary from which my remarks will deviate are 1) a fixation on the disruptive presence of the past without regard to the changing status of the future in Kluge's oeuvre and 2) a default assumption that Benjaminian motifs of fragmentation and montage figure only in non-narrative ways for Kluge.⁴ Rather than rehearse an all too familiar tale of Kluge's indebted-

---

2 Kluge is well known for explicitly assigning primary influence to Adorno, a key connection that will be discussed at length in the second section of Part One on Kluge's cosmic miniatures. The present study makes no claims to a comprehensive account of figures of influence in Kluge's writing—a very long list that would also have to include names such as Kant, Clausewitz, Marx, Fourier, Bloch, Kracauer, Korsch, Sohn-Rethel, Eisenstein, Tretyakov, and Luhmann, just to mention a few—nor does this section of Part One aim to track all the Benjaminian influences, motifs, and references in Kluge's oeuvre. Benjamin explicitly appears for example as something akin to a character in "Geister, wie Walter Benjamin sie beschreibt" ["Ghosts as Walter Benjamin describes them"] and "Walter Benjamin kommt bis Halberstadt" ["Walter Benjamin comes as far as Halberstadt"] (Kluge, "Door to Door with an Other Life" 556, 571–574), and Benjamin certainly plays a role in the figuration of urban settings, mass culture, and revolutionary histories in Kluge's stories from "The Gap the Devil Leaves Us" as well. This first section of Part One aims instead to identify crucial structural aspects of Kluge's approach to futurity that can be understood only by situating what I call his cosmic miniatures in relation to Benjamin's critical theory early in the 20th century and changing conditions of temporality and narrative today.
3 For another example, see Eshel, who speaks of Kluge's writing in terms of "the curiosity of a poet standing in front of history's catastrophic pile of debris" ("The Past Recaptured?" 72).
4 Bernard Malkmus speaks of "Kluge's patchwork of texts and images," for example, in terms of "a nonnarrative arena of competing discourses grouped around certain shifting centers of metaphorical or thematic gravity" (251). See also Andrew McGettigan, who notes that, "[i]n the *Arcades Project*, Benjamin insists that the past 'decomposes into images not narratives'" (27). For new critical insights into the nexus of narration and montage for Benjamin and others in the Weimar Republic, see Patrizia McBride, *The Chatter of the Visible*, as well as her independent article on Benjamin's *Einbahnstraße* [*One-Way Street*] between *Bildung* and German Constructivism (Adelson and Fore, *Futurity Now* 233–247). Devin Fore's masterful study of "realism after modernism" also offers many rich new perspectives on narration and montage in the Weimar Republic. On "realism after modernism," see Steve Giles as well, who focuses on Brecht, Lukács, and Adorno. There are also critical voices remarking, as Harro Müller notably did as early as

ness to Benjamin in terms of a shared resistance to grand linear narratives of hegemonic history—or even to narrative writing as such—Part One probes relations between futurity and narrative form, in dimensions both large and small, in what I call Kluge's cosmic miniatures.[5] This term refers to short prose pieces of literary experimentation in which the narrative functions of cosmic motifs (e.g. suns, planets, stars, extraterrestrials, astrophysics, and outer space) in Kluge's writing pivot on narrative uses of futurity as experiential portals in time. Kluge's use of futurity in stories for the 21st century becomes a pivot point for critical and phenomenological relations between cosmic horizons and human life teetering between hope and destruction. This first section of Part One aims to illuminate Kluge's indebtedness to and his distanciation from Benjamin in four key respects. The first (in order of importance for present purposes) concerns the "heliotropism" of Benjamin's fourth thesis on historical materialism (1940); the second pertains to the "end" of storytelling in Benjamin's seminal essay "Der Erzähler" ["The Storyteller"] (1936); the third involves the non-hermeneutic "use" of the future in *Einbahnstraße* [*One-Way Street*] (1923/1928); and the fourth relates to, in Andreas Huyssen's coinage, the "modernist miniatures" written by Benjamin and others early in the 20th century. A close reading of Kluge's cosmic miniature "Hoffnung bei Sonnenaufgang" ["Hope at Sunrise"] from the story collection "Door to Door with an Other Life" (2006) will be complemented by analysis of Kluge's interventions in the telling of time and futurity especially, the status of hope for him in contradistinction to utopia, and the task of his storytelling for the 21st century. Subsequent sections of Part One address the narrative status of hope, utopia, and futurity in Kluge's storytelling relationship to Theodor W. Adorno's own heliotropic miniature from *Minima Moralia: Reflexionen aus dem beschädigten Leben* [*Minima Moralia: Reflections from Damaged Life*], and to the extraterrestrial configuration of living "door to door with an other life" discussed in the Introduction.

Part One should also be understood in relation to our contemporary moment, as a simultaneously fractured and globalized present applies unprecedented pressure on the very concept of futurity in many fields (Adelson 2013). Aleida Assmann speaks in more general terms of "transformations of the modern time regime" and "a 'continental shift' in the structure of Western temporality" ("Transformations of the Modern Time Regime" 41). Kluge himself has publicly

---

1982, that montage and narration are not mutually exclusive for Kluge: "With his multifaceted montage technique, Kluge does not abandon the use of narrative schemes" ("'In solche Not'" 890).

5 Verso has recently published a collection of Benjamin's own exercises in storytelling in English translation (*The Storyteller: Short Stories*).

associated the end of communist states in Europe with the hopeful opening of new "horizons" of imagination and futurity rather than the putative end of history and loss of utopia that have preoccupied so many others (see for example Kluge, "Der große Sammler der Wahrheit" ["The Great Collector of Truth"] and "'Ich liebe das Lakonische'" ["'I Love the Laconic'"], two interviews from 2000, and Kluge's comments about 1989 in the preface to *Die Lücke, die der Teufel läßt* in 2003).[6] Far beyond historic transformations associated with German unification or the demise of the Soviet Union, however, the 21st century to date is rife with proliferating obsessions and anxieties about futurity, survival, and time. Hans Ulrich Gumbrecht's assertion of a growing primacy of the present is but one example of this, as is the competing claim that our now is one in which a 20th-century "'time of *diagnosis*'" yields to the "'time of *prognosis*'" instead (Brandstetter, Peters, and van Eikels 9).[7] Both claims would surely be anathema to Benjamin as the author of "Madame Ariane: Second Courtyard on the Left," one of the many entries in *One-Way Street*, a book that Miriam Hansen describes as beginning "to theorize" in the 1920s the "*undoing*" of "the alienation of the senses that preoccupied Benjamin in his later years" (*Cinema and Experience* 80). Dedicated to a fortune-teller, this entry figures for us in Benjamin's phrasing two competing forms of futurity. They entail the interpretive

---

6 In 2000 Kluge observed: "I always need a horizon of hope in order to write. Strangely, the implosion of the Soviet Union and our reunification opened the horizons" [*Ich brauche immer einen Hoffnungshorizont, um zu schreiben. Seltsamerweise hat die Implosion der Sowjetunion und unsere Wiedervereinigung die Horizonte geöffnet*] ("Der große Sammler der Wahrheit"). Fewer than half of the entries in *Die Lücke, die der Teufel läßt* are included in the English translation by Martin Chalmers and Michael Hulse under the title *The Devil's Blind Spot* (2004). For the foreword to the English translation Kluge also changed the original German reference to 1989 to "1991" as a reference to "the disintegration of the Russian imperium" (vii).

7 Focusing on Germany since 1945 but also speaking more generally and autobiographically, Gumbrecht argues that we no longer have futures. Drawing considerable inspiration from Kluge's film titled *Der Angriff der Gegenwart auf die übrige Zeit* [*The Assault of the Present on the Rest of Time*] (1985), Christopher Pavsek astutely assesses Kluge's longstanding concerns with the "temporal imperialism" of an expanding present (*The Utopia of Film* 173 et passim); for both Kluge and Pavsek, however, the persistence of differential temporalities remains critically key. Brandstetter and her co-editors cite philosopher Paolo Virno from an interview conducted in 2004 by Jun Fujita Hirose; their source is <http://multitudes.samizdat.et/De-la-diagnosi-a-la-prognosi>. For interdisciplinary investigations of futurity between "prophecy and prognosis," see for example Weidner and Willer's German anthology, as well as Heinrich Hartmann and Jakob Vogel's earlier *Zukunftswissen*. For relevant commentary on an international scale, see especially Arjun Appadurai's distinctions between competing ethics of probability and possibility in *The Future as Cultural Fact*, and Elena Esposito's *The Future of Futures: The Time of Money in Financing and Society*.

mode of prognosis, which he rejects, and a split-second "presence of mind" [*Geistesgegenwart*] that he favors because that presence entails an "extract" [*Extrakt*] of the future, the precise disjunctive awareness of which is far more important than any advance knowledge of that which is temporally "most distant" [*Fernstes*]. "Omens, presentiments, signals pass day and night through our organism like wave impulses. To interpret them or to use them: that is the question" [*Vorzeichen, Ahnungen, Signale gehen ja Tag und Nacht durch unseren Organismus wie Wellenstöße. Sie deuten oder sie nutzen, das ist die Frage*] ("One-Way Street" 482–483; *Einbahnstraße* 113). Yet even if we can intuit a critique of hermeneutics here that Kluge would share,[8] what precise use of the future is at stake for Benjamin or for Kluge, and are they compatible *in* their orientations to the future? For Niklas Luhmann, in whose systems-theoretical account the modern European future famously "cannot begin," a structurally "open" future ("The Future Cannot Begin" 131), that is to say, one that is not merely undecided but fundamentally undecidable, has been a defining feature of European modernity as a particular "interpretation of reality," and Luhmann defines time itself as an "interpretation of reality with regard to the difference between past and future" (135). If we shift—with Benjamin and Kluge alike—from interpretation to use as our critical focus, what "use" of the future palpitates Benjamin's historical theses and their afterlife in Kluge's recent prose?

The use of the future in the fortune-teller entry and the concluding one titled "To the Planetarium" in *One-Way Street* can be grasped only in relation to the larger array of star-studded or sidereal motifs that inform Benjamin's oeuvre. His use of stars, suns, planets, outer space, and so on underwrites, according to Philipp Weber, all of Benjamin's key concepts from aura, mimesis, script, language, redemption, to constellation (8 et passim).[9] Weber's point is not that Ben-

---

[8] For a multifaceted analysis of the relationship between Kluge's poetics and hermeneutics, poststructuralism, and anthropological Marxism, see Winfried Menninghaus, who also notes certain affinities between Kluge and Benjamin, especially in relationship to the latter's theory of language (266).

[9] Weber also reviews relevant scholarship by Lorenz Jäger, Stéphane Mosès, Wolfgang Bock, Bettine Menke, and others while noting: "Specialized studies of Walter Benjamin's star-image are still not especially numerous" (10). Weber begins his own book with the opening lines of Georg Lukács's *Theory of the Novel*, which characterize premodern humans in relation to the "starry sky" [*Sternenhimmel*] as "die Landkarte der gangbaren und zu gehender Wege" (which Anna Bostock's translation renders as "the map of all possible paths" but which could also be translated as "the map of those paths that could, should, and must be traveled") and modern subjects by contrast (in a later section for Lukács) in terms of "transcendental homelessness" (see Weber 9). On the figure of constellation Weber observes: "An essential hinge in Walter Benjamin's philosophical thought is cognition as a constellative procedure" (45).

jamin's use of sidereal motifs is conceptually consistent over time but rather that the figuration of the sidereal is the means by which Benjamin develops and articulates his dialectical mode of thought. If Benjamin's *Denkbilder* or thought-images form the "matrix" of his theoretical reflections, as Sigrid Weigel once put it (*Entstellte Ähnlichkeit* 16), for Weber, all of Benjamin's core *Denkbilder* or dialectical images are in varying senses also *Sternbilder* or star-images, sidereal relations between humankind and the cosmos signaling for Benjamin "the lost natural unit with the aid of which concepts become recognizable as dialectical" [*die verlorene natürliche Einheit, an der die Begriffe als dialektische erkennbar werden*] (Weber 8–9). Whether discussing "the Copernican turn of remembrance" of Benjamin's *Passagen-Werk* or Arcades Project [*die kopernikanische Wendung des Eingedenkens*, in Convolute K1, 3 on "Zukunftsträume" or "future dreams"], tensions between micro- and macrocosmic dimensions of "non-sensual similarity" [*unsinnliche Ähnlichkeit*] in the 1933 essays on mimesis, or Benjamin's theory of magic reading, Weber illuminates how Benjamin's sidereal *Denkbilder* index "something that stands outside the world and nevertheless extends into it" from an elevated perspective [*ein außer der Welt Stehendes, das dennoch in sie hineinragt*] (Weber 95). The lights and movements in the distant heavens by which humans orient themselves on earth underwrite Benjamin's articulations of the "non-identity" of modern life, the difference between the ancients and the moderns, the disjunctive "temporalization" of relations between what is near and what is far, and the residual utopian potential that remains hidden but recognizable in alienated life as loss and lack.[10] Ahead and back, close in and far away, animate and inanimate, the multidirectional looking that sidereal relations require and the "flash" of insight [*Aufblitzen*] that sidereal critique affords must not be understood in terms of sheer "categorical negation" [*kategorische Negation*] though, as Weber rightly notes, but "rather in the detection of qualitative moments of perception as they can be excavated, at least unconsciously and in residual form, through to modern humans" [*vielmehr im Aufspüren qualitativer Wahrnehmungsmomente, wie sie residual bis zum modernen Menschen zumindest unbewußt zu eruieren sind*] (25). The lack characterizing modern human life for Benjamin is thus not absent but present and accessible to the dialectical critique that his *Denkbilder* entail.

Weber cites the "heliotropism" of Benjamin's fourth historical thesis in passing as one example of the philosopher's "Copernican turn of historical thought"

---

10 Weber writes: "Star-images serve [Benjamin] [...] for the representation of precisely that non-identical element, that improbability or even denial of access [*Entzogenheit*], that are at the same time necessary for his thought" (94–95). As Weber further notes, this occurs for Benjamin under "signs of temporalization" (95).

(38–39), but it is worth taking a longer look at the relevant passage in the original because it will resonate in the discussion of the Kluge miniature to come.[11] Benjamin comments on the intangibles of class struggle—one might count hope among them—as "things" [*Dinge*] that "have retroactive force" [*in die Ferne der Zeit zurück [wirken]*] (Benjamin, "Theses on the Philosophy of History" 255; "Über den Begriff der Geschichte" 252).[12] In the language of likeness he continues: "As flowers turn toward the sun, by dint of a secret heliotropism the past strives to turn toward that sun which is rising in the sky of history. A historical materialist must be aware of this most inconspicuous of all transformations" [*Wie Blumen ihr Haupt nach der Sonne wenden, so strebt kraft eines Heliotropismus geheimer Art, das Gewesene der Sonne sich zuzuwenden, die am Himmel der Geschichte im Aufgehen ist. Auf diese unscheinbarste von allen Veränderungen muß sich der historische Materialist verstehen*] ("Theses on the Philosophy of History" 255; "Über den Begriff der Geschichte" 252). This horizon given as if in natural likeness is thoroughly historical in Benjamin's dialectical sense and thus subject to change at any moment. Andrew McGettigan uses this passage to parse the "'secret heliotropism'" of Benjamin's "philosophy of historical *experience*" as an adaptation of Henri Bergson's non-linear "memory-image," that is to say, as that which addresses the present from the past by means of actualized perception oriented in the main not to knowledge but to action (McGettigan 25–28). For Benjamin, McGettigan expands: "[...] far from being inert objects of study, *historical* pasts address the present equivocally and heterogeneously. In the *Arcades Project* this dialectical structure is expressed by the concept of 'legibility'," which is constellative in its figuration (29; see also Weber 45).[13] For Fritz Breithaupt, who reads Benjamin in a phenomenological vein, "Benjamin locates the event of history in the making-phenomenal of the nonphenomenal nucleus" of historical things. The capacity of such things to have an afterlife however necessarily entails that "something remains open for the future," which is "unknown." Benjamin's own formulation of a "historical index" or "secret

---

11 Here I provide my translation of Weber's phrasing, which reads "die kopernikanische Wendung des historischen Denkens" (38). Above I relied on the English translation by Howard Eiland and Kevin McLaughlin, which renders Benjamin's "kopernikanische Wendung des Eingedenkens" as "Copernican turn of remembrance" (Benjamin, *The Arcades Project* 389).

12 The intangibles that Benjamin explicitly lists are "Zuversicht," "Mut," "Humor," "List," and "Unentwegtheit." The Zohn translation lists only "courage, humor, cunning, and fortitude," thus omitting "confidence." Benjamin does not say these items are the "refined and spiritual" things he means, but only that the "things" he means are "alive" in and appearing *as* them. The Zohn translation ("manifest themselves in this struggle as [...]") de-emphasizes the sense of liveness that my translation underscores.

13 McGettigan refers here to Convolute N3,1 of the Arcades Project.

index, by which [the past] is referred to redemption" turns on the figure of "heliotropism" in the fourth thesis (Breithaupt 191–192).[14] Here I would say that a sidereal lack is perceptible but the future as such is not. This distinction is crucial. What happens when the sun rises for Kluge?

"Hope at Sunrise" is one of Kluge's 350 "new stories" published under the title "Door to Door with an Other Life." The figure of "parallel worlds" with which this collection's foreword begins does not conjure separate worlds at all but realities cast as necessarily entwined. "A reality that destroys human beings is 'real.' Human beings deny reality that shows them its inhuman side: this is also 'real.' Thus we live of necessity in parallel worlds: DOOR TO DOOR WITH AN OTHER LIFE" [*Eine Realität, die Menschen vernichtet, ist 'wirklich'. Eine Wirklichkeit, die sich gegenüber Menschen nicht-menschlich zeigt, wird von ihnen verleugnet: das ist ebenfalls 'wirklich'. So leben wir notwendig in Parallelwelten: TÜR AN TÜR MIT EINEM ANDEREN LEBEN*] (7). With this necessary entwinement in an "other life" in mind, how can Kluge's storytelling of the recent past be understood as "new" not only in but also for the 21st century? Longstanding social and conceptual relations between futurity and modernity are subject in Europe and elsewhere to growing pressures of globalization, which refashions the story of modernity from any number of economic, political, and cultural perspectives. And yet Kluge has always been concerned with the production of alternative European and German modernities, as the frequent scholarly description of his creative work as counter-history suggests. In what sense then do the forms and stakes of Kluge's intensified preoccupation with storytelling at this contemporary moment respond to or reshape the future as an acute problem in thought and time?[15] "Hope at Sunrise" provides a useful point of entry for thinking about his cosmic miniatures in this vein.

---

14 The Benjamin quotations in Breithaupt's second paragraph on p. 192 are drawn from the second and fourth historical theses and from Convolute N3,1 of the Arcades Project. The phrase "secret index, by which it is referred to redemption" is from the second thesis, though the Zohn translation renders the index here as "temporal" rather than "secret." Writing "On Lyric Poetry and Society" in the 1950s, Theodor W. Adorno will speak of poetic form "as a philosophical sundial telling the time of history" [*das Gedicht als geschichtsphilosophische Sonnenuhr*] (*Notes to Literature*, Vol. I, 46).
15 For Luhmann, the future can be understood only as a "problem" in thought ("The Future Cannot Begin" 137, 145 et passim; "Describing the Future" 64). For Eshel's definition of futurity stressing open constructions of possibility from a comparative literary perspective, see *Futurity* (4) [*Zukünftigkeit* (15)]; Eshel's chapter devoted to Kluge is notably subtitled "Literature as Orientation" (53–66) and addresses the ironic hopefulness of texts from "Chronicle of Feelings." Another chapter provides a motif-based reading of Kluge's use of "'horizons of hope'" and irony in a story about the infamous Wannsee Conference of 1942 that is also included in

This short text is one of many numbered entries in a longer book section titled "Wir Glückskinder der Ersten Globalisierung" ["We Fortunate Children of the First Globalization"]. There globalization connotes the geobiology of planet Earth 630 million years ago and a quantum physics of temporality in which realities of hope and destruction co-exist in the present. Kluge's "hope at sunrise" revolves in this instance around a recognizably human figure—albeit one rendered in minimalist strokes—and the narrative is brief enough to be shared here:

> A still young woman—whose clinical condition, in the fourth hour of night, when a weakness befalls the body, had taken a rabid turn for the worse—still saw, in truth, entirely by indirection, the dawning red sky [*Morgenröte*]. She observed it as a luster on the metal of the medical instruments that surrounded her. She could not see the window from her bed in the intensive care unit.
>
> If there were any windows in the room at all, which was tuned to defend against foreign influences. She was still alert. She registered that she had not expected that she would still experience the end of this terrible night. Urban life began to flood through the hospital. The nurses and young doctors were noisily bustling back and forth. This is how she immediately took hope, before, around seven o'clock in the morning, she lost all control of her circulation and quickly, after a dose of morphine, died.
>
> [*Eine noch junge Frau, deren klinischer Zustand in der vierten Nachtstunde, in welcher den Körper eine Schwäche befällt, sich rabiat verschlechtert hatte, sah noch, und zwar ganz indirekt, die Morgenröte. Sie beobachtete sie als einen Glanz auf dem Metall der medizinischen Geräte, die sie umgaben. Das Fenster konnte sie von ihrem Bett in der Intensivstation aus nicht sehen.*
>
> *Wenn es überhaupt in dem auf Abwehr von Fremdeinflüssen gestimmten Raum Fenster gab. Noch war sie aufmerksam. Sie registrierte, daß sie nicht erwartet hatte, das Ende dieser schrecklichen Nacht noch zu erleben. Städtisches Leben begann die Krankenanstalt zu durchfluten. Die Schwestern und Jungärzte lärmten hin und her. So faßte sie unverzüglich Hoffnung, ehe sie gegen sieben Uhr früh jede Kontrolle über den Kreislauf verlor und rasch, nach einer Beigabe von Morphium, starb.*] (27)

In this narrative sequence a young woman in hospital takes a turn for the worse at night, observes a virtually Homeric rosy-fingered dawn "entirely by indirection," feels hope amidst the hustle and bustle of morning life and the realization

---

"Door to Door with an Other Life" (Kluge 151). See Eshel, *Futurity* (227–228). For key conceptual and historical reflections on "How to Use the Future" in relation to probability, affect, and modernity, see Rüdiger Campe. For Richard Langston, Kluge's televisual innovations in the 1980s already "represent an intensification of his storytelling" to the degree that his stories in that medium "are compressed into literal images that flash on the screen" (*Visions of Violence* 226). Langston associates this with a Benjaminian "compactness of storytelling" (225) that—in Kluge's hands—shifts from Benjamin's achronic messianism to "the anthropology of laboring bodies" (226). On the latter point, Langston refers to Fredric Jameson's essay "On Negt and Kluge" of 1988.

that she had not expected to survive the night, and dies with the aid of an ancient god of dreams at least nominally present in the reference to morphine. Is this a hopeful text? Insistent syntactical interruptions with which the story begins and the doubtful, heterodiegetic voice of narration that midway through shatters any sense of immersion take readers by surprise and unsettle efforts to orient oneself in the world of the text.[16] To illuminate Kluge's cosmic miniatures as one form of storytelling for the 21st century, I shall highlight three dimensions of this unsettlement.

First, regarding time and futurity, "Hope at Sunrise" commingles references to the cyclical advance of clock time, natural cycles of nighttime turning into daytime (indexed in part through the cultural commonplace or *topos* of a rosy dawn inaugurating a new day in both temporal and figurative senses), and the hospital patient's "use" of the future as textually evidenced by expectations that twice prove false, first when she expects to die but doesn't and then when she takes hope in the morning but dies exactly when the story too comes to an end. Scalar dimensions of time are in play as elements from the life and death of one human being are narrated in relation to the earth's rotation around the sun. As David Couzens Hoy details in his book on temporality as what he calls "the grid of lived [rather than scientific] intelligibility," modern philosophy has long stressed objective-subjective distinctions between "the time of the universe" and "the time of our lives" (92–93). As a phenomenologist writing against this philosophical tradition, Hoy claims that all time is "'lived time'" with lived time underwriting any interpretation of the world. Hoy is not concerned with futurity, but his mapping of human time and cosmic time helps bring into relief for us that Kluge's "Hope at Sunrise" presents the temporality and futurity of large and small—in this particular case of relative size, cosmic and human—as fundamentally relational, at least in the narrative economy

---

16 As Andreas Huyssen insightfully noted in 1995 in reference to Kluge's "new stories" for the late 20th century: "Reading Kluge's stories produces strange effects. Given their sheer number and the shortness of many, it is inevitable that the reader will forget a lot of them quickly. But eventually one feels the cumulative impact of his kind of storytelling, which operates on a paradigmatic rather than a syntagmatic level. And then there emerge those stories that begin to work in one's head. The gaps and fissures left by Kluge's minimalist narrative strategy beg to be filled in. The reader is hooked" (Huyssen, "An Analytic Storyteller" 147). Many features Huyssen finds operative in Kluge's 20th-century writing are also operative in the author's 21st-century storytelling. My project, in fundamental dialogue with Huyssen's important work, aims to address both continuities and shifting emphases in Kluge's writing for the 21st century.

of this very short text.[17] In this sense Kluge's "Hope at Sunrise" appears compatible with Benjamin's sidereal configuration of historical experience.

One could interject here that Paul Ricoeur, in *Time and Narrative*, understands narrative *tout court* as that which establishes a relationship between two otherwise incommensurable temporalities, namely, the objective time of the universe and the subjective time of our lives. In Ricoeur's hermeneutic undertaking, "narrative *is* the human relation to time" (Cobley, *Narrative* 17). Kluge's operative approach to narrative differs from this in crucial ways that also begin to tip him away from Benjamin. For example, Kluge's point of departure is not the radical incommensurability but the very entanglement of cosmic and human time, and this entanglement for Kluge is often narratively configured in terms of approximation rather than alienation or incommensurability. The fact that this is rarely if ever construed as continuous approximation for Kluge should not distract us from recognizing that some kind of approximation is in play nonetheless.

Contrastive consideration of Ricoeur additionally highlights for us that the sense-making of Kluge's storytelling is not hermeneutic but something like a cross between phenomenology, materialism, critique, and puttering as a form of labor. I would say that his storytelling exercises "future-making" to the degree that futurity, for Kluge, is a kind of long-distance sense organ that many of his narratives work on and operatively cultivate. The temporal nucleus of his cosmic miniatures becomes phenomenal. Writing in the first published version of *Geschichte und Eigensinn* in 1981 about social labor on historical relationships "as something concrete" [*als einem faßlichen Gegenstand*] (777), Oskar Negt and Alexander Kluge distinguished between the work of "short-distance" and "long-distance" senses. "The short-distance senses are working; the long-distance senses have not been worked on. Above all, they generate no society. That is a political problem of the present and a distortion in our basic relationship to history" [*Die Nähesinne arbeiten, an den Fernsinnen ist nicht gearbeitet worden. Sie bilden vor allem keine Gesellschaft. Das ist politisches Problem der Ge-*

---

[17] In a televised exchange between Kluge and Joseph Vogl in 2000, Vogl begins: "Wherever one has thought about time, one has turned one's gaze to the sky. As to the sun, which always returns, day after day [...]." To this Kluge replies, echoing the term that Lukács had also invoked: "[...] and to the starry sky" [*Sternenhimmel*] (Kluge and Vogl 261). In this interview, incisively titled "Zeit ohne Raum" ["Time Without Space"], Vogl retains a philosophical distinction between subjective time and world time (265). This is a distinction that I believe is tendentially undone in Kluge's cosmic miniatures. In reference to the geobiological globalization discussed above, it is worth noting that, in this exchange, Kluge associates "a first globalization" with the onset of locomotives in the 19th century (263).

genwart und Verzerrung des Grundverhältnisses zur Geschichte] (597). The "long-distance sense" [*Fernsinn*] Negt and Kluge had in mind in 1981 was history. In my assessment Kluge's storytelling practice today cultivates futurity as another long-distance temporal sense, albeit one that his cosmic miniatures bring very close in narrative form.[18]

To return to "Hope at Sunrise," the second dimension of unsettlement I wish to highlight concerns the status of hope for Kluge in contradistinction to utopia. The hospital room becomes an explicit site of hopeful orientation to a new day and continued life when the patient perceives "entirely by indirection" the light and color of dawn reflected on medical equipment in the room. This observed observation is immediately followed by a complete sentence in a narrative voice that could still be considered homo- though not autodiegetic. This voice tells us that the window in the room could not be seen from the patient's bed. However, what we encounter next is a decidedly heterodiegetic narrative voice, albeit one that conveys epistemological uncertainty as to whether there *are* any windows in the room. This uncertainty manifests in the only incomplete sentence in the story, a syntactical fragment that gives rise to an implied question. If the light of dawn is not generated by natural sources, what unnatural factors account for the "foreign influences" that might nonetheless enter even a windowless room in the form of hope? The *thematic* allusion to "foreign influences" suggests that hope comes from elsewhere—a place not given in the story world—but the *narrative* unsettlement in "Hope at Sunrise" suggests that hope is already present, not nowhere (as the etymology of *u-topia* would have it) but possibly everywhere.[19] This does not negate the textual fact that the young woman's

---

[18] Edited by Devin Fore, a partial English translation of *Geschichte und Eigensinn* appeared as *History and Obstinacy* with Zone Books in 2014. The two passages I have cited in my translation from the German original are not included in the Zone publication. On "future-making" in relation to both anthropology and globalization, see Arjun Appadurai, *The Future as Cultural Fact*.
[19] Kluge's configuration of space and time here is both compatible with and divergent from what Reinhart Koselleck has described as a paradigmatic shift from the spatialization to the temporalization of utopia in European modernity. His essay "The Temporalization of Utopia" (translated by Todd Presner for inclusion in Koselleck's *Practice of Conceptual History*, 84 – 99) speaks of the modern "onset [*Einbruch*] of the future in utopia" (85). Jakob Böhme's mystical treatise of 1612 titled *Aurora oder Morgenröte im Aufgang* ["Aurora or Dawn Rising"] and the "windowlessness" of Gottfried Wilhelm Leibniz's early 18th-century monads also merit mention in relation to Kluge's "Hope at Sunrise." Here too I would say that Kluge is both deeply engaged with long-standing traditions of sensibility and cosmology, on the one hand, and with unprecedented contemporary problematics, on the other. For a refined reading of Leibniz's windowless monads in relation to early modern theories of sensibility and metaphysics, see Hubertus Busche. Challenging conventional readings that associate the windowlessness of Leibniz's monads with a putative lack of insight, influence, and relationality between individuals (100), Busche details how

hopes and expectations prove false relative to apparent evidence, but neither does it relegate hope—the only word of the title to be repeated in the story itself—to the status of illusion. Hope is cast here precisely not as a logical result of causal sequence or even faith but as an incipient phenomenological orientation toward a different yet perceptible temporality. This alternative or parallel temporality becomes accessible only through a narrative voice that disrupts its own narration and becomes in this sense more rather than less reliable in inverse proportion to its cognitive certainty. If hope can take place everywhere, the question of access is still key. The absent-present conjunction of hope may be compatible with Benjamin's sidereal dialectic, but the phenomenology of narration for Kluge is arguably closer to sensual labor than epistemological critique.[20]

The third dimension of unsettlement in "Hope at Sunrise" pertains to the task of Kluge's storytelling project for the time of our 21st-century lives. Here I suggest the following contrast with the philosophy of hope articulated by Ernst Bloch on the cusp between totalitarian dictatorship and post-fascist democracies in Germany. Bloch's conceptualization of the "not-yet" of what he called a becoming of "concrete utopia" [*konkret werdende Utopie*] was intended both as a Marxist corrective to Marxist economism (which Bloch considered a "false concept of matter") *and* as a Marxist anthropology restoring the human to its rightful conceptual place as the material core of political transformation ("Zur Ontologie des Noch-Nicht-Seins" ["On the Ontology of Not-Yet-Being"] 57–58, 63). Benjamin's historical materialism also has its anthropological dimensions, as Rainer Nägele, Miriam Hansen, Devin Fore, Sigrid Weigel, and others have discussed—in relation for example to *Leib, Kreatürlichkeit*, image, and media as modern phenomena—though Benjamin's anthropological materialism predates in all senses those 20th-century catastrophes that have such centrifugal force in Kluge's writing. The anthropological valence of Kluge's stories of hope is

---

Leibniz's critique of Cartesian scholasticism leads Leibniz to a more complex conclusion instead: "Monads need no windows because, through the very medium of perception, they are always already with the Other. They do not *have* any windows because—mediated through the divine logos of self-activated mediation—they *are* themselves the window to the Other" [*Monaden brauchen keine Fenster, weil sie durch das Medium der Perzeption hindurch immer schon beim Anderen sind. Sie h a b e n keine Fenster, weil sie—vermittelt durch den göttlichen Logos selbsttätiger Vermittlung—das Fenster zum Anderen selbst s i n d*] (115).

20 Kluge and Benjamin are both famously committed to materialist critique in the cause of human freedom, and both also focus much of their work on language, though Benjamin is far better known for the latter than Kluge. My argument that Kluge's phenomenology of narration is closer to sensual labor than epistemological critique remarks a relative emphasis, especially in connection with futurity, rather than an absolute distinction in relation to Benjamin.

far less clear.[21] It may be apt to recall Benjamin here—"What draws the reader to the novel is the hope of warming his shivering life with a death he reads about" (*Illuminations*, "The Storyteller" 101)—and "Hope at Sunrise" might suggest an anthropological thrust given Kluge's emphasis in "Door to Door with an Other Life" on a kind of biopolitical "stock of hope in us" [*Hoffnungsvorrat in uns*] (7). Yet if his storytelling has an anthropological dimension, this does not describe general or even historical conditions of human life but instead entails an intensified investment in storytelling as necessary for survival now. Benjamin famously links the "art of storytelling" [*Kunst des Erzählens*] and the "impartability of experience" [*Mitteilbarkeit der Erfahrung*] in terms of a 20th-century decline in his essay of 1936 on the 19th-century Russian writer Nikolai Leskov, but Benjamin cautions us even then to think of the approaching "end" of storytelling in terms of changing "forces of productivity" [*Produktivkräfte*] rather than decay [*Verfall*].[22] He also links the art of storytelling to a certain proximity to death, and Kluge's oeuvre is nothing if not riddled with the dead and dying. Benjamin additionally praises the ancient storytelling of Herodotus in ways that could apply to Kluge's "Hope at Sunrise." Storytelling "does not exhaust itself" in recourse to information, Benjamin writes, and Herodotus's especially dry style "explains nothing," he claims (392). Kluge's intensified investment in written forms of storytelling that "explains nothing" entails—among others—that form of short prose that I will now discuss more generally as cosmic miniature. Like Benjamin, Kluge mobilizes the figuration of the sidereal to write past, present, and future history "against the grain" of modern alienation and lack. Diverging in other respects from Benjamin's temporal configuration of sidereal relations nearly a century ago, however, Kluge's narrative experiments in literary form for the 21st century yield new relations to the futurity of hope and the culture of storytelling in turn.

Cosmic motifs abound in Kluge's multimedial oeuvre, both before and since 2000, including his writing about cinema as distinguished from film. For exam-

---

21 Nägele notes that Benjamin's "'anthropological materialism'" marked his "unbridgeable distance to Adorno" (172–173), a claim that the second section of Part One will revisit. For astute remarks on rethinking the nexus of anthropomorphism, narrative, and perspective in early 20th-century literature and art, see Fore. Fore relates Negt and Kluge's term "a deficient mutant" [*Mangelmutante*] and their "materialist anthropology" to early 20th-century debates about anthropology left and right (8). More will be said about this too in the next section.
22 Benjamin calls the "end" he has in mind a "concomitant symptom" [*Begleiterscheinung*] of such productivity ("The Storyteller," *Illuminations* 83, 87). See also Alexander Honold (375). See especially as well Jeanne Marie Gagnebin's book chapter on the so-called "end" of storytelling in Benjamin's approach to modern memory, and Patrizia McBride's new insights into Benjamin's conceptual approach to storytelling, narrative, and montage (*The Chatter of the Visible*).

ple, his foreword to *Cinema Stories* posits cinema as "immortal" in contrast to film and attributes this to the claim, "that we can share with one another in public something that 'moves us inwardly'" [*daß wir etwas, das uns 'innerlich bewegt', einander öffentlich mitteilen*] (*Cinema Stories* n.p.; *Geschichten vom Kino* 7). Something "'like cinema'" will continue to function long after the film technologies we know cease to be relevant, we read. In the print piece "The Cosmos as Cinema" a disembodied narrative voice paraphrases 1846 claims that all world history is "traveling through the cosmos as MOVING SEQUENCES OF IMAGES," and summarizes the gist of such claims: "all of prehistory is stored in the universe in tracks of light" (*Cinema Stories* 91). In the narrative economy of this text however 20th-century astrophysics highlight the concomitant "problem" of what cannot be seen, even as the rest of this cosmic miniature references writing and reading technologies associated with "dark energy," advertising columns [*Litfaßsäulen*], papyrus, x-ray and infrared machines, and the miniature's medium of print (91–93).

Yet the mere presence of cosmic motifs is insufficient to justify the rubric of cosmic miniatures, as Kluge's sprawling *Lernprozesse mit tödlichem Ausgang* [*Learning Processes with a Deadly Outcome*] attests. First published in 1973, this wordy experiment in time takes us from the Third Reich and the Battle of Stalingrad via revolutionary China and planetary destruction to Martian orbit in 2103. Large and small arcs of history, futurity, and narration play key roles here (see Adelson, "Experiment Mars"), but this text is not a cosmic miniature. To repeat, in my usage the term refers to short prose pieces of literary experimentation in which the narrative function of cosmic motifs pivots on narrative uses of futurity as experiential portals in time.[23] These specific uses of futurity become linchpins for engaging varying relations that Kluge's miniatures set into motion

---

[23] Some Kluge scholarship addresses the narrative status of contingency and causality in Kluge's prose in relation to modern literary traditions known as "kleine Prosa" [literally: small prose]. See for example Sascha Michel. I focus on the narrative status of futurity instead. Because I also focus on Kluge's cosmic miniatures as a form of print literature, these miniatures should not be confused with Kluge's newest form of "micro-texts" [*mikrotexte*], which are explicitly composed "for the digital generation" in reference to technologies such as Smartphone and Kindle (see for example Kluge, "Die Entsprechung einer Oase" ["Corresponding to an Oasis"]). According to editorial information provided with the "oasis" piece, this micro-text "derives from a telephone conversation with Alexander Kluge" in 2012. Dirk Göttsche analyzes small-prose forms of contemporary German literature with no mention of Kluge or futurity, though Göttsche does associate a "distinct aesthetic temporality" [*ästhetische Eigenzeit*] with "small prose," a temporality that "cancels out" modern time through "deceleration of perception" ("Zeitpoetik in Kleiner Prosa der Gegenwart" 250; see also 251). For a historical retrospective and literary examples drawn from the present too, see also Göttsche, *Kleine Prosa in Moderne und Gegenwart*.

between cosmic horizons and human life teetering between hope and destruction. Kluge's longstanding attention to hegemonic "strategies from above" and human survival "strategies from below"—for example, in his 1977 account of the Allied air bombing of Halberstadt in World War II (the account that prompted Sebald to liken Kluge to Benjamin's angel of history)—is well known.[24] While

---

24 The Appendix entry "Above and Below (*oben und unten*)" in Negt and Kluge's *History and Obstinacy* in 2014—which cites among others the example of systemic breakdown in "the German Democratic Republic in 1989," a historic event that took place eight years after *Geschichte und Eigensinn* was first published—still discusses destructive power from above and seeming defenselessness from below with an eye to moments when "[r]elations between the two are inverted" (424). (For the German, see Kluge, "Landkarte der Begriffe: Ein Glossar zu *Geschichte und Eigensinn*," in *Glass Shards: Echoes of a Message in a Bottle* [Richard Langston, Gunther Martens, Vincent Pauval, Christian Schulte, and Rainer Stollmann 38].) The longer section titled "Oben und unten" in *Geschichte und Eigensinn* (786–790) in 1981 cites historical examples from the 1920s and 1940s but foregrounds similar relations of inversion (see especially 790). Here the authors conjure cosmic examples of a "Lagrangian point" [*abarischer Punkt*] in celestial physics to explain what a decisive moment of such inversion could look like: "An impulse must therefore struggle 'uphill' against Earth's gravitational force, then climbs to the crest of the gravitational mountain. From there it goes 'downhill' into the much smaller gravitational funnel of the moon" (790). For present purposes it is important to note that, despite the telluric imagery Negt and Kluge invoke here in the metaphor of the mountain, "**Above** and **Below** do not designate any emplacements [*Örtlichkeiten*], but rather a position in the relationship to history," that is to say, "points and formations in time" [*Zeitpunkte und Zeitgestalten*] (789). The possibility of both temporal inversion and social conversion is given in this configuration, which Negt and Kluge explicitly posit against any linear "concept of progress" (789). In this temporal connection in particular, see also Fore's comparison of "recursive and even reversible" structures of time in "microhistories" discussed by Negt and Kluge in their later book *Maßverhältnisse des Politischen* ["Politics as Relations of Measure"] and by Yuri Lotman in his Russian study, *Kul'tura i vzryv* [*Culture and Explosion*], both books having been published in 1992 (Fore, "The Old, the New, and the Now: Points of Orientation at the End of the Cold War"). Reviewing *Geschichte und Eigensinn* for the journal *Telos* in the mid 1980s, and invoking Rudolf Burger's comparison of Negt and Kluge with Foucault, Andrew Bowie also stressed inversion, albeit with a different point of comparison: "With Foucault, the authors are interested in the 'microphysics of power,' but they give it a more complex materialist foundation than the largely Nietzschean one Foucault provides. [...] According to Burger, they actually *invert* Foucault's perspective. What Foucault 'describes "from above" as a strategy of disciplining from the viewpoint of power centers dispersed over the surface of the social body, Negt and Kluge describe "from below"'" (Bowie 185). Stressing more than mere inversions of spatial hierarchies of power, my focus on cosmic miniatures in Kluge's literary prose helps illuminate temporal aspects of "above and below" relations that have long played a certain role in his work, but for which familiar spatial approaches based primarily on his 1977 text about the aerial bombing of civilians in Halberstadt in 1945 cannot account. The inversion of vertical hierarchies of power continues to matter in Kluge's work, but this alone cannot explain the temporal conversion of catastrophic history into what Adorno

these strategies of "above" and "below" might be thought to be replicated in figural tensions between outer space and earthly ground, Kluge's cosmic miniatures give us different scalar dimensions and narrative relations to engage for the 21st century.

Here I shall briefly sketch the sorts of cosmic miniatures one encounters in Kluge's rapidly proliferating work and discuss two additional conceptual touchstones for contemplating their significance. Among Kluge's cosmic miniatures written in the 21st century one finds minimalist accounts of invisible extraterrestrials whose presence can be felt and known, according to the terms of Kluge's narration (as a later section of Part One will demonstrate), several stories commingling the geopolitical history of astrophysics as a branch of knowledge production with hapless but only loosely drawn anthropomorphic figures to whom affects of disappointment, resentment, yearning, and *Ausdauer* or endurance attach, and seemingly straightforward scientific metanarratives about the long arc of cosmic formations resulting in stars, planets, and galaxies. Narrative strategies for negotiating futurity vary from text to text but can nonetheless be grasped under my proposed rubric of cosmic miniatures as defined. Subsequent sections of Part One will analyze examples of the first two sorts of cosmic miniatures described here, while a discussion of the third will be reserved for Part Three, which primarily concerns what we might call Kluge's German miniatures for an otherwise global 21st century. Readers familiar with Kluge will not be surprised to discover that some degree of categorical overlap is impossible to avoid if one is to do any justice to his prose. Part One nonetheless details some salient features of Kluge's cosmic miniatures in particular.

One of the key conceptual historians of European modernity, Reinhart Koselleck published his seminal study of "futures past," in part, to track history inhering in concepts as not merely descriptive but generative.[25] Like many other scholars of modernity, Koselleck sees particular forms of futurity as constitutive of modern society, politics, philosophy, economy, and culture. These forms tend to grasp the future as both different from and better than the past, to the degree that the modern concept of "progress" pertains (see also Luhmann in this regard from the perspective of systems theory). For Koselleck, modern concepts of "'space of experience' and 'horizon of expectation'" entail "different orders" (259) of relating past and future in the present. "Experience once made is as

---

once called—as we shall see in a subsequent section of Part One—"future without life's miseries." For that, we need to tend to Kluge's human and cosmic horizons of futurity.

25 *Vergangene Zukunft* was first published in 1979. I will be citing from the English translation, *Futures Past*, and focusing on the chapter, "'Space of Experience' and 'Horizon of Expectation': Two Historical Categories" (255–275).

complete as its occasions are past; that which is to be done in the future, which is anticipated in terms of an expectation, is scattered among an infinity of temporal extensions" (260). Koselleck elaborates: "The horizon is that line behind which a new space of experience will open, but which cannot yet be seen. The legibility of the future, despite possible prognoses confronts an absolute limit, for it cannot be experienced" (261). Despite all variations for which he allows, this modern temporality renders the "space of experience" as closed and integrative—the experienced past "assembled into a totality" (260), a mode of integration to which Benjamin would never subscribe—and the "horizon of expectation," for Koselleck, as necessarily open and inaccessible to experience. At the same time, as Koselleck's analysis elucidates, temporal tensions between experience and expectation characterize modernity as a historical phenomenon and yet are changing *in* historical time.[26] In my reading of "Hope at Sunrise" as a cosmic miniature for the 21st century, the changing horizon of hope is rendered— with and *contra* Koselleck—*accessible* to experience by virtue of the *legibility* of futurity in narrative form. Precisely because it becomes structurally accessible to experience, however, this heliotropic futurity cannot be understood to be deferred. This marks a significant departure from Benjamin's historical materialism.

Huyssen coined the term "modernist miniatures" to lend a name to a form of writing that emerged early in the 20th century in response to "an epochal crisis" of experience associated with "the destruction of experience in the trenches" of World War I, mass media and changing forms of social life in urban settings, and what Benjamin "diagnosed [as] the end of storytelling," as Huyssen put it ("Modernist Miniatures" 27–28).[27] My term "cosmic miniatures" in reference to Kluge's new "new stories" is inspired by Huyssen's coinage and should be understood as being in dialogue with his work on modernist miniatures as a so-called minor genre that has paradoxically played a major role—in Huyssen's assessment—in the literary history of modernism and the cultural history of modernization in Europe (29, 32).[28] Reading the short-prose practice of writers such as Rilke,

---

[26] For Koselleck, "space of experience and horizon of expectation are not to be statically related to each other" (263). Shifting relations in speed and proximity between lived spaces of experience and not-yet-experienced horizons of expectation are two of the main types of historical change in the modern era that Koselleck discusses.
[27] See also Huyssen, "The Urban Miniature" and especially *Miniature Metropolis*, which will be discussed in the next section.
[28] Although Huyssen distinguishes modernist miniatures from earlier forms of short prose, his account of the former is compatible with the claim advanced by the editors of *Kleine Prosa* ["Small Prose"] when they write: "In this function of productive disturbance, Small Prose remains to this day a model form of literary innovation, self-reflection, and boundary transgres-

Musil, Kafka, Kracauer, Benjamin, and others, Huyssen calls the modernist miniature "a specific mode of writing" that entails "the modernist transformation" of older forms of both storytelling (*Erzählung*) and other short prose forms such as "aphorism, fragment, sketch," and so on (29–30). The specificity of these urban miniatures turns for Huyssen on "the micrological observation of metropolitan space" (32), deep links between narrative temporality and spatial experience (however broken they both may be), and "a foregrounding of vision" as writers and theorists alike adapted feuilleton forms to navigate a disorienting "crisis of perception" precisely through "reading and seeing the city" (32).[29]

Kluge is undoubtedly heir to these modernist miniatures. However, his cosmic miniatures for the 21st century distinguish themselves in three key ways. First, Kluge's cosmic miniatures are more centrally concerned with invisible rather than visible phenomena, as the recurring figure and problem of unseen extraterrestrials suggests.[30] Second, the shift from urban settings to outer space alters the valence of experience because experience in these miniatures becomes an emphatic function of futurity rather than space as a scene of reading.[31] Third, whereas the modernist miniatures respond to conjoined crises of experience,

---

sion that has participated significantly in the transformational processes of literary modernity" [*In dieser Funktion produktiver Störung bleibt die Kleine Prosa bis heute ein Formmodell literarischer Innovation, Selbstreflexion und Grenzüberschreitung, das an den Transformationsprozessen der literarischen Moderne wesentlichen Anteil hat*] (see Althaus et al, ix). For Huyssen's more extensive account of the specifically literary role played by the modernist or "metropolitan miniature" from Baudelaire to Adorno, see *Miniature Metropolis: Literature in an Age of Photography and Film*. For other perspectives on small prose forms in European or broader international traditions, see for example A. Lehr (*Kleine Formen*), Ottmar Ette (*Nanophilologie*), and Daniel Kampa (*Kurz und bündig: Die schnellsten Geschichten der Welt*). According to Ette, "A micronarrative always signals its macrocosm," by which he means the macro-structural conditions of reading, writing, and understanding in literary narrative (3). This hermeneutic position is not entirely compatible with the modernist miniatures analyzed by Huyssen.

29 For Huyssen, the crisis of perception that modernist miniatures engaged was itself "the creation of a modernist urban imaginary as an embodied material fact" on a much broader scale, in significant part through photography and film (*Miniature Metropolis* 4).

30 This claim is not absolute. Many of Kluge's stories before and since 2000 also feature numerous motifs drawn from the history of optics and the science of vision as well as perspective. As Huyssen discusses in some detail, some modernist miniatures also feature a "form of spatial terror" associated with invisibility ("Modernist Miniatures" 34–35).

31 Analyzing stories from "The Gap the Devil Leaves Us," Matthew Miller stresses the "spatial coordinates" of Kluge's "diabolical dialectics." According to Miller, these examples of Kluge's writing entail a commitment on Kluge's part to "enlightenment's renewal from out of its blind spots" (320). See also Christopher Pavsek, who makes a different but related argument about "failure" as a constitutive element of Kluge's engagement with cinema and revolution (*The Utopia of Film*).

perception, and narration, Kluge's cosmic miniatures teeter between hope and destruction under the aegis of what he calls "an extremely extended chance" [*eine extrem langgestreckte Chance*] ("Our Ancestors, the Stars," "Door to Door with an Other Life" 42).

Postclassical narratologist David Herman lists the basic building blocks of narrative as situatedness, event sequencing, worldmaking or "world disruption," and "what it's like" or experience (*Basic Elements of Narrative* xvi). While there is certainly setting in "Hope at Sunrise," most of Kluge's cosmic miniatures are only minimally situated without being fully emplaced—on this planet or any other. Whole worlds—even disrupted ones—are rarely given despite frequent threats to Earth's survival. And thoughts and feelings of anthropomorphic figures are so scarcely sketched, one can certainly not speak of experience as Herman or Koselleck defines it. On this point Kluge is much closer to Benjamin's concept of experience as socially and historically under siege. If Kluge's cosmic miniatures—as a subset of his new "new stories" for the 21st century— qualify as narrative, as I believe they do, they do so at the outer reaches of contemporary narrativity with a stress on non-linear sequencing.[32] This form of sequencing plays an even greater role in Kluge's global miniatures, which will be discussed in Part Two. Before we can turn to them, it is especially important to note at this juncture that the temporality of his cosmic miniatures serves the cultivation of futurity as an experience to be had in reading Kluge's prose, while the "extract" of the future in Benjamin's sidereal and heliotropic model of historical change remains non-phenomenal.[33]

This is not at all to say that Benjamin's overall project is confined to epistemological critique. The point here is rather that the form of futurity that Benja-

---

[32] On the more general and ongoing importance of "non-linear narration" for Kluge, see also Christian Schulte, who focuses on Kluge's relationship to Benjamin, and Wolfgang Reichmann, who focuses in part on Kluge's 21st-century miniatures too. *Cosmic Miniatures* will also address some exceptions to "non-linear" predilections in Kluge's writing practice.

[33] By contrast, Eric Downing incisively suggests that Benjamin's account of "'magic reading'" in the latter's essays on mimesis and similitude entails a temporality of speed that not only establishes contact with "the extract of things," but "also, in however weakened a form, achieves a contact with the future, or an extract of the future" (210). The weak form of "contact with the future" that Downing underscores in Benjamin's "'magic reading'" offers a bridge to Kluge that the non-phenomenal temporal nucleus of Benjamin's "secret heliotropism" does not provide. I argue that a phenomenological experience of futurity is considerably strengthened in reading Kluge's prose. For extended analysis of textual relationships between futurity and reading in 19th-century realist and 20th-century modernist prose, see Downing's forthcoming monograph, tentatively titled *The Chain of Things: Magic, Reading, Sympathy, and the Future in German Literature and Thought 1850–1940*.

min invokes in the service of that larger project is resolutely inaccessible to phenomenal experience. In this particular regard, Benjamin's orientation to the future arguably thus remains conventional in Koselleck's modern sense. By contrast, Kluge diverges from Benjamin and Koselleck alike in his narrative use of futurity as an experience to be had in reading his cosmic miniatures. In *The Utopia of Film* Christopher Pavsek writes that Kluge's "essential gesture" is a temporal "utopian imperative," always "toward a redeemed future" (1, 22–23), by which Pavsek means a future that is always necessarily and repeatedly deferred in time.[34] I wonder if this is true. Reading Kluge's cosmic miniatures in and for the 21st century leads me to suggest that complex historical futures are both closer and more useable than we might otherwise sense. Reading suns and stars in Kluge's recent prose helps refine our grasp of the author's narrative poetics, his heliotropic relationship to Benjamin, and his phenomenological contributions to futurity as a cosmic dimension of contemporary literature.

2 Heliotropic Narrative with and beyond Adorno

2.1 Something Missing and Counterfactual Hope

The relationship between Kluge's cosmic miniatures and Benjamin's sidereal futurity is structurally configured as a form of *Abschied*, itself a recurring motif in Kluge's multimedial oeuvre. Derived from the transitive verb *abscheiden*, which generally means "to separate" but in its intransitive variant can also mean to take one's leave as in "to die," the noun is usually translated as "farewell." The title of Kluge's first feature film, *Abschied von gestern* (1965–1966), though rendered in English as *Yesterday Girl*, is thus commonly understood in terms of a "farewell to yesterday." This might appear underscored by the film's often-cited

---

[34] Pavsek, who considers Kluge "perhaps the most significant heir to Adorno's thought working in Germany today" (150), ascribes differentiated types of influence on Kluge's cinematic oeuvre to Adorno in particular with regard to utopia; Pavsek has relatively little to say in *The Utopia of Film* on Kluge in relation to Benjamin or literature. However, Pavsek's pointedly temporal configuration of utopia in the conjoined service of critical theory and revolutionary praxis would offer a bridge to Kluge's interests in Benjamin and literature too. In this regard see also Pavsek's 1993 essay on Kluge's storytelling in relation to Benjamin, with which the present study shares certain affinities. For example, Pavsek makes the following observation about Kluge in 1993: "the question of narrative is a matter of practice, of just how one might go about initiating learning processes that would lead to an outcome other than a deadly one" (86). However, Pavsek stresses uses of storytelling as a form of labor without specifically addressing the narrative status of futurity in Kluge's writing practice.

epigraph: "Uns trennt von gestern kein Abgrund, sondern die veränderte Lage." Miriam Hansen renders this correctly in English translation this way: "We are separated from yesterday not by an abyss, but by the changed situation" ("Reinventing the Nickelodeon" 404). Her astute analysis of Kluge's films stresses how he responds to both historical catastrophe and postwar change in Germany by relocating "his utopia of cinema to a different construction site" (404), which is to say, different from what the past alone in either political or cinematic terms can afford. For my purposes, an alternative translation of the epigraph to *Yesterday Girl* might conceivably read: "We are not separated from yesterday by an abyss, but by the changed situation." This slight syntactical alteration underscores both conjunctive and disjunctive temporalities in our posited relationship to yesterday, and this relationship enabled by a "changed situation" must also be construed as one to an historical abyss. In this sense we are not separated from yesterday after all, and yet it is equally important to note, for Kluge as both a filmmaker and a writer, that this datum of not being separated is itself subject to differentiating change. This multidirectional relationship to yesterday is one that the judge in a key courtroom scene in *Yesterday Girl* both represents and blocks when he introduces knowledge that the defendant before him comes from a Jewish family victimized by Nazi genocide, on the one hand, and then brusquely imposes a courtroom taboo on the historical connection, on the other: "But let's leave that, it lies behind us" [*Aber lassen wir das, es liegt zurück*]. Yet neither the filmic figure of Anita G. nor the earlier literary version that prompted her cinematic incarnation bids farewell or leaves the past behind as the judge in *Yesterday Girl* would have it.[35] By divergent aesthetic means, Anita G. instead signals in both works extended engagement with a catastrophic and criminal past, precisely through Kluge's reconfiguration of possible relationships to yesterday.[36] This form of leave-taking constitutes something closer to a

---

[35] On German relations of taboo to murdered Jews, see Gertrud Koch ("Between Fear of Contact and Self-Preservation"). The female protagonist of *Yesterday Girl* is Anita G., and this name also serves as the overarching title of twelve related but also quite different narrative entries in Kluge's earliest literary collection (*Lebensläufe*). The judge and courtroom scene that play such a prominent role in the film, for example, appear only peripherally in "Anita G." (see Kluge, "Chronicle of Feelings," Vol. 2, 734–748). For Kluge's more recent thoughts on negating the negation of farewell in film, see "Kein Abschied von gestern."

[36] Heide Schlüpmann, whose feminist analysis discusses the problematics of "living after Auschwitz" as one of the two main themes of *Yesterday Girl*, the filmic Anita G. is "a seismograph whose reactions are observed" but who herself remains incapable of producing a critical perspective on this historical problematic (74). Miriam Hansen notes that "most of Kluge's female characters" function as "allegorical constructions" ("Reinventing the Nickelodeon" 403). On the judge's remarks in *Yesterday Girl*, see also Thomas Elsaesser (*German Cinema* 97).

branching or veering off from an existing path or trajectory rather than a definitive farewell. The form this takes in Kluge's global miniatures for the 21st century will be taken up again in Part Two's discussion of a section of "Door to Door with an Other Life" titled "Abschied von den Lokomotiven" ["Farewell to Locomotives"]. There we will see that deviating from tracks laid in the past yields narrative work on time despite the imagery of relays, links, and railway connections that might initially appear to favor the telluric and spatial instead.

The relationship between Kluge's cosmic miniatures and Benjamin's sidereal futurity can thus be construed more as an operative de-viation than a definitive farewell.[37] Even more crucially, however, the recognition that the futurity of Kluge's cosmic miniatures becomes phenomenal and accessible to experience—by virtue of its legibility in narrative form—allows us to understand a pivotal absence or lack in Kluge's storytelling in a fundamentally new way. This will also require us to understand that the legibility of futurity in Kluge's prose miniatures must not be confused with what Adorno once condemned in his pithy characterization of traditional European metaphysics as merely the "legible constellation of that which exists."[38] Kluge's literary experiments are ironically full of what we might say is not there, only hardly there, or barely detectable: remnants, residue, fragments, gaps, blind spots, and in cosmic terms, black holes of various orders

---

[37] Writing on Ernst Bloch and Walter Benjamin as iconoclastic "users of the utopian tradition," Barry Maxwell characterizes the "overriding imperative" of that tradition as fundamentally spatial, its figurative repertoire reliant on "continual variations on metaphors of the road, the path, the street, or more abstractly perhaps 'ways' (*Wege*)." As Maxwell argues, Bloch and Benjamin's refunctioned approaches to utopian thought in the European tradition can therefore mobilize a rhetoric of diverse paths and *Wege* "to further utopian progress" without succumbing to teleological models of linearity ("The Paths in the Midst of Collapse" 217–218 and 226). Maxwell does not account for the "temporalization of utopia" that conceptual historian Reinhart Koselleck posits as paradigmatic for European modernity. As we shall see, Kluge's striking fascination with "ways out" or *Auswege* nonetheless ties him to spatial and temporal dimensions alike in the tense relationship between critical theory and utopian thought.

[38] Here I deviate slightly from Ashton's translation of this passage from Adorno's *Negative Dialectics*, which Ashton renders as "a legible constellation of things in being" (407). Ashton's translation underscores Adorno's critique of ontology; mine brings his critique of empiricism more sharply into view. Adorno crafted his *Negative Dialectics* against the European tradition of metaphysics, which in his critical German assessment was "möglich allein als lesbare Konstellation von Seiendem" (*Negative Dialektik* 399). The legibility of futurity in Kluge's work is closer to what Adorno by contrast conceived in *Negative Dialectics* as "metaphysical experience" (*Negative Dialectics* 372–375; *Negative Dialektik* 365–368). Pavsek, who analyzes both compatibilities and differences between Adorno and Kluge in reference to the latter's work on film, finds that the two figures share a distinctly somatic interest in the "figure of utopia" beyond the "'merely existent'" (*The Utopia of Film* 197).

of magnitude in both knowledge and space. This is in part related to Benjamin's philosophical concept of historical materialism as reading fragments "against the grain" of 19th-century historicism and narrative traditions of continuous linear progress (see Kai Lars Fischer's elaboration of this connection with regard to Kluge's extensive writing on the Battle of Stalingrad), just as it is also related, in even stronger part, to Adorno's micrological concerns with "holes, gaps, and blind spots" [*Löcher, Lücken und Leerstellen*], as Joseph Vogl puts it in describing the paratactical "aphoristic structure" of Adorno's own writing and arguments in *Minima Moralia* (Vogl, "Woher der Storch die Kinder bringt" 44).[39] Yet Kluge's own writerly obsession with gaps, holes, and blind spots also signals his more general indebtedness to 20th-century contestations across the political spectrum over the Weimar Republic's legacy of philosophical anthropology. As Devin Fore observes in his trenchant study of modernism and realism entwined in Weimar-era thought and culture, philosophical anthropology modeled the human being as an "unfinished, world-open (*weltoffen*) creature," and Arnold Gehlen—the figure most prominently and most controversially associated with philosophical anthropology in early 20th-century Germany—"defined the human animal as a 'deficient being' (*Mängelwesen*) and a constitutional mimic. Unlike other animals, Gehlen wrote, man is born into the world ill equipped and featureless, possessing neither the instinctual drives nor the concrete matériel necessary for survival" (*Realism After Modernism* 7). Given Gehlen's formal association with the National Socialist Party as early as 1933 and the at times "proto-fascist" conclusions drawn by some proponents of philosophical anthropology, Fore continues, "philosophical anthropology was for decades publicly proscribed among the Left" (7). Notable exceptions underscored by Fore from the period following World War II include figures one could hardly associate with right-wing politics:

---

39 Adorno's own elaborations on related matters in the essay titled "Parataxis," which is devoted to the importance of Friedrich Hölderlin's poetics for both critical method and historical analysis, is included in Volume 2 of Adorno's *Notes to Literature*. There he argues that Hölderlin wrote against the grain of both philosophical idealism and poetic realism. Adorno ties this to a critique of capitalism. "The realistic principle in poetry duplicates the unfreedom of human beings, their subjection to machinery and its latent law, the commodity form" (127). As Susan Buck-Morss details, Adorno's critical method of "negative dialectics" is itself indebted to the early Benjamin (64–65 et passim). On Adorno's particular appreciation of what he called Benjamin's "'microscopic gaze'" in this connection, see Buck-Morss (74–76). On Adorno's gaps more generally, including in relation to ancient Greek as well as Christian theological traditions, see also Raymond Geuss. Referring to the translation of Kluge's *Lebensläufe* that appeared as *Case Histories*, Pavsek argues that Kluge's "micrological narratives" from the 1960s "continue the formal gesture of Adorno's *Minima Moralia*" (*The Utopia of Film* 174).

Étienne Balibar on citizenship, Bernard Stiegler on technicity, and Oskar Negt as well as Alexander Kluge on Marxist critical theories of labor.[40]

Citing from social theory co-authored by Negt and Kluge in 1981, Fore vitally notes: "[t]wo of the leading voices of German critical theory today, Oskar Negt and Alexander Kluge, have built their materialist anthropology of labor on a definition of the human as a 'deficient mutant' (*eine Mangelmutante*), a 'life form which, according to its metabolism, is not autonomous, but enters into concrete associations with others. Which is to say: it is a being that requires society'" (8).[41] This emphasis on social relations as constitutive of human life in need (and not merely the more functionalist reverse) is a precept that Kluge and Adorno share. For both, one could say what Peter Uwe Hohendahl claims in *Prismatic Thought* in the chapter on "The Social Dimension," which concerns Adorno's approach to aesthetic mediation. "This is not a matter of the artwork *reflecting* social conditions but rather a matter of human labor" on those conditions (150). However, one could scarcely consider Adorno a philosophical anthropologist. Aside from public disagreements between Adorno and Gehlen aired on German radio in 1965 concerning the role of "the human" in sociology (Adorno and Gehlen),[42] and aside from "provisional 'Notes towards a New Anthropology'" that

---

40 The primary exception Fore lists for the mid-20th century is Mikhail Bakhtin, the "great theorist of otherness," for whom philosophical anthropology explicitly served "as the master rubric for his entire moral system" (8).

41 Fore cites here from note 3 on p. 23 of the original German edition of Negt and Kluge's *Geschichte und Eigensinn* (1981). The original footnote cited by Fore in *Realism after Modernism* is not included in *History and Obstinacy* (2014), though the main text translated there does include another reference to "auxotrophic mutants [*Mangelmutant*]" (94). On the significance of anthropology for Negt and Kluge's theoretical work, see Fore's introduction to *History and Obstinacy*, the first section of which is titled "The Anthropology of Capital" (15–24).

42 Stefan Müller-Doohm summarizes Adorno's position in this broadcast, one of four public debates that Adorno conducted with Gehlen: "The relationship between individual and society was like the negative identity of universal and particular. In his famous radio debate with Arnold Gehlen in 1965, [Adorno] argued that this was neither an anthropological constant nor a historical necessity, but the product of a historical and social development" (390). Lambert Zuidervaart situates the stance that Adorno takes vis-à-vis both philosophy and anthropology in *Negative Dialectics*, first published in 1966, specifically in relation to the cold war and the future of Marxist critical thought: "Although Adorno shares many of Marx's anthropological intuitions, he thinks that a twentieth-century equation of truth with practical fruitfulness had disastrous effects on both sides of the iron curtain. The Introduction to *Negative Dialectics* begins by making two claims. First, although apparently obsolete, philosophy remains necessary because capitalism has not been overthrown. Second, Marx's interpretation of capitalist society was inadequate and his critique is outmoded. Hence, praxis no longer serves as an adequate basis for challenging (philosophical) theory. In fact, praxis serves mostly as a pretext for shutting down the theoretical critique that transformative praxis would require. Having missed the moment of its re-

Adorno had hoped to contribute to his collaborations with Max Horkheimer during the exile years in California (Müller-Doohm 274), Adorno's critical philosophy of "negative dialectics" and much of his other writing too articulate a sharp critique of philosophy itself, to the degree that philosophical concepts aim to capture universal truths, including universal truths about what it means to be or become human.[43] Susan Buck-Morss describes Adorno's philosophical dynamic or "'logic of disintegration'" most succinctly in *The Origin of Negative Dialectics*:

> Adorno was engaged in a double task of seeing through the mere appearances of bourgeois reality and the alleged adequacy of bourgeois concepts used to define it. As with Hegel, contradiction, with negation as its logical principle, gave this thinking its dynamic structure and provided the motor force for critical reflection. But whereas Hegel saw negativity, the movement of the concept toward its 'other,' as merely a moment in a larger process toward systematic completion, Adorno saw no possibility of an argument coming to rest in unequivocal synthesis. He made negativity the hallmark of his dialectical thought precisely because he believed Hegel had been wrong: reason and reality did not coincide. As with Kant, Adorno's antinomies remained antinomial, but this was due to the limits of reality rather than reason. Non-reconciliatory thinking was compelled by objective conditions: because the contradictions of society could not be banished by means of thought, contradiction could not be banished within thought either. (63)

Hohendahl puts it even more succinctly when he avers in *Prismatic Thought* that Adorno's pointed resistance to any form of "grand design" in writing and thought "breaks up and displaces the elements of the philosophical tradition" (vii).

---

alization (via the proletarian revolution, according to early Marx), philosophy today must criticize itself: its societal naivete, its intellectual antiquation, its inability to grasp the power at work in industrial late capitalism. While still pretending to grasp the whole, philosophy fails to recognize how thoroughly it depends upon society as a whole [...]. Philosophy must shed such naivete. It must ask, as Kant asked about metaphysics after Hume's critique of rationalism, How is philosophy still possible? More specifically, How, after the collapse of Hegelian thought, is philosophy still possible? How can the dialectical effort to conceptualize the nonconceptual—which Marx also pursued—how can this philosophy be continued?" (n.p.).

43 "For Adorno, reason *is* that gap that separates reason from itself," Andreas Hetzel summarizes in recourse to Adorno's contributions to *Dialectic of Enlightenment* but also more generally (Richard Klein et al., *Adorno-Handbuch* 395). Tiedemann claims that, like Marx and Horkheimer, Adorno was not simply interested in understanding society as the "substratum" of philosophy—which he transformed but did not renounce—but also in changing society with an eye to a better future (45; see also 16–17 on Adorno's profound commitment to critical philosophy after Auschwitz). Paul Piccone, the founding editor of *Telos*, by contrast, in his 1977 introduction to *The Essential Frankfurt School Reader*, criticizes Adorno's "'dehistoricized'" dialectic and Critical Theory for "'not even attempt[ing] to prefigure the future by elaborating the mediations necessary to bring it about'" (as cited in Hohendahl, *Prismatic Thought* 6).

The same could be said just as accurately of Kluge's many writing projects and cosmic miniatures too, in which not only philosophical ideas but philosophers themselves sometimes appear to figure literally, albeit in defamiliarizing guise, as we shall see later in this section when I discuss "Samstag in Utopia" ["Saturday in Utopia"], one of Kluge's several experimental miniatures featuring a philosopher with an especially strong resemblance to Adorno ("The Gap the Devil Leaves Us" 444–448).[44] However, I shall contend in this section that Kluge deviates from Adorno despite their shared critical passion for gaps, holes, and blind spots in their equally shared causes of human survival, happiness, and freedom under social conditions bent on preventing them. Sidereal motifs abound in Adorno's avowedly antisystematic writings too—thinking in "constellations" (see especially *Negative Dialectics*), the "night side" [*Nachtseite*] of history (*Dialectic of Enlightenment*), a blistering critique of the popular astrology column in *The Los Angeles Times* ("The Stars Down to Earth"), for example—and some form of negative dialectical gap is crucial to all of them.[45] Yet Kluge's

---

[44] This miniature is not included in published English translations from "The Gap the Devil Leaves Us" in either *The Devil's Blind Spot* or Tara Forrest's anthology, *Alexander Kluge: Raw Materials for the Imagination*. While some miniatures feature historical philosophers by name—such as Marx, Benjamin, and Adorno all together in "Gußeiserne Balkons als Saturnring oder Saturnring aus Gußeisen" ["Cast Iron Balconies as Saturnian Ring or Saturn's Ring out of Cast Iron"] ("The Gap the Devil Leaves Us" 890–892) or Adorno seeking advice in love from Luhmann over *Sauerbraten* and "Rumpsteak à la Voltaire" in entry 12 of "Die Küche des Glücks" ["The Kitchen of Happiness"] (*Labyrinth der zärtlichen Kraft* ["The Labyrinth of Tender Power"] 513–517)—"Saturday in Utopia" does not feature Adorno by name except as the author of the epigraph from *Minima Moralia* with which this Kluge miniature begins. The philosopher in this miniature is "by profession" a "refuser" [*Verweigerer*] and is married to "G.," who will play an especially important role in my reading of this text. For a mix of facts and gaps in knowledge concerning Luhmann's substituting for Adorno at the University of Frankfurt in 1968, see Thomas Anz. Richard Klein comments on the "pluralization of Adorno's reception" since the early 1990s in particular and in this connection appreciatively mentions "Alexander Kluge's eminently precise and humorous writing about the great father figure" (Klein, Kreuzer, and Müller-Doohm 443). For Harro Müller, "Adorno's person and his work are for Alexander Kluge media of aesthetic, poetic formations" ("Verwendungsweisen des Authentizitätsbegriffs bei Theodor W. Adorno und Alexander Kluge" 62).

[45] Buck-Morss comments that Adorno considered replacing the term "constellations" with a more Brechtian *Versuchsanordnungen* or "trial combinations" as early as 1931 but that he kept using "constellations" into the 1960s despite his misgivings about "horoscopes and astrology as a 'culture industry'" (254, n. 84). Both the Cumming (231) and Jephcott (192) translations of *Dialectic of Enlightenment* render *Nachtseite* as "dark side" rather than "night side" and thereby obscure the cosmic connection. For the critique of the *Los Angeles Times* astrology column from the early 1950s, see Adorno, *Stars Down to Earth* (46–171). In separate entries in the *Adorno-Handbuch* Richard Klein and Andreas Hetzel both note in passing a methodological connection

"aesthetics of the gap" (Claudia Brauers; see also Carolin Bohn) in my reading pivot on a form of futurity that Adorno—for all his philosophical, experiential, and aesthetic interests in human suffering, somatic horizons, and the differential temporality of historical truth, the *Zeitkern* or "temporal core" of aesthetics and society conjoined—could not foresee.[46] This futurity manifests in Kluge's small- and large-scale narrative experiments for the 21st century, which break with the modern concept of future time by allowing readers literally to exercise the future sense as a long-distance sense organ of cosmic and human relations.

Two key terms that suggest themselves at this juncture for getting a firmer grasp of what it might mean to think of futurity in this way are utopia and hope, and not surprisingly, Adorno had a lot to say about both, before as well as after Auschwitz.[47] His personal friendships and intellectual exchange with

---

between Negt and Kluge's *History and Obstinacy* [*Geschichte und Eigensinn*] and Adorno's thinking in "constellations" (Klein, Kreuzer, and Müller-Doohm 395, 443).

46 Adorno stresses "the temporal core of art's truth content" in *Aesthetic Theory* (219). The term *Zeitkern* ["temporal core"] also figures in *Dialectic of Enlightenment* (in relation to the concept of a totally administered society) and in *Negative Dialectics* (in relation to "metaphysical experience"). For the work of art, this temporal core entails "engagement with empirical reality" beyond mere "reflection of reality, as Lukács prescribed" (Hohendahl, *Prismatic Thought* 198). As Hohendahl elaborates, Adorno makes an especially strong claim in this regard inasmuch as the artwork, as Adorno understood it, is "exposed to historical time" at its aesthetic core and not merely in its reception (199). Many Kluge scholars draw attention in various ways, implicitly and explicitly, to the "aesthetics of the gap" [*Ästhetik der Lücke*] in Kluge's writing. This is usually explained in terms of contingency logic or cinematic montage but rarely in relation to futurity as a temporal structure beyond frequent allusions to a different and hopefully better future. One significant exception to this is Eshel's *Futurity*, which first appeared in German translation as *Zukünftigkeit* and includes a chapter on Kluge miniatures drawn from "Door to Door with an Other Life." I shall discuss one key difference between Eshel's project and mine later in Part One when we consider to what degree a "gap" in Kluge's prose can also serve as an "Ausweg" or exit, as Kluge scholars so often claim (see n. 60). When Brauers speaks of Kluge's "aesthetics of the gap," she specifically refers to the original German version of Kluge's *Learning Processes with a Deadly Outcome* (1973). Highlighting Kluge's experimental miniatures in and for the 21st century instead, I do not mean to suggest that Kluge's writing shifted altogether from one form of gap to another in 2000 but rather that gaps function in various ways in Kluge's prose and that some of those differences—especially those concerning futurity—are intensified under present conditions.

47 For a sampling of scholarly positions and heated debates over Adorno's relationship to utopianism, see Seyla Benhabib, Richard Wolin, Fredric Jameson (*Late Marxism* and *The Seeds of Time*), Joel Whitebook, Christoph Menke, Nigel Gibson and Andrew Rubin, Rolf Tiedemann, Kathleen League, and Peter Uwe Hohendahl (*The Fleeting Promise of Art*). Slavoj Žižek's contribution to *Thinking Utopia* in the 21st century addresses the passing of "the age of the really existing socialism (RES)" and associates this end with a rejection of "belief in the possibility of a self-transparent organisation of society which would preclude political 'alienation'." Calling this

Benjamin and Ernst Bloch, author of *The Spirit of Utopia* (1918/1923), *Traces* (1930), *Heritage of Our Times* (1935), and *The Principle of Hope* (1938–1947/ 1959), date back to the 1920s, and as Hans-Ernst Schiller details, in private correspondence and professional commentary alike, Adorno was both deeply sympathetic to and profoundly critical of Bloch's philosophical approach to utopian temporality as the "not-yet" [*Noch-Nicht-Sein*] of better life that real human need requires. Adorno too was keenly oriented to a "future without life's miseries" [*Zukunft ohne Lebensnot*] (*Negative Dialectics* 398). As Buck-Morss explains, for Adorno:

> There was also a utopian dimension to nonidentity as it related to the concrete particular. The transitoriness of particulars was the promise of a different future, while their small size, their elusiveness to categorization implied a defiance of the very social structure they expressed. Reading the nonidentity of the particular as a promise of utopia was an idea Adorno took from Ernst Bloch. Insisting on recognition of the 'not-yet-existing' (*Noch-nicht-seiende*), Bloch grounded hope for the future in those nonidentical 'traces' (*Spuren*) of utopia already experienced within the present. (76)[48]

Yet Adorno's characteristic inclination to locate "utopian hope" in "small things" (Buck-Morss 76)—small things already riven with the gap of alienation in subject-object relations that modern life imposes—did not prevent Adorno from con-

---

"the resigned 'post-modern' acceptance of the fact that society is a complex network of 'subsystems', which is why a certain level of 'alienation' is constitutive of social life, so that a totally self-transparent society is a utopia with totalitarian potentials," Žižek goes on to say, in a characteristically provocative aside: "In this sense, it is Habermas who is 'post-modern', in contrast to Adorno, who, in spite of all his political compromises, to the end remained attached to a radically utopian vision of revolutionary redemption" (256). In *The Fleeting Promise of Art*, Hohendahl underscores that "for Adorno the social and the aesthetic are necessarily linked," and that the particular "utopian moment that defines the direction of Adorno's theory" pivots on this link. For this reason, Hohendahl details, Adorno's "utopian perspective makes it difficult and precarious to 'update' Adorno," especially if those undertaking such efforts attempt to sever that link (16). Hohendahl's primary contrastive examples here are Wellmer (on Adorno in relation to Habermas) and Menke (on Adorno in relation to Derrida). Hohendahl's own updating efforts focus on Adorno in relation to Kantian aesthetics and judgment.

48 Buck-Morss goes on to note the importance of these ideas in Adorno's philosophy of music as early as 1928: "That the locus of utopian hope was in the small things, in details which slipped out of the conceptual net, was an idea Adorno had already expressed in his philosophy of music, and it remained important in his aesthetic theory" (76). The *Adorno-Handbuch* edited by Richard Klein and others includes many more references and analyses of the importance of music in Adorno's thought.

demning his friend's philosophy of "concrete utopia."[49] Despite their shared affinities, including to selected aspects of Marxist thought, anticapitalist critique, and what Adorno would call "metaphysical experience" (*Negative Dialectics* 372–375), Adorno's rejection of Bloch's concrete utopia had in key part to do with Bloch's configuration of Marxist philosophy, as Adorno understood it. For Adorno, Bloch's model of concrete utopia was much too anthropocentric and his style of writing about utopia much too expressive, epic, and "'undialectical'"—Bloch himself a mere "'teller of fairy tales'" [*Märchenerzähler*] (Schiller 26–27). By Adorno's negative dialectical reckoning, these features were anathema to critique, for they belie the gap between reason and reality, a gap that Adorno understood emphatically as a real threat to human life—and also as a chance, however small, to resist that threat. For Adorno, Bloch's Marxism—as a model of thought—was at its core incompatible with the utopian impulse itself to the extent that a concretely imagined social utopia in the service of a "better society" (Schiller 28), even in the name of Marx and especially under the shadow of Stalinism, threatens or negates the concrete particular.[50] Adorno put his negative dialectical objection in especially stark terms in his public radio debate with Bloch

---

49 See Schiller (30) and the Adorno biographies by Müller-Doohm and Lorenz Jäger for further details on major rifts in Adorno's friendship with Bloch. Martin Jay notes that Adorno tended to prefer the Marxist term "reification" to "alienation" when discussing capitalist modernity in particular (*Marxism and Totality* 267), though *Dialectic of Enlightenment* indicts "all of Western history" (261).

50 Contrary to long held assumptions in Marxist scholarship, the stances that Marx and Engels themselves took towards "utopian socialism" were not uniformly negative or historically consistent, as scholars such as Steven Lukes, Henri Maler, Roger Paden, David Lovell, and David Leopold have insightfully shown. Lukes speaks of their "anti-utopian utopianism" (155; see also Paden 67). From different critical perspectives, Paden and Leopold are especially helpful in explaining positive attitudes that Marx and Engels also expressed vis-à-vis utopian socialism and its early proponents in particular. Whereas Paden stresses "Marx and Engels' ambiguous relationship" (67) to utopianism, which he examines from five methodological vantage points, Leopold insists that Marx and Engels' multifaceted relationship to utopianism is not "ambiguous" at all. Ruth Levitas explains some key aspects of Bloch's understanding of a utopian "impulse" as follows: "In Bloch's view, Freud regarded the unconscious as a kind of rubbish bin of repressed material that was no longer conscious; this overly negative approach on Freud's part disregarded the additional and countervailing characteristic of the unconscious, that of being a creative source of material on the verge of coming to consciousness. The unconscious is also the pre-conscious, is intrinsically creative and the source of the utopian impulse, which Bloch appears to regard as a fundamental human propensity" (101). Fredric Jameson's *Archaeologies of the Future*, which relies heavily on Bloch's "utopian impulse" to consider science fiction as a pointedly utopian undertaking since the end of state communism in Europe, refers to the 1990 edition of the monograph by Levitas, who stresses a "structural pluralism" in utopia as a concept with destructive, critical, and creative elements (Jameson 3, n. 2).

in 1964 on the subject of utopia: "where the threshold of death is not at the same time considered, there can actually be no utopia" (Adorno, Bloch, and Krüger 10; see Schiller 28 for additional commentary and Adorno's original German phrasing, which sharpens the contradiction: "'wo die Schwelle des Todes nicht zugleich mitgedacht wird, da gibt es eigentlich auch keine Utopie'").[51]

Aside from invoking a line from Bertolt Brecht's libretto for *The Rise and Fall of the City of Mahagonny* (1930), the mere title of Adorno and Bloch's riveting debate (audio segments of which are available in German on YouTube under the modified title *Möglichkeiten der Utopie heute* ["Possibilities of Utopia Today"]) recalls elements of philosophical anthropology, German Idealism, Marxist theory, and centuries of utopian thought in Europe: "Something's Missing." Something is missing in Kluge's cosmic miniatures for the 21st century too, but it is certainly not the ubiquitous "threshold" to death in social, political, and historical terms. And we have already ascertained that hope in these miniatures—"door to door with an other life"—is not nowhere but possibly everywhere. What else must we consider about Adorno on utopia and hope before we turn more directly to Kluge's experiments in writing at the crossroads of hope and destruction? Like Bloch but unlike Bloch, Adorno also favored "*concrete utopian projections* in more than a metaphorical sense," as Richard Wolin observes (41). According to Hohendahl, Adorno saw the modern "artwork as a historical witness" with

---

[51] On the importance of "threshold" for Adorno's philosophical approach to totality and truth, see Philipp von Wussow (112). Schiller pinpoints ways in which Adorno misunderstood some of Bloch's arguments, including Bloch's relationship to both Kant and Marx. For recent analysis of ways in which utopia, as distinguished from nostalgia, "plays a central role in Adorno's social critique," see S.D. Chrostowska (93 et passim). She argues that what nonetheless links Adorno's utopianism to "reflective" nostalgia is above all "not spatial but temporal and affective" (94). Some features that she ascribes to Adorno's critical thought are relevant to Kluge's work too, while others are challenged by the discussion of hope in Adorno and Kluge that will follow here. For example, at one point Chrostowska stresses the importance of "alert somnolence" (95) for Adorno (especially in *Minima Moralia*), and as we shall see in my analysis of Kluge's cosmic miniature "Saturday in Utopia," the text's most important figure ostensibly withdraws to take a nap. (One might compare Adorno and Kluge regarding this motif with Jonathan Clary's recent critique of "24/7 capitalism." In his book *Late Capitalism and the Ends of Sleep*, he writes for example: "Sleeplessness is the state in which producing, consuming, and discarding occur without pause, hastening the exhaustion of life and the depletion of resources" [17].) However, Chrostowska misses something important in Adorno when she argues that his utopian orientation is to to the past "rather than the future" (95), and that his utopianism does not "anticipate" a future-oriented politics of freedom but is meant only to "inspire" such politics instead (101). To understand what Kluge both inherits and adapts from Adorno, in this section of Part One we will by contrast need to look more precisely at the workings of differential temporality and counterfactual hope in each of these writers.

a "utopian dimension" that Adorno implicitly posited as a literary "foreshadowing of what is repressed in modern social systems" (*Prismatic Thought* 85–87). This *fore*shadowing bespeaks a temporal orientation to an other life, and Adorno's own idiosyncratic usage of "antezipieren" for "anticipate" in his work on aesthetic theory reminds us of this as well.[52] Adorno's understanding of *Antezipieren* is hardly compatible with 21st-century prognostic orientations in futurity, which tend to seek knowledge about possible futures, largely for the purpose of planning for and effectively managing future scenarios.[53] While we might be inclined to think of Adorno's temporalization of the utopian dimension as one example of what Koselleck has analyzed as the epochal "temporalization of utopia" in European modernity, this would be misleading for two main reasons.

---

52 For this one needs to consult the German version of *Ästhetische Theorie* (251, for example). Robert Hullot-Kentor uses the standardized "anticipate" in his English translation of the relevant passage. "The aesthetic We is a social whole on the horizon of a certain indeterminateness, though, granted, as determinate as the ruling productive forces and relations of an epoch. Although art is tempted to anticipate a nonexistent social whole, its non-existent subject, and is thereby more than ideology, it bears at the same time the mark of this subject's non-existence. The antagonisms of society are nevertheless preserved in it. Art is true insofar as what speaks out of it—indeed, it itself—is conflicting and unreconciled, but this truth only becomes art's own when it synthesizes what is fractured and thus makes its irreconcilability determinate. Paradoxically, art must testify to the unreconciled and at the same time envision its reconciliation; this is a possibility only for its nondiscursive language" (168).

53 Arjun Appadurai also speaks in *The Future as Cultural Fact* of nefarious forms of prognostic futurity that profit from future disasters. Drawing on work by both Naomi Klein ("disaster capitalism") and Michael Lewis ("nature's casino"), Appadurai speaks of the 21st-century "growth of a casino capitalism which profits from catastrophe and tends to bet on disaster" (295). Calling this an "ethics of probability," he favors an "ethics of possibility" instead, which he derives from Bloch. For more extensive historical and analytical reflections on the imbrication of prognostics with other forms of futurity and especially prophecy in epistemology, religion, and arts, see Weidner and Willer. For seminal commentary on literature and probability, see especially Campe ("How to Use the Future" and *The Game of Probability*). Gerhard Richter's chapter on the final miniature in Adorno's *Minima Moralia*, "Toward the End," offers this insightful commentary, which is relevant here: "for Adorno, no conjunction of philosophy and art even would be needed if it did not also, in the alterity of its own negativity, point to an elsewhere that has not abandoned a structure of promise, prayer, and the thinking of an unknown, and potentially worthwhile, futurity" (70). As Richter elaborates, "for Adorno the overconcretization of that futurity, what he prefers to call a mere *Auspinseln*, dooms even the dialectically charged artwork to endorse yet another humanism and to repeat the failure of what already is" (70). The conclusion to Richter's own chapter implies that elements of Adorno's investment in futurity may be a necessary antidote to our contemporary moment of "geo-political empire building" and "a tireless affirmation of self-identity" (70). Kluge would no doubt agree, though as I shall argue, Kluge's relationship to Adorno on the matter of futurity is itself prismatic and deviational.

First, the "before" and "after" of Adorno's utopian orientation to historical time are always dialectically entangled in Adorno's negative sense. There is for him no utopia that could be located, contained, or even imagined in an altogether different time zone. This core entanglement of differential temporalities—conjunctive and disjunctive alike—has also been of core concern to Kluge since the 1960s.[54] One political scientist writing from a "cross-national perspective" on utopian thought in the 21st century suggests that utopia and dystopia are so inextricably tied to each other now that we might think instead only of a "eutopia" instead that "develop[s] within the confines of the dystopia" (Lyman Tower Sargent 6).[55] Though the mutual impingement of so many concrete social utopias and their inverse in the world today has perhaps intensified in global terms, Sargent's term would not be very helpful in parsing the grammar of Kluge's futurity, precisely because of Kluge's deep connection to Adorno. Adorno adhered in his aesthetic theory and negative dialectics to a radical *Bilderverbot* concerning what the positive social content of utopia would be (see Gertrud Koch, "Mimesis and the Ban on Graven Images").[56] As a filmmaker and user of many different types of images in various media, Kluge can of course not be construed as falling under a literal ban on images in any general terms. However, it does seem to apply concerning the utopian futurity of his prose miniatures. Although these texts contain many implicit and explicit references to past utopian and dystopian visions alike, Kluge's miniatures paint no portrait of what a future society should be (see Adelson, "Experiment Mars" in this regard concerning *Learning Processes with a Deadly Outcome*).

---

54 Despite Koselleck's insistence that the modern future is categorically inaccessible to experience and that "'*uchronia*'" thus prevails in the modern utopian tradition, he does claim that *representations* of temporalized utopias must "assume temporal continuities regardless of whether they are openly thematized or not." That is to say, even for Koselleck, albeit only with regard to requirements of representation and not structures of time: "The entire utopia of the future thus lived off *points of connection* not only in the realm of the fictive but in the empirically redeemable present" (87, 88, emphasis added).
55 For various approaches to considering the interlacing of utopia and dystopia in European communism since 1989, including in German contexts (which Sargent's essay does not address), see especially Susan Buck-Morss (*Dreamworld and Catastrophe*), Boris Buden, and Boris Groys. For especially insightful literary analysis in this regard, see Katrina Louise Nousek's "Pasts with Futures."
56 Bloch's *Principle of Hope* also insisted on distinguishing between the "'*intention* towards utopia'" and utopian "'*content*'," which remained beyond the reach of poetry and philosophy (see Schiller 28 and Levitas 119). On Adorno's relationship in this regard to Marx's own critique of utopianism in his time, see Adriana S. Benzaquén, who argues that "Adorno's thought never abandoned the space opened up by Marx's [eleventh] thesis [on Feuerbach]," namely that the point is to change the world and not merely interpret it (149).

Second, Adorno's temporalization of the utopian dimension eludes the conceptual grasp of Koselleck's temporalization of modern utopia because Adorno's orientation to this dimension is not only temporal but affective too. This affective orientation is necessarily tied to somatic experience rather than cognitive expectation, however much in excess of that which already exists.[57] This is why there is no emphatic utopia in Adorno but considerable "utopian longing" (see Wolin 33 on this aspect of Adorno's work in relation to the Frankfurt School more generally). Kluge's work also evidences this longing, though I find that he additionally diverges from Adorno to the extent that Kluge's writing actively cultivates the temporal extension to utopian horizons by exercising the future sense as an experiential phenomenon.[58] Perhaps we can then say about both Kluge and Adorno what Barry Maxwell, who analyzes the figurative importance of non-teleological paths and "'ways' (*Wege*)" in Critical Theory's articulations of "utopian progress," has said of Bloch and Benjamin: "[They] are not makers of utopias, but users of the utopian tradition" (217). What then do we say about a problem like hope, which figures in such important ways for Adorno and Kluge too? How do their uses of hope in utopian dimensions differ?

Writing in 2012 and analyzing the key role that hope plays in mediating critically between normative principles and human happiness for Kant as well as Adorno, Tilo Wesche remarks how little serious attention scholars have paid to hope in Adorno, despite the fact that "nearly half of Adorno's texts end with

---

[57] For Bloch too, as Schiller insists, the utopian principle of hope never meant "confidence" in future outcomes (29). See also Richter on Bloch's understanding of "the radical disappointability of hope" (164–168). By contrast, as Tilo Wesche explains, for Kant, hope cannot be "disappointed" because of the factual primacy of reason (62). For new critical insights into Adorno and affective culture in postwar Germany, see especially Anna Parkinson's "Adorno on the Air Waves" and her monograph *An Emotional State*. See also Amy Villarejo's book chapter titled "Adorno's Antenna," which links Adorno's critical theory, queer theory, and media theory to analyze televisual temporality, social desire, and cultural forms of identification that resist the identity principle that Adorno associated with catastrophe (*Ethereal Queer* 30–65). Here readers will find a pathbreaking discussion of Adorno's keen critical interest in the early US-American situation-comedy series known as *Our Miss Brooks*.

[58] Here I differ from Corinna Mieth, who also speaks of a "utopian dimension" and utopian "longing" in Negt and Kluge's approach to history and anthropology. But in her reading, the "structure of this longing" is paradoxically tied to an impasse that makes social change impossible. She ascribes the same utopian impasse to Adorno. "Utopische Modelle bleiben, so meine These, wie in Theodor W. Adornos *Ästhetische[r] Theorie*, einer Sehnsuchtsstruktur verhaftet, die sich gesellschaftlich nicht umsetzen läßt. Am Ende steht nicht die Herstellung einer anderen Gesellschaftsordnung im Vordergrund, sondern die menschliche Sehnsucht wird zum literarischen Modell utopischer Phantasie" ("Die utopische Dimension" 181–182).

thoughts on hope" (63).⁵⁹ According to Wesche, "counterfactual hope," for both Kant and Adorno, is "more than wishful thinking but less than knowing" (50; see also 59). For Kant, the "phenomenon of hope" is what links ethical ideals and human happiness together (55), and hope can be described more precisely as that phenomenon "which is able to bridge the gap [*Kluft*] between ethical ideals [*Moral*] and praxis" (49). Since gap and linkage alike are constitutive of Kant's enlightened conceptualization of reason, hope in this framework is susceptible to neither disappointment nor certainty (58, 62). An oscillation (*Schwanken* in Kant's terminology) attends hope by virtue of its necessary but precarious relation to reason (61–62), and this oscillating hope is therefore not mere fantasy or desire but "'grounded'" in reason (58). In order for hope to have the bridging capacity that Kant ascribes to it between ideals and praxis, however, Wesche explains, Kant must introduce a third element to which hope necessarily refers "even though" nothing in reason, knowledge, or probability can guarantee it: the possibility of "counterfactual success" (57). This will be important for Adorno's negative dialectical approach to hope—and also for Kluge's relationship to Adorno's modification of Kant—because in Kantian terms counterfactual hope becomes a fact whether or not the specific content of such hope is ever realized. As Wesche tells us: "The ground for *counterfactual* hope in something that in light of certain knowledge is neither possible nor impossible is—this is Kant's basic insight—itself a *fact:* the fact of reason" (62). As Wesche then elucidates, Adorno adapts Kant's understanding of this bridging capacity of hope in several pivotal ways, even as Adorno shares Kant's precept of counterfactual hope as "something that can be neither proven nor disproved by empirical knowledge." First, Adorno understands "'despair'" as the "placeholder for the blank spot [*Leere*] against which Kant's primacy of reason showed itself to be unassailable." Second, Adorno's negative dialectical approach to counterfactual hope breaks with the Kantian concept "inasmuch as the ground of counterfactual hope"—for Adorno—"cannot itself exist in an unchallenged fact" (62). Third, in Adorno's negative dialectic, that which is negative is not something missing as sheer "lack" [*Mangel*] but "as a *contradiction*" (65). And fourth, in this contradiction

---

59 Wesche's primary example of the oversight is Nicholas H. Smith's essay on "Hope and Critical Theory," which omits Adorno altogether but Wesche finds otherwise laudable (63, n. 62). The positive exception he cites in the same footnote is Helmut Holzhey, "Hoffnung und Wahrheit," in Georg Kohler and Stefan Müller-Doohm's anthology, *Wozu Adorno?* (292–306). Micha Brumlik's entry "Theologie und Messianismus" in the *Adorno-Handbuch* from 2011 includes a section on hope and hopelessness, especially but not only in relation to Auschwitz (Klein, Kreuzer, and Müller-Doohm 300–303). For new scholarship on one of Kant's key philosophical questions, see Andrew Chignell's forthcoming study, *What May I Hope?*.

the negative acquires an "independent force vis-à-vis another force, the positive, which it stands against" [als eigenständige Kraft einer anderen Kraft, dem Positiven, gegenübersteht] (65).

Here I have highlighted and numbered Wesche's points about Adorno that become especially important for considering Kluge too: a structural nexus of hope and despair in the face of catastrophe, the factuality of hope that can nonetheless not be grounded in reason that goes unchallenged, and something missing as a real force at odds with hegemonic forms of identity. There is nothing pure or self-identical about this counterfactual hope, and it should be clear that there is nothing in Adorno's or Kluge's use of it that falls into the category of counterfactual histories in the service of normalization (see Gavriel Rosenfeld on contemporary German culture in this regard), though Kluge's writing can be and has been discussed as a kind of social fiction in the service of alternate histories and especially "counter-histories" [Gegengeschichten]. Yet the factual possibility of counterfactual success that Adorno derives from Kant, with modifications, and that Kluge adopts from Adorno, with modifications of his own, is not strictly speaking bound by the empirical past, even though both hope and despair are historically and structurally linked to past and future alike. This distinction between linkage and bondage is important to note because it sets Kluge's counter-histories apart from those alternative fictions that hinge on rewriting the past. Kluge's literary experiments rewrite the future instead, and they do so, I wish to suggest, in narrative forms that exceed the mere indexing of possibility.[60]

---

[60] In this regard I both agree with but also differ from Eshel's important emphasis on futurity in contemporary literature. Writing against the "many critics" who see our age "as deprived of futurity altogether" (*Futurity* 176), Eshel wisely foregrounds instead those literary works (in his German, English, and Hebrew examples) that he sees "as actually tying together the past and the future [...] and thus as signaling futurity" (179). For Eshel this means that such works "investigate the human capacity to reduce social and political unfairness by taking concrete, often mundane action, thus affecting tangible political conditions" (179). This has largely epistemological, ethical, and behavioral implications for politics and society. Eshel's definition of futurity underscores this: "Contemporary literature creates the 'open, future, possible' by expanding our vocabularies, by probing the human ability to act, and by prompting reflection and debate" (4). (The citation within Eshel's definition is to David Grossman's phrasing in a 2007 lecture on Kafka, "this postcatastrophic world," and the "seemingly insoluble Israeli-Palestinian conflict" [4].) My reading of Kluge's futurity focuses instead on the realm of the sensible as distinguished from the empirical, on literary labors on the human capacity to sense historical time in its cosmic dimensions, and thus to expand the human sense of time in the 21st century. On the relationship between fiction genres of alternate histories and the narratological concept of "future narratives" (Christoph Bode and Rainer Dietrich), see especially Kathleen Singles, who maintains

As is widely noted, the forces at work in Adorno's thinking in constellations about hope and despair are at once epistemological and historical in the sense that the contradiction of counterfactual hope that Wesche describes manifests only in "real historical conflicts and crises, the radicalization of which"—for Adorno, in Wesche's assessment—"is Auschwitz" (65). Micha Brumlik, addressing the status of "theology and messianism" in Adorno's thought (Brumlik calls the critical philosopher a "hedonistic materialist" and a messianist in the subjunctive [302]), likewise reminds us that the radical cruelties of the Third Reich, as Adorno himself wrote, radicalized his thoughts about the possibility of even thinking "damaged life" (Brumlik 307; Adorno, *Negative Dialektik* 394, *Negative Dialectics* 402). If the various forms of real suffering that Adorno's work speaks to include those associated with Fordist and monopoly capitalism, European totalitarianisms, eliminationist anti-Semitism and the Nazi genocide of the Jews, and the instrumental rationality of the "culture industry," Auschwitz signaled for him the really existing "regress of civilization into barbarism" that Marx had only feared as a future possibility (Tiedemann 14). For Adorno, as Tiedemann puts it, Auschwitz was "a chasm that could no longer be bridged" (21). And yet he never abandoned the need to philosophize about hope and despair, partly to counter tendencies, which he associated with Heidegger, to ontologize catastrophic experience (16–17).[61] If this chasm was an unbridgeable chasm in affect, the negative dialectical structure of counterfactual hope for Adorno remained a bridge that—for the sake of hope and despair together—could not quite be crossed. Auschwitz radicalized, among many other things, Adorno's relationship to futurity. Yet as Peter Uwe Hohendahl has carefully demonstrated in new work on Adorno's essays "Progress" and "Resignation" from the 1960s (see Adorno, *Critical Models*, for Henry Pickford's English translations), Adorno actively continued to think "the future of humanity" (Hohendahl, "Progress Revisited: Adorno's Dialogue with Augustine, Kant, and Benjamin" 243). Vis-à-vis Benjamin Hohendahl finds in Adorno a "deradicalization of the

---

that "alternate histories rewrite history" (111) and pursues "the question of why they are *not* FNs [Future Narratives]" as she understands the latter (109–146).

61 Brumlik recalls Adorno's clear indebtedness to Benjamin in Adorno's own stance on the necessary conjunction of hope and despair (300), which pivots on differential temporalities of experience. The final line of Benjamin's essay on Goethe's *Elective Affinities* is key: "Only for the sake of the hopeless ones have we been given hope" (Benjamin, "Goethe's Elective Affinities" 356). Steven Helmling also notes Adorno's debts to Benjamin and claims that Adorno's "critical 'unhappy consciousness' [...] pre-dated the news of Auschwitz itself" (8). However, he argues that Benjamin saw critique as "identification with the dead and with death itself," whereas Adorno's "vibrant, highly cathected affect [is] quite different from that of the 'saturnine' or 'melancholy' Benjamin" (8–9).

theory of history and by the same token a distinctly more positive assessment of the concept of progress" (254). For Adorno, progress remains "a problematic yet indispensable idea" (254).⁶²

For Rainer Nägele, Benjamin's "'anthropological materialism'" marked his "unbridgeable distance to Adorno" (172–173). Here I suggest we consider Kluge himself a vibrant and oscillating bridge between the two.⁶³ Nägele's phrasing (in contexts not concerned with Kluge) might lead us to imagine that Kluge's own investment in a "materialist anthropology of labor," as Fore puts it, would necessarily situate his experiments in writing closer to Bloch's philosophical anthropology of need in a Marxist vein than to Adorno's negative dialectics of suffering and hope. As Thomas Schwarz Wentzer sees it in a recent anthology of new dialogues between anthropology and philosophy in the 21st-century world of globalization, Bloch actively sought "to develop a certain sense for the New: the 'anticipatory sense' vis à vis the future, which discovers possibilities that lie open in any given situation" (87).⁶⁴ As is well known, and together

---

62 For additional reflections on Adorno and Kant in relation to "human freedom and the autonomy of art," see the first chapter in Hohendahl, *The Fleeting Promise of Art*. In his contribution to the *Adorno-Handbuch* titled "'Ende des Individuums'," Markus Schroer alerts us to a common misunderstanding of Adorno as a resigned pessimist, which Niklas Luhmann echoed in the 1980s when he equated Adorno's position in this regard with that espoused in Gehlen's philosophical anthropology (Klein, Kreuzer, and Müller-Doohm 280). See also Martin Jay's discussion of Adorno's positions on hope and despair in the broader context of the Frankfurt School (*Marxism and Totality* 241–275). Jay allows for "residues of a utopian insistence on the possibility of radical change" in Adorno's thought over time but finds that "Adorno's utopian hope was by far the weaker and most muted of [hope and despair]" (242). Jay also notes that Adorno's *Negative Dialectics* "warned against the primacy of philosophical anthropology" (270). With regard to Kluge, Matthew Miller notes that Negt and Kluge's understanding of "obstinacy" [*Eigensinn*] moves "beyond the conceptual labor of negation (in Marx, as well as Adorno) on which Negt and Kluge [simultaneously] rely" ("*Eigensinn* in Transit" 94).
63 Kluge compares his own filmmaking, specifically with regard to *Nachrichten aus der ideologischen Antike: Marx—Eisenstein—Kapital* ["News from Ideological Antiquity: Marx—Eisenstein—Capital"] (2008), to Adorno and Benjamin's modes of writing (Candace Wirt). Speaking of theoretical work co-authored by Kluge and Negt, Langston notes that *Geschichte und Eigensinn* entails both "indebtedness" to and "departure" from Adorno as well as Benjamin with regard to "time and history" (*Visions of Violence* 43). Many scholars note various debts that Kluge owes to these particular predecessors without underscoring the stronger claim that Kluge's own creative-critical writing marks a bridge between them with specific regard to anthropological materialism.
64 Wentzer discusses Bloch and Hannah Arendt's thoughts on "the human condition" as "anthropologies of the possible" and includes some discussion of emotions and affect in this connection. For historical and epistemological links between core affects of hope and fear in rela-

with his magnum opus on "the principle of hope," Bloch also had a great fondness for short prose forms such as anecdotes and fairy tales. Yet here we would be mistaken in my view to align Kluge's cosmic miniatures too closely with Bloch's materialist anthropology of need, futurity, and concrete utopia as opposed to Adorno. This is largely because of Adorno's crucial and explicit objection to Bloch's philosophical anthropology of human need and social transformation: "Hope is not a principle" (Adorno, *Notes to Literature* [Vol. 1] 213). Despite the fact that "[Bloch's] philosophy overflows with materials and colors, it does not escape abstractness. What is colorful and particular in it serves largely to exemplify the single idea of utopia and breakthrough," and "[t]he color Bloch is after becomes gray when it becomes total" (213). For our purposes, it is especially interesting to note the contrast that Adorno himself draws between Benjamin and Bloch, which he uses—all criticisms of Benjamin aside—to lambaste Bloch further on philosophical and stylistic grounds. "In contrast to Benjamin"—Adorno refers here to *One-Way Street*—"Bloch does not give himself over to the miniature but instead uses it expressly as a category." For Adorno, as we have seen, this raises the specter of reification and alienation in the practice of philosophy. For Bloch, he writes, "[e]ven the microscopic remains abstract, too big for itself. Bloch declines the fragmentary." And in going "beyond what forms the basis of his experience," Adorno charges, Bloch becomes "an idealist *malgré lui*" (213).[65] If Kluge shares greater affinities with Adorno than with Bloch on philosophical, stylistic, and to a certain degree Marxist grounds alike, what materialist anthropological valence of labor does accrue to Kluge's configuration of hope in the deep and chilling embrace of disaster?[66] My readings of Kluge's

---

tion to the early modern development of mathematical probability, see especially Rüdiger Campe ("How to Use the Future").

[65] Ulrich Plass, who analyzes the role of language and history in *Notes to Literature*, also highlights Adorno's objection to hope construed as "'a principle'" and remarks: "Hope is one of the strongest impulses in Adorno's work" (*Language and History* xxxv).

[66] Hohendahl, who also addresses the "temporal core (*Zeitkern*)" of Adorno's aesthetics (*Prismatic Thought* 198 et passim), devotes considerable attention to those elements of Marxist theory that Adorno retained, sidelined, or ignored. "As strange as it may sound," Hohendahl writes, "Adorno's understanding of social criticism is much closer to Marxist theory than is generally assumed" (174). "As much as Adorno consistently criticized mechanical versions of Marxist theory and their undialectical notions of the base/superstructure model or reflection theory (he accuses Lukács of both), he relied on core Marxian concepts—forces of production, relations of production, commodity fetishism, reification—in his sociological as well as his aesthetic writings" (174). This is also the ground on which Hohendahl takes issue with Jameson, both for considering *Negative Dialectics* a "'massive failure'" in *Marxism and Form* (1971) and for the specific way in which he later reverses his position to make the "radical claim" in *Late Marxism: Adorno or the Persistence of the Dialectic* (1990) "that Adorno's work represents the legitimate form of

narrative uses of futurity as experiential portals in time aim to show that his cosmic miniatures, even more than Adorno's negative dialectics allow, labor to expand the human sensorium of time.⁶⁷ If hope is an oscillating bridge for Adorno that one could not quite cross without falling into the trap of ideological illusion and capitalist reification, there is far more movement still on the bridge of futurity in Kluge's cosmic prose, and it proceeds in non-linear fashion by miniscule degrees of major proportions. The figure of hope in these storytelling projects is the temporal, affective, and phenomenological orientation to that futurity as a long-distance sense organ in time.

Kluge's aesthetics of gaps, holes, and blank spots is thus tied to a structure of counterfactual hope as an orientation to futurity. This orientation appears in Kluge's case as an experiential form of sense perception, something to be made by human labor in relation to the cosmos.⁶⁸ In theoretical terms this is a structure that must be understood as at once historical and cosmic, which is to say, this-worldly and off-worldly (*weltentrückt*) too (see Introduction for discussion of Kluge's social fiction in relation to extraterrestrials).⁶⁹ But what allows this ori-

---

Marxism for the [postmodernist and poststructuralist] 1990s" (Hohendahl 4, 6). To Hohendahl's mind, "Jameson undercuts the central point of Adorno's theory: the dialectic of the artwork in advanced capitalism" and thus "displaces the culture industry from the aesthetic sphere" (148). Jameson's specific approach to a Marxist concept of "totality," in which Jameson wishes to replace a concept of mediation with a concept of "transcoding as a way of reconnecting a fragmented world of special codes," therefore overlooks Adorno's own Marxian interventions regarding "forces of production" in the cultural sphere (177). Reviewing Jameson's revised reading of Adorno in *Late Marxism*, Eva Geulen astutely remarks that the advantages of Jameson's approach also come with "a price—namely the acceptance of the whole," which she identifies as the dialectic. In her words, Jameson "allows the particular (Adorno's dialectic) to vanish into the universal (the dialectic as such)" ("A Matter of Tradition" 155).

67 See also Jacques Rancière, who remarks in *The Politics of Aesthetics: The Distribution of the Sensible:* "The idea of modernity would like there to be only one meaning and direction in history, whereas the temporality specific to the aesthetic regime of the arts is a co-presence of heterogeneous temporalities" (26). For Kluge however, art makes no claim to aesthetic autonomy that life itself could not also claim, and this distinguishes him perhaps most distinctly from Rancière and Adorno alike.

68 In *Negative Dialectics* Adorno assails "what the vulgar drive to higher things calls the question of the meaning of life." In this connection he continues: "The concept of sense involves an objectivity beyond all 'making': a sense that is 'made' is already fictitious" (376). Here Adorno is using the German word *Sinn* in its connotations of "meaning" rather than sense perception.

69 With regard to Kluge's cosmic miniatures, I prefer to translate *Leerstelle* as "blank spot" rather than "blind spot," though scholars refer to both, sometimes interchangeably. For my purposes, "blind spot" tends to stress an epistemological and visual problematic, whereas "blank spot" suggests instead a site that has not yet been coded or lived and is thus more readily experienced as open.

entation to come alive in narrative form and actively to work on the utopian dimension of futurity without being merely an epistemological insight into contingency or simply an affective alternative or companion to despair in the face of historical-political catastrophe? The rest of Part One will wrestle with this question, which, rather surprisingly, rarely seems to percolate in scholarship on Kluge generally or on Kluge specifically in relation to Adorno.[70] While critique, insight, and affect all have their roles to play in Kluge's aesthetics of the gap, as many others have elaborated with great acuity, I argue here that these are necessary but not sufficient conditions for the utopian dimension of Kluge's prose to be rendered—in scalar terms—more rather than less real. More will need to be said about Kluge's elusive understanding of reality shortly, especially because —and this may surprise some readers—it especially concerns narrative. Before we turn to a text-analytical comparison of Adorno's heliotropic narrative in *Minima Moralia: Reflections from Damaged Life* with two cosmic miniatures taken from Kluge's "Door to Door with an Other Life" and "The Gap the Devil Leaves Us," however, we must briefly consider two final terms that play important though I would say different roles for Adorno and Kluge. These two terms are *Ausweg* [way out], which is sometimes also rendered in English as exit or escape, and *Totalität* [totality], which commentators sometimes equate with other con-

---

[70] For a rather different configuration of relationships linking contingency, affect, narrative, and theory as a sphere of "non-conceptuality," see Hans Blumenberg's late work on "anecdotal narration" as a philosophical mode (Paul Fleming, "On the Edge of Non-Contingency" 27 et passim). Fleming illuminates how stars and the universe figure in Blumenberg's account of particular anecdotes, including one about Einstein's roofer, which "mobilize[s] subjective experience as an element of cosmic theory" (28–31, 35). For present purposes it is important to note that Kluge and Adorno favor the short prose form of miniatures, not anecdotes. However, Blumenberg's riveting essay "On a Lineage of the Idea of Progress" pointedly assigns special status to astronomy in conceptualizing the idea of progress as binding "time quantum and achievement quality" together (7). Tracing the history of astronomical thought from Hipparchus to Galileo, Blumenberg essentially identifies a modern paradigm of progress that a) has its roots in antiquity and b) is not predicated on goals of "perfection" (27). This presumably explains why neither Kant nor the Enlightenment is once mentioned in Blumenberg's "lineage of the idea of progress." Kluge's own critical interests in the trajectory of astrophysics and imperfection of progress resonate in many ways with Blumenberg's keen attention to entangled histories, and yet Kluge remains beholden to Kant and the dialectic of Enlightenment, largely through the legacy of counterfactual hope that he inherits from Adorno and reworks for us. For additional thoughts on the relevance of Blumenberg for Kluge, see Langston, "'Windows are to a House...': Marx, Blumenberg, Negt and Kluge." See Part Three of the present study for extended discussion of Blumenberg's astronomical reflections on "the idea of progress."

ceptual terms such as "the whole" [*das Ganze*] for Adorno or for Kluge with "relationality" [*Zusammenhang*].[71]

2.2 Gap Aesthetics and "Ways Out"

As the titles of the two Kluge collections just mentioned already suggest, even the devil leaves a gap (Matthew Miller analyzes this in terms of Kluge's "diabolical dialectics"), and doors mark thresholds to other lives. Can readers cross such thresholds, however incrementally, to begin to sense and not merely contemplate what a "future without life's miseries" could feel like? Many things speak against this, not least of them Kluge's indebtedness to Adorno and Adorno's own insistence that there is no outside—in time or space—to the reach of modern reifica-

---

[71] Marx and Hegel loom large, in one way or another, for Adorno as well as Kluge. As Adorno famously wrote in his inversion of the Hegelian dialectic: "The whole is the untrue" (*Minima Moralia* [Redmond translation] 47). The translators of Negt and Kluge's co-authored *History and Obstinacy* have in my view chosen the most appropriate translation of one of Kluge's favored terms, *Zusammenhang* ("relationality"). The German word literally means "the quality or state of hanging together." The rendering of this in the published English translation as relationality is certainly apt, especially but not only because the choice underscores the connection to Marx's concept of commodity fetishism and social relations as "the 'phantasmagorical form of a relation between things'" (see Negt and Kluge, *History and Obstinacy*, "Commentary 10: The Violence of Relationality" 250–255). Cosmic and human relations in time need to be considered as well for an understanding of Kluge's experimental prose miniatures. Scholarly commentary on Kluge's writing sometimes speaks of *Zusammenhang* as totality or also "context," the latter of which corresponds to everyday usage of the term in modern German. To my mind, the translation of Kluge's *Zusammenhang* as "totality" or "context" is highly problematic for reasons that become clear in the discussion to follow. The multifaceted approach that Kluge takes to *Zusammenhang* as "relationality" in his experimental prose miniatures shares many features of the "intellectual promiscuity" that Sabine Haenni, drawing on Miriam Hansen's work, attributes to both early cinema and media studies in the digital era. However, Kluge's promiscuous cosmic miniatures also demonstrate that one need not look to "digital humanities projects" alone to discover "content that is 'relational,' a scale that is adjustable, and an archive that is animated" (Haenni 201; see also *Digital_Humanities* by Anne Burdick et al. [22], to which Haenni refers). In this sense I would disagree with Haenni's inclination to dismiss "the miniature, as practiced," for considering "the exigencies of twenty-first-century critical discourse" (202). There she clearly has Benjamin and Kracauer's modernist miniatures from the early 20th century in mind (on "modernist," "urban," and "metropolitan" miniatures, see especially Huyssen, *Miniature Metropolis*). Kluge's 21st-century miniatures in print literature cultivate a relational "promiscuity" (to borrow Hansen and Haenni's inspired term) that arguably rivals that of digital humanities without necessarily relying on digital media of consumption.

tion under capitalist conditions.[72] Describing Adorno's prose miniatures from the midst of damaged life as "the utopia of an infernal ideology," Bryan N. Alexander likens *Minima Moralia* to Benjamin's articulation of modernity as "'the time of Hell'" (Alexander 55). Moreover, as Koselleck serves to remind us, the very habit of modern European thought renders better and worse futures alike categorically inaccessible to experience. Jameson's portrait in 1990 of Adorno's oeuvre stresses, in related veins, the critical philosopher's "unique emphasis on the presence of late capitalism as a totality" of subject-object relations in concepts, artworks, and lives. For Jameson, "Adorno's life work stands or falls with the concept of 'totality'" (*Late Marxism* 9; see also Buck-Morss, *Origin of Negative Dialectics* 73–74, Martin Jay, *Marxism and Totality* 241–275, and Ulrich Ruschig, "Materialismus: Kritische Theorie nach Marx"). This is not a category of resignation for Jameson but an indispensable category of Marxist critique of reified or—in Adorno's term—"damaged life." Yet even those scholars who, from entirely different perspectives, illuminate Adorno's continual undercutting of totality in language, thought, and art miss something important, according to Hohendahl (who is not willing to accept Jameson's Adorno wholesale), if they fail to recognize totality as "the absent term that influences the trajectory of negative dialectics, giving significance to the breaks and gaps" to which Adorno is no less committed in his conjoined analyses of society and aesthetics (*Prismatic Thought* 212, 214). For Adorno, writing on 20th-century contestations over positivism in German sociology, totality is both "'what is most real'" and "'also illusion—ideology'" (*The Positivist Dispute in German Sociology*, as cited in Jameson, *Late Marxism* 232). This dialectical paradox yields at times a metaphor of "the maze—a place seem-

---

[72] Adorno writes in *Negative Dialectics* that "Hegel's theory of the identity of chance and necessity" obtains even beyond the Hegelian dialectic. For Adorno, the identity principle and contingency are fundamentally interlocked with each other: "Contingency is thus not only the form of a non-identity mangled by causality; contingency itself coincides with the identity principle. And this principle—as merely posited, imposed upon experience, not arising from the nonidentical in experience—in turn carries chance in its inmost core" (345). According to Jameson, Adorno's "attitudes towards 'actually existing socialism' were clearly class-conditioned (as was his lack of sympathy or understanding for Third World revolutions" (*Late Marxism* 7). For more recent work, from various perspectives, on Adorno's usefulness for revisiting critical theories of postcolonialism, exile, and mimesis, see for example Antonio Y. Vázquez-Arroyo ("Minima Humana"), Zahid R. Chaudhary (*Afterimage of Empire* and also "Subjects in Difference"), and Enzo Traverso's thoughts about what Adorno and C.L.R. James might have had to say to each other in *L'histoire comme champ de bataille*. Langston revisits Kluge's relationship to Adorno's concept of "permanent catastrophe" in focused discussion of the Chernobyl disaster as a watershed event in modern history ("Permanent Catastrophe and Everyday Life"), though this essay does not address Critical Theory's relationship to the Second World as such.

ingly without an exit" and yet no "dead ends" (Hohendahl, *Prismatic Thought* 155, 167). I would say that Adorno's focus on the category of totality is thus not "unswerving," as Alexander puts it (55), but fundamentally swerving or *schwankend* in modified Kantian terms of oscillation, as discussed by Wesche and above. If Adorno's negative dialectics aims to indict from within and undo a socio-economic totality of modern alienation "at the same time" (Hohendahl, *Prismatic Thought* 168), this irresolvable oscillation can perhaps best be explained as a function of Adorno's configuration of counterfactual hope, in which critical horizons are imagined just beyond the temporal reach of actualized experience.[73] For Adorno, the indexical marker for such horizons in aesthetic form is to be found in the gap, the break, the cut, a contradictory lack: something missing that both is and isn't really, potentially there.

How much orientation—beyond wishful thinking—can there be to an exit or escape where none exists?[74] Explicitly likening what he calls Kluge's anti-realist "utopian program" to Benjamin's angel of history, Christian Schulte unintentionally makes Kluge sound closer to the Adorno of counterfactual hope described above when Schulte foregrounds, as Kluge's aim in writing, "the construction of relations of experience [*Erfahrungszusammenhänge*] under conditions of a loss of experience [*Erfahrungsverlust*]" (11). Any notion of experience on Adorno's terms would have to be understood as "metaphysical" in a combined this-worldly and off-worldly sense, and Kluge himself occasionally reminds us that Benjamin's angel of history "keep[s] company with two or three other angels that aren't quite as destructive" (Kluge and Gertrud Koch, "Undercurrents of Capital" 367). Kluge's other angels in this quip are not theological but something akin to his extraterrestrial figures of cosmic relations. This-worldly and off-worldly senses must both be kept in view if we are to understand why translating Kluge's use of *Zusammenhang* as "totality" alone could so easily lead us astray, even though the multidimensional relationality that *Zusammenhang* accentuates is al-

---

[73] For Jameson, Adorno's Marxism "turns" philosophically on a temporal "vision of postponement and lag, deferral and future reconciliation" (*Late Marxism* 231). When Jameson writes that Adorno's "future-oriented" philosophy "prophesies catastrophe and proclaims salvation" (*Late Marxism* 231), he implicitly invokes a much cited line from Adorno's concluding entry in *Minima Moralia*: "The only philosophy which can be responsibly practiced in face of despair is the attempt to contemplate all things as they would present themselves from the standpoint of redemption" (247, Jephcott translation).

[74] Benzaquén concludes that critical theory in the lineage of Marx, Adorno, Horkheimer, and Benjamin "understand change not as the move toward a pre-determined utopian future, but in terms of escape out of present intolerable circumstances. What it needs to guarantee is that *the move out of the present* is possible. Critical thought is thus thinking against the limits to the possibility of the future" (159, 160).

ways posited in relation to the inescapable, this-worldly *ubiquity* of modern life's destructive tendencies.[75] This is why we can find so many seemingly contradictory descriptions of Kluge's *Zusammenhang* in the scholarship, and why so many of them are nonetheless correct. For Rainer Stollmann, who stresses "free association" and that which cannot be systematized—"at least not without remainder" ("Zusammenhang, Motiv, Krieg" 83, 86)—the *Zusammenhang* of concern to Kluge consists of "breaks" and "disturbance" [*Störung*] in the very concept of *Zusammenhang* as coherence (84). As Schulte and many others have noted, this indexes both the "lack" at modernity's core, the "missing" wholeness that unalienated life would entail, and also Kluge's aesthetic strategies for remedying that very situation, for seeking "ways out" by probing "the possible, however improbable" ("Konstruktionen des Zusammenhangs" 50, 53).[76] Yet "Kluge's labor on the historical context of catastrophe [*Katastrophenzusammenhang*]" is also seen to yield "a fragmentary universe," a "communication" that "encompasses past, present, and future, the totality [*Totalität*] of history" (55–56, 60).[77] Adorno's legacy circulates actively in such formulations whether the philosopher is explicitly invoked or not.[78] This is in part because Adorno doubted that any "'co-

---

[75] Two clarifications are in order here. First, off-worldly should also not be confused with otherworldly in a strictly separate sense of alternative utopian worlds. Second, I speak here of Kluge's use of *Zusammenhang* in his social-fiction miniatures in order to avoid simple conflation with Negt and Kluge's co-authored theoretical elaborations of the term in works such as *Public Sphere and Experience* and *History and Obstinacy*. Kluge's theory and storytelling are clearly connected —as the title of his Frankfurt aesthetics lectures in 2012 also suggests—yet I would additionally insist that reading his stories makes an experiential difference for which theory alone cannot allow. For early and incisive commentary on Negt and Kluge's theoretical approach to *Zusammenhang* in relation to the "subjective factor" as a blind spot in the Marxist tradition of conceptualizing experience and "living" rather than dead labor, see Rainer Stollmann ("Zusammenhang, Motiv, Krieg").

[76] For thoughts on ways in which Kluge's approach to forms of remedy in this regard might entail different concepts of media, remediation, and "second-order mediation of experience" than Niklas Luhmann, Jay David Bolter, and Richard Grusin allow, see Langston, "Permanent Catastrophe and Everyday Life" (115, 121).

[77] Elsewhere Schulte stresses Kluge's "encyclopedia of experience" as distinguished from a "totality of knowledge" (see his editorial introduction to *Die Frage des Zusammenhangs* 11). For elaborations on Kluge's writing as "encyclopedic literature," see Gunther Martens ("'Wann wird man so weit sein'").

[78] In "Konstruktionenen des Zusammenhangs" Schulte explicitly conjures Benjamin as Kluge's virtual mentor far more frequently than he does Adorno, partly because, according to Schulte, reparative forms of *Zusammenhang* are "producible" [*herstellbar*] only through active recourse to "remembrance" [*Erinnerung*] (67). The horizons of futurity are thus not entirely wrong but severely limited when Schulte tells us that historical catastrophes, for Kluge, appear "as 'writings

herent theory'" could adequately account for "'contemporary society'" (Dirk Braunstein and Stefan Müller-Doohm 248), and Adorno's own formulations regarding "the coherence of the nonidentical" [*die Kohärenz des Nichtidentischen*] continuously invert the relationship between *Zusammenhang* as connection and *Zusammenhang* as wound (see *Negative Dialectics* 25–26; *Negative Dialektik* 36).[79] For Adorno, one cannot be thought without the other.

Adorno's legacy also circulates vibrantly—as an oscillation, I would say—in Kluge's own writerly tangle of gaps, holes, and connective constellations, for reasons related to but also different from what Richard Langston designates as "the legacy of permanent catastrophe" bequeathed to Kluge by Adorno "as a condition" of critique ("Permanent Catastrophe and Everyday Life" 103, n. 11). At several junctures in personal correspondence and published work Adorno did use the term "permanent catastrophe" from the mid 1930s on, along with related terms such as "total catastrophe" (both can be found in *Minima Moralia*, for example) and "the permanent threat of catastrophe" ("The Position of the Narrator in the Contemporary Novel," *Notes to Literature* [Vol. 1] 34). In his posthumously published *Aesthetic Theory* he wrote of art's "*tense relation* to permanent catastrophe" (135, emphasis added).[80] (We should pause to note that Kluge will use the language of "permanent revolution" instead in his first poetics lecture in Frankfurt in 2012 on his "theory of storytelling." Part Two will revisit Kluge's use of this language in narrative form.) Langston focuses on Kluge's televisual responses over time to the nuclear meltdown of 1986 at Chernobyl in order to demonstrate two main things: 1) how Kluge acknowledges Chernobyl as both a distinct "historical catastrophic event" and an insidious index of catastrophe's

---

on the wall,' as advance messengers of further disasters in the future" (47). I argue that Kluge's cosmic miniatures entail other differential forms of futurity as well.

79 The Ashton translation speaks of infringement rather than wounding—"the very thing infringed by deductive systematics" (26)—but Adorno's use of the past participle *verletzt*, which means wounded or violated, is more apt for his argument about concrete particulars even though he is at this juncture not talking about human beings as such but about "a thing itself" (25). Here we might also note that the abstraction "Kohärenz" is etymologically derived from Latin expressions connoting relations of "hanging together" (Seebold 508). In his eclectic overview of philosophical literature on *Zusammenhang* Herbert Holl notes that Kant considered *Zusammenhang*, "in contrast to gravitation," a "merely 'disjunctive'" surface phenomenon (132, n. 3). See also Negt and Kluge's comments on the two faces of capital itself: "capital's generative and combinatory potency, on the one hand, and its interconnected exploitative potency, on the other" (*History and Obstinacy* 82).

80 Many commentators also reference Adorno's essay on Beckett, "Trying to Understand *Endgame*," in this connection. On Adorno's use of the term in private correspondence with Benjamin in 1937, see Birgit R. Erdle, "'Sticking to our language'" 11).

structural transformation from exceptional event to an everyday, "ubiquitous *condition* [...] of planetary life" (101), and 2) how Kluge is able "to redress" the catastrophic "imperceptibility" of catastrophe in this vein "using the tools of filmmaking and television broadcasting" (103). Langston's analysis is astute, and he effectively illuminates how "Kluge engenders in his Chernobyl broadcasts temporal and spatial differences that information-driven television literally has no time or space for" (121), notably by showing us how Kluge's televisual productions rework perception of dimensional relations between what is near and far as well as between what comes, large and small, from above and below. However, with an eye to the cosmic miniatures and critical horizons under discussion in Part One, I must disagree with Langston on two primary grounds. First and foremost, he paints a one-sided portrait of Adorno's "permanent catastrophe," such that the philosopher's commitment to counterfactual hope (and not merely despair) as a social fact itself becomes imperceptible. In temporal terms—here again I stress the temporal—the "permanent threat" and ubiquitous presence of catastrophe are, even for Adorno, not permanent and fixed but wavering on a bridge he could not cross. This oscillation is also part of what Adorno bequeathes to Kluge as a lived though not fully embodied challenge.[81] And second, while I agree with Langston that Kluge goes farther with his creative work in expanding the dimensions of the possible than Adorno could with his critical theory, I would hesitate to ascribe Kluge's spirited affects, as Langston does concerning "élan" and "amazement," to the domain of the "utopian" *tout court* (120).[82] They more properly bespeak an affective orientation to the utopian dimension, with an emphasis on the complex *dimensional* quality of future time. Kluge's engagement with counterfactual hope as a productive social fact takes precedence in his cosmic prose miniatures, and the temporal structure of futurity at this hope's gapping core operates differently from his telluric televisuals and deviates from Adorno too in ways we will now be better equipped to recognize when we turn to the "Heliotrope" miniature in *Minima Moralia*.

The desire and quest for *Auswege* or "ways out" of social circumstances pitched to ongoing misery and systematic destruction are constant companions to Kluge's storytelling labors on hope and despair in the midst of everyday and

---

[81] In this sense my discussion of Kluge's futurity also focuses on different relations of embodiment and the human sensorium of history than those that Langston analyzes in *Visions of Violence* under an avant-garde rubric of a post-fascist "historical realism."

[82] Another scholar who stresses both Kluge's inheritance and divergence from Adorno is Harro Müller, who analyzes Kluge's "equivocal" reworking of Adorno's concepts of authenticity and "coherence" [*Stimmigkeit*] ("Verwendungsweisen des Authentizitätsbegriffs bei Theodor W. Adorno und Alexander Kluge" 59 et passim).

extreme historical catastrophe. Stefanie Harris, who compares and contrasts Kluge's multimedial writing projects from the 1970s with several since 1989, correctly identifies the concern with *Auswege* as the very "core" of Kluge's entire initiative (295). While most Kluge scholars address or invoke this motif in one vein or another, however, few are able to tell us how such *Auswege* could convert ubiquitous catastrophic conditions into possibilities for non-catastrophic experience. Harris comes close to addressing this crucial question when she shifts her emphasis from "spatial incommensurability" to "temporal asynchrony" as key (297, 310), and when she considers Kluge's use of texts in terms of a "'cool medium'" as Marshall McLuhan defined the term. In Harris's summary a cool medium is "open-ended—improvised and involved," that is to say, requiring high degrees of active participation by readers for anything meaningful to occur.[83] And yet, like so many other Kluge commentators too, Harris ultimately relies on an understanding of Kluge's "counter-histories" that sees them only as an index of possibility, one with which ideological narrative models are imaginatively challenged and cognitive awareness is raised that things could have been and could yet be different.[84] This is not sufficient to help us understand how Kluge deviates from Adorno's configuration of counterfactual hope as a real force in the world. For that we need a more robust sense of operative forms of narrative futurity in Kluge's cosmic miniatures, since any chance for

---

83 In 1982 Harro Müller described Kluge's early work as relying on a "strategy searching for *Ausweg*" ("'In solche Not'" 894). According to Müller, Kluge's use of montage in that regard aimed to activate in his readers "the development of a *relationship to history*" and not simply a critical understanding of history (891). Regarding hot and cool media, Marie-Laure Ryan argues that the digital age defies McLuhan's characterization of immersion and interactivity as "polar opposites" in reading (2, 347). As she elaborates: "A hot medium facilitates immersion through the richness of sensory offerings, while a cold medium opens its world only after the user has made a significant intellectual and imaginative investment," and "the type of involvement that McLuhan associates with cool media is much closer to the interactive than to the immersive dimension of virtual reality" (348). Given the large amount of historical and scientific data that some of Kluge's stories entail, which McLuhan would associate with the information saturation of hot media, Kluge's texts cannot be neatly or consistently divided into hot and cold categories.
84 See also Schulte, who repeatedly stresses in "Konstruktionen des Zusammenhangs" the particular efficacy of Kluge's storytelling strategies, "at least in the imagination" (62 et passim). Harris makes an important observation when she notes that Kluge's counter-histories do not merely tell the "other side of the story" or "a different story" but rather, "in their content and their forms stubbornly refuse permanent and definitive ordering" (310). Eshel's analysis of Kluge stresses the ethical stakes of rethinking "human agency" through "an ongoing process of charting a future course of action" that could avoid the horrors of catastrophic pasts (*Futurity* 63, 65). By contrast, Jörg Drews found in 1985 that Kluge's "anarchic, liberating" form of "conceptual slapstick" ultimately leaves readers "resigned in behavior" (26–27, 30).

conversion from catastrophic conditions to something that could allow for non-catastrophic experience—for human happiness and even sheer survival, including survival of the planet—hinges on a sense of futurity that is not consistently deferred.

Kluge's constellations of living and dying "door to door with an other world" at first glance suggest a spatial figure of passage that is belied by the differential temporalities of his miniatures. Writing on "door logic" as a processual "cultural technique" involving human and non-human actors alike, one in which categorical distinctions between inside and outside are both established and recursively undone, Bernhard Siegert remarks a particular "paradox" that arises with the invention of the revolving door in 1888: "One walks through a door that is permanently closed" (201; see also 13–14 and 192–205).[85] This phrasing, together with the temporal element that Siegert's processual recursions imply, sounds remarkably close to what Adorno bequeaths to Kluge: a critical horizon of counterfactual hope oscillating in the ubiquitous presence of permanent catastrophe. And Siegert, who identifies not with German Critical Theory but with a post-postwar turn in German media theory, even begins his book chapter on the cultural technique of door logic with a partial tribute to Adorno before he closes the door on his relevance for thinking about doors today. Citing a passage on doors and fascism from *Minima Moralia* ("Do Not Knock"), Siegert on the one hand counts Adorno "among those philosophers of culture who already in the 1940s confronted the fundamental significance of cultural techniques" (192). On the other hand and in the next breath, however, Siegert mistakenly claims that Adorno saw culture only as "'refinement'," as "something that only pertains to people who associate with things anthropomorphically" (192). Here Siegert fails to account for the deep entanglement of culture and barbarism as a Benjaminian echo in Adorno's own thought. Additionally he conflates Adorno's anthropocentrism—his foundational concern with human suffering—with an alleged commitment to anthropomorphic forms of cultural representation and critique. This conflation cannot capture Adorno's negative dialectical approach to subject-object relations in society or art. More to the point for present purposes, however, Siegert's door logic is insistently cast from a theoretical perspective on "humanoid-technoid" cultural techniques that above all "focuses on empirical historical objects" rather than "philosophical idealizations" (9, 193). Yet Adorno and Kluge alike reject empiricism as well as idealization. For Adorno, as we have seen, the possibility

---

[85] For a narratological approach to "portal" as one key "metaphorical expression of the experience of time" as figured in "spatially based cognitive schemata," see Dannenberg (74). She notes that, "[i]n narrative fiction, the motif of the doorway to another world has [...] long been one of the most evocative means of suggesting escape" (76).

of metaphysical experience oscillating between historical disaster and utopian dimensions remained key to critical thought. And for Kluge, vibrating tensions between this-worldly and off-worldly aspects of differential time make for thresholds and door logic of a different order (cosmic and human, beyond empirical histories), one that still bespeaks a temporal and affective longing for a real future without life's miseries.[86]

Kluge's aesthetics of the gap, of a profound discrepancy between the destructive mode of what is and the future-oriented mode of what could escape systematic destruction, are thus inextricably tied to the figure of *Ausweg*. Is this only a matter of imaginative and cognitive recognition of contingent forms of possibility and ideology critique? It will be clear by now that Part One argues for a non-symptomatic reading of Kluge's cosmic miniatures that extends Adorno's legacy of counterfactual hope beyond a mere index or distant horizon of possibility. This poses two overarching dilemmas for analysis of Kluge's stylistics in prose. First, as discussed in the Introduction, major commentators on Kluge's 20th-century writing about war such as W.G. Sebald and Fredric Jameson attribute narrative impasses in Kluge's work to either the absolute systematicity of wartime destruction or an absolute aporia of social life in modern warfare. And second, Adorno's micrological insistence on gaps and holes in aesthetic form is always coupled with what he calls the *Lückenlosigkeit* (*Negative Dialektik* 33)—the very quality of having no holes—that he attributes to social reification, categorical abstraction, and systemic oppression of human desire for life as could be rendered present "from the standpoint of redemption" (*Minima Moralia*,

---

[86] Siegert's analytical paradigm is informed by Lacanian categories of the Imaginary, the Symbolic, and the Real. These categories do not generally play a decisive role for Kluge, though some of his miniatures explicitly or implicitly refer to Lacan (see for example "Futur antérieur" ["Future Anterior"] in "The Gap the Devil Leaves Us" 221–222). Siegert characterizes his own approach to cultural techniques as "posthermeneutic" in contradistinction to a late 20th-century phase of German media theory, which he describes as "antihermeneutic" (6). The post-postwar turn in media theory he means speaks of "cultural techniques of hominization, time, and space" and "unequivocally repudiates the ontology of philosophical concepts" (9). Siegert explains that the theory of cultural techniques is not "anti-ontological" but "moves ontology into the domain of ontic operations" (9). For this reason he notes that "[o]ne could also speak of empirical transcendentals" (209, n. 25). However, he would not likely speak of metaphysical empiricals, and that is where we still need Adorno to follow Kluge's temporal trajectory of door logic. Referring to other work by Siegert, Fore remarks a certain similarity between Siegert's approach to media history and Negt and Kluge's theoretical work on social relations, to the degree that Negt and Kluge's approach to the human species resonates with Siegert's understanding of human subjectivity as "an effect of relays and lags in transmission"(see Fore's Introduction to Negt and Kluge, *History and Obstinacy* 31).

Jephcott translation 247).[87] Yet we have already seen that even Adorno, by reputation the intractable pessimist, never stopped actively thinking "the future of humanity," as Hohendahl put it, and that such thinking was always tied for Adorno to styles of writing between hope and despair. If Kluge scholars have long and rightly emphasized Kluge's own aesthetics of the gap as a means of cultivating "ways out" of disaster and despair, how does this work beyond imaginative and epistemological nods to future possibility in the modern sense? And if Kluge's cosmic miniatures render a changing horizon of hope accessible to experience by virtue of the legibility of futurity in narrative form, as I have contended above and will argue in textual detail below, how do specific narrative forms in Kluge's constellations of relationality resist being merely legible constellations of "that which exists" on empirical this-worldly grounds alone?

Since the 1970s, as is often remarked, Kluge has insistently appealed to what he describes as the radically contradictory nature of social reality. "Reality is real in that it really oppresses human beings. It is unreal in that every oppression only displaces energies [*Kräfte*]. They disappear from sight but they continue to work underground" ("The Sharpest Ideology: That Reality Appeals to its Realistic Character" 191, translation modified).[88] His anti-realist realism is motivated by "protest" rather than "confirmation of reality" (192) and radically committed, as Kluge put it in 1975, to "the uncompromising production of realistic products [as] itself the means of changing the horizon of experience" (194). This double-track perspective on realism also explains why Marijke Visch keenly observed as early as 1983 that historical documents and critical fictions so easily merge in Kluge's writing (43; see also related media-theoretical remarks by Georg Stanitzek, "Massenmedium Kluge" 248).[89] In another section of his 1975 book on his

---

87 The Ashton translation inexplicably renders "Lückenlosigkeit" as "validity" (*Negative Dialectics* 22). Hohendahl translates the "Lückenlosigkeit" of "the systemic character of modern mass culture" in Adorno's thought as "seamlessness" (*Prismatic Thought* 130), which is far more felicitous. Nonetheless, for understanding Kluge's critical dialogue with Adorno, it seems important to stress that it is not seams but holes that are missing in Adorno's formulation of systematicity.

88 For the original German, see Kluge's *Gelegenheitsarbeit einer Sklavin: Zur realistischen Methode* (215). I have modified the Roberts translation only to restore Kluge's "Menschen" to "human beings" rather than "men."

89 Visch claims however that they do so "seamlessly" [*bruchlos*], whereas I would insist on Kluge's stylistic use of the gap even when one is being bridged. See also Harro Müller's remark in 1982 that documentary and fictive elements in Kluge's writing "cannot be distinguished in binary fashion" ("'In solche Not'" 890). Klaus Scherpe cites Kluge's anti-realist realism in his broader exposé of a foundational dilemma attending literary realisms "on the trail of the real" ("Dem Realen auf der Spur" 141–142).

sensual "realist method" Kluge makes a related claim: "Forms running counter to historical sensuality do exist in subdominant experience really. Yet, on the scale of values, they are not validated as being especially sensual. Instead one would be inclined to call them analytical or abstract, which they are not" (*Gelegenheitsarbeit einer Sklavin* ["Part-Time Work of a Domestic Slave"] 212–213). Here Kluge is mainly though not only talking about what he appreciatively calls "'cinema impure'" ("The Sharpest Ideology" 195); the productive cultivation of real if new forms of sense perception also applies to his storytelling, albeit with different formal means. As Pavsek suggests in his account of Kluge's "reworking of Benjamin," for Kluge, "the question of narrative is a matter of practice" ("The Storyteller in the Age of Mechanical Reproduction" 86). What many Kluge commentators fail to underscore is that the critical "counter-histories" they celebrate in Kluge must also be narrated or told in the irresolvably ambiguous dual sense of the German verb *erzählen*. Such shared telling or constellated narration in Kluge's terms is both blocked and opened by the gaps and holes that historical oppression entails, a permanently closed door that his texts nonetheless tease us to walk through in time. For Kluge, it was "the task of the 20th century" precisely "to narrate" and "to tell" counter-histories [*Gegengeschichten zu erzählen*] (*Theodor Fontane* 23; see also "The Sharpest Ideology" 196). His cosmic miniatures for the 21st century may also be grasped in this connection—the past is never entirely past for Kluge—but only if we also tend to the sensory dimensions of futurity that these stories help produce by intensified narrative means.

This claim is at odds with a dominant strand in Kluge reception over the decades, which has tended to regard the disjunctive, fragmentary, and oppositional features of montage as a set of aesthetic principles that would preclude any commitment to narrative as necessarily affirmative (for random examples, see Bernard Malkmus, Bernd Stiegler, and Wilhelm Voßkamp). Others allow for Kluge's sustained and multimedial interest in "non-linear" narration (see for example Wolfgang Reichmann, Tara Forrest, and Kai Lars Fischer).[90] Yet by and large one will find far more invocations of "montage" than "narration" in critical analyses of Kluge's experimental aesthetics. This may have something to do with the fact that Kluge's reputation as a critical *auteur* was first established in the realms of film, television, and theory, though it no doubt has far more to do with the longstanding legacy of volatile tensions over the antagonistic relationship be-

---

90 Langston argues in *Visions of Violence* that Kluge's "television programs beginning in the eighties represent an intensification of his storytelling" and then elaborates: "These stories are compressed into literal images that flash on the screen" (226).

tween montage and narrative dating back to the Weimar Republic. Patrizia C. McBride offers stunning new insights into "the unorthodox notion of narrative that at times authorizes" what she calls "the paradoxical interweaving of perception and meaning that marks the montage aesthetics of artists associated with Dada, Constructivism, and the New Objectivity" (*The Chatter of the Visible* 6). As she explains:

> The idea that montage at this time may have offered ways for rethinking narrative would have struck many contemporaries as counter-intuitive. After all, [many] montage artifacts conspicuously lack the basic ingredients of traditional narrative: obvious causality or motivation, logical concatenation, or a stable perspective. Instead, they present a world splintered in a cacophony of ill-fitting fragments that are barely held together by makeshift connections. In this world the parts do not amount to a whole but rather engender a disorienting game of endless permutations, one that seems refractory to the ordering principles of narrative. (6)

This description could readily mesh with many descriptions of Kluge's prose as well (see for example Harris 310). And as Huyssen ascertained over twenty years ago in reference to Kluge: "All traditional notions of narration—such as plot, character, and action—are suspended, and one has great difficulty orienting oneself" ("An Analytic Storyteller in the Course of Time" 146). According to McBride, montage practices of the historical avant-garde in Weimar-era culture have a narrative objective too, which "is no longer to 'represent' reality through artifacts that are endowed with meaningful semblances, but rather to produce experience altogether by shaping the encounter between individuals and the forms of the incarnated world." Her critical intervention in montage studies in the phenomenological sense she describes thus "reconceptualize[s Weimar-era] narrative as an exploration of the limits and potential of embodiment unfolding as an exteriorized repetition and manipulation of objects and forms" (9).[91] The international legacies that Kluge does and does not take up from the historical avant-gardes and his reworking of futurity in lived relation to the cosmos are not McBride's concern, and my analysis of Kluge's cosmic miniatures does not address the multimedial or technological aspects of his overall engagement with storytelling. The analysis I propose of Kluge's narrative experiments in print literature—experiments that render future and off-worldly horizons accessible to

---

91 For her own project, McBride explicitly draws on Monika Fludernik's narratological consideration of "experientiality," which in Fludernik's usage "describe[s] the effects of narrative beyond the strictures of plot-driven accounts" (McBride 10). For additional critical perspectives on a deep-seated admixture of narrative and montage in the historical avant-garde in both Germany and the Soviet Union, see Fore, *Realism after Modernism*.

experience through their legibility in storytelling form—nonetheless resonates with McBride's revisitation of montage aesthetics in the early 20th century when she speaks of montage narrative as effecting "a direct realignment in reality's relational network" (10). This vocabulary has a certain kinship with Kluge's perspectives too, though realignments in his writing are never "direct."

A quieter strand of Kluge reception has alerted us from early on to the co-figuration of narrative and montage in his aesthetic work, especially with regard to print literature. Harro Müller does so most explicitly when he points out that narration and montage are not at all mutually exclusive for Kluge's "montaged stories" [*montierte Geschichten*] ("'In solche Not'" 890), that is to say in terms Kluge uses to describe his own writing, stories that are themselves cut or put into "constellative" relationship with each other (see for example his poetics lectures on a "Theory of Storytelling"). These stories need not rely on narratological precepts of plot, character, or action to turn on other possible types of narrative ordering, however tentative and fungible that ordering may be. Kluge once defined montage as a "theory of relationality" [*Theorie des Zusammenhangs*] and immediately clarified that, for his work in film, montage was a "cipher" [*Chiffre*] for something missing, that is to say, a "contrast between two perspectives" [*Kontrast zwischen zwei Einstellungen*] that pivots on a gap, which can itself not be seen or visually represented (Eder and Kluge 97–98).[92] The book at hand considers the narrative futurity of Kluge's storytelling miniatures as such a gap between what is and what could be. This gap in my reading is not inert but alive in orientation in Kluge's experimental prose. According to David Roberts, who has written expertly on both montage and *Zusammenhang* in Kluge's 20th-century writing, the disjunctive properties of montage are always tied for Kluge to the conjunctive associations of *Zusammenhang*, at least as a "question" ("Alexander

---

[92] Christina Scherer speaks of Kluge's "'something third'" as a filmic excess that she understands as "a purely mental image" (90). Kluge himself speaks of montage alone as "an absurdity" [*eine Absurdität*] (Eder and Kluge 98). For relevant reflections on Kluge's approach to storytelling in fim, see Hansen, "The Stubborn Discourse: History and Story-Telling." There she notes Kluge's indebtedness to Benjamin and Bloch, "who, in their peculiar blend of messianic utopianism and Marxism, locate the blindly reproducing power of history in a dialectical relationship between fictions of linearity and the actual discontinuity, non-synchronicity, arbitrariness of historical processes." She then highlights a significant difference, since "Kluge (whose intellectual persona is less that of a theorist than that of a teacher and organizer) conceives of the gap between the two kinds of history—official versions of history and whatever they suppress, erase from memory—as a space for historical practice, raising the question of a historically changeable relationship of individuals to their own history. This translates, in more pragmatic terms, into the question of access to the means of enunciation, hence Kluge's long-standing concern with the organization of the public sphere" (122–123).

Kluge und die deutsche Zeitgeschichte" 81– 83; see also "Die Formenwelt des Zusammenhangs"). We might push this further and call it a quest, one that acquires greater urgency in the 21st century, as the future of humanity and the planet alike are imperiled. Recent scholarship evidences a sea change in analytical emphasis as greater attention is paid to Kluge's work on storytelling too and not just montage. The editors of the new scholarly journal devoted to Kluge stress for example that his work—"*erzählend* und *montierend*"—actively engages in both (Christian Schulte, Richard Langston, Gunther Martens, Vincent Pauval, and Rainer Stollmann, *Vermischte Nachrichten* 10; see also Susanne Marten's discussion of Kluge's "narrative means" of bridging gaps in Kluge's story "Kot von Außerirdischen" ["Extraterrestrials' Shit"] from "The Gap the Devil Leaves Us"). This heightened interest might be pragmatically explained by the massive increase in Kluge's own literary productivity since the millennial turn, but it most certainly also has to do with key roles that the narration of counter-histories has played in their production over decades. This cannot be explained in terms of breaks, cuts, gaps, and holes alone. My readings of Kluge's cosmic miniatures therefore contribute to the growing field of critical interest in Kluge's narrative strategies as a storyteller by analyzing the co-figuration of disjunctive and conjunctive features—the gap and the bridge—in his experimental prose. Because of the legacy of counterfactual hope that Kluge inherits from Adorno, however, this cannot yield "a new whole," as Kai Lars Fischer claims it does in reference to montage (57). At most it yields an experiential approximation, this-worldly and off-worldly at the same differential time, to sensing a "future without life's miseries."

Adorno famously rejected montage as an art form, not out of a preference for narrative as such but because he was inclined to see the juxtaposition of montage elements as a "static" replication of that which exists.[93] Erhard Schütz alludes to this in drawing a clear distinction between Kluge and Adorno, noting in the process that "the future" is part and parcel to Kluge's "kaleidoscopic montage aesthetic" (61). Yet Miriam Hansen, in her "Introduction to Adorno" concerning the philosopher's 1966 essay "Transparencies on Film," suggests both that Adorno modified some of his harsher positions on montage and that Adorno and Kluge influenced each other, through nuanced disagreement and exchange, to think more capaciously about the critical capacities of montage (194– 97; see also Kluge, "Die Aktualität Adornos" ["The Actuality of Adorno"] and Ul-

---

93 See Gustav Falke (142) for one of several critical entries in the *Adorno-Handbuch* on Adorno's problematic positions on montage and music. See also Hohendahl on Adorno's dismissal of Surrealist montage as "restricted to shock value" (*Prismatic Thought* 88).

rich Plass, "Dialectic of Regression" 142–144).[94] For present purposes, it is important to note that Adorno's 1966 essay on film addresses "the practice of montage as arranging things 'in a constellation akin to that of writing'" (Hansen 196). And for Adorno the only promising forms of writing are those that are not mere reproductive "script" but those that call for "a critical deciphering" (Hansen 197). Hansen sees Adorno's thoughts here "as crossing with Kluge's endeavors," especially concerning "montage as an interference of discourses which attempts to provoke a more active participation on the part of the spectator" (197). I would suggest that Kluge and Adorno also cross in their configurations of counterfactual hope as a project in writing, but that Kluge as storyteller deviates from Adorno by expanding the sensual possibility of *Ausweg* as a temporal experience. For Adorno, the lack of holes in a social system fostering "total catastrophe" relegates small hope to micrological domains, and we have already seen that, while Adorno remains oriented to utopian horizons, his critical engagement with them is repeatedly beholden to possibility and impossibility alike.

For Kluge, however, the conjunctive, "cooperative" aesthetics of the gap yield what seems to be a surprisingly optimistic mantra: "in relationality [*Zusammenhang*] there is always a way out" ("Das Politische als Intensität alltäglicher Gefühle: Theodor Fontane" [1979] in *Fontane–Kleist–Deutschland–Büchner* 13; see "The Political as Intensity of Everyday Feelings" 286 for Andrew Bowie's translation, which renders Kluge's *Zusammenhang* as "connections"). And as an oddly determined metereological expert in "terraforming" Earth with Siberian ice avows in one of Kluge's cosmic miniatures from "The Gap the Devil Leaves Us," "There has to be some way out" [*Irgendeinen Ausweg muß es geben*] (758). Kluge is trickster of his own narrative recursions, so learning that "there is always a way out" also entails a Lenin citation of sorts (Kluge, Schulte, and Stollmann, *Verdeckte Ermittlung* 57) may give us pause. Affective orientations in Kluge's miniatures are never easily deciphered and rarely speak for themselves. Nevertheless Kluge's continual narrative stagings of the quest for ways out of catastrophic histories signal a more radical commitment than Adorno could muster to expanding the human sensorium of differential time. In Kluge's case this involves special regard for futurity and not just history as a long-dis-

---

94 Plass argues that "Kluge's and Adorno's film aesthetics converge" in their approaches to regression as a potentially progressive force, and in their use of "gaps between the images" (144). For more detailed discussion of Adorno's approaches to "constellation" as well as "montage" in small forms of writing, with an emphasis on the philosophical traditions on which Adorno draws and with which he also breaks, see A. Lehr (133–183 and 184–230). Lehr also notes that Adorno held varying views of montage at times (200), and Lehr explicitly characterizes *Minima Moralia* as a "variant of montage" (226).

tance sense that needs to be worked on, cultivated, and exercised. Experiential but not empirical and therefore not presentist either, this use of futurity also points to Kluge's ongoing and deepening anthropological interest in humans as living creatures with "something missing." What could lived future time in utopian dimensions feel like beyond what modernity and ideology allow? What narrative forms encourage us to entertain this question as a quest on which human happiness and survival depend? The rest of Part One turns to the texts themselves.

2.3 Utopian Longing and Narrative Orientation

Adorno is a legacy that Kluge openly, repeatedly, and avidly claims. Asked about his philosophical lineage in 2001, for example, Kluge responded that he comes "by way of Adorno" [*von Adorno her*] (Alexander Kluge and Jochen Rack, "Erzählung ist die Darstellung von Differenzen" 74). There are personal, historical, political, intellectual, and aesthetic reasons for this, as many commentators over time have noted either in passing or in analytical detail. These interlaced reasons came together in concentrated form in 2009 when the city of Frankfurt am Main awarded Kluge its prestigious Adorno Prize for distinguished accomplishments in philosophy, music, theater, and film (in Kluge's case, for his work in writing and film). Kluge's September 11th acceptance speech was titled "The Actuality of Adorno," thus echoing the title of Adorno's inaugural lecture in philosophy at the university of Frankfurt in 1931 on "the actuality of philosophy."[95] In his own speech Kluge highlights Adorno's predilection for "associative networks" in historical form and critical thought, and Kluge claims to follow Adorno "faithfully" in the latter's capacity as a working "seismograph" for gaps and blind spots in perception between "rescue and doom" (67, 69). The conjunction of these perspectives is invoked in the differential date of Kluge's public address, which ties Kluge's award at once to Adorno's birth date in 1903 and hellish disaster in New York City in 2001.[96] Some personal reminiscences of Adorno figure

---

[95] For discussion of the "dialectical ambiguity" of the term *Aktualität* in German, see Max Pensky's introduction to *The Actuality of Adorno* (1–2). For the print version of Kluge's acceptance speech from 2009, which is not identical to the version posted on Kluge's Web site, see Kluge, *Personen und Reden* (67–75). For those citations for which pagination is available, I cite the print version.

[96] Noting too that he and Negt had dedicated *Öffentlichkeit und Erfahrung* [*Public Sphere and Experience*] to Adorno by name and dates in 1973, Kluge makes these chronological and associative links explicit in the early part of his speech. For reflections on the methodological impor-

in Kluge's speech as well, as does a shared insistence that Auschwitz and, in Kluge's words, "everything that today and in future looks different but repeats Auschwitz" (71) must not be repeated. Yet Kluge's Adorno is no pessimist but a dedicated seeker of necessary "ways out." For Kluge, this means an active "doubling of reality" (70). With Adorno he considers the falseness of damaged life "powerful and hermetic" and at the same time "unreal and full of holes like a sponge" (71–72).

The polyphonic and temporal dimensionality that Kluge ascribes to Adorno is cast in anything but bleak terms, for Kluge's speech in 2009 gives us Adorno as a kind of "partisan" fighting systemic lies and a bringer of "unshakeable hope that, if necessary in the form of a message in a bottle, somewhere on our shores fragments or pebbles of true aliveness will arrive" [*unbeirrbare Hoffnung, dass notfalls in Form einer Flaschenpost, an irgendeiner Stelle unserer Strände Fragmente oder Kieselsteine von wahrer Lebendigkeit ankommen*] (Web version, n.p.).[97] The "planetary bridge through time" (74) that Kluge claims to share with Adorno on this occasion does "not aim for something impossible" [*nicht auf etwas Unmögliches gerichtet*] but something necessary for happiness as well as survival (Web version, n.p.). On this particular September 11th Kluge's Adorno indeed sounds closely related to the one I describe in Part One and much less like the resolute pessimist for which Adorno is so often taken. Yet what Kluge takes from Adorno may well be more than what Adorno's own writing bequeathes without the loving labors of his storytelling heir. Other scholars have provided excellent fine-grained analyses of motifs and methods that Kluge inherits, in whole or in part, from Adorno as his friend, mentor, and a partner in critical thought. These include for example Christopher Pavsek on "non-identity" and "negative dialectics" (see especially *The Utopia of Film*), Richard Langston on "permanent catastrophe," Miriam Hansen on "montage" and "constellation" in writing, Harro Müller on anti-empirical "authenticity" and "coherence" [*Stimmigkeit*] (see Müller, "Die authentische Methode"), and Corinna Mieth on "post-teleological utopia" as a "dialogue with the dead" (*Das Utopische in Literatur und Philosophie*). In what follows I shall focus on Adorno's legacy of counterfactual hope as a social fact and Kluge's reworking of this pivotal inheritance as an experiential horizon of futurity in narrative form.

---

tance of such non-chronological rearrangements of dates, books, and stories, especially with regard to Negt and Kluge's *Der unterschätzte Mensch* ["The Underestimated Human Being"], see Barbara Hahn, who underscores the constant renewability of text in the temporally rearranged "moment of reading" (105).

97 This passage is omitted from the print version of Kluge's acceptance speech in *Personen und Reden* (67–75) and appears only in the Web version.

Written between 1954 and 1958, two entries in the first volume of Adorno's *Notes to Literature* shed relevant light on this critical philosopher's perspectives on narrative form. Both ascribe a certain utopian longing or "utopian intention" in the sense of orientation to a form of narrative prose (13, 36). Under bourgeois conditions of social life, Adorno contends, the "true subject matter" of the European novel since the 18th century has been "the conflict between living human beings and petrified relations" ("The Position of the Narrator in the Contemporary Novel," *Notes to Literature* [Vol. 1] 32, translation modified).[98] The objective epic perspective on totality demanded by Lukács is no longer possible in what Adorno calls "the contemporary novel" because "the permanent threat of catastrophe no longer permits" either aesthetic distance or subjective immediacy in the form of individuation (34). Here Adorno identifies a paradoxical pulse in the heartbeat of the modern novel: "it is no longer possible to tell a story but the form of the novel requires narration" (30). The crux of this paradox lies for Adorno in both the non-identity of modern experience and the figure of the narrator, to the degree that this figure is generally tied to the pretense of "internal continuity" (31). Narrative standpoint for Adorno thus risks complicity in "the lie of representation" (34), and the novel must become "anti-realistic" in order to be real (32). This is what Adorno calls the novel's "metaphysical dimension" (32) in relation beyond empiricism to what he in *Minima Moralia* gives the name "damaged life." Although Kluge will never be called a novelist, not even in Adorno's favored company of modernist writers such as Proust, Kafka, Joyce, and Mann, we should pause here to note that Adorno's essay, "The Position of the Narrator in the Contemporary Novel," pinpoints narrative standpoint in particular as the crux of the matter, a crossroad at which subject-object dilemmas under conditions of alienation come together as a problem in literary form. We shall have occasion to recall this in our discussion of heliotropic narration in *Minima Moralia* and Kluge's cosmic miniatures too.

First published in Volume 1 of *Notes to Literature* in 1958, Adorno's long essay on the essay itself as a prose "form" ("The Essay as Form" 3–23) also takes up the constellative "force field" of utopian longing (13), the tense structural entanglement of "continuity as discontinuity" (16), and "individual human experience *held together in hope and disillusionment*" (8, translation modified and emphasis added).[99] For Adorno, the essay is "the critical form par excellence"

---

98 Shierry Weber Nicholsen renders Adorno's "versteinerte[...] Verhältnisse[...]" from *Noten zur Literatur* (Vol. I, 43) as "rigidified conditions" (32). Adorno's strong rhetorical contrast between life and stone warrants the corrected translation.
99 Adorno's German phrasing gives us "die in Hoffnung und Desillusion zusammengehaltene einzelmenschliche Erfahrung" (*Noten zur Literatur* [Vol. 1] 15). The published English translation

(18) precisely because "it thinks in breaks," as the broken reality of capitalist modernity demands (16, translation modified).[100] The purpose of the essay form Adorno envisions is not simply to replicate that reality, however, but to allow for its transformation. Citing Max Bense's thoughts from 1947 on essayistic prose, Adorno casts the French-derived word "essay"—attempt or *Versuch* in German—literally as experiment in this transformative vein (18). The very "lack of a standpoint" [*Standpunktlosigkeit*] (18) that Adorno ascribes to the essay as a critical discursive form is a cunning "parody" against "*mere 'perspectives'*" (18, emphasis added), its experimental procedure "methodically unmethodical" (13). As an experimental form of writing, the essay in Adorno's sense challenges both the philosophical ideal of "certainty" (13) and categorical presumptions about what is being all there is or could be. The essay "coordinates elements instead of subordinating them" (22) and "wants to [...] release the latent forces" in what existing concepts cannot see (23), he writes. Above all, for present purposes, it is important to note that Adorno's interest in the essay as form hinges on experiment rather than genre, and that he attributes the essay's relevance for the 20th century specifically to its "anachronism" (22). Kluge's anachronistic experiments in transformative narration take the form of cosmic miniatures instead.

The narrative tradition in literary modernism and critical theory that Kluge's miniatures come closest to emulating is not the novel or the essay but the long "misrecognized" major strand of modernist prose from Baudelaire to Adorno that Huyssen has identified and analyzed under the rubric of the "metropolitan miniature" (*Miniature Metropolis: Literature in an Age of Photography and Film*, ix et passim).[101] Reading his material against the grain of both genre theory as such and new media at the turn from the 19th to the 20th century, Huyssen sees the metropolitan miniature as a kind of "remediation in reverse" (8). In his reading, a particular mode of literary writing that first appeared in the feuilleton sections of major European newspapers did not simply mimic or appropriate formal strategies borrowed from photography and film, for example, but experimented instead with literature's own capacities for new perception under

---

renders this as "individual human experience, maintained through hope and disillusionment" (8).

100 The published English translation reads instead: "It thinks in fragments, just as reality is fragmentary" (16).

101 In essays on the subject that preceded the publication of *Miniature Metropolis*, and in the monograph itself, Huyssen also occasionally uses the terms "modernist miniature" and "urban miniature" for the metropolitan miniatures he means.

accelerating conditions of urban modernization.[102] As Huyssen puts it, an internally diverse range of metropolitan miniatures by several different authors yielded "new forms of spatialized writing" (10) in which a somatically new "urban imaginary" was "characterized by unstable subject positions, the breakup of plot, discontinuous narrative, hallucinatory imaginaries, and fragmented spaces of perception" challenging any internal-external divides (5, 6, and 10). Resisting both "realistic description" of urban settings and "fleshed-out characters" moving through them (10), the metropolitan miniature as Huyssen describes it achieved two key things. It made the modern metropolis "both legible and visible" to human perception (5), and it "always implied a critical theory of bourgeois society" for Marxists and non-Marxists alike (3). Huyssen identifies "perspectival" orientation itself as that which "metropolitan experience threw into turmoil" (16), and the modernist miniatures that reflect this share the unsettling and "ever-recurring motif of *Leere* and *Hohlraum*, void and hollow space" (6).

Kluge's aesthetics of the gap are schooled in part in reading the metropolitan modernist miniatures of writers such as Rilke, Kafka, Kracauer, Benjamin, Musil, and Adorno too. Yet as I have demonstrated above, Kluge's cosmic miniatures for the 21st century deviate from the literary tradition Huyssen describes by underscoring opportunity rather than crisis, by making legible what remains predominantly invisible rather than visible, and above all by shifting the scene of reading from urban space to the temporal dimension of futurity (see also Adelson, "Horizons of Hope"). Huyssen is undoubtedly correct in naming Kluge as an "author who still works with the legacies of the modernist miniature today" (13)—perhaps in the same way in which Kluge can be said to use the utopian tradition without being a maker of utopia himself—though I would modify Huyssen's suggestion that Kluge's preferred medial modes of storytelling run the risk of becoming "obsolete" (13). Given Kluge's storytelling investment in the differential and changing temporality of futurity, emphatically "anachronistic" would be a more accurate descriptor. Huyssen names good reasons for ending his study and the trajectory of the modernist miniature with Adorno rather than Kluge—notably, widespread urbanization since 1945 and Kluge's own growing interest in global connections and "planetary" concerns (13)—but *Miniature Metropolis* leaves an important one unmentioned: Kluge's cosmic and global miniatures for the 21st century work above all on the changing dimensional quality of futurity in narrative form.[103]

---

[102] For other perspectives on "mediating modernity" in relation to German literature around 1900, see Stefanie Harris.

[103] Huyssen's analyses of the modernist miniatures to which *Miniature Metropolis* is devoted do speak of pointedly literary "*Zeitaufnahmen*" or snapshots and "chronotopes" (21). As he

2 Heliotropic Narrative with and beyond Adorno — 91

Adorno's *Minima Moralia* plays an important role in Huyssen's critical map of the metropolitan miniature and in my account of Kluge's off-worldly approach to counterfactual hope and heliotropic narration. For Huyssen too, Adorno is no mere "doomsday prophet" (281), and the "sliver of hope" Huyssen associates with Adorno's writing also comes in the form of "reflections," as Huyssen puts it, "*from* rather than *about* a damaged life" (279). Huyssen sees the subjective turn associated with Adorno's much later radio speech, "What Does Coming to Terms with the Past Mean?" (1959), "already foreshadowed in *Minima Moralia*" (281), the three parts of which were written in American exile between 1944 and 1947, in the orbit of the urban metropolis of Los Angeles.[104] Huyssen focuses his incisive readings of *Minima Moralia* on the first part, written in 1944, "before an end to exile had become a real possibility" (281–282) for Adorno and his wife, Gretel Karplus Adorno. This selection underwrites Huyssen's keenly sustained dual reading of *Minima Moralia* as both the end of the metropolitan miniature as a specific form of literary writing since Baudelaire, and "as an exilic text par excellence written at the outer limits of the Western world," under the shadow of German fascism and the exterminationist anti-Semitism of the Holocaust (270–271; see also 270–296). This linkage between formal and lived constellations is crucial, for the "micrological gaze" and future-oriented "message in a bottle" that Huyssen finds in *Minima Moralia* are tied to miniature stylistics with high historical stakes (271). These are, in Adorno's terms as discussed above, modernist miniatures with an oscillating "temporal core." The linkage between textual stylistics and historical stakes (never merely contextual or empirical) applies for Adorno even when the ostensible subject matter of a given miniature appears relatively banal, such as shutting a door, walking a dog, or keeping house (see for example the entries "Do not knock," "Great and small," and "Behind the mirror" [a literal housekeeping title that Jephcott translates figuratively as "Memento" instead).

When Huyssen cites from "Memento" in *Minima Moralia* to give us Adorno's own description of well crafted writing, we can therefore recognize both a stylis-

---

puts it, the metropolitan miniature "in its sequential verbal composition opens up a dimension of temporality in the movement of reading itself" (17). Given Huyssen's emphasis on urban forms of "spatialized writing" in the modernist miniature one might conceivably consider Kluge's 21st-century stories of Shanghai and other global cities as a new kind of metropolitan miniature under contemporary conditions of globalization. See for example "Door to Door with an Other Life."

104 Finding it "puzzling that *Minima Moralia* has rarely been analyzed in relation to its express commitment to subjective experience," Huyssen refers to Alexander Düttmann's *So ist es* as a key exception (273; see also 333, n. 7).

tic description and the lurking presence of what Adorno considered permanent catastrophe under fascist and capitalist conditions too: "'Properly written texts are like spiders' webs: tight, concentric, transparent, well-spun and firm. They draw into themselves all the creatures of the air. Metaphors flitting hastily through them become their nourishing prey. Subject matter comes winging towards them'" (as cited in Huyssen 271; Adorno 87 in Jephcott translation). Kluge's miniaturized aesthetics of the gap are much less tightly drawn than this. One would be hard pressed to call his cosmic miniatures "tight," "concentric," "transparent," or "firm." They often appear sprawling and pliable, with proliferating gaps instead. And yet Huyssen's discussion of Los Angeles—"the city of angels"—as "an absent presence" structuring the subjective form of *Minima Moralia* and its interpretive significance sharply reveals the twinned indexical gesture of Adorno's metropolitan miniatures as indictments of this-worldly horrors associated with politics and culture, on the one hand, and expressions of Adorno's real hope, however small, for "some countervailing force," on the other (275, 276, 280–281).[105] This is why we need to recall the understanding of counterfactual hope in Adorno that we have gleaned from Wesche in order to go beyond even Christian Thorne's otherwise unsurpassed short description of the form that *Minima Moralia* takes: "short, chiseled essays, each a thesis just waiting to be canceled by one of its fellows, their sentences a fun-house ride of whiplash reversals, if we could imagine a fun-house ride that was dense and deliberate and sad. *Minima Moralia* is an elaborate, startling exercise in aphoristic antinomy" (92). This captures the subjective mood and formal tensions stressed by Huyssen as well, albeit without the indispensable historical reading that Huyssen brings into view. Whatever might appear merely mundane in *Minima Moralia* is always attended, in my terms now, by this-worldly catastrophe and off-worldly cosmologies of possible transformation as well.

The entries in *Minima Moralia* are both numbered and named. In Adorno's case this signals two competing, alternating, and contrapuntally resonant modes of ordering the material at hand, one sequential and continuous, the other associative and discontinuous. The sequentiality of uninterrupted numbers for individual entries is not repeated in the table of contents, where three parts are numbered and the list of starting pagination for single entries conjures a gap in the numbering where a written entry will appear, like a promise almost kept.

---

[105] Huyssen essentially suggests that the German anthology of new readings of *Minima Moralia* edited by Andreas Bernard and Ulrich Raulff in 2003 does not and cannot read the exilic dimensions of Adorno's modernist miniatures because those new readings overlook the structural role of Los Angeles as "an absent presence" in *Minima Moralia* (276).

The associative titles appearing as a vertical list in the table of contents evoke social conventions, folksy adages, institutional transactions, dialectical thought, fairy tales, literary masters, gardening motifs, popular culture, operatic traditions, foreign expressions from Latin, French, and Italian to English, and much more.[106] Some titles do connote political themes explicitly, such as "Asylum for the homeless" (in the Redmond translation) and "To them shall no thoughts be turned" (in the Jephcott translation), and the corresponding entries do address the crisis-ridden social politics of *Minima Moralia*'s time. But even these entries surprise us in their thematic focus and rhetorical turns. Written in 1944 and assigned to Part One, "To them shall no thoughts be turned" opens with a reference to the "past life of emigrés" who have fled fascist brutality being "annulled" (46), though where we might expect a presciently ironic indictment of post-genocidal failures of memory to come, this miniature impeaches the statistical processing of émigré "'background'" checks by host countries instead. "Anything that is not reified, cannot be counted and measured, ceases to exist" (47). Walter Benjamin, who had committed suicide in September 1940 after finding his escape route out of Vichy France blocked on the border to Spain, had written earlier that year, in his theses on the philosophy of history, that "*even the dead* will not be safe from the enemy if he wins" (255). Benjamin's ghost surely whispers along in "To them shall no thoughts be turned" when Adorno writes in 1944: "even the past is no longer safe from the present, whose remembrance of it consigns it a second time to oblivion" (47 in Jephcott translation).[107] Here the permanent threat of catastrophe also manifests in the statistical forms of information gathering meant to aid emigrés escaping Nazi-occupied Europe and not to kill them. "Asylum for the homeless," also included in Part One, explicitly mentions "Hitler," "the labor and concentration camps," the wartime "destruction of the European cities," and the presumably Soviet failure of "socialistic society," but the poignant rancor of this miniature is reserved for the ubiquitous impossibility of "dwelling" in any form at all. No housing or "private life"—and certainly not the "musty pact" of familial "refuge"—is untainted by catastro-

---

[106] On Adorno's pivotal perspectives on the use of "words of foreign derivation and utopia," as Yasemin Yildiz puts it, see her Adorno chapter in *Beyond the Mother Tongue* (67–108).
[107] Huyssen may have such passages in mind when he writes that *Minima Moralia* is not only a "coda" to the literary tradition of the metropolitan miniature but also "an epitaph to Walter Benjamin's suicide" (291). We know that Adorno must have had access to a typescript of "On the Concept of History" that Benjamin mailed to Gretel Adorno in New York in the late spring of 1940 (Eiland and Jennings 662). As cited in Eiland and Jennings, the personal letter that Benjamin sent Gretel Adorno along with his unpublished theses described them "'more as a bouquet of whispering grasses'" (662).

phe for Adorno, and this miniature concludes with what scholars consider *Minima Moralia*'s hardest hitting line: "There is no right life in the wrong one."[108]

However, it is worth noting that the associative, discontinuous entry titles in *Minima Moralia* yield many surprising constellations in the miniatures themselves, and not necessarily the dialectical inversions of value or association we might predict. Written in 1945, the miniature titled "Great and small" for example challenges the "division of the world into important and unimportant matters, which has always served to neutralize the key phenomena of social injustice as mere exceptions" (Jephcott translation, 125), but this miniature does not simply elevate what is lowly, small, and minor in stature to higher echelons in "a hierarchy of importance" or magnitude (125). An "antidote" (126) is proposed instead, whereby "large themes" (125) manifest "in broken and eccentric ways" [*gebrochen und exzentrisch*].[109] Here too Adorno associates the blindly obstinate and dangerous "barbarism" of categorical hierarchies with the mathematics of "administrators" (125–126). His critical miniature in this instance draws on another small thing as itself a caricature of routinized hierarchies in European philosophy, the figure of a "dog out on a walk," in search of base relief.

> [...] at some unexplained spot he stands and sniffs, tense, unyielding, earnestly displeased —and then relieves himself, scrapes the ground with his feet and trots on his way in uncorn. In primitive times life and death may have depended on such things; after thousands of years of domestication they have become an unreal ritual. Who can help being reminded of them when observing a serious committee weighing the urgency of problems before turning over the carefully defined and time-tabled tasks to the attentions of their colleagues? There is something of this anachronistic doggedness in all importance, and to use it as a criterion of thought is to impose on thought a spellbound fixity, and a loss of self-reflection. (Jephcott translation, 125)[110]

---

108 Here I have mainly cited the Redmond translation of this particular miniature (33–35), with the exception of Jephcott's "musty pact" and "refuge" (38). Adorno's concluding line in German reads "Es gibt kein richtiges Leben im falschen" (43), which Jephcott translates as "Wrong life cannot be lived rightly" (39).

109 Here I deviate from Jephcott as well as Redmond, who both translate Adorno's original phrasing (142) as "refractedly and eccentrically" (Jephcott 125; Redmond 133).

110 Adorno explicitly includes both "war economies" and the "progressive philosophy" of thinkers such as "Bacon and Descartes" in this critique (124–125), though he only implicitly alludes to these and other philosophers' varying uses of canine tropes in their own conceptual articulations. On the role that dogs and other animals played for Adorno himself, see Ulrich Plass (147–148). On Kluge and the philosophical life of dogs, including with Kant and Marx, see Rainer Stollmann, "Das Private und die verwaltete Welt" ["The Private Sphere and the Administered World"]. Laika, who in 1957 was the first dog to orbit planet Earth but did not survive, also figures in some of Kluge's cosmic miniatures. See for example "Hündchen Laika" ["Little Dog Laika"] in "The Gap the Devil Leaves Us" (96–97). The collection that appeared in 2015

This anachronistic "doggedness"—*Sturheit* in Adorno's German and "obstinacy" in Redmond's translation—is a form of routinized anachronism that cannot serve the cause of human freedom, critical thought, or counterfactual hope for either Adorno or Kluge. For that we turn now to the spirited anachronism of heliotropic narration as it appears—large as well as small, broken and eccentric—in a key miniature from Part III of *Minima Moralia*.

2.4 Adorno's "Heliotrope" and Oscillating Perspective

"Heliotrope" is the 114th of the 153 miniatures assigned Arabic numerals in the German publication of *Minima Moralia* and both the Jephcott and Redmond translations. The final entry in this grouping ("Zum Ende" or "Finale" for Jephcott and "At the end" for Redmond) also marks the end of the published translations, whereas the Suhrkamp edition that postdates Adorno's death in 1969 includes ten additional entries selected by editors in 1979 from the author's previously unpublished excerpts. These ten additions are assigned Roman numerals, such that yet another ordering system is introduced, and we can see that even the end does not end for Adorno. This motif figures in the "Heliotrope" miniature itself when a house guest coming "from afar" disrupts everyday routines, more than delighting the child whose parents the invited guest has come to see (177–178, Jephcott translation). "Her appearance promises the child a world beyond the family, reminding him that it is not the ultimate" (178).[111] Something marvelous lies "beyond" this family sphere, though by and large this childhood portrait mainly appears benign and caring, in striking contrast to the one we encounter in "The bad comrade," an entry dated 1935 about the torments of bullying classmates that appears out of chronological order in the book's third part. That miniature begins with the line: "In a real sense, I ought to be able to deduce Fascism from the memories of my childhood" and

---

as *Kongs große Stunde* ["Kong's Great Hour"] also includes a miniature titled "Katzen im Weltraum" ["Cats in Outer Space"] (586–588).

111 Most of the references to the "child" [*Kind*] in this miniature are gender-neutral, in keeping with grammatical usage, while the gender of the "lady visitor" is highlighted throughout. However, the first line of the miniature also assigns masculinity to the child in a way that straddles grammatical convention and particular description. Adorno's biographers have identified the perfume-bearing house guest in "Heliotrope" as Else Herzberger, an especially close friend of the Adorno family who later provided some material assistance to Benjamin and other emigrés in great distress (see Müller-Doohm 55, 214, and 501, n. 9; and Lorenz Jäger 14–15). According to Detlev Claussen, "Adorno was distantly related to Benjamin" through Else Herzberger, with whom Adorno eventually fell out (47–48).

concludes: "In Fascism the nightmare of my childhood has come true" (192–193). The title "Heliotrope" however at first glance suggests harmless domesticity inasmuch as the word denotes both a fragrant flowering plant and a nice purplish color.[112] The miniature bearing the name "Heliotrope" provides no image of flowers at all though, and the only colors conjured are either textually associated with the phantasmatic "demon" with which bourgeois parents instill the terror of misdeeds in their own children or the faded, distorted colors of "washed-out" life (178).[113] These are cues to the reader that the scene of delighted childhood presented here is anything but idyllic, cues heightened by the racist rhetoric in "the frightful image of the black man" as the punitive "demon" that parents themselves create to discipline their children (178). The excitement that the arrival from afar generates in the child does not stem from gifts the visitor brings but from the horizon of "transformed life" (177, translation modified) that her visit prompts him to anticipate. Ordinary timetables for going to bed and going to school may be lifted, and categorical distinctions "between the generations too are suspended" (178). The child finds his way back again, this time "without fear," to his even younger "yearning" for "unformed joy" and ecstatically imagines that he is already "sitting at table with all humankind [*Menschheit*]" (178, translation modified). This in my opinion is an emphatically temporal portrait of the utopian dimension as Adorno envisions it.

The adult visitor bringing fantastic things from distant and not-so-distant places (Asian lands and "the caravanserais of Switzerland and the South Tyrol" [177]), arrives, we are told, as a "soothsaying gypsy" and is herself "transfigured into a rescuing angel" (178). The information she imparts to the boy is riddled with family gossip, but the manner in which she speaks to him—"seriously without condescension, to the child of the house"—is what transports him in time, "just as fairies talk to children in fairy-tales" (177). This rescuing

---

112 A 19th-century German invention, the heliotrope is also a surveying instrument that relies on reflected sunlight and triangulated calculations to measure long-distance relations. I thank Erik Born for alerting me to this additional meaning of heliotrope, which I would see as indirectly relevant to Adorno's narrative triangulations as well.

113 For other miniatures in Part Three of *Minima Moralia* with floral allusions in their titles, see also "Hothouse plant" and "All the little flowers." Eva Geulen analyzes the latter in relation to *Minima Moralia*'s motifs of sexual intimacy, eroticism, pleasure, and love as articulations of Adorno's theoretical "fidelity to the transitoriness of life" and that which is necessarily transient and "doomed to fail" (108–110). Erotic experience in this analysis thus does not signal compensation for flawed social life in Adorno's thought but a "logic of failure" that "seems primarily destined to renew longing" instead (111, n. 8). On Kluge's cinematic and conceptual relation to a "generative notion of failure" as a revolutionary project he shares with Adorno, see Pavsek (*The Utopia of Film* 152 et passim).

angel "removes the curse from the happiness of the nearness closest in," we read, "by wedding it to outermost distance" (178, translation modified).[114] Here Adorno's language faintly recalls Benjamin's "immense wooing of the cosmos" from the "To the Planetarium" miniature in *One-Way Street*, a cosmic wooing that Benjamin saw "enacted for the first time on a planetary scale" in the destructive technologies of World War I ("One-Way Street" 486–487).[115] The child of this heliotropic household cannot simply dwell here either, and Adorno's miniature concludes with "the child's whole being" oriented to "waiting," with "[l]ove count[ing] the hours" until the rescuing angel will cross his threshold once more and "restore [the] washed-out colours" of a life wedded to catastrophe (178).[116] Here we can recognize the pulsating co-presence of hope and despair that has been identified as a hallmark of Adorno's critical philosophy as well as his metropolitan miniatures, and we can also recognize the temporal registers to which the miniature repeatedly draws our attention even as it maps out a spatialized "threshold" event. But what exactly makes "Heliotrope" heliotropic in its associative and narrative gestures, and on what basis can we say that this has something to do with futurity that is not permanently deferred?

Surprisingly little scholarly attention has been paid to Adorno's "Heliotrope" miniature since its first publication in 1951, and only in 2010 did Robyn Marasco identify what must now seem both obvious and crucial. The associative title of this domestic miniature distinctly alludes to Benjamin's fourth philosophical thesis on the concept of history, in which he speaks of a "secret heliotropism"

---

114 Adorno's phrasing in German reads: "Sie nimmt vom Glück der nächsten Nähe den Fluch, indem sie es der äußersten Ferne vermählt" (202). Jephcott's English translation reads: "From the joy of greatest proximity she removes the curse by wedding it to utmost distance" (178). I have modified the translation to underscore Adorno's negative dialectical commitment to "happiness," to stress the intended cosmic blurring of merely spatial distinctions between near and far, and to weaken the hierarchical subject-object implications of Jephcott's superlatives. "Outermost" is more conducive to my reading of cosmic horizons as off-worldly, whereas "utmost" connotes distance that is measurable rather than relational. The Redmond translation reads: "She dispels the curse on the happiness of what is nearest of all, by wedding it to what is most distant" (191). This is not entirely felicitous for two reasons. Redmond dispels the possibility that domestic "happiness" curses itself (as opposed to something else having cursed it), and his choices also uphold spatial distinctions between "near" and "far."
115 For more idyllic biographical reminiscences of Adorno's childhood, see Reinhard Pabst. For relevant analytical remarks on the co-figuration of progression and regression, see Ulrich Plass's comparison of Adorno and Fritz Lang ("Dialectic of Regression").
116 The literal ending of the miniature is itself doubled in the Jephcott translation, which includes a poetic citation of return from afar by Eduard Mörike and a superscriptural Arabic numeral directing readers' attention elsewhere, in this case, to an informational footnote at the bottom of the page. Only the Mörike quotation as such is provided in the original.

of historical transformation, as discussed in the opening section of Part One of the present study. "As flowers turn toward the sun, by dint of a secret heliotropism the past strives to turn toward that sun which is rising in the sky of history. A historical materialist must be aware of this most inconspicuous of all transformations" (*Illuminations* 255; see also Marasco 656).[117] And yet, as I have argued above, Benjamin's heliotropic orientation to the future remains conventional in Koselleck's modern sense of being phenomenologically inaccessible to experience even if one can experience lack—the sense that something is missing—as such. Marasco calls Adorno's title for this miniature "significant" though she invokes Benjamin's "heliotropism" almost as if in passing (656), in the sense that she is not concerned with critical theory's sidereal motifs, cosmic horizons as such (though she does speak metaphorically of wanting "to resist the idea that the revolutionary horizon has for ever receded" [645]), or differential models of futurity. What does concern her is what she considers a nefarious "return of love" in 21st-century political theory, especially as associated with various critical theorists such as Michael Hardt, Antonio Negri, Slavoj Žižek, Alain Badiou, and Terry Eagleton (643–644). To Marasco's way of thinking, their contemporary discourse of political love serves only "to feminize political subjectivity, rendering it passive and wholly derivative of the dominant order" (643) without offering any revolutionary solutions for "frustration and despair" (645). For Marasco, Benjamin's historical theses recall harder-edged affects and emotions for revolutionary forces instead (650), and she finds that Adorno's dialectical configuration of love in *Minima Moralia* "seizes upon the utopian potential harbored in the wait without resting a politics on the fragile arrows of *amor*" (655). In her reading, "hope for the future" is necessary but insufficient for radical social change (654), and with Adorno's "Heliotrope" in particular, "love establishes the scene for a childlike hope of 'transformed existence' that can never come to rest comfortably in any extant amorous relationship" (656; see also Geulen, "'No Happiness without Fetishism'" 111 et passim, for ways in which "Adorno desires desire" without coming to rest in erotic objects of "fulfillment"). Adorno, in Marasco's analysis, out-radicalizes even Simone de Beauvoir's feminist critique of women as the "ones who wait" in mere consciousness of their unhappiness (651, 657). Marasco thus ascribes a politically necessary but limited utopian function to the young

---

117 Without any mention of either Benjamin or Adorno, Jacques Derrida's essay "White Mythology: Metaphor in the Text of Philosophy," originally published in 1971, discusses the rhetorical figure of heliotropes in philosophy (especially in relation to suns and flowers) to consider a dual gesture of philosophy as such, whereby "metaphor *comes back* to *physis*, to its truth and its presence" (244). For Derrida, the heliotrope becomes "the very figure of that which doubles and endangers philosophy" (271).

boy who waits in Adorno's "Heliotrope," which indicts, as she puts it, "a pernicious kind of forgetfulness," one that "relinquishes those childhood dreams of a world beyond and outside of our own" (657). The family's magical adult female house guest "stands in for radical alterity" in her assessment.

Marasco's feminist analysis of Adorno's "Heliotrope" is by far the most extensive reading to date, and it underscores Adorno's renewed importance for both a "poetics of thinking" in critical theory for the 21st century and specifically the figure of "utopian potential" for devising "some *way out*" of damaged life (643, 652, 655). But her discussion of utopian dimensions in *Minima Moralia* as necessary but insufficient for real change leaves us with a familiar dilemma of how to account for conversion beyond the mere indexing of possibility in either Adorno or Kluge, who claims to follow Adorno faithfully. In short, Marasco's treatment of "Heliotrope" ignores the factor of counterfactual hope as a real social force both in and off world. And the "radical alterity" she assigns to the miniature's "lady visitor" bypasses the negative dialectical approach that Adorno takes to virtually everything. That is to say, the critical difference that utopian longing affords for Adorno is not radically exogamous; it does not come from a radically different space, time, or subject but—as Huyssen has already in part reminded us in reference to *Minima Moralia* as consisting of modernist miniatures—*from* what I would call the temporal non-identity of damaged life in deep relation to off-worldly horizons of the cosmos.[118] In this sense Adorno's "Heliotrope" does not simply signal the happy cosmopolitanism of spatial "openness to the world" that Lorenz Jäger assigns to it (14) or the radiant wonders of world travel that Detlev Claussen describes (47), though it does have to do with what Adorno called "'the utopia of not being oneself'" and hope as being operative "only as a broken, a secret energy source of thought" (as cited in Claussen 46, 356).[119] The house guest in "Heliotrope" does come "from afar," but the things her child host associates with the excitement she sparks are not so much foreign things in a strictly demarcated sense as they are *Allotria* already hidden

---

118 This might also mark a point of departure for distinguishing Adorno's approach from Foucauldian notions of heterotopia.
119 The first citation stems from "The George-Hofmannsthal Correspondence," and the second from Adorno's public letter to Max Horkheimer on the occasion of the latter's 70th birthday in 1965, the English translation of which Claussen includes in his Appendix. On the active utopian dimensions of inauthenticity in even childhood "attempts at self-relation," see also Geulen, "'No Happiness without Fetishism'" (101). There she cites Adorno's "Gold assay" miniature from *Minima Moralia*, which asserts that all such childhood attempts "contain an element of imitation, play, wanting to be different" (153).

in the domestic sphere.[120] *Allotria* is the term Adorno uses in the German version of "The Essay as Form," which unfortunately gets lost in the English translation, where it is rendered only as "a trivial endeavor" (*Noten zur Literatur* [Vol. 1] 10; *Notes to Literature* [Vol. 1] 4). The Greek-derived term in Adorno's German sense refers to things in the plural that do not fit into an assigned topic or conceptual category. These are not trivial things at all but quite crucial things in Adorno's associative mode of writing. The association between experimental essay and *Allotria* in "The Essay as Form" follows shortly after Adorno's association of essayistic writing with "the leisure of a childlike person" and the aphoristic assertion: "The essay [...] does not let its domain be prescribed for it" (4).[121] The material things the young child in "Heliotrope" associates with the family's visitor belong in various senses as much to him as they do to her. He "breathes" her perfume, which reminds him of "memory even though he breathes it for the first time," and the travel cases she bears from elsewhere appear to him in declarative terms as things he has presumably absorbed through immersive reading that precedes her: "chests in which the jewels of Aladdin and Ali Baba, wrapped in precious tissues—the guest's kimonos—are borne hither from the caravanserais of Switzerland and the South Tyrol in sleeping-car sedan chairs for his glutted contemplation" (177).[122] While the house guest explicitly appears as "the figure of all that is different" (178), we might say the child appears in more important ways *as* the figure of the essay or at least as its kin. What work on the matter of perspective then can Adorno's "Heliotrope" miniature be said to do?

As a historical, cosmic, and critical orientation in time, the futurity of Benjamin's secret heliotropism remains inaccessible to experience. The futurity of Adorno's heliotropic miniature in *Minima Moralia* is hidden but intermittently available to experience through narrative oscillations between hope and despair. This is not only a matter of resonant motifs but also, in a core temporal sense, of oscillations in narrative perspective. With only two exceptions, both of which mark the child's disfiguring discipline of his own child-like "yearning" grammatically in the simple past (178), the "Heliotrope" miniature is written almost en-

---

[120] Huyssen remarks that the entire literary tradition of the metropolitan miniature as a major phenomenon in European modernism had been "hiding in plain sight" (*Miniature Metropolis* ix). On the "tension between proximity and distance" that Adorno ascribes to "the given," including the figure of the visitor from afar in "Heliotrope," see Philipp von Wussow (114–115).

[121] The political stakes are very high here too, for Adorno associates the risk of thinking outside prescribed thought with being "marked with the yellow star" (4), a clear—and sidereal—allusion to anti-Semitism in the Third Reich.

[122] Ulrich Plass notes in another context that Adorno and his wife also had a dog named Ali Baba ("Dialectic of Regression" 147).

tirely in the present tense. This comes as a surprising realization, given the especially vibrant impression the text conveys of something distinct already having happened and something even more wonderful yet to come. Differential relations of past, present, and future infuse the present-tense narrative throughout and point to gaps in the child's experience as well, gaps suggesting that lost longing can be redeemed in future adult life oriented to the utopian dimension. Adorno's "Heliotrope" thus also articulates a different temporal relationship to the figure of the child, and not only to the figure of heliotropism, from the one most commonly associated with Benjamin. Writing on *Berlin Childhood around 1900*, Benjamin's collection of childhood miniatures written in first-person voice from the 1930s, literary theorist Peter Szondi focuses on Benjamin's affinity to and significant divergence from Marcel Proust with regard to the temporal valence of childhood memory in literary prose. Proust's magnum opus in novel form and Benjamin's short prose are both centrally committed to the "search for time past," Szondi writes before explaining their essential difference:

> Proust sets off in quest of the past in order to escape from time altogether. This endeavor is made possible by the coincidence of the past with the present, a coincidence brought about by analogous experiences. Its real goal is to escape from the future, filled with dangers and threats, of which the ultimate one is death. In contrast, the future is precisely what Benjamin seeks in the past. [...] Proust listens attentively for the echo of the past; Benjamin listens for the first notes of a future which has meanwhile become the past. Unlike Proust, Benjamin does not want to free himself from temporality; he does not wish to see things in their ahistorical essence. He strives instead for historical experience and knowledge. Nevertheless, he is sent back into the past, a past, however, which is open, not completed, and which promises the future. Benjamin's tense is not the perfect, but the future perfect in the fullness of its paradox: being future and past at the same time. (499)[123]

For our purposes, it is important to note a key aside in Szondi's discerning essay of 1961, in which he cites from the "Finale" miniature of *Minima Moralia* to suggest that hope comes from the future for Adorno, in sharp distinction from Benjamin, for whom hope and an open future alike come from the past (502). Szondi has the opening lines of "Finale" in mind when he writes this, where Adorno calls upon philosophy responsible to "the face of despair" to consider "all things as they would present themselves from the standpoint of redemption" rather

---

[123] The scholarship on the figure of childhood in Benjamin's larger oeuvre is too voluminous to be reviewed here. For an updated overview of the convoluted publication history of Benjamin's *Berlin Childhood*, see Huyssen (*Miniature Metropolis* 184–186). The sixth chapter of Huyssen's monograph on modernist miniatures illuminates Benjamin's relationship to French Surrealism and Louis Aragon in particular through Huyssen's analysis of Benjamin's miniatures in *Berlin Childhood around 1900*.

than "reconstruction" (Jephcott translation, 247). This is also where Adorno issues an imperative to produce "[p]erspectives" that would "reveal" from such future light the "rifts and crevices" of this world of human suffering (247). I think Szondi is more rather than less correct in drawing this particular distinction between Adorno and Benjamin, inasmuch as Benjamin forecloses his open futurity to experience. However, Szondi's keen observation in 1961 goes against the grain of much Adorno scholarship, which likes to cite an explicit and later proclamation from *Negative Dialectics* instead, where Adorno tells us that hope comes "from the past" [*aus dem Vergangenen*] (378). Mobilizing metaphors of color, and invoking Benjamin on the entanglement of hopelessness and hope, Adorno elaborates:

> Grayness could not fill us with despair if our minds did not harbor the concept of different colors, scattered traces of which are not absent from the negative whole. The traces always come from the past, and our hopes come from their counterpart, from that which was or is doomed; such an interpretation may very well fit the last line of Benjamin's text on *Elective Affinities:* "For the sake of the hopeless only are we given hope." (377–378)

Hope never appears as a word in Adorno's heliotropic miniature but shapes the text in its temporal and affective orientation. This heliotropic hope is rendered experientially present in complex narrative perspective rather than metaphoric color, and this hope comes for Adorno from the future as well as the past. This too is reflected in the miniature's narrative perspective and use of voice.

"Heliotrope" presents a remarkably intimate portrait of a child's invigorating excitement over a scene of hospitality with known autobiographical elements. So it may be puzzling to realize that the first-person voice of singular narration appears only once in this miniature, and it does so in the self-distancing form of intertextual citation when Adorno concludes his miniature with a poetic citation from Eduard Mörike: "'Here I am again/returned from the endless world'" (178). What kind of intimacy is this in Adorno's own writing, an intimacy to which no "I" appeals? For an initiating clue we must turn to the first word to follow the miniature's title. In Adorno's German this first word entails a subjective, anthropomorphic reference to the child whose experience is about to be narrated, but the reference appears in the estranging indirect mode of a singular masculine pronoun in the dative case, which immediately figures the person about to be conjured as an indirect object. "Dem, zu dessen Eltern Logierbesuch kommt, schlägt das Herz mit größerer Erwartung als je vor Weihnachten" (201). Jephcott opts for elegance over precision when he translates the opening line this way: "When a guest comes to stay with his parents, a child's heart beats with more fervent expectation than it ever did before Christmas" (177). And Redmond chooses to convert Adorno's grammatical indications of determinate gender into consistent ungendered plurals such as "the children of the house" and "the parents' guests" (190, 191), even though Adorno's miniature gives us only one child and a single guest. A more literal translation of the opening line of "Heliotrope" would read something like this instead: "To him to whose parents company comes, the heart beats with greater expectation than it ever did before Christmas."[124] This is a perfectly naturalized use of a dative object in German, but Redmond's instinct to multiply the subjective reference to the child whose beating heart we are made to sense is in one sense correct. This is because the text presents the child's subjectivity in ways that are both broken and proliferating, and breaks and proliferation alike come to us in the fragmented voice of the third person, which in Adorno's usage entails a relational commingling of subjective and objective registers that are anything but omniscient or self-identical. This particular commingling marks the utopian temporal horizon of Adorno's heliotropic miniature, so we should take a closer look at what happens not merely to but with the voice of the third person in this important but little remarked entry in *Minima Moralia*.

Recent scholarship on so-called unnatural voices in the interdisciplinary field of postclassical narratology will be helpful to us here in certain limited senses. One of the major proponents of this newer branch of narratological inquiry, Brian Richardson proposes an "inductive" rather than deductive approach to "the creation, fragmentation, and reconstitution of narrative voices." The inductive approach in his view allows narrative theory and narratologists in particular to account more effectively for "the permeability, instability, and playful mutability of the voices of nonmimetic fictions" (*Unnatural Voices* ix, xii). Three of his overarching reasons for proposing such an approach are of special interest here. As Richardson puts it, narrative theory that proceeds from predetermined categories of narrative voice tend to overlook existing strategies of narrative representation that do not match conceptual categories; even postclassical narratology needs better tools to account for the "modernist origins and historical antecedents of the anti-realist practices of so many contemporary works" of literary fiction; and since the age of late modernism and the historical avant-garde, first-person narration has grown "increasingly eccentric" and the putative omniscience of third-person narration "increasingly inauthentic" too (ix, xi, 46). The legacy that Adorno bequeathes to Kluge thus also concerns what we might in this sense call, to borrow Richardson's term, "unnatural voices."[125] One of the

---

[124] As is well known, Adorno was baptized at birth in the Catholic church, in keeping with his mother's religious affiliation, while his father's family background was Jewish. For additional details see Müller-Doohm (15–24).
[125] For additional commentary on the growing field of scholarship and nuanced debates on "natural" and "unnatural" voices in narrative theory, see for example Jan Alber, Henrik Skov

core narratological concepts that Adorno's use of perspective implicitly questions is that of perspective itself or "point of view," and another is voice. Regarding the "unnatural" capacity of third-person narration to undo common-sense perceptions of voice, Richardson cites Roland Barthes's damning quip from the 1970s to the effect that third-person narration effects "'a sort of murder by language'," and in 2006 Richardson himself concludes with equal pith and less drama: "The third person is not what it used to be" (9). With this he means that long-held presumptions of omniscient perspective tied to the objective distance of third-person narration no longer hold for contemporary narrative forms and may not always apply to older narrative forms either. Be that as it may, we know that historical murder and mayhem tarry in everything Adorno writes, and we would hardly expect the master of negative dialectics to leave any narrative voice unquestioned. And yet Adorno is not Barthes, for his use of the third person in this miniature creates a utopian horizon of future life not murder. To what extent can we say that Adorno's highly variegated and always grammatically correct use of third-person forms in "Heliotrope" effects an "unnatural voice" of narration in this future-oriented sense? How does this work?

One common third-person voice of narration in everyday German usage is the impersonal *man* or "one." As Alber, Nielsen, and Richardson observe, literary narratives written in this voice "tend to resist the binary opposition of first and third person or Genette's homo- and heterodiegetic stances" (355), thus ren-

---

Nielsen, and Brian Richardson's co-authored overview in *The Routledge Companion to Experimental Literature* ("Unnatural Voices, Minds, and Narration"); Jan Alber and Monika Fludernik's 2010 anthology, *Postclassical Narratology: Approaches and Analyses*; Richard Walsh, *The Rhetoric of Fictionality*; as well as several contributions by Fludernik: *Towards a 'Natural' Narratology*, "New Wine in Old Bottles," "Natural Narratology and Cognitive Parameters," and "How Natural is 'Unnatural Narratology'?" Both Richardson and Fludernik take issue with long held positions on voice and person articulated by Gérard Genette as an especially influential classical narratologist, and Alber, Fludernik, Nielsen, and Richardson all seem to agree that their analyses of natural and unnatural voices in narration complement each other. Fludernik's cognitive studies approach nonetheless tends to stress ways in which readers "project real-life parameters into the reading process" in multidirectional interaction with narrative ("New Wine" 623), while Alber, Nielsen, and Richardson are more interested in ways in which "[u]nnatural narratives present specific challenges to or entirely violate common-sense understandings of narratives and of fictional voices and narration" (351). For another fine-grained approach to narrative strategies of "recursiveness in representation," especially with regard to narrative voice, see Richard Walsh, "Person, Level, Voice: A Rhetorical Reconsideration." Walsh challenges both communicative models of narration as "transmission" and Genette's rigid typologies of narrative "person" and "level." Walsh, who remains indebted to Plato for two of his own preferred categories, differentiates three different functions of narrative voice to counter Genette: instance (diegetic), idiom (mimetic), and interpellation (ideological).

dering "unnatural" those first- and third-person voices that have come to be naturalized.[126] In "Heliotrope" Adorno invokes the seemingly impersonal *man* just once, albeit in a particularly significant association: "The single visit makes Thursday a feast-day and in the hubbub [*Rauschen*] one seems to be sitting at table with all humankind" (178, Jephcott translation modified). The noun that Jephcott translates as "hubbub" and Redmond as "euphoria" (191) associatively conjures both a kind of transportive ecstasy and the undifferentiated sound of strong movement. The grammatical subject in this instance strains in multiple directions, all of which are associated with the child's perspective, which itself appears broken and refracted. This perspective is doubly estranged in this clause, to the extent that the third-person voice as such signals subjectivity at some remove, and the third-person voice in the impersonal form of "one" suggests a higher degree of remove into a sphere connoting both objective and collective properties. This child-like subject is not identical with itself, but it is certainly not alone or indulging in ineffectual fantasy.[127] Some real shift in subject-object relations begins to happen at this table, and the extraordinary status of this ordinary act of sitting down to a festive meal when special company comes is echoed in the semantics of "euphoria" and "all humankind" as well. The broken perspective of this essayistic figure—the broken perspective of the child—is also tied to breaks, gaps, and conjunctions too in time, which together carry an "inkling of true promiscuity" (178). This is the temporal promiscuity of utopian orientations, which allow one to sense the possibility that school could be missed tomorrow and "all humankind" could be dining in one's home right now. The present tense in Adorno's "Heliotrope" relies on this temporal future sense.

The narrative perspective that comes to us in third-person voice and child-like time is even more complicated though. Does the "to him" with which this heliotropic miniature begins refer to a particular child—the one whose actual experience is being described by the narrative instance, which speaks in the voice of an adult? Or does the inaugural "to him" introduce a generic (though not uni-

---

126 Scholars in the field tend to mean various processes of naturalization and de-naturalization rather than any ontological distinctions between "natural" and "unnatural" voices. Fludernik, who provides an overview of Genette and Stanzel's key disagreements concerning narrative voice, also ascribes "one major theoretical drawback" to Genette's model, inasmuch as he "takes the existence of a narrator (or a narrative voice) for granted" ("New Wine" 621). For extended challenges to "natural" and even "unnatural" categories in postclassical narratology, see the anthology *Strange Voices in Narrative Fiction*, edited by Per Krogh Hansen, Stefan Iversen, Henrik Skov Nielsen, and Rolf Reitan.
127 For analysis of fantasy as an especially productive element in Negt and Kluge's Marxian social theory, see Langston ("Toward an Ethics of Fantasy").

versal) child of sorts, one belonging to that cohort of possible children to whom such visitors might come? The third person of the single word *dem* ("to him") carries both possibilities, and in this sense too Adorno gives us a refracted third-person voice of narration that straddles the particular and the possible. The vectors of third-person narration multiply yet again in "Heliotrope" when Adorno introduces the third-person voice in the interrogative form of "he who [*wer*]" (178). This third person figures twice in the miniature, and the contrast is instructive. When it first appears, we read that "the order of the day" might be magically suspended and "he who at eleven o'clock has still not been sent to bed has an inkling of true promiscuity" (178). This grammatical usage appears mainly descriptive, though the semantic proximity of "true promiscuity" in time and the generic co-presence of other possible children who might not be sent to bed by eleven resonate here too. Something significantly different happens when the interrogative form of the third-person voice returns near the end of the miniature, this time with an urgent imperative of utopian dimensions attached. The "rescuing angel" who comes in the form of a house guest "removes the curse from the happiness of the nearness closest in," we read, "by wedding it to outermost distance" (178, translation modified). The miniature then concludes, in Jephcott's translation: "For this the child's whole being is waiting, and so too, later, must he be able to wait who does not forget what is best in childhood. Love counts the hours until the one when the guest steps over the threshold and imperceptibly restores life's washed-out colours: 'Here I am again/returned from the endless world'" (178). This use of the "he who" construction is no longer descriptive or generic but decidedly utopian. This third-person voice in the utopian dimension belongs not only to the future, but also to a future rendered at least partially accessible to present experience through Adorno's narrative turn to this non-empirical but nonetheless real imperative.[128] This future literally informs the very grammar of Adorno's heliotropic prose, notably through the refracted voices of its third-person narration.

One of the "unnatural voices" discussed by Richardson is that of the "'permeable narrator'," a form that "slips (or is collapsed)" into other perspectives and in this sense "speaks what should be impossible for it to know" (ix.) Writing in 2006, Richardson notes that a permeable narrator "threatens to violate the principle of an autonomous, individual consciousness that is presupposed by all current theories of the narrator" (95). Adorno's negative dialectical critique

---

[128] While the pressures Walsh has in mind when speaking of interpellation are largely oppressive, one might conceivably think of Adorno's use of third-person voice in "Heliotrope" as a kind of interpellation to the utopian dimension of "damaged life."

of bourgeois subjectivity and philosophical precepts of autonomous individualism that attend it is well established. But in what sense can we say that the specific unfolding of narrative perspective or "point of view" in "Heliotrope" relates to the multiplicity of third-person voice in this prose miniature? Ulrich Plass provides an especially insightful and relevant account of the role that the figure of childhood plays in Adorno's overall "dialectic of regression," although Plass does not address questions of narrative perspective and voice.[129] His starting point is the observation that Horkheimer and Adorno's *Dialectic of Enlightenment* is usually taken to signal that "there is no progress without regression" in capitalist modernity and the so-called culture industry (127). Drawing on Adorno's extensive correspondence with his close friend and émigré filmmaker Fritz Lang, and on miniatures from *Minima Moralia* that pivot on childhood songs (see Plass 135–136 on the latter), Plass demonstrates instead that regression is not an "exclusively negative or derogatory term" for Adorno but something that points to the possibility of an other life as well (127). Furthermore, "Adorno's critique of regression in the culture industry" was linked to "his insistence on the philosophical relevance of experiences pertaining to childhood" (129). As Plass argues, for Adorno, this more open-ended possibility of experience is "associated primarily with qualities pertaining to childhood: naïveté, silliness, playfulness, and an uninhibited capacity for wonder" (128). There is little silliness in evidence in "Heliotrope," but serious play, rather sophisticated naïveté, and a persistent capacity for wonder despite internalized inhibitions and socially imbued fears do seem to apply. Third-person voice in this miniature does not suggest objectifying distance but, as we have seen, subjective approximation to a utopian horizon with claims to real effect. We might take this to mean, in agreement with Plass, there is no regression without progressive remainder. Adorno's "Heliotrope" does not stress regression, however, but a longing much more strongly oriented to progress and transformation in life. The narrative perspective subtly underwriting the miniature's multiple third-person voices echoes this in the sense that an adult point of view recalls the child's point of view—with all its somatic excitement, temporal anticipation, and transformative delight—with-

---

129 For additional commentary on the importance of the figure of childhood for Adorno's negative dialectic, especially in relation to mimesis and utopia, see Matt F. Connell ("Childhood Experience and the Image of Utopia" and "Body, Mimesis and Childhood in Adorno, Kafka and Freud"). See also John Milfull ("Short Stories?") and Reinhard Pabst ("Ein Sohn aus gutem Hause").

out consigning the child's perspective to memory alone or illusion or even affirmation.[130]

The figure of the child comes alive here in the present and presence of company "from afar," and this child, who actively remembers his own past terrors, senses a vibrant future freed of fear ahead. Yet the narrative perspective that relays this scene of childhood to us at some intimate remove is that of an adult who also looks backward as well as forward. The adult's temporal relationship to this childhood scene is similarly refracted in the co-presence of differential temporalities. If the child feels himself taken up into "the mighty and mysterious league of the grown-ups, the magic circle of the people of sense" [*die magische Runde der vernünftigen Leute*] (178), the narrative perspective on the utopian dimension comes to us from this adult realm of instrumental rationality (in Horkheimer and Adorno's parlance) and not in unmediated fashion from the child's "uninhibited capacity for wonder" (Plass). The house guest who appears as the figure of a radiant other life appears as "their friend" to the adults at the dinner table too ("Heliotrope" 178). And the adult narrative instance that shares a utopian admonition with us as readers—"so too, later, must he be able to wait who does not forget what is best in childhood" (178)—is both contemplating and sharing a heliotropic horizon that exceeds the experience of any particular child.[131] The imperative "not" to "forget" is thus tied here more acutely to the cultivation of a future sense in the present, however minute, than to a past harboring hidden secrets of redemption. And yet, the adult narrative instance admonishing us not to forget the utopian dimension is not one with the utopian dimension, since in the heliotropic narrative terms of Adorno's miniature, this dimension remains beyond the adult's current temporal grasp. We have after all no way of knowing whether he who narrates this miniature will also be he who does not forget. Together with third-person voices that oscillate between subjective and objective registers, between intimate remove and heliotropic proximity in time, this snippet from Adorno's reflections from damaged life also relies on recursively broken and conjoined orientations, child-like and adult, in narrative perspective. If we can understand the child in "Heliotrope" as kin to the figure of the essay, the more elusive adult he may or may not have already become comes to us in the

---

[130] This is important to underscore, since celebrating the child's perspective as inherently pure in its utopian orientation would require us to overlook the catastrophic effects of the racist rhetoric that the child has already unwittingly internalized. This is another reason why we must turn to Adorno's use of narrative form in "Heliotrope"—and not the child's figural perspective as such—to appreciate the utopian dimension of this miniature.

[131] There is some irony in speaking of utopian admonition here, but the term is warranted in Adorno's sense of negative dialectics.

reserved figure of human suffering whose hopes for a "future without life's miseries" have nonetheless not died. At least in this miniature, which we should understand as being in dialogue with Benjamin's secret heliotropism of catastrophic history, counterfactual hope comes to Adorno from the future as much as it does from the past. Unlike with Benjamin, however, this future is not permanently deferred but arguably practiced in tiny turns of narrative writing.

Counterfactual hope is accorded some degree of real experiential effect in Adorno's "Heliotrope" miniature, even though it shares the pages of *Minima Moralia* with many others as well, including an impressive range of temporal affects and narrative gestures.[132] Even if Adorno could not permanently cross his historical bridge between hope and despair, he could and did begin to exercise in incremental ways what Kluge's storytelling will work on more intensively in the form of a future sense. Narrative articulations are key to such exercises for Adorno and Kluge alike. Adorno's heliotropic miniature and Kluge's cosmic miniatures of much later vintage do function as "unnatural narratives" to the degree that they "violate common-sense understandings" (Alber, Nielsen, and Richardson 351) of narrative perspective, voice, person, and narrative itself as an ostensibly communicative act of linear transmission (see especially Walsh's critique of communicative models of narratology). We must conclude this section on Adorno though with one important caveat regarding the applicability of the term "unnatural narratives" in reference to Adorno and Kluge. Experts in the narratological field explain that unnatural narratives "transcend real-world possibility by projecting physically, logically, or humanly impossible scenarios or acts of narration" (Alber, Nielsen, and Richardson 351; see also Richardson, *Unnatural Voices*, and Alber, "Impossible Storyworlds"). The editors of *Postclassical Narratology* similarly point to unnatural narratives as "anti-mimetic narratives that challenge and move beyond real-world understandings of identity, time, and space by representing scenarios and events that would be impossible in the actual world" (Alber and Fludernik 14). Adorno and Kluge may challenge and violate many common-sense understandings of social and even physical reality in their writings, but these dialecticians would not subscribe to an entirely "anti-mimetic" logic that dichotomously pits impossibility against possibility or real-

---

132 See for example "Little Hans" in Part Two of *Minima Moralia*, a miniature in which Adorno scathingly indicts the dangers of intellectuals living "as a 'third person'," as if they and "the objective quality of their work" were untouched by "economic brutality." The entwined motifs of childhood and adulthood figure here too when this miniature concludes: "Whatever the intellectual does, is wrong. He experiences drastically and vitally the ignominious choice that late capitalism secretly presents to all its dependants [sic]: to become one more grown-up, or to remain a child" (132–133).

ism against anti-realism.[133] The notion of counterfactual hope as a social fact speaks in a different tongue. The unnatural narratives we encounter in Adorno's "Heliotrope" and Kluge's cosmic miniatures challenge real-world limits to off-world aspirations of futurity by expanding rather than accommodating the human sensorium of possible experience.[134]

2.5 Kluge's Flawed Beauty and Unnatural Narration

Kluge's aesthetics of the gap are in large and small parts inspired by Adorno's temporal configuration of counterfactual hope in micrological writing against

---

[133] Marie-Laure Ryan points to distinctions between classical physics and modern physics or "quantum mechanics" that radically alter perceived relationships between possibility and impossibility. "With modern physics, the natural and the impossible seem to exchange places: whereas in classical physics the impossible lies outside of nature, in modern physics, especially quantum mechanics, nature often seems to incorporate the logically impossible. By defying logic, literature and the visual arts rival the power of modern science to challenge the imagination" ("Impossible Worlds" 368). The observation of such inversions is arguably more relevant to Kluge's project than any classical models of possibility, though we should be careful not to assume that Kluge's experiments rely on merely inverted categories of "natural" possibility. This is because nature is not at all a natural category for Kluge's writing or his Marxist theory. Hitherto subdominant strands in even postclassical narratology—strands that exceed mere contrast between "natural" and "unnatural" modes of narration to stress for example "the fact that literary narratives excel in the construction of and playing with the strangeness of the written, narrating voice"—might thus prove both more relevant to Kluge's writing and more interested in his experimental prose. See for example *Strange Voices in Narrative Fiction*, co-edited by Per Krogh Hansen, Stefan Iversen, Henrik Skov Nielsen, and Rolf Reitan, whose joint introduction I have just cited (4).

[134] For this reason Fludernik's narratological concept of "experientiality" rather than experience would not apply to writers such as Adorno and Kluge, who are each, in different ways, committed to transforming the reality of social life. Blending narrative studies and cognitive studies to account for representations of experience, Fludernik defines experientiality as "the quasi-mimetic evocation of real-life experience" (*Towards a 'Natural' Narratology* 12) and explains that in her usage mimesis does not mean "imitation" but the "implicit though incomplete homologization of the fictional and real worlds" (35). Adorno prefers to speak of historical experience and to allow for "metaphysical experience," however, both of which he would see as radically distinct from "real-life experience," which he would associate with empiricism. On experientiality as a narratological concept, which Fludernik coined, see Marco Caracciolo's online entry in *The Living Handbook of Narratology* as well as Caracciolo's *The Experientiality of Narrative: An Enactivist Approach*. Here it should also be noted that the off-world aspirations to futurity Adorno and Kluge attempt to foster are at odds with the kind of spatial appropriation and cosmic conquest Peter Szendy discusses in relation to Carl Schmitt's "nomos of the cosmos" (see Introduction).

the grain of empirical history. Kluge's writing in and for the 21ˢᵗ century however bespeaks a more variegated cultivation of possible "ways out" of ubiquitous catastrophe than we find in *Minima Moralia* or even—at least in terms of intensity—in Kluge's publications prior to 2000. Kluge's intensified quest for *Auswege* also entails a more dedicated expansion of the future sense than Adorno's negative dialectics can provide in their oscillations between hope and despair. Where Adorno gives us a somatically inflected pedagogy of critical thought, Kluge gives us an apprenticeship in non-empirical but nonetheless experiential labor power, even as his entire body of work also encourages us to think critically and creatively about overcoming social conditions bent on destroying human life. Composed in a very uncomposed 1944, Adorno's final entry in Part One of *Minima Moralia* is itself titled "Lücken" ["Gaps"] (Jephcott translation, 80–81). This miniature indicts a Cartesian insistence on clarity and seamlessness in intellectual thought, on the grounds that such analytical and rhetorical perfection is doomed to "mere repetition" of that which already exists or the "categorical forms" we invoke to describe empirical reality (81). For Adorno, as one might expect, the true "value of a thought is measured by its distance from the continuity of the familiar," and any reduction in "this distance" constitutes the objective devaluation of thought (80). The "guilt" or debt thought owes its object (to which it remains in Adorno's original phrasing "allemal etwas schuldig" [91]) is itself cast as a kind of break or gap, a constellation explicitly likened to life as "deviating" from its prescribed course (Jephcott translation, 81).

> This inadequacy [of thought] equals that of life, which runs a crooked, deviating course, disappointing by comparison with its premises [sic], and yet which only in this actual course, always less than it should be, is able, under given conditions of existence, to represent an unregimented one. If life fulfilled its vocation directly, it would miss it. (Jephcott translation modified, 81)¹³⁵

---

135 My modifications in Jephcott's translation make Adorno's relevance for Kluge's own modified style of writing clearer. Here it is especially important to note that the necessary inadequacy attributed by Adorno to thought does not simply "resemble [...]" the course of life, as Jephcott's translation would have it, but "equals" [*gleicht*] it, albeit in a way that does not add up to equivalence. Jephcott also gives us life "which describes a wavering, deviating line," whereas Adorno's choice of the verb *verlaufen* and the adjective *verbogen* suggests running a course that is crooked or bent rather than "wavering." The adjective that Jephcott and I have both translated as "deviating" [*abgelenkt*] is technically a past participle that could also be translated as "distracted." Finally, I have altered Jephcott's "a life fulfilled" to correspond with Adorno's emphasis in this sentence on "life" rather than an individuated life.

This is where Adorno's miniature devoted to gaps suddenly opens one up for us with recourse to both a third-person voice and a temporal motif familiar from our reading of "Heliotrope."

> He who were to die old and in the consciousness of seemingly blameless success [*schuldenlosen Gelingens*], would secretly be the model schoolboy who reels off all life's stages without gaps or omissions, an invisible satchel on his back. Every thought which is not idle, however, bears branded on it the impossibility of its full legitimation, as we know in dreams that there are mathematics lessons, missed for the sake of a blissful morning in bed, which can never be made up. Thought waits to be woken one day by the memory of what has been missed, and to be transformed into teaching. (81)[136]

The horizon for this utopian dream however is not the blissful hours actually spent in bed but the missed hours of "mathematics lessons" [*Mathematikstunden*] irrevocably lost to the unidirectional arrow of time. In Adorno's world these are not the math lessons taught in the formal classroom but those numbered hours oriented to human happiness and a future without life's miseries.

The memory of something missing in past and present alike will awaken future-oriented thought, Adorno writes in 1944, and transform thought "into teaching." The multidirectional temporal structure ascribed to thinking in gaps here recalls the narrative relationship between child figure and adult voice in "Heliotrope," and Adorno's "teaching" [*Lehre*] is aligned with the utopian horizon of "what is best in childhood" as metaphysical experience. Counterfactual hope is clearly oscillating in Adorno's temporal configuration of pedagogy. Yet futurity is once again deferred, and the word *Lehre* is ambiguous to the extent that it can signal not only lessons taught but also a codified social form of labor apprenticeship in the European tradition of craftsmanship.[137] Adorno and Kluge alike are far more interested in interlocutors than masters, regardless whether teaching or labor is at stake. Whereas Adorno remains keenly committed to critical thought as a social form of pedagogy, even and especially in Germany after Auschwitz (see above all his radio broadcasts between 1959 and 1969, published

---

[136] Jephcott accurately and elegantly translates Adorno's "Wer alt [...] stürbe" as "Anyone who died old [...]." Here I have opted for "He who were to die" in order to underscore a resonance with the use of the third-person interrogative and also the future orientation in "Heliotrope." Roger Behrens summarizes Adorno's general relationship to mathematics by noting that Adorno was not very good at this subject in school and that Adorno's critical philosophy associates mathematics with "reification," erasure of difference, and a form of "identification without remainder" (148–149).

[137] Geuss by contrast briefly discusses the reference to *Lehre* at the end of Adorno's "Gaps" as a theological allusion to Benjamin's thoughts on Jewish doctrinal law (175).

in German as *Erziehung zur Mündigkeit* and included in Henry Pickford's English translations in *Critical Models*), Kluge's critical and creative pedagogies of public life must additionally be understood as a material form of apprentice labor without any master contract.[138] This study of Kluge's experimental miniatures is mainly concerned with Kluge's growing narrative investment in storytelling as labor on human time, historical catastrophe, and counterfactual hope in relation to cosmic constellations. This investment on Kluge's part repeatedly invites readers to exercise their inchoate future sense as an experiential organ of off-worldly perception. Where then does hope come from for Kluge in narrative terms of perspective and voice? How do his aesthetics of disjunctive and conjunctive gaps create narrative linchpins for experiential forms of futurity?

One of the cosmic miniatures in Kluge's storytelling collection situated "door to door with an other life" bears the title "Das Schöne ist fehlerfrei" ["The Beautiful is Flawless"] ("Door to Door with an Other Life" 34–35). It appears as the fifth numbered entry in a sequence of seven stories comprising a book section titled "We Fortunate Children of the First Globalization" (29–40), which is itself embedded in a longer book section bearing the same title (9–55). Kluge's narrative play with titles that resonate with or repeat each other, and with numbered sequences that invoke and violate linear sequentiality at the same time, is in evidence here, and the third section of Part One will analyze three other numbered entries from Kluge's subsection "We Fortunate Children of the First Globalization" in order to demonstrate how those entries can serve as a guide to reading uses of futurity in Kluge's cosmic miniatures more generally. At this juncture

---

[138] Invoking Kluge's own assessment, Schulte notes that Kluge's approach to film has more in common with "school recess" [*Schulpause*] than "classroom lessons" [*Schulstunde*] ("Kritische Theorie als Gegenproduktion" 43). On Adorno's postwar commitment to critical pedagogy, see for example Alex Demirović, Max Pensky ("Beyond the Message in a Bottle"), Anna Parkinson ("Adorno on the Air Waves"), and Jaimey Fisher ("Adorno's Lesson-Plans"). See also Henry A. Giroux on the Frankfurt School's more general commitment to critical thought through pedagogy. Giroux focuses on Adorno, Horkheimer, and Marcuse because, as he puts it in reference to the transnational field of critical pedagogy, "so much of the work on the Frankfurt School being used by educators focuses almost exclusively on the work of Jürgen Habermas" (27). Kluge's stories, films, and theoretical work from the 1960s on are riddled with motifs of teaching and learning; see for example *Learning Processes with a Deadly Outcome*, the history teacher around whom the film *The Patriot* is centered, the disciplining of "the obstinate child" in *History and Obstinacy*, and the many miniatures featuring philosophers affiliated with the Frankfurt School whom Kluge gratefully considers "my teachers" (*The Devil's Blind Spot* viii). On Kluge's relevance for school curricula, see a special issue of a professional journal of German pedagogy devoted to *"Man kann nicht lernen, nicht zu lernen": Alexander Kluge im Unterricht* ["'One cannot learn not to learn': Alexander Kluge in the Classroom"] (Jens Birkmeyer, Torsten Pflugmacher, and Ulrike Weymann).

however we turn to the "flawless" beauty of the fifth entry in Kluge's subsection in order to highlight some narrative features that straddle conventional and experimental aspects of narration and critical theory in Kluge's own cosmic prose. The first thing we might notice about this entry is that its title and storytelling substance implicitly invoke centuries-old debates among philosophers from the ancient Greeks on concerning flawlessness, perfectability, and teleologies in life, thought, morality, truth, and art. Key figures in addition to Kant from the German tradition dating to the 18th century would be Christian Wolff, who defines beauty as perfection manifesting in coherent and well ordered form, and Alexander Gottlieb Baumgarten, who coined the term "aesthetics" in 1735 and introduced "an emphasis on the emotional impact of art that is lacking in Wolff," who stressed cognitive ontology overall (see Paul Guyer, "18th Century German Aesthetics," for philosophical, historical, and bibliographical details). Baumgarten's work on "empirical psychology" posits sense perception as a flawed and "'confused'" but necessary means of higher cognition, and for Baumgarten, beautiful thought and art alike are characterized by harmony and coherence (see Guyer, who cites at length from Baumgarten's *Metaphysics* and *Aesthetica*). Yet as we have already seen, values such as perfection, clarity without remainder, and coherence without critique are anathema to Adorno, for whom such things convey the violence of modern catastrophe. Commenting on Adorno's general relationship to pre-Christian, Christian, and "post-Christian" concepts of "the imperfection and inadequacy of human life" (167, 171), for example, and on the "Gaps" miniature from *Minima Moralia* in particular, Raymond Geuss argues that Adorno invariably favors the "superiority of failure" in writing (164).[139] For Adorno, thinking is best "when not being perfect" (171).

The title of Kluge's miniature on "flawless" beauty is thus richly ironic, and the text unfolds in oddly poignant and comic ways when the category of beauty is projected onto both a "beautiful Greek woman" attending a conference of astrophysicists in Hawaii and the elegant "equations" [*Gleichungen*] she writes on the board in chalky hand despite the presence of sophisticated electronic technology, while the presenting astrophysicist herself "reserves the word beauty exclusively for the cosmos and the world of nanospheres" (34). This Greek scientist stresses relations between "what is INFINITELY SMALL and TEMPORALLY BRIEF" [*das UNENDLICH KLEINE und ZEITLICH KURZE*], on the one hand, and "what is COSMICALLY LARGE" [*dem KOSMISCH GROSSEN*], on the other.

---

[139] See also Pavsek's discussion of the importance of both Adorno and failure for Kluge's cinematic approach to revolution (*The Utopia of Film*). On Kluge's overall conceptual commitment to imperfection rather than perfection, see Schulte, "Kritische Theorie als Gegenproduktion" (42).

To her mind, the beauty of her mathematical equations attests to their correctness and "coherence" [*Stimmigkeit*], that is to say, their ability to capture "realities that lie so extremely distant from each other" [*so extrem auseinanderliegende Realitäten*] (34–35). Adorno's distrust of mathematical formulae rings in our ear, especially so when we read of the ones the beautiful scientist writes on the board: "The equations arranged themselves sequentially without complication" [*Die Gleichungen reihten sich aneinander ohne Komplikation*] (34). Yet this is Kluge writing after all, and some complication must come from somewhere. In the first part of the "flawless" miniature discussed so far though, the narrative as such presents no complications. Third-person narration proceeds here in naturalized conventions yielding a descriptive if thematically alienating scene. The third-person narrative instance appears to maintain objective distance from the figures so described, and character focalization also seems firmly in place when we read that "most of the specialists in the room considered this woman as well as her elegant formulae" to be "'beautiful'" and that the Greek astrophysicist "reserved" the word for the cosmos and her nanoscientific equations (34–35). Aside from whatever negative dialectical reservations we may harbor toward the miniature's cosmic motifs of flawlessness, equivalence, and the objectification of the Greek beauty, nothing appears to disturb the narrative field just yet, and none of the figures described in the first paragraph—including the woman—is brought close enough or long enough to arouse a strong sense of readerly interest.

This changes—which is to say: something different happens—in the last two parts of the miniature, which consist, first, of a dialogic disruption featuring the Greek scientist and an unspecified interlocutor, and second, of a narrative paragraph introducing a "young male physicist" attending the annual convention for the first time (35). This newcomer, who may or may not be the unspecified interlocutor in the dialogic segment, is infatuated with his "goddess" of a colleague, who appears to him in all her mesmerizing beauty as "unattainable" even though the two share tea after her talk (35). Here too Kluge uses an objectifying form of third-person narration and an internalizing form of figural focalization in ways that conform to naturalized conventions of reading. The infatuated young physicist is brought only slightly closer to readerly interest than the Greek lecturer though, precisely because of his sensual interest, and were it not for two important disturbances in the progression of this text, readers could feel comfortably or uncomfortably distant from the scene at hand.[140] This type of affective

---

140 Here I draw on James Phelan and Peter J. Rabinowitz's contribution to the chapter on "Time, Plot, Progression" in *Narrative Theory: Core Concepts and Critical Debates* by David Her-

and temporal distance is all too familiar and should not be confused with the kind of critical distance coupled with proximate danger that Adorno associates with the true value of thought in "Gaps." To recall, Adorno writes there that the "value of a thought is measured by its distance from the continuity of the familiar." The "continuity of the familiar" in the case of Kluge's "flawless" miniature is paradoxically the objectifying distance inscribed in the third-person voice of narration as Kluge deploys it here. Almost imperceptibly but distinctly, the nature of its use nonetheless shifts in the final two sentences of the miniature, and the temporal effect of this final shift directs us back to the dialogic disturbance in the narrative field, a disruption that in this sense continues to reverberate even after the narrative instance has had the last word. This requires some explanation.

Readers may notice one sort of temporal disturbance early on in the miniature when textual description draws attention to the anachronism of the presenting physicist writing by hand on a board behind her despite all the high-tech conference equipment in the room. This is a subtle allusion to Kluge's recurring motif of historical catastrophes and biblical "'writings on the wall' to be deciphered as messengers of more disasters" yet to come (Schulte, "Konstruktionen des Zusammenhangs" 47), messages coming from the future so to speak. But the third-person voice of narration is as such undisturbed and undisturbing here; it describes what any observer in the room could see and hear. Descriptive sensory adjectives alone heighten our attention as we read that the chalk marks made by the beautiful Greek woman are "powerful" [*kräftig*] and "grating" [*knirschend*] (34). At the miniature's ostensible conclusion, by contrast, the narrative voice,

---

man, James Phelan, Peter J. Rabinowitz, Brian Richardson, and Robyn Warhol (57–83). Phelan and Rabinowitz prefer to speak of "progression" rather than "plot" in order to challenge a single-minded emphasis on "events" in narrative theory in favor of "thinking about the larger principle of organization of a narrative, one grounded in the link between the logic of the text's movement from beginning to middle through ending (what we call textual dynamics) and the audience's temporal experience (readerly dynamics) of that movement" (58–59). Commenting in another context on competing facets of 18th-century German aesthetics, Micha Huff stresses the importance of aesthetic dispositions that were long deemed "peripheral" to "the beautiful," including dispositions such as "amazement, attention, and interest." Drawing on the terms of 18th-century debates themselves, these categories of so-called peripheral orientations to aesthetic perception, especially in relation to "the beautiful," are all especially important for Kluge's experimental writing as well. On 18th-century aesthetic discourses of interest and the "art of attention," see also Johannes Wankhammer. Kluge's cosmic miniature "The Beautiful is Flawless" bespeaks the relevance of 18th-century concerns most clearly with regard to "interest." Schulte underscores in general terms the cultivation of "attention" [*Aufmerksamkeit*] as a key feature of Kluge's critical work in film ("Kritische Theorie als Gegenproduktion" 38).

signaling as Dmitri Nikulin puts it in more general terms "a minimum of corporeality" (75), shifts away from both the objectifying observation and figural focalization that characterize the other narrative segments of the text. Having just conveyed, in the focalization of the preceding sentence, the young man's conviction that beauty requires "untouchability" [*Unantastbarkeit*] (35), the narrative voice suddenly manifests as an interested party though not an embodied character. While narratologists might wish to ascertain whether this voice has homodiegetic or hetereodiegetic status, on negative dialectical grounds we would have to leave this question unresolved and say more precisely instead that Kluge's flawed narrator has both this-worldly and off-worldly interests in this scenario of human-cosmic relations.

For Adorno and Kluge alike, one world necessarily bleeds into another. Amidst but not among the astrophysicists, the narrative voice in this instance asks, "[h]ow could [the young man] possibly have displayed the beautiful woman in his lab or his bachelor's residence," a speculative question that the narrative voice itself proceeds to answer in a rather disturbing way: "Only as a statue would that have been possible" [*Nur als Statue hätte das geschehen können*] (35). Here the third-person narrative voice exceeds all prior focalization to speculate in the subjunctive mood about counterfactual possibility, only then to foreclose it. The interest expressed at this juncture appears to belong to the narrative voice itself as it transgresses the conventions it has established in the brief span of the otherwise "flawless" miniature. The answer this voice provides is disturbing rather than hopeful, for the horizon of possibility conjured in this conference setting would allow only for the conversion of a living person into inanimate form. The threat of death lurks between the lines here too in an implied inversion of the Pygmalion and Galatea motif from Ovid's *Metamorphoses*, and the stakes of this micrological speculation are correspondingly high. Yet we would be missing something important about Kluge's "flawless" miniature if we concluded the textual analysis here. This is because the narrative voice not only asks a flawed question (to the extent that the category of beauty is never challenged) and provides a flawed answer (in the sense that reification would prevail), but because the third-person voice at this juncture also draws attention to its narrative status as an uncertain voice of transgressive interlocution. This voice is neither reliable nor unreliable but interesting, perfectly flawed to make readers sense that something is amiss in this scene of utopian longing.[141]

---

[141] Brian Richardson discusses overarching debates about "narratorial reliability in contemporary fiction," arguing that "additional work is needed to encompass the more extreme kinds of unreliability postmodernism delights in producing" (*Unnatural Voices* 103). See also James Phelan's seminal refinements to typologies of reliability and unreliability in *Living to Tell About It: A*

This has consequences for how we understand Kluge's writing in relation to both the concept of unnatural narrative in contemporary narratology and the status of literary dialogue in negative dialectics. Brian Richardson analyzes "three extreme forms of narration" in his monograph *Unnatural Voices: Extreme Narration in Modern and Contemporary Fiction* (79–105). Arguing in the main against intractable categories of narration and not at all concerned with Kluge, Richardson nonetheless offers us an especially helpful term that does apply to one of the most striking features and recurring structures in Kluge's cosmic miniatures, including "The Beautiful is Flawless." This is the narrative voice of "the interlocutor," which Richardson situates among "the most significant and extreme narrating agents which exist at the very boundaries of narration" (79). As he defines this narrative instance, "[t]he interlocutor is a disembodied voice that poses questions which the narrative goes on to answer" (79). We have a clear example of this at the conclusion of Kluge's "flawless" cosmic miniature, though more often than not Kluge's disembodied—or only barely embodied—voices of interlocution raise questions that are either never answered or inadequately answered or else answered in such a way that confusion and more questions result.[142]

"The Beautiful is Flawless" provides an example of this as well in the dialogic disturbance mentioned above, but before we turn to that in more detail, we should recall more of what Richardson has to say about the interlocutor as a narrative voice that has probed the outer limits of narration since the onset of modernism at least. Richardson's primary literary example is the "Ithaca" chapter of James Joyce's *Ulysses*, a famously befuddling chapter consisting entirely of questions and answers. (David Herman is another prominent postclassical narratologist, who has written at length in *Story Logic* on the Mutt and Jute dialogue in

---

Rhetoric and Ethics of Character Narration and "Estranging Unreliability, Bonding Unreliability, and the Ethics of *Lolita*." Richardson additionally introduces types of "posthumanist narrators and voices that have superseded the traditional figure of the narrator as a person who is telling a story and who is subject to the normal abilities and limitations of a human being or humanlike narrating agent" (103). Of the five types he discusses in *Unnatural Voices*—"fraudulent," "contradictory," "permeable," "incommensurate," and "dis-framed"—only the description of "incommensurate narrators" applies to Kluge's most frequent and varying uses of narrative voice. As Richardson explains, incommensurate narrators as he defines them "are those who cannot be the single source of the heterogenous voices of texts they seem to narrate," and the "heterogeneity of the materials [...] must exceed our ability to postulate a single, realistic consciousness responsible for all of them" (105).

142 For related remarks on Adorno's approach to "stupidity" as a mode of "thinking in times of danger" and to language as "the organ, not the instrument of theory" (265), see Erdle's contribution to *Futurity Now* (260–270).

2 Heliotropic Narrative with and beyond Adorno — 119

Joyce's *Finnegan's Wake* to tease out key socio-linguistic functions of dialogic structures in literature more generally.) For Richardson, a "key feature" in Joyce's usage and many other instances of interlocutive narration is "the protean nature of both questioner and respondent" (82). More precisely, he understands the disembodied voice and narrative stakes of the interlocutor this way:

> [...] the interlocutor [...] is an unstable and inherently protean figure (or kind of discourse) that regularly oscillates from one function or status to another as it evokes familiar categories like narrator and narratee in order to blur their edges or transgress them altogether. As such it would seem to be a new category that deserves inclusion in a poetics that attempts to circumscribe the narrative experiments of *Ulysses* and postmodern fiction. In this, it resembles the phenomenon of second person narration, which often resembles yet eludes the adjacent forms of first and third person narration. (85)

This account of the interlocutor as a protean narrative voice predicated on functional oscillation is useful for thinking about Kluge's many narrative figures of interlocution oscillating between horizons of hope and conditions of despair. Three caveats nonetheless apply.

First, in the contemporary arena, Richardson associates the interlocutor with postmodern fiction and unreliability, while Kluge's narrative interlocutors overall tend to gain in reliability as they lose their cognitive footing, and Kluge's writing style is so steeped in the aspirations, failures, and differential temporalities of modernity that the adjective "postmodern" hardly seems to apply. And as Langston has argued in reference to the many textual, filmic, and televised dialogues that Kluge has cultivated over decades with his co-theorist and friend Oskar Negt, the sociologist and the polymath are passionately committed to an Enlightenment project associated with "Kant's autonomous thinking subject" ("Toward an Ethics of Fantasy" 285), albeit with heightened interest in "sensual experience" (278), "fantasy work" (291), and the living "maieutic labor of relationships" (285). For Negt and Kluge, Langston summarizes, the autonomy of reason in part entails "the labor of thinking with others" (289). Dialogic form in Langston's account is tied, not to content resolution or communicative rationality in a Habermasian vein, but to "the promise of making an infinite number of possible connections—both reasoned and erroneous ones—within and between fractured subjects, the multiple worlds they inhabit, and the present impressions, past wishes, and future will fulfillments those subjects have experienced" (290).[143]

---

[143] Langston argues that Negt and Kluge also "part ways with Kant" by "uproot[ing] the imagination from the timeless ontology subtending Kant's *Sollen* and transplant[ing] it in the historically critical province of a Freudo-Marxian *Sein*" (289). While I am sympathetic to Langston's attention to sensual experience and the social stakes of fantasy in Negt and Kluge's work, his

Kluge's literary writing too thus participates through narrative interlocution in the ongoing but non-teleological project of European modernity.

A second caveat concerns Richardson's claim that, with some narrative voices, "there may be no 'they' there—with postmodern fiction, we often have mere discourse that unconvincingly occupies the space of a standard narrator. It is this rejection of the personified narrator," Richardson contends, "that the figure of the interlocutor finally reveals" (*Unnatural Voices* 86). While it is tempting to appropriate this phrasing for Kluge's interlocutive narrators as well, since they do not figure as persons, we must not forget that Kluge, like Adorno, is fundamentally concerned with human suffering, human happiness, and the labor power required to convert the history of one into real possibilities for the other. And third, Richardson describes the interlocutor as a "disembodied voice," which may be a contradiction in terms if we take this part of Richardson's definition literally. In the case of Kluge's cosmic miniatures it would be more accurate to say that the narrating interlocutors we encounter are not inscribed with a strong or full sense of embodiment. No apparent body attaches to these narrative instances of interlocution (as opposed to minimally drawn characters who are also engaged in dialogue), and yet voice as such signals, to recall Nikulin, "a minimum of corporeality." This reminds us in turn that Kluge's interlocutive third-person narrators are also situated on that oscillating bridge between this-worldly catastrophe and off-worldly horizons of a "future without life's miseries." In this sense, we might think of the figure of interlocution in Kluge's cosmic miniatures as an experiment in what James Phelan in other contexts has termed "crossover narration," one form of "departure from the mimetic code" whereby the effects of narration in one ostensibly "independent" set of events are transferred to another "independent" set ("Implausibilities, Crossovers, and Impossibilities" 168–169). To the degree that counterfactual hope takes on real effects in Kluge's cosmic miniatures through the experiential accessibility of futurity, a form of "crossover narration" may be in play that Phelan, who begins with "the mimetic code," may not have envisioned. For Adorno and Kluge alike, as we have already seen, any critical realism worth its salt necessarily conjoins mimetic and anti-mimetic strategies.

Counterfactual hope would appear to be fairly ineffectual in "The Beautiful is Flawless" if we focus on the narrative turn to the voice of interlocution at the

---

analysis does not sufficiently distinguish between sensual and empirical experience for my purposes. For my analysis of the future sense in Kluge's cosmic miniatures, relations between this-worldly and off-worldly dimensions are key. Langston's emphasis on dialogic process creating "conditions of possibility of thinking autonomously in the company of other thinking subjects" (290) also leaves the dilemma of actual conversion intact.

miniature's conclusion: "Only as a statue would that have been possible." If the narrative voice begins to come alive here on its own behalf, the shocking deadness of its limited vision only underscores an unspoken tension in the text between life and death. The future possibility indexed by this voice of interlocution is—at this point—grammatically confined to the past and cognitively constrained by a logic of limitation. This conveys future possibility only in the language of empirical constraint, which is to say it does not convey possibility as open at all. This narrative voice of speculative resignation might literally have the last word in this cosmic miniature, but the constrained futurity it expresses is undone elsewhere in the miniature through the very form of interlocution. This form operates in another key in the dialogic disturbance that textually separates the scenic description of the lecture hall and the introduction of the young astrophysicist pining away for his unattainable goddess. As is so often the case in Kluge's experimental prose, this snippet of dialogic exchange is framed by but not embedded in narration. Verbal sparring is delivered in direct discourse left personally unmarked, and it is therefore not always clear who speaks. The dialogue disrupting the narrative in "The Beautiful is Flawless" certainly involves the Greek presenter as one participant, since she is asked whether she means "'beauty'" or "'radiance'" [*Pracht*] when speaking in her lecture of a galactic constellation extinguished long ago (35). However, the identification of her partner in conversation is not at all clear. This other voice could belong to the embodied young physicist, even though this character is explicitly introduced only after the dialogue has taken place, when readers learn that he has enjoyed some temporal "moments" [*Augenblicke*] over tea with the object of his adoration. Yet this other voice in dialogue could belong instead to a textual interlocutor as narrative instance interacting with the Greek woman in dialogue. In that case, some distance between the diegetic levels of third-person narration and narrated figure would be closed, and the answers to questions posed by the narrative interlocutor would appear in the form of the lecturer's dialogic response. This particular conjunction of dialogue and narration however is most interesting for yet another reason.[144] For this interlocutive function of the narrative voice—both preemptive-

---

144 As David Herman notes in more general narratological terms, one basic "principle for storyworld design involves the creation of mental models for speech acts performed by participants. Although research on speech representation in literature predates the heyday of structuralist narratology, the advent of a formalized theory of narrative had led to an explosion of interest in the ways in which stories can embed as well as result from verbal acts. Most broadly, this research is based on the intuition that the ontology of narrative encompasses Sayings as well as Doings, or rather that it includes verbal as well as nonverbal modes of Doing" (*Story Logic* 171; see also Herman's chapter on "dialogues and styles" [171–207]).

ly and retroactively, we might say—reanimates the life force that the final word of resigned interlocution at the text's end seems to extinguish. The narrative voice also takes on second-person presence in this reading and thus becomes deictically more rather than less real.

We should pause to note that reanimation transpires here on the basis of interlocutive form and not content statement alone. The sequence of questions posed by the interlocutor in this dialogue invites the accomplished scientist to clarify what she means by the beauty of a no longer extant galaxy. Is this beauty regular or complicated perhaps? Her answers are increasingly elusive as she replies by means of negation. "Nothing about it is regular" (35). Neither is it "complicated," she says. When she asserts in a positive vein that this beauty is "autonomous" [*eigenständig*] instead, the interlocutor probes further by asking whether she means obstinately "resistant" [*widerspenstig*]. To this she replies again in the negative: "Not vis-à-vis my equations" (35). While critical associations of autonomy, obstinacy, and resistance circulate in even this brief exchange, three features of the text are important to highlight here. First, stepping out of lecture mode, the Greek woman alerts us at this juncture to a dimension of relational realities that her beautiful mathematics recall but the text itself does not fully express. On textual terms, something percolates or effervesces beyond her sentences and equations alike.[145] Second, both the Greek character and the interlocutive narrator come more alive in this conversational exchange as a functional transgression of reality levels in Kluge's miniature. Third, the narrative voice of minimally embodied interlocution becomes more protean in temporal terms as well, because its very status as interlocution oscillates between the closure of resignation and an openness to life beyond deadening equivalence. The specific form of dialogic disturbance we encounter in the text's middle continues to provoke a readerly sense of future possibility even after a later instance of interlocution in the same text appears to close that door.

Marie-Laure Ryan's otherwise brilliant essay on "temporal paradoxes in narrative" cannot account for Kluge's interlocutive narrative engagement with futurity, precisely because she too, to a certain extent and like Phelan, takes a mimetic code as her point of departure. For the mimetic code that Ryan addresses, the past is by definition "that which cannot be changed" (145). Ryan is especially good at illuminating various ways in which literary narratives and modern astro-

---

[145] Human-cosmic relations also resonate associatively when we read that the Greek astrophysicist's luxuriant hair lies around her "crown" [*Haupt*] and that one of the galactic constellations she discusses in her lecture is named after "Berenice's Hair" (34), a name that carries with it various allusions to the histories of astronomy, mythology, warfare, and empire. See Erik Gregersen.

physics alike can and do break with this aspect of an anthropocentric mimetic code, but for Kluge as well as for Adorno, the dimensional past of catastrophic histories can and must be changed from what Adorno called the "standpoint of redemption." This is the sense in which Kluge's active cultivation of counterfactual hope that is at least partially accessible to experience serves the future of humanity in temporal and qualitative terms, even though Kluge's writing is also emphatically predicated on the actual destructiveness of empirical histories too. Citing A.N. Prior's comment that according to everyday experience and logical precepts, "'the future has an openness to alternatives that the past does not have'" (157), Ryan unintentionally draws our attention to two aspects of the mimetic code that Kluge's micrological writing does uphold, namely, that human futures are not yet decided and can therefore be meaningfully influenced (147). Yet for Kluge, this does not mean (not even as a mimetic premise), as it does for Koselleck as a conceptual historian of modernity or Ryan as a postclassical narratologist working on fiction, that an established past cannot be changed or that an unknown future cannot be experienced at all. Ryan's analysis of temporal paradoxes of Anglophone narrative in literary work by writers such as Philip K. Dick, Audrey Niffenegger, D.M. Thomas, and others provides an especially helpful critical vocabulary for differentiating between competing and variously non-mimetic models of temporal directionality in literature as well as life—physical, biological, causal, cognitive, intentional, chronological, and historical, for example (144–149)—and she also recalls for us that third-person voice has long counted as "the most reliable mode of narration" (159). Kluge's relevance for contemporary discussions of unnatural voice in narrative theory may therefore lie in his radical experiments with third-person voice, perspective, and interlocution at the temporal crossroads of empirical destruction and counterfactual humanity as a future-oriented horizon accessible to sensory experience through reading.

Dmitri Nikulin's philosophical critique of the antagonistic roles that dialogue and dialectic have themselves played in the history of European philosophy help us see more sharply in turn how Kluge's writerly obsession with proliferating voices of interlocution and confusion also aims to redeem the modern history of dialectical thought. Kluge arguably does so through his micrological experiments in narrative form. The interplay of third-person interlocution and second-person exchange in "The Beautiful is Flawless" analyzed above takes on another critical register when considered in relation to Nikulin's *Dialectic and Dialogue*. There Nikulin faults seminal philosophers such as Plato, Hegel, and Gadamer, among others, for sacrificing the living dimensions of conversational dialogue over time to the monologic demands of a universal dialectic. In his historical-philosophical account:

> [...] dialogical practices give birth to procedures that are first used and then codified, reflected on, and systematized as dialectical methods that are then understood either as a universal method or 'tool,' like the art of reasoning, or as the most valuable part of philosophy. Dialogue, therefore, is abandoned as philosophically unproductive, unsystematic, and utterly accidental to the process and acts of reasoning. Philosophical thinking thus conceives of itself as having 'outgrown' confused and disoriented dialogue and having turned to monological, strict, and conclusion-oriented thinking. (72)

Nikulin explicitly wishes to reclaim the ontological value of conversational dialogue for contemporary philosophy and dialectics in particular.[146] He does so by arguing for four basic properties of conversation that connect dialectic and dialogue "to each other" (72). These four qualities include the indispensable presence of a "personal other" (75), the irreducible singularity and simultaneous plurality of even a minimalist "voice" (76), the "unfinalizability" of conversational exchange as distinguished from information-sharing (77–78), and what Nikulin terms "allosensus" as a kind of "dissonant yet [mutually] engaging polyphony" that is unlike either consensus or dissensus (78–80). To Nikulin's way of thinking, philosophical dialogue has in a sense become the historical victim of philosophical dialectics, which in its dominant strain drives life out of thought. The dialectical schools of thought he indicts are in his terms decidedly *"impersonal,"* since a given argument deemed valid can belong to everyone and no one at the same time. "Somebody has to be the first to discover an argument," he writes, "but anybody can repeat, reproduce, and use it" (87). This type of reasoning results, he claims, only in claims to "a universal abstract truth" (87).

As will already be clear from Nikulin's appeal to the ontological value of conversational life, there are some significant differences between his critical project and Kluge's. Nikulin's particular emphasis on crucial relations between dialogue and dialectics in the history of philosophy (relations that have been remarked by many other philosophers as well, from different perspectives) is nonetheless worth noting with regard to Kluge, because Nikulin ultimately casts narration as a kind of enlivening force that works against the deadening effects of universal reason. In his words: "Narration is what allows dialogue to be dramatic and to express the process of either discussing a point or disclosing the personal other. Unlike dialogue, dialectic does not require narration [...]" (87). Nikulin puts his distinction between dialogue and dialectic in harsh terms on specifically narrative grounds.

---

[146] One might fruitfully consider the most recent issue of the *Alexander Kluge-Jahrbuch* in this regard as well. Published in 2016, the third volume of this scholarly journal explicitly devotes one long section to Kluge's "art of conversation" [*Gesprächskunst*] (Christian Schulte, Winfried Siebers, Valentin Mertes, and Stefanie Schmitt, *Formenwelt des Dialogs* 127–351).

> Discursive thinking is not narrative: it tells a story about correct reasoning, but the plot in such a story is an ordered argument and the only character that coincides with the author is discursive reason itself. Unlike dialogical narration, the dialectical story, once it is proven correct, cannot ever be otherwise, although it is possible that there is a different way of expressing the truth about something—that is, a different proof of a universal statement. Therefore, the dialectical order of an argument is not that of narration. (87)

While readers frequently encounter narrative voices with radically variable degrees of embodiment in Kluge's experimental prose between "damaged life" and "an other life," and while his cosmic miniatures draw on historical dialectics and conversational dialogue alike, it will be equally clear by now that dialogue and dialectics for Kluge are inextricably intertwined. Nikulin rather bizarrely does not address negative dialectics in his otherwise very impressive study, and somewhat alarmingly, Adorno appears only in a very short note on Hegel (163, n. 12). Kluge's storytelling habitation of Adorno's legacy for critical theory opens up different avenues for philosophically engaging dialogue, in which negative dialectics faces historical death and still breathes cosmic life, notably through Kluge's whimsical and high-stakes experiments with narrative form. More than fantasy is at labor here, as we have seen in the experiential narrative temporality of the future sense in "The Beautiful is Flawless." What then happens with narrative voice, temporal dimensions, and critical horizons in "Saturday in Utopia," where Adorno and some of his personal others appear figurally in Kluge's 2003 collection, "The Gap the Devil Leaves Us"? Here too some surprises await us.

2.6 Kluge's Future Narrative: "Saturday in Utopia"

The German title of Kluge's cosmic miniature "Samstag in Utopia" ("The Gap the Devil Leaves Us" 444–448) involves translational features that are lost in the English rendition of the title as "Saturday in Utopia." There are two reasons for this, and they both bespeak gaps manifesting only with language, gaps with conjunctive as well as disjunctive qualities. Associative and translational, these gaps cleave and also suture time as a socio-historical dimension. First, the use of the Latinized Greek word "Utopia" rather than the naturalized modern German version available as "Utopie," which will figure in important ways in the final sentence of this miniature, recalls Sir Thomas More's seminal philosofictive reflections published in book form as *Utopia* in 1516.[147] Kluge's title simultane-

---

[147] The term "philosofictive" stems from Peter Szendy, as discussed in my Introduction. Szen-

ously conjures More's spatialized paradigm for imagining societal perfection and the later "temporalization of utopia," which Koselleck considers one of the hallmarks of modern thought and rhetoric. Second, the word *Samstag* is one of two possible German names for the day of the week known in English as Saturday, which in English alludes to both a planet and the Roman god Saturn. The German alternative to *Samstag* in equally colloquial usage is *Sonnabend*, which literally means "sun's eve" or the evening that will lead up to the day of the sun known among the days of the seven-day week as Sunday [*Sonntag*]. The notably 'other' way of speaking time that goes unnamed but not entirely unarticulated in this narrative miniature thus hints at both anticipatory and heliotropic orientations in the title alone. According to the authoritative etymological dictionary of the German language, *Samstag* is "the only day of the week" for which no god's name is invoked in any Germanic language (Seebold 784). Any heliotropic appeal to metaphysical dimensions here therefore also signals Kluge's extended engagement with Adorno's stance on "metaphysical experience" and counterfactual hope, oscillating between this-worldly catastrophe and off-worldly horizons of human happiness and utopian longing. The tiny word "in" linking a mundane designation for a day of the week with no etymological trace of transcendental aspiration, on the one hand, and a spatialized tradition for imagining societal perfection, on the other, points to the interior setting of Kluge's textual miniature. The setting is more detailed than is often the case in Kluge's cosmic miniatures, this time taking us not only into an emphatically "private apartment" where a married couple resides, but also into a "guest room" within that is reserved for the husband's erotic assignations with his beautiful young mistress, a "model" from Munich. When she embraces him upon arrival, the scene is figured in decidedly spatialized and privatized terms of a utopian ideal projected deictically onto a narrative present: "Here, in the nowhere space [*im Nirgendwo*], in the hallway between door and little guest room, in the extraterritorial arena of personal happiness" (445). The narrative voice overlays empirical description and utopian imaginary here in ways that the temporal configuration of narrative perspective in "Saturday in Utopia" will otherwise belie.

Ostensibly utopian relations are also complicated by a third character in the mix, the philandering husband's wife "G." (445), who physically prepares the spare room for the desirous pair and then goes off to nap elsewhere in the apartment, while the lovers do their thing in the guest room as "a space outside real-

---

dy's focus is neither More nor utopia but Kant and extraterrestrials. On Kluge's overall preference for associative modes of fantasy and montage, especially in film, see Schulte, who additionally speaks of a "rhizomatic structure" ("Kritische Theorie als Gegenproduktion" 41).

ity" (445). If this is utopia, G.'s actions and the miniature's use of narrative voice lend this mixed-use apartment many temporal twists and turns in the utopian dimension. When we read that G. is a "realist" from a family of leather manufacturers whose facility "used to produce gloves" (448), that her husband in 1967 is a philosopher known professionally for his commitment to negation and refusal (444), and that the miniature's epigraph is a marked citation from Adorno's *Minima Moralia*, we may too readily conclude that Kluge's "Saturday in Utopia" is simply about the empirical historical constellation of Adorno, his wife Gretel Karplus Adorno, and one of the philosopher's many known mistresses. While there is some biographical motivation for certain aspects of the miniature's portrayal,[148] the analytical focus here will be on specific ways in which "Saturday in Utopia" can be read as a cosmic miniature pivoting on experimental narrative uses of futurity as experiential portals in time. In what sense does this miniature labor productively on temporal aspects of the utopian dimension in the this-worldly and off-worldly terms of this claustrophobic apartment, and what crucial uses of narrative voice and unnatural perspective does Kluge activate and enliven here? If many of Kluge's literary miniatures signal an intensified quest for *Auswege*—ways out of historically real catastrophe—it is especially perplexing to read in "Saturday in Utopia" that G. takes herself "out of the way" [*aus dem Weg*] of the two lovers for whom she has prepared a trysting room. What narrative role does G. play in this cosmic miniature? My interpretation will hinge on this critical question. Does G. as a figure of narration belong to the utopian dimension or not? Does the miniature present the philosopher's wife only as a figure of passive endurance, patient waiting, and loving tolerance for displacement—or something more? Whatever biographical truths may attach to this text, the close reading that follows here entertains the four figures that Kluge gives us in "Saturday in Utopia"—the philosopher resembling Theodor Adorno, the philosopher's wife resembling Gretel Adorno, the philosopher's mistress resembling one of Adorno's lovers from the 1960s, and the narrative instance resembling

---

148 See Müller-Doohm's well researched book chapter "Éducation sentimentale" in *Adorno: A Biography*, 52–63; Ina Hartwig's speculations; Heinrich Adolf's essay on Arlette Pielmann in *Adorno-Portraits*; and Martin Jay's online comment in 2012 that we still know far too little about Gretel Adorno, the life partner and thinking interlocutor who took detailed minutes of so many of the Frankfurt School's critical conversations ("Theodor Adorno and Max Horkheimer"). Jay additionally refers to Staci von Boeckmann's 2004 dissertation and 2007 article on Gretel Adorno's contributions to the Frankfurt School of Critical Theory. Adolf's essay on Arlette Pielmann repeatedly draws on Kluge's "Saturday in Utopia" as if it were a historical document, even while acknowledging that Kluge's text has been fictionalized (see 311, 322, and 326).

no one we quite know yet—as working philosofictive models that help us engage the future sense through narrative form.

As with Adorno's "Heliotrope" miniature and Kluge's "The Beautiful is Flawless," "Saturday in Utopia" features a narrative instance implicitly addressing readers in third-person voice. For Kluge, this voice here too is largely disembodied, though the narrator in "Saturday in Utopia" does have quite a lot of information to impart and also seems to have read its Adorno. This narrative voice begins by describing the philosopher of refusal in ways that both recall the negative dialectical motifs of childhood and adulthood from "Heliotrope" and oscillate between character focalization through the philosopher, on the one hand, and interested if somewhat critical judgment of the philosopher, on the other. "[W]ithout any qualms" [*bedenkenlos*], we read, this professional philosopher had "refused since childhood to become an adult" (444).[149] As the narrative voice goes on to explain: "In this sense he was neither a child (because no one can remain a child by force of will), nor had he become an adult." A judgment immediately follows: "A thinker with weak sides in his living habits, since in his program there was little room for direct experience" (444–445). This narrative voice is knowledgeable but not neutral, and the narrator's parenthetical aside makes a point of asserting a reality principle at odds with Adorno's negative dialectical approach to childhood desire. The text of Kluge's miniature actually begins with a direct citation of Adorno's philosophical voice from *Minima Moralia*. This marked excerpt does not come from "Heliotrope" or any other "damaged life" miniature with a focus on childhood though, but from an Adorno miniature turning on adult motifs of sexuality, romance, and commerce. Titled "Ne cherchez plus mon coeur" [look for my heart no longer], an unmarked line from Baudelaire, Adorno's own text, entry 107 from Part Three of *Minima Moralia*, opens onto "the negative anthropology of mass society" (Jephcott translation, 167). As Adorno puts it here, in socio-historical terms: "The exchange relationship that love partially withstood throughout the bourgeois age has completely absorbed it" (167).

The radiant horizon of the wondering child in "Heliotrope" seems long gone when Adorno draws on his exile experience to capture this social aporia in cosmic and sexual allusions conjoined.

> The quality of every one of the countless automobiles which return to New York on Sunday evenings corresponds exactly to the attractiveness of the girl sitting in it. – The objective dissolution of society is subjectively manifested in the weakening of the erotic urge, no lon-

---

[149] A miniature on evolutionary development in Kluge's "Kong's Great Hour" refers to Adorno and Benjamin alike sharing "an aversion [...] to becoming adults" (611).

ger able to bind together self-preserving monads, just as if mankind were imitating the physicists' theory of the exploding universe. The frigid aloofness of the loved one, by now an acknowledged institution of mass culture, is answered by the "insatiable desire" of the lover. (168)[150]

The only excerpt from Adorno's miniature actually cited in the epigraph to "Saturday in Utopia" however is the one contrasting the women Adorno ascribed to modern society and mass culture with those willing to give themselves sexually to Casanova. "When Casanova called a woman unprejudiced, he meant that no religious convention prevented her from giving herself: today the unprejudiced woman is the one who no longer believes in love, who will not be hoodwinked into investing more than she can expect in return" (168). Ultimately "Ne cherchez plus mon coeur" decries the de-eroticization of "de-inhibited sex" and the social erasure of "ecstasy" as having no utopian value at all (169). We might then expect the Adorno-like philosopher in "Saturday in Utopia" to represent the insatiability of desire, a longing for longing itself. As Eva Geulen astutely reminds us, in his philosophical approach to writing about sexual intimacy in *Minima Moralia* overall as a collection devoted to failure, "Adorno desires desire" without coming to rest in erotic objects of "fulfillment" (Geulen, "No Happiness without Fetishism" 111 et passim).

The Adorno-like character we encounter in Kluge's miniature is cast in a different mold, for this embodied figure—whom the narrator describes as a "child's soul with capable hand" (446)—seems rather keenly interested in empirical fulfillment when he sits down, "full of hope" (445), with his mistress on the guest room bed. With the utopian mathematical ending of Adorno's miniature "Gaps" still in mind, we might even be inclined at first to read "Saturday in Utopia" as redeeming those blissful hours actually spent in empirical beds after all. Yet Kluge like Adorno is after something more here. We just cannot rely on the Adorno-like philandering philosopher in "Saturday in Utopia" to know or even sense what that more might be. Through narrative focalization, readers perceive the sense of masculinist competition the wayward husband feels, even in the "isolation" [*Abgeschiedenheit*] of the private apartment keeping the outside world at bay, with other "men's eyes" desiring "the young idol" in his arms (445). On negative dialectical grounds established by Adorno, this pseudo-Adorno seems doomed to failure too, though not in the critically generative ways that

---

150 For Adorno, as Buck-Morss summarizes, the concrete particular was never categorically generalizable or "identical to itself" (*Origin of Negative Dialectics* 76). On the importance of Leibniz's early 18th-century *Monadology* for Adorno's thought in this regard, see Buck-Morss (76, 86, and 244, n. 101).

Geulen ascribes to *Minima Moralia* or Pavsek analyzes in Kluge's films. How then in narrative terms do critical horizons of futurity become accessible to experience in "Saturday in Utopia"?

Kluge's miniature gives us an Adorno that is figurally not identical to itself, and in this sense "Saturday in Utopia" takes up and continues Adorno's critical, historical, and philosophical legacy of non-identity that is always more than a categorical concept. To answer the question of how Kluge's storytelling strategies render critical horizons of futurity accessible to experience in this miniature, however, we must enlist the aid of two other partisans hard at work at the unnatural limits of narrative experimentation in the confined space of the conjugal apartment. One is the third-person voice of narration, which here too plays a range of roles, and the other is the realist figure of G. herself, who hardly has a word to say and arguably plays the most important role of all. We turn first to the third-person voice of narration, which as already noted introduces itself in naturalized conventions of focalization, description, and something akin to objective commentary if not omniscient perspective. The consciousness behind this voice has at least done its Adorno homework. This narrative voice also engages in speculation involving both a counterfactual temporality and descriptive specification. With an eye to the sparsely appointed guest room where "no books" and "no useable tools of quotidian worth" [*keine Gebrauchswerkzeuge des Alltags*] are stored, we read: "If the window were barred, this could be a prison cell" (444). One of the most significant functions of the narrative voice in the first (and unnumbered) segment of the miniature however is that of interlocution. To recall Richardson's definition of the interlocutor as one understudied strategy of experimental narration, "[t]he interlocutor is a disembodied voice that poses questions which the narrative goes on to answer" (*Unnatural Voices* 79). In narratological terms the interlocutor in this sense is considered experimental because it highlights "the protean nature of both questioner and respondent" and a functional oscillation between narrator and narratee (82, 85). The third-person narrator of "Saturday in Utopia" speaks as an interlocutor in this sense when the narrative voice takes on a pedagogical tone and appears to mimic Adorno in a virtual encounter between Adorno's "Heliotrope" and Kluge's "Saturday in Utopia," the very text that requires this narrating voice for the miniature to exist temporally in the first place. At this juncture the narrative voice of interlocution speaks to readers in Adorno-ese:

> How on earth can one enjoy a happiness that is not at all possible for children, a happiness that requires the use of adult genitalia? Happiness is the fulfillment of a child's wish. It is possible because the differentiation between child and adult does not exist at all in bodies

and soul. This boundary is unreal, not the sentence about a child's wish. This is how, just as the real does not exist. That is the secret of all philosophers.

[*Wie nur kann man ein Glück genießen, das Kindern gar nicht möglich ist, das den Gebruach der erwachsenen Genitalien erfordert? Glück ist die Erfüllung eines Kinderwunsches. Es ist möglich, weil es die Unterscheidung zwischen Kind und Erwachsenem in den Körpern und in der Seele gar nicht gibt. Diese Grenze ist unwirklich, nicht der Satz vom Kinderwunsch. So, wie es das Reale nicht gibt, das ist das Geheimnis aller Philosophen.*] (445)[151]

Other narrative functions will accrue to the narrative voice in "Saturday in Utopia," as we shall see, but at this point the third-person interlocutor disturbs any surety about levels of diegesis, while its own voice seems to have been at least partially infiltrated by the character the narrator has just been describing. This goes beyond mere focalization, since neither the historical Adorno nor his textual double would ascribe his critical insights into the unreal nature of the real to "all philosophers."

Another possible though unlikely instance of narrative interlocution can be found in an especially brief dialogic exchange—the only direct dialogic exchange in the entire miniature—shortly after the philosopher's paramour has arrived in the apartment. "Some water?" someone asks, to which another unspecified voice replies: "How so?" [*Wieso?*] (445). While we might readily imagine either the host offering his guest some water to drink after her train ride or the guest requesting the same, the reply that comes in the form of another question makes no apparent sense, especially given the ways in which these two characters are sketched overall (he as polite and attentive and she as petty and self-aborbed with no real passion to be with her aging lover). Even if we were to leap across the breach to imagine the narrator taking direct part in this dialogic exchange—the most reasonable explanation in fact being that the narrative instance itself requests a glass of water, only to be rebuffed by the lovers in scene—the miniature as such offers no textual evidence to support or to challenge such a reading. At most we can confidently say that this minimally embodied dialogue, which consists only of two questions, violates the common-sense understanding of the "cooperative principle" (Paul Grice) of sociolinguistic dialogue itself.[152] Since the do-

---

151 I have taken a minor liberty in translating „wie nur," which could be translated as „but how," as „how on earth" instead to reflect a more colloquial and telluric tone that seems warranted in this instance, since the narrator's initial point of departure in raising this question is empirical. While I have opted to translate „Satz vom Kinderwunsch" as the „sentence about a child's wish," one could conceivably also translate this phrase as the „sediment of a child's wish."
152 See David Herman on the "presumption of coherence that interlocutors and readers bring to the utterances comprised by texts, discourses, and conversations" (*Story Logic* 179), and Irene

mestic scene of a leisurely Saturday in utopia at first blush seems to rely on quite a bit of figural cooperation, we might now also look elsewhere for traces of disturbance in the cooperative field.[153]

In the story collection devoted to "the gap the devil leaves us," the critical-theory miniature "Saturday in Utopia" is located in chapter 7, which consists of "foundational stories" [*Basisgeschichten*] with the overarching title "Mit Haut und Haaren" [literally: with skin and hairs] ("The Gap the Devil Leaves Us" 437–506). This is a common German expression of embodiment taken to mean, in a figurative sense, "unconditionally" or "completely," that is to say, with one's whole being. Another miniature in this chapter, which revolves around personalized discussions of the "minimum," the "maximum," and "the whole" [*das Ganze*] in sexual relations, and which also bears the title "Mit Haut und Haaren" (449–451), immediately follows "Saturday in Utopia." For these and other reasons we might be tempted to conclude that the wifely figure resembling Gretel Adorno loves her husband unconditionally and therefore accedes to his romantic affairs without remainder, and that she does so with her entire being. The third-person narrative voice at first renders this figure present in a way that facilitates such a reading by aligning G. with both utter pragmatism and self-sacrificial affection. G. also serves as a temporal marker. The narrative shift to an experiential present tense occurs only once G. is introduced. We read in declarative terms indicating practiced repetition: "It is Saturday. She lays wool blankets, purple in color, made from Canadian wool, onto the wooden cot that serves in the guest room as a bed. She puts out water, and hand towels" [*Es ist Samstag. Sie legt wollene Decken, purpurfarben, aus kanadischer Wolle, auf die Holzpritsche, die im Gastzimmer als Bettstatt gilt. Sie stellt Wasser hin, Handtücher*] (445). G. appears to represent pure acquiescence to the empirical realm, and a bit later on the page, the narrator links the wife's actions and her afternoon nap to love: "She got herself out of the way, that's what love is capable of" [*Sie hat sich aus dem Weg geschafft, das ist, was Liebe vermag*] (445). This is striking in textual terms, since—if the hallway leading to the little guest room is where utopia lies—love appears to be sleeping behind another door. For most of the unnumbered opening segment of "Saturday in Utopia," however, the narrative instance focuses its perspective on the philosopher and his breathy

---

Kacandes on the logical expectation that "paired utterances [are] issued by alternating speakers" (*Talk Fiction* 3).

153 See also Alexis Radisoglou, whose 2015 dissertation on destructive effects of neoliberal globalization and Kluge's 21st-century critical fictions of planetarity aims "to move Kluge more closely in the vicinity of thinkers for whom the re-appropriation of the political impulse proper is predicated on a strongly anti-consensual model of the political" (17).

mistress—"excited by the traveling wind of her own lively person" [*erregt durch den Fahrtwind der eigenen, lebendigen Person*] (445). As this first segment approaches its own terminus, readerly attention is drawn to a "certain closeness" [*gewisse Nähe*] (445) between the trysting pair and to the anticipatory temporality they share: "A long afternoon lies ahead of them both" [*Ein langer Nachmittag liegt vor den beiden*] (446). The experimental narrative instance in this first segment of the miniature straddles naturalized conventions and unnatural voices of storytelling perspective, as we have seen. A significant shift in voice and perspective occurs however just after the final period in this unnumbered segment, and this shift comes in the form of a numbered footnote, the only one in the miniature as such and one in which the narrative voice once again proves non-identical with itself and—for the first time—makes us see G. in a different light.

Kluge often does tricky things with numbers, and one odd thing about the only footnote in "Saturday in Utopia" is that it appears both above and below as number 2. There is indeed a footnote numbered 1 on the same page on which "Saturday in Utopia" begins, but this footnote is an interloper from a different miniature. Numbers and equations will figure in our analysis again when we get to the four numbered narrative supplements that also belong to "Saturday in Utopia" as a mutating story of sexual commerce, romantic exchange, and utopian longing. Here we turn though to footnote 2, which uses numbers in a different way to highlight G., the empirical epitome of pragmatic resignation, in agentive relation to cosmic dimensions. Kluge effects this first with rhetorical tone and then with destabilized perspective. The narrative footnote opens with a sentence in which the third-person voice appears in familiar, descriptive guise: "The philosopher's wife is responsible for furnishing the apartment" [*Für die Einrichtung der Wohnung ist die Frau des Philosophen zuständig*] (446). The next several sentences are entirely different in tone, for the narrative voice emerges here as a bureaucratic bean-counter on the subject of love. "There are 186 various aggregate conditions of love. The one someone needs when he receives his mistress is not receptive to practical ideas" [*Es gibt 186 Aggregatzustände der Liebe. Derjenige davon, den einer braucht, wenn er seine Geliebte empfängt, bleibt für praktische Ideen unempfänglich*] (446). This rhetorical register aligns the narrative voice with the language of reification and confirms G.'s apparent function as being in charge of rationalized practicality when her lovesick husband is otherwise engaged. The next sentence in the footnote alters this by opening a rhetorical and temporal door to another perspective. "This program," we read, "let us call it 184a, shares a sisterly bond with unearthly love" [*Dieses Programm, nennen wir es 184a, ist der unirdischen Liebe verschwistert*] (446). Several things are important to note about this sentence. Shifting to the first-person plural, the bureaucratically inclined narrator at this crossroad draws us as readers into the perspective of rationalized labor and bureaucratic administration. This perspective is hardly utopian at all. The narrator's use of the word "program" additionally echoes the narrator's earlier description of the philosopher as having little place for direct experience "in his program." This would align the philosopher himself with the instrumental rationality of "administered society," as the critical theorists of the Frankfurt School famously put it, and the resonant use of "program" here might also make us think that program number 184a marks the philosopher's impractical desire for love that's out of this world.

I would like to suggest a different reading. Even though the third- and first-person voices of collective narration speak the language of bureaucracy here—a language that Adorno associated with "permanent catastrophe" in modern life—nothing prevents us from reading the referential ambiguity of "program," as it is used in the footnote, in relation to the philosopher's wife instead of her besotted husband. In this alternative reading, what the narrative voice explicitly classifies as a "program" lies in G.'s everyday practicality, which readers can now additionally recognize as related to "non-telluric love" and G.'s own non-identical self (hence the "sisterly" bond). This philosopher's wife is no one-dimensional woman, and G.'s narrative status as an agent of disruption is indirectly confirmed by the narrative observer, even though this observational voice addresses us in footnote 2 in the register of bureaucratic classification: "This [program] explains why the bed appears unrealistically narrow for two persons and inappropriate for a certain comfort in sex life. The wife chose it this way" [*So ist es zu erklären, daß die Liege für zwei Personen unrealistisch eng und für eine gewisse Gemütlichkeit des Liebeslebens unangepaßt erscheint. So hat es die Frau ausgesucht*] (446). In narrative terms this bespeaks anti-realist disruption rather than psychological revenge alone. More than the philosopher resembling Adorno, and far more than the beautiful model resembling one of Adorno's many mistresses, Kluge's "Saturday in Utopia" gives us G. as a storytelling cipher of both this-worldly and off-worldly relations. Footnote 2 steps out of the flow of narrative time in this miniature and uses narrative perspective to reveal the secret heart beating counterfactually at the temporal core of this text. This is no mere index of possibility, and G.'s temporal orientation to cosmic horizons and utopian longing is not one of waiting. Her figural orientation to an "other" time that is not merely past or wholly present is radically rooted in the lived and endangered hours of her everyday, even and especially on a peaceful Saturday at home. Can we then say that G. functions not only as a figure of narration but also as a voice of narration in Kluge's miniature? In footnote 2 the narrative voice after all still treats her as an object of narration, and while this voice claims to have enough knowledge about G.'s consciousness to "explain" her actions, this knowledge is not narratively focalized through her. The figure of G. thus arouses our readerly curiosity even as her actions are supposedly explained, and something about her, as a figure of narration, remains temporally just beyond our perceptual ken. Does she ever manifest as a voice of narration in the differential temporalities of Kluge's miniature? To answer this question, which no narrative shape shifter poses in "Saturday in Utopia," we turn to Supplement 4, the miniature's final segment, which ends with an equation.

The narratively rich first segment of "Saturday in Utopia" is followed by a series of four numbered supplements, each of which is explicitly labeled as such [*Zusatz 1, Zusatz 2, Zusatz 3*, and *Zusatz 4*] and additionally assigned a subtitle: "Lethargy" [*Trägheit*] for the first, "Relation of Exchange" [*Tauschverhältnis*] for the second, "Shouldn't he have given her something?" [*Hätte er ihr nicht etwas schenken müssen?*] for the third, and in quotation marks, "'Indifference destroys everything'" ["*Gleichgültigkeit zerstört alles*'"] for the fourth. The temporal order of this sequence is chronological, with the first two situated on the Saturday in question, with varying degrees of narrative distance from the arrival scene described. The third supplement takes place "months later," after the philosopher's girlfriend has dumped him, much to his lovelorn chagrin, and the fourth entails a kind of narrative summation with a focus on G., once a "lover, demoted decades ago, and now a wife" [*vor Jahrzehnten herabgestufte Geliebte, jetzt Ehefrau*] (448). Despite the directional order of this chronological sequence, each of the supplements also highlights, in one way or another, a differential relation to time. Each of the four supplements also invokes, in one way or another, economies of value and exchange in love, sex, and capitalism. The repetitive German term that Kluge uses to designate these textual supplements—*Zusatz*—itself bears associative traces of 19th-century critiques of capitalist exploitation into the miniaturized scenes of private living and lovemaking arrangements.

William Thompson, an Irish supporter of the so-called Cooperative Movement and author of *An Inquiry into the Principles of the Distribution of Wealth Most Conducive to Human Happiness* (1824), whose work was known to Karl Marx, uses both "additional value" [*Zusatzwert*] and "surplus value" [*Mehrwert*] in his analyses of labor and capitalist production (166–167). Marx's chapter on "Constant Capital and Variable Capital" from Volume One of *Capital* uses the German term *Zusatz* to speak of "the addition of new value to the material of [a worker's] labour," in part, in relation to the "twofold nature" [*Doppelseitigkeit*] of his working relationships to time as well as value (*Capital* 307; for the German, see *Das Kapital* 188).[154] For Marx in *Capital*, "*Zusatz*" is also a term for a textual

---

[154] The relevant paragraph concerns the simultaneous co-presence of two different labor processes linking time, material, and value in different ways (one serving preservation and the other

supplement in the form of a footnote or an edition. Other rhetorical and conceptual associations with Marx also reverberate in the chapter of foundational or "base stories" [*Basisgeschichten*] in which "Saturday in Utopia" appears, a chapter given the umbrella title "Mit Haut und Haaren," as noted above. Marx uses this particular colloquialism to advance his analogy of value relations in capitalist economies and social relations of categorical identifications in thought. In *Capital*'s opening chapter on "The Commodity" Marx writes in a footnote:

> In a certain sense, a man is in the same situation as a commodity. As he neither enters into the world in possession of a mirror, nor as a Fichtean philosopher who can say 'I am I', a man first sees and recognizes himself in another man. Peter only relates to himself as a man through his relation to another man, Paul, in whom he recognizes his likeness. With this, however, Paul also becomes from head to toe, in his physical form as Paul, the form of appearance of the species man for Peter. (144, n. 19)

What Ben Fowkes has rendered "from head to toe" in English translation, to mean Paul's entire empirical embodiment, appears in Marx's German as "mit Haut und Haaren," to indicate Paul's entire bodily existence itself becoming the form in which the generic category of "human being" [*Mensch*] appears (*Das Kapital* 28). Here too we recognize echoes of Adorno's concern as well as Kluge's with gaps between empirical and metaphysical dimensions, on the one hand, and the life-threatening or life-sustaining engagements with those gaps in language and labor, on the other. More to the point for present purposes, Kluge's associative interpellations of Adorno and Marx in "Saturday in Utopia" underwrite this miniature's experimental labor on the narrative value of time and the narrative value of futurity in particular.[155]

---

creating new value) and converting the "value of the means of production" into "the value of the product" (307). As Marx elaborates: "The worker does not perform two pieces of work simultaneously, one in order to add value to the cotton, the other in order to preserve the value of the means of production, or, what amounts to the same thing, to transfer to the yarn, as product, the value of the cotton on which he works, and part of the value of the spindle with which he works. But by the very act of adding new value he preserves their former values. Since however the addition of new value [*der Zusatz von neuem Wert*] to the material of his labour, and the preservation of its former value, are two entirely distinct results, it is plain that this twofold nature of the result can be explained only by the twofold nature of his labour; it must at the same time create value through one of its properties and preserve or transfer value through another" (307). For present analytical purposes, it is especially important to note that Marx casts these distinctions in terms of a worker's bifurcated or multidirectional relationship to time in the guise of simultaneity.

155 The phrase "mit Haut und Haaren" arguably also alludes to a provisional chapter that Kracauer envisioned in 1940 for his study of early cinema in relation to the material world; see Mir-

The Adorno-like philosopher and the mistress-like model in "Saturday in Utopia" spend a lot of time contemplating the value of their time together and their futures in Kluge's first three designated supplements, although the third-person voice of narration dominates here too and draws more overt attention to the young beauty's obsession with her own variable social status in relations of exchange. Supplement 1 for example presents the young lover as having "an excited temperament" on the train and being "a lethargic person" in the philosopher's guest room, where she is "not unhappy" with her "extended" [*lang hingezogene*] passivity and her role as "sheer bringer of happiness" [*schiere Glücksbringerin*]. "After a time she gets hungry," and we read: "She expects to receive a gift at a later point in time" [*Für einen späteren Zeitpunkt erwartet sie ein Geschenk*] (446). Labeled "Relation of Exchange," Supplement 2 takes place a bit later "on this Saturday" afternoon, and the narrative voice lets us know through character focalization commingled with Marxist rhetoric that the young woman is mostly "satisfied with the exchange" [*mit dem Austausch einverstanden*], content with the "exchange value" [*Tauschwert*] of her beauty in the philosopher's eyes and the "use value" [*Nutzwert*] she delivers when she visits him (446). The narrative account of the philosopher's perspective as he lies "on top of her" [*über ihr*] is focalized through a different rhetorical register, as he—as if beside himself in pillow talk with her—speculates on cosmic dimensions instead: "Perhaps [...] there is no reciprocity in love, no exchange; crystals look at each other in silence. Heavenly bodies [*Gestirne*] slide past each other in separate orbits; they know each other not" [*Vielleicht [...] existiert in der Liebe keine Gegenseitigkeit, kein Tausch, stumm blicken Kristalle einander an. In ihren Bahnen gleiten Gestirne aneinander vorüber, die sich nicht kennen*] (447). Whether he's right or not has no consequence for her momentary satisfaction, we read, and in the guest room she is decidedly "indifferent" [*gleichgültig*] to her lover's fame. Pliant, peevish, and calculating at the same time, she does think to herself what their shared futures might hold: "At his funeral she would appreciate it if she were mentioned in his eulogy. That lay far ahead" [*In einer Grabrede wüßte sie es zu schätzen, wenn sie genannt worden wäre. Das lag fern*] (447).

Not surprisingly then, we learn in Supplement 3 that man and mistress have parted ways in anger and that she is now brooding over their "UNEQUAL EXCHANGE" [*UNGLEICHEN TAUSCH*]. "Shouldn't he have given her something" be-

---

iam Hansen ("'With Skin and Hair'") for important methodological reflections on tensions between Kracauer's Marseille notebooks and the much later published version of his *Theory of Film: The Redemption of Physical Reality.*

yond his actual gifts, she wonders, such as a career, a marriage, an inheritance, or even "UNBRIDLED HAPPINESS" [*UNBEZWINGLICHES GLÜCK*] (447)? Having "stolen her youth" [*ihre Jugend gestohlen*], the aging philosopher hadn't proved useful "to her futures" [*ihren Zukünften*] at all (447). The model's displeasure now also applies to G., who had never greeted her or acknowledged her personal presence, and whom the ex-mistress "months later" begins to hate "belatedly" [*nachträglich*] (447–448). The wife's "indifference" [*Gleichgültigkeit*], she fumes, had "devalued" [*abgewertet*] the younger woman's very stay in utopia (446, 448). Lest we conclude too quickly that the jilted philosopher looks pretty good by contrast with this picture of pettiness—his desire unbroken, his efforts to regain his onetime lover's affection infused "with unquenchable longing" [*mit unstillbarer Sehnsucht*] (447)—Adorno himself reminds us in a voice from "damaged life" in the 1940s that unattainable woman and insatiable male are stock characters in a capitalist script that mass culture has written (see the passage cited above from "Ne cherchez plus mon coeur," *Minima Moralia* 168). The trysting couple's tormented reflections on their time-sensitive affair thus underscore the non-identity of Kluge's Adorno-like figure in subjective and objective dimensions alike. Temporal entanglements of the 1940s, the 1960s, and the 21st century too resurface in intensified narration in Supplement 4, this time with heightened and new narrative attention to the figure known only by the initial G.

The logic of consecutively numbered supplements suggests that Supplement 4, empirically the final addition to "Saturday in Utopia" as presented, could in theory be followed by unknown others yet to come. This vaguely conjures both the open-ended structure of modern futurity as a temporal paradigm and the serial figurality of Adorno's mistresses as a biographical model too. The seriality of the latter makes only a tempered appearance in the narrative unfolding of Kluge's miniature, inasmuch as G. herself appears in Supplement 4 anachronistically as "a mistress from 1941" [*eine Geliebte von 1941*], whom her distressed but thoughtful husband was unable to "translate into the year 1967" [*in das Jahr 1967 übersetzen*] (448). The prominence of the word "indifference" in the supplement's subtitle and the epigraphic idiom "'Love blinds'" [*"Liebe macht blind"*] put a spotlight on G. as well, even as the subtitle's linkage of "indifference" and ubiquitous destruction—"'Indifference destroys everything'"—simultaneously ties the historical-philosophical figure of Adorno to this supplement too. We shall return to this subtitle as citation in additional time. For now we note various ways in which this fourth supplemental narrative directly cultivates readerly attention to G. in particular. This is where the text lends her more biographical detail and also where the narrative voice as such insists that this figure merits intensified curiosity, ours as well as that of the doomed lovers in their inner sanctum.¹⁵⁶ This insistence and intensification come in the narrative form of interlocution, the voice of experimentation that we have already seen push the narratological limits of counterfactual capabilities and functional oscillation elsewhere in Kluge's heliotropic prose in a cosmic dimension. Here the voice of interlocution extends its own durational temporality by opening with four questions revolving around G. as an object of interfigural awareness, and then attempting to answer these questions in a long paragraph in which a few more questions and additional answers follow.

> Were the two in the neutrally appointed little chamber blinded? Did the learned lover and the woman who had traveled here to see him feel at all what went on in the wife, who had spent these hours in retreat? Did they try to understand it?
> What should they have understood?
>
> [*Waren die Zwei im neutral ausgestatteten Kämmerchen verblendet? Empfanden der gelehrte Geliebte und die Herangereiste, was in der Ehefrau, die sich zurückgezogen hatte für diese Stunden, etwa vorging? Suchten sie das zu verstehen?*
> *Was hätten sie verstehen sollen?*] (448)

Blurring narratological boundaries between third-person narration and any intended audience of a communicative transmission, this unnatural voice of interlocution seems to be having a lively conversation with its disembodied self and inviting us to align our readerly perspectives on social exchange with both sides of this narrative split.

This would appear to transpire in a realist register, which the voice of interlocution repeatedly and explicitly ascribes to G. as a character in the story. Yet the voice of interlocution in textual fact is paradoxically the only voice in the miniature to cultivate this register. As we have already noted, G. never speaks at all. Or does she? The interlocutor in this final paragraph at times seems to focalize perception through G., as for example when we read that G. saw her "competitor" [*Konkurrentin*] off when the other woman departed to catch her train home, and the interlocutor intervenes to ask and immediately answer: "But competition how so? The image was not thought through" [*Wieso aber Konkurrenz?*

---

156 The miniature lends G. biographical details on primarily textual grounds, not necessarily those that would justify presumption of an exact correspondence between G.'s imagined biography and Gretel Adorno's actual life. For example, Supplement 4 refers to G. as "a mistress from 1941," whereas we know that Gretel Karplus met Adorno in 1923 and married him in 1937. Müller-Doohm's Adorno biography mentions a love affair that ended badly between Adorno and Renée Nell in 1942, but even if we assume that Kluge might toy with dates, in textual terms it is unlikely that Kluge is introducing a second, unnamed lover at this juncture in "Saturday in Utopia."

Die Vorstellung war undurchdacht] (448). But whose perception is faulty here? The wife's or the interlocutor's? The interlocutor clearly focalizes perceptions in the storyworld through G. when the narrative voice tells us the pragmatically minded realist "honestly loved the strange, somewhat child-like scholar, imagined under the condition of her own death" [*den eigenartigen, etwas kindlichen Gelehrten aufrichtig liebte, vorgestellt unter der Bedingung ihres eigenen Todes*] (448). Two things are worth noting about this indication of heightened focalization through G. at this juncture. First, especially in tandem with the text's earlier reference to the philosopher's death on his mistress's anticipatory horizon, this focalized futural reference to G. imagining her own death resounds like a very unrealistic incantation of Martin Heidegger, Adorno's philosophical nemesis, in the interior space of the married couple's "private" residence. For Heidegger, "Being-towards-death" is a generic condition of the ontology of human existence. "Anticipation [of mortality] makes Dasein *authentically* futural," he writes in *Being and Time*, "and in such a way that the anticipation itself is possible only in so far as it is futural in its Being in general" (373). For Adorno's negative dialectics however, death marked no ontological condition but a socio-historical threshold, and as we will recall from his 1964 radio broadcast with Bloch, for Adorno, there can be "no utopia" without consideration of this particular "threshold of death." Second, the voice of interlocution Kluge gives us in "Saturday in Utopia" explicitly raises a question of utopian temporality in conjunction with G.'s realism. "What after all was she missing that would have been hers if the traveling mistress were out of the picture? Would she have had a share in the energies of the utopian Saturday hours? Under realist conditions?" [*Was entbehrte sie denn, was ihr zugekommen wäre, wenn die Herangereiste entfiele? Hätte sie an den Energien der utopischen Samstagsstunden Anteil gehabt? Unter realistischen Bedingungen?*] (448).

Here the experimental voice of interlocution itself strikes another realistic chord, only to align with a characteristically Klugean anti-realist realist perspective with the next caveat: "Even if reality is invalid" [*Auch wenn Realität nichts gilt*] (448). In the last question-and-answer stretch of Supplement 4, the narrative interlocutor appears both to sympathize with G. and to push her affective orientation and narrative position into increasingly realistic terrain. The slippage is subtle and deadly. "That love confirms this rule [i.e. the rule that reality is invalid] is demonstrated in the fact that she [G.] arranged the pavilion for the two contracting agents, whom she took care of and tolerated, without luxury, without accommodations, without fantasy" [*Daß Liebe diese Regel bestätigt, zeigt sich darin, daß sie den Pavillon der beiden von ihr betreuten, geduldeten Kontrahenten nicht luxuriös, nicht angepaßt, nicht phantasievoll gestaltete*] (448). The interlocutor's curious sympathetic perspective in this case proves deadly because it confines G. to a space of resigned empirical realism without remainder on her laboring behalf. The experimental interlocutor at this point ceases to oscillate between one narrative trajectory and another, opting functionally to close rather than widen the gap of experiential possibility. Fortunately "Saturday in Utopia" might not give this interlocutor the miniature's last words after all. This is the reading I will now pursue.

Stakes are especially high when the empirical limits of existing reality cease to oscillate, for that would leave us reading only that which merely "exists," as Adorno put it in *Negative Dialectics* when condemning European metaphysics for its complicity in catastrophe (347). The subtitle of Kluge's last apparent supplement to "Saturday in Utopia" gives us more writing on the fourth wall of the page in and beyond this miniature interior space. This claim could be justified by various textual features evident so far: deadening motifs of capitalist reification and social exchange, ineluctable commercialism in so-called private life, and narrative experiments in anti-realist realism and unnatural transformation, for example. (This would also include the transformation of type-casting stock figures and categorical identifications such as "the scholar," "the mistress," "the wife," and "the realist" into the narratively distinct figure of G., who is both "the wife" and has a secret name indexed by a particular element making its way out of a merely alphabetical sequence.) But with Kluge there is always more. The sentence marked as a citational speech act in the supplement's subtitle is a modified quotation and translation from spoken words addressed to a government-sponsored conference on "Holocaust Era Assets" in the Czech Republic in 2009 by Noach Flug from Israel. President of the International Auschwitz Committee and himself a survivor of several concentration camps in the Third Reich, Flug addressed present and future audiences in the commingled voices of historical memory and living grief: "I speak on behalf of the survivors of the German concentration camps and ghettos. We remember our murdered families and the million [sic] of victims who remain in the places of the ashes. They are with us always; we will never forget them" (268–269). Flug invokes written testimony of aging survivors as a document delivered to government leaders of the Federal Republic of Germany, the Czech Republic, and the European Council in 2009 but "directed towards the future," and the curiosity of the young as representing "hope" that this catastrophic "knowledge will live on into the future" (269). Flug's appeal for future historical memory, 21st-century governmental reparations, and constant social vigilance against the persecution of difference is underwritten by his penultimate statement: "Indifference destroyed everything and everyone; we have experienced it" (270).

The genocide of the Holocaust plays no overt narrative role in Kluge's "Saturday in Utopia," though it does certainly figure in Adorno's critical understanding of "permanent catastrophe" as discussed above. Kluge operates as Adorno's heir in "Saturday in Utopia" too, though not without some significant differences. Converting the simple past of Flug's "destroyed" into the ubiquitous present of "destroys" in his supplemental subtitle, Kluge's German translation additionally foregrounds two vectors of relationality at the same time. The German word for indifference—*Gleichgültigkeit*—literally denotes the abstract quality of being equally valid; the word thus extends the miniature's strong motif of oppressive equivalence without remainder and indicts, as Adorno would, the social risks and historical threats of categorical abstraction. At the same time—and here it is important to point out the obvious—the German words that Kluge uses in the title and subtitle of Supplement 4 for indifference, destruction, and even supplement are German. That is to say, they partake of concrete particular histories of language, society, life, death, and horizons of thought. This will be important to recall when we come to the end, where Kluge in a surprising twist reverts to the sign of equivalence, but does so in a way that allows both us and G.—in a temporal sense—to begin again.

Supplement 4 and "Saturday in Utopia" come to an apparent end with two declarative statements: "Love has no place. Utopia=no place" [*Liebe hat keinen Ort. Utopie=kein Ort*] (448). Which narrative voice speaks here, and what perspective prevails? The logical assumption would be that the voice of interlocution extends into this terminus too, in uncritical realist mode, since the voice of interlocution otherwise fills the entire supplement, betraying its experimental narrative function only when it resolves G.'s figural status near the end on empirical grounds alone. This reading would be unsatisfying though because it would adhere to the reality principle that the experimental interlocutor in bureaucratic guise effectively undoes in footnote 2, as discussed above. This is the footnote in which G.'s figural relationship to a cosmic horizon of relationality comes into view. A realistically resigned reading of the supplement's conclusion would mainly fail to satisfy though because it would be nonsensical in an unexperimental and boring way, and Kluge's writing is nothing if not experimental in its temporal core. If the otherwise oscillating narrative voice of "Saturday in Utopia" is ultimately overwhelmed by its own empirical claims, the final lines of the supplement yield only what we already know on an empirical plane—there is "no place" for the wife's love in her own marriage and the Greek word meaning utopia literally means "no place—or what makes no descriptive scenic sense (since we know the wife does have a place to sleep in the apartment). The life would go out of the miniature in such indifferent narrative analysis, but it comes back in rather than out if we attune our readerly perspective to G. manifesting here for the first time as a narrative voice and not merely as a narrated figure. Coming from her emergent perspective, "love has no place" violates the spatial and temporal constraints of utopian traditions alike. The alternative futurity of her conversion to an "other life" is made accessible to present experience through G.'s twofold narrative transformation into third-person voice and "unearthly" perspective. This is Kluge literally and heliotropically exercising our future sense in narrative form. And if the miniature's concluding assertion of equivalence under a mathematical sign does come from G.'s enlivening narrative perspective, we should take a closer look, and not only because "Saturday in Utopia" repeatedly warns us not to put our faith in calculations of equivalence and exchange, or because "no place" echoes the refrain of negation and nonidentity in Kluge and Adorno alike.

The grammatical subject of the supplement's final declaration in an ostensibly realist key is not in fact "utopia" but a German word related to and resembling it spelled "Utopie." The little letter "e" is what encourages us as readers to begin again, all empirical history of destruction to the contrary, since the miniature's ending marks socio-historical difference, not in chartable space but in the utopian dimension of an experiential futurity that would not be indifferent to the destruction of everything. The retroactive narrative tension that arises, through reading this text, between "Utopie" as a non-equivalent cipher of differential time, on the one hand, and the Latinized, Greek, and generic invocation of "Utopia" in the miniature's title, on the other, refers us to G. as far more than a mere figure of utopian redemption.[157] The narrative voice that "Saturday in Utopia" labors to give her opens up a more capacious, experiential, temporal perspective on critical perspective itself. Kluge's intensified storytelling investment in this future sense exceeds the metaphysical constraints of Adorno's own radical experiments with third-person narration and counterfactual hope in the modernist miniatures and "damaged life" of *Minima Moralia*. "Saturday in Utopia" additionally articulates, in narrative form oscillating between fact and fiction, a critical perspective on Gretel Karplus Adorno's life-and-death contributions to the Frankfurt School of Critical Theory that has long been denied her. Kluge rewrites the future rather than the history of this theory when he presents G. as a philosofictive figure of utopian orientation in time who does much more than take 'minutes' of dialectical exchange, and when this silent figure undergoes a functional conversion from wordless character to narrative voice.[158] The

---

[157] See also David Leopold's comments on the etymology of Thomas More's "neologism" *utopia* (446), which indirectly remind us that the language of "utopia" is itself never generic.

[158] See also Staci von Boeckmann's 2004 dissertation and subsequent article on the "life and work" of Gretel Adorno. For scholarly commentary on various roles that women and gender play in Kluge's work in visual culture and social theory, see Heide Schlüpmann, Miriam Hansen ("Alexander Kluge, Cinema and the Public Sphere"), Joanna Gilbert, and Michael Bray. Gilbert

cosmic dimensions of this incalculable utopian equation mark this doubly as a kind of "crossover narration," once in James Phelan's intended sense of unnatural experimentation, and at the same time in violation of Phelan's definitional claim that the events involved are originally "independent" of each other (168–169). For Kluge, the narrative events of hope and despair, protest and destruction, death and life are socio-historically and cosmically related at root, through gaps and leaps in storytelling.

Kluge's 21st-century cosmic miniatures "The Beautiful is Flawless" and "Saturday in Utopia" also share and deviate from key features of experimental narrative that contemporary literary theorists have specifically associated with futurity. For Albrecht Koschorke, a leading literary and cultural theorist from Germany who offers a masterful overview of a "general theory of narrative" in *Wahrheit und Erfinding* ["Truth and Invention"], "future fictions" fall into three different heuristic categories (229–236). These include literary fictions, in which an artificial future and "alternative world" are "relieved of customary reality" [*von der gewöhnlichen Realität entlastet*] (229); "social fictions" of so-called imagined communities (in the terminology of Benedict Anderson's seminal work on political communities of social bonding), with social fictions for Koschorke always commingling imagined and real effects to some degree (229); and pointedly modern fictions of societal formation predicated on a temporal consciousness of futurity as open and "uncertain, but precisely for that reason pliable" (230). As Koselleck and Luhmann both put it in their own conceptual terms, this structural notion of an open future is an indispensable marker of European modernity as such. For Koschorke: "Future fictions serve to give this [temporal] uncertainty a place in society's imaginative economy, to incorporate it at the same time into the present, and also, in the other direction, to open a given present up to that which will come" (230). For this reason, Koschorke argues, "an

---

specifically addresses the interplay of a transgendered analytic and categorical concepts of gender in Kluge's films. To date scholars have paid little sustained analytical attention to gender and narrative form in Kluge's literary social fictions. Hansen raises different medium-specific but related issues of voice, narration, character, and gender with regard to Kluge and cinema: "The status of character in Kluge's films is inseparable from its relation to the voice-over, the absent narrator who intervenes, seemingly, to mediate the character for the spectator. The relationship of voice-over to character inevitably provokes criticism for its gender-specific division of labor: a male voice—that of the filmmaker himself—speaks a female figure. The validity of this criticism hinges, in part at least, on the dimension of authority and closure traditionally associated with voice-over narration, especially in its documentary usage." As Hansen astutely observes in her analysis of Kluge's voice-over of Gabi Teichert in the film *Germany in Autumn:* "the figure takes on a life of its/her own, as she is engaged in a project that neither narrator nor spectator as yet understand" (66–67).

open temporal horizon is indispensable" to social function in modern life, and referencing futurity both "secures social integration" (230) and sparks political conflict over who controls future events and their social meaning (232). Koschorke is especially helpful for parsing a "porous" boundary between prognostic planning and "artistic fantasy" in the social life of social fictions (231), and some of his insights into social narrative are especially apt for Kluge, for example, when Koschorke writes: "The urgent pressure [*Andringen*] of the new tears gaps [*Lücken*] into the co-presence of past and present" (234). However, Kluge's literary social fictions also stand in tension with Koschorke's general claims in three particular ways. Kluge's philosofictive miniatures of catastrophic history and counterfactual hope are never "relieved of customary reality" but struggle to draw critical breath precisely there. Their futurity is open to possibility but also—and this is crucial—increasingly accessible to experience too, in ways for which the modern imaginary of future time does not or does not yet allow. Last but not least regarding Koschorke, Kluge's cosmic miniatures in and for the 21st century call for particulate narrative analysis, for the legacy of negative dialectics and counterfactual hope that Kluge inherits from Adorno and reworks for his readers is not unproblematically open to a general theory of anything.

Another approach to the arrival of something "new" in contemporary theories of narrative storytelling opens with a quotation from speculative fiction writer William Gibson: "'The future is already here—it's just not very evenly distributed'" (Christoph Bode and Rainer Dietrich, *Future Narratives* 1). For Christoph Bode and Rainer Dietrich writing in the domain of 21st-century narratology, "future narratives" represent a distinct type of narrative form, one that is not so much new in the sense of never having existed before (though Bode and Dietrich make this claim after a fashion too [3]), but more significantly "new" in the sense of having been "hitherto unidentified" by classical or postclassical narratology, even though future narratives abound in many "past narratives" that narratologists have already studied in some detail. For Bode and Dietrich, "the key feature" of what they call future narrative is that it is based on "nodal" situations rather than "past events" alone as a matter of narrative form (1). This sounds at first promising for an analysis of Kluge's cosmic miniatures, since his narrative experiments with counterfactual hope function as oscillating nodes of possible transformation from catastrophic existence to what Adorno termed a "future without life's miseries." Yet past historical events matter quite a lot to Kluge's own version of critical theory and narrative creativity, so it might be premature to ditch them altogether in a rush to embrace the newest narratological "kid in town" (2). Bode and Dietrich nonetheless discuss the formal structure of future narrative in some ways that resonate with Amir Eshel's analysis of literary "futurity" in crosscultural comparison as a fundamentally ethical way of addressing historical catastrophe too. Though not directly concerned with political histories or social catastrophes, by contrast, Bode and Dietrich explain that future narrative in their definition "does not only *thematize* openness, indeterminacy, virtuality, and the idea that every 'now' contains a multitude of possible continuations," but also "goes beyond this by actually *staging* the fact that the future is a space of yet unrealized potentiality, [...] by allowing the reader/player to enter situations that fork into different branches and to actually *experience* that 'what happens next' may well depend upon us, upon our decisions, our actions, our values and motivations" (1).

Bode and Dietrich's emphasis on actual experience may sound compatible with the argument I have been advancing about ways in which Kluge's narrative experiments render futurity accessible to experience through exercises in reading, but it is not. This is because Bode and Dietrich rely entirely on the modern European definition of futurity as inaccessible to experience, and the reading experience they mean is empirically identical to itself. In their phrasing, future narratives also "*preserve and contain* what can be regarded as defining features of future time, namely that it is yet undecided, open, and multiple, and that it has not yet crystallized into actuality. It is by virtue of their capability to do exactly this—to preserve the future *as future*—that these narratives are here called 'Future Narratives'" (1). The nodal ground of these future narratives begins to sound much less enticing from the narrative perspective of Kluge's miniatures, since it would be difficult to tell where desire or hope for transformation might come from or why change would matter. Things get worse—again, from a perspective schooled in Kluge's very social idiosyncrasies—when Bode and Dietrich insist on two more formal aspects of the future narratives they mean. "Future Narratives are always about how we see ourselves in relation not to 'things as they are', but in relation to *things to come*" (3). And "finally and fundamentally," they claim with regard to the new node-based category of narrative form that was long overlooked and they have now called into being through identification: "often what appears to be different can, in fact, be shown to be fundamentally *the same*. Which is, after all, what an *identification* is" (3). For Kluge and Adorno alike, as many other commentators on various aspects of their extensive and intensive bodies of work have shown, an ethical imperative attends experiments in social life and artistic form, especially in modern German culture at the crossroads of catastrophic histories and critical theory, and the ethos of experiments in what I would call narrative futurity and literary form runs against the grain of identification, including the self-identical identification of futurity as narrative form. The utopian orientations of heliotropic narration in Adorno's *Minima Moralia* and Kluge's cosmic miniatures give us a different critical language for engaging the future sense of utopian dimensions.

3 Extraterrestrial Speculations with and beyond Kant

This section of Part One revisits the figure of extraterrestrials, which concerned both Kant in the 18th century and us in the Introduction to this study of Kluge's cosmic miniatures. This is where the narrative figuration of extraterrestrials in Kluge's experimental writing practice will help us extend our exploration of key questions raised in the Introduction. How do non-destructive strategies from "above" in an off-worldly sense manifest in future-making strategies from "below" in the miniscule details of Kluge's experimental prose? How does something not of this world enter into the story scenes of his making, where threats to life are everywhere and world-making—long considered a staple feature of literary narrative and science fiction alike—is constantly undone? If Kant's extraterrestrials serve an enlightened concept of autonomous reason favoring the realm of intelligible understanding, Kluge's creative exercises in unalienated life work in more concentrated fashion on the realm of the sensible, including sensibilities of time. Kluge is clearly indebted to a German critical tradition that begins historically with Kant and pivots, for Kluge as a writer of miniatures, on Adorno. Yet as we have seen for Kluge and Adorno alike, albeit in different measure and narrative turns, the realm of the sensible is never confined to empirical perception alone. The future sense that Kluge's cosmic miniatures cultivate necessarily draws on this-worldly and off-worldly dimensions alike, and in this section of Part One, Kluge's invisible extraterrestrials will help us see how Kluge's narrative uses of futurity come to function as experiential portals in utopian time at this dimensional nexus.

For one prominent literary theorist of the late 20th and early 21st centuries, known for his many contributions to critical theory in a Marxist vein (and to heated debates about the actuality of Adorno, as we have already seen), something historically significant about 1989 in a broad political sense infused new life into a particular literary genre. In *Archaeologies of the Future* Fredric Jameson conflates science fiction and utopian literature in order to posit that utopian impulses lost to the world with the demise of European communism in 1989 find new life in contemporary science fiction. Jameson does not mean to suggest with this that science fiction since 1989 necessarily subscribes to Marxist thought, but to underscore instead how utopian desire acquires renewed relevance in a new marking of time.[159] Celebrating the thick descriptions, elaborate

---

[159] Jameson is thinking of the time of post-communism in Europe, but the heightened importance he ascribes to science fiction since 1989 is not by his account confined to Europe. See also Eric D. Smith, who draws on Jameson's *Archaeologies of the Future* and *The Geopolitical Aesthetic* alike to advance a postcolonial critique of imperialist forms of science fiction. Invoking James-

narratives, material challenges, and extensive character development in Kim Stanley Robinson's red, green, and blue *Mars* trilogy of the 1990s, for example, in which unprecedented difficulties on a hostile planet are overcome in social process, Jameson's endeavor pivots on a concept of totality in conjoined dreams of social betterment and exercises in literary form. I argue instead that literary engagements with futurity in the century still unfolding evidence a more variegated palette of both concerns and forms than a categorical fixation on the genres of science fiction, utopian writing, or dystopian speculation allows. In the present study, futurity in the most general terms denotes a broad range of aesthetic practices in contemporary literature that revolve around the future in some still undefined ways—practices for which we are still developing the kind of sophisticated critical vocabulary applied to memorial cultures and the historical past in literary guise.[160] Stylistically distinct and even obstinate without being simply idiosyncratic, Kluge's cosmic miniatures also contribute to this larger trend in contemporary literature and critical theory, albeit one that has only recently begun to unfold and cannot be captured in the language of totality or even a philosophy of time.[161] A closer look at Kluge's extraterrestrials will demonstrate that they too foster the future sense as a long-distance organ of temporal perception in very particular ways.

The frequency with which future-oriented time travel and extraordinary parallel worlds figure in Kluge's prose is striking. Although these motifs have been present in his work for decades, they receive intensified attention in works writ-

---

on's *Archaeologies* for example, Smith characterizes utopia as "not a static locus of achieved meliorist or millenialist fantasy but rather the roving imaginative principle and restless dialectical figuration of social possibility itself" (48).

160 For a range of important and methodologically varied critical interventions in this regard, see especially Erdle (*Literarische Epistemologie der Zeit*), Eshel (*Futurity*), the ten essays included in Adelson and Fore (*Futurity Now*), Willer's various publications on prognostics, generation, and the epistemology of futurity (including the rich anthology co-edited with Benjamin Bühler under the title *Futurologien*), and Assmann ("Transformations of the Modern Time Regime"). On international "booms" in memorial cultures and memorial criticism late in the 20th century, see Huyssen (*Twilight Memories* and *Present Pasts*) and Neumann (*Shifting Memories*).

161 See Adelson's "Experiment Mars" for a comparison of Martian motifs in *nâzım hikmet: auf dem schiff zum mars* ["nâzım hikmet: on the ship to mars"] by Berkan Karpat and Zafer Şenocak with those in Kluge's *Learning Processes with a Deadly Outcome*, first published in German in 1973 and republished with minimal change in 2000 as part of Kluge's two-volume "Chronicle of Feelings." A lacuna around futurity was until recently especially evident in German Studies, where postwar literary history has long been concerned with the legacy of a violent and genocidal past. While these concerns remain relevant, varying modes of futurity in German literature of all periods are coming more clearly into critical focus now, along with global capital.

ten since 2000, a period that coincides with heightened talk of "parallel societies" in German discourses of immigration and "parallel universes" in scientific research in quantum physics. Both of these arenas are centrally concerned with contested and changing conceptions of time (for example, when rural Turks or Muslims are discursively portrayed as literally behind the times in Europe or when astrophysicists debate the temporal structure of the cosmos).[162] Neither quantum physics nor immigration politics can simply serve as cipher texts for decoding the literary motifs of time travel and parallel relations in Kluge's recent work though. These larger frameworks of debate might rather be understood themselves as parallel tracks for considering the changing parameters of both human life and material worlds on various scales. Quantum physics nonetheless play an indispensable role in Kluge's 21st-century writing, as we shall see. Unlike Jameson, I will not focus on categories of science fiction, utopianism, or totality, but on more odd little texts in which motifs of miniaturization help to create large perspectives on futurity in prose.[163] The experimental writing at issue in this section of Part One will again be drawn from Kluge's 350 "new stories" published in "Door to Door With an Other Life," the same collection that contains "Hope at Sunrise" and "The Beautiful is Flawless." Like "Hope at Sunrise," the miniatures to which we turn here can all be found in "We Fortunate Children of the First Globalization" (9–55), the first numbered segment of Kluge's volume explicitly devoted to portals in time.

Much incisive scholarship on the author's prose relies on conceptual categories of "montage" and "counter-history" to argue that Kluge both continues artistic traditions of the historical avant-garde and breaks with totalitarian histories. These combined features ultimately tell—by this scholarly account—a story

---

[162] Wilhelm Heitmeyer first used the term "parallel societies" in 1996 in reference to dangers associated with Islamic fundamentalism in Germany and then in the more widely cited study that he co-edited with Joachim Müller and Helmut Schröder titled *Verlockender Fundamentalismus* ["Alluring Fundamentalism"]. See Werner Schiffauer for an excellent overview of competing uses of the German term and its increased usage in the wake of 9/11. On this see also Werner Köster's anthology *Parallelgesellschaften* ["Parallel Societies"], the contributors to which date the most frequent usage of the term in German print media to 2005 and 2006 (53, 69). On the "new physics" tied to both parallel worlds and a "new notion of time" see Fred Alan Wolf, *Parallel Universes*, which however predates many of the more dramatic technological and cognitive developments in theoretical physics since the book's first publication in 1988. For a more rigorous account see Michio Kaku, *Parallel Worlds: The Science of Alternative Universes and our Future in the Cosmos*. As Kaku observes, the scientific "concept of time" has not been static but has itself evolved "over the centuries" (128).

[163] My essay "Experiment Mars" from 2008 instead analyzes motifs of fragmentation in relation to futurity in works by Kluge, Karpat, and Şenocak.

of redemptive possible futures or at least "conditions for a redemptive future" in Langston's exemplary formulation (*Visions of Violence* 20).[164] As noted in the Introduction, Sebald approaches Kluge's writing in this light too. Concentrating on Kluge's writing about Allied bombing raids on German cities in World War II, he sees Kluge as a kind of archaeologist of catastrophe looking backwards while being propelled forward, much like Benjamin's angel of history in Sebald's explicit comparison. When scholars throughout the humanities speak of the end of the 20th century in terms of a "global crisis" in ideologies and images of "future time," Kluge's commitment to writing about "conditions for a redemptive future" would seem to be just the reading tonic we need.[165] Yet not all of Kluge's writing experiments engage futurity in the same way, and as we have seen, many of them do not operate in narrative terms in redemptive mode at all. If Benjamin's angel of history moves toward the future in Kluge scholarship in more or less familiar ways on a path to redemption, what unfamiliar forms of futurity do Kluge's interplanetary cosmic travelers present?[166]

---

164 Langston, who devotes a chapter of his book to analyses of Kluge and the embodiment of time, posits a decisive break between the historical avant-garde and avant-gardes after 1945 because, in his view, "post-fascist avant-gardes" lay claim to a certain kind of "historical realism" in their approaches to fascist violence done to human bodies (20–22). Langston also refers to an "ineluctable literary core of Kluge's efforts" and the author's own "insistence on being an author foremost" (198, 291); see also Helmut Heißenbüttel's early prediction in this connection. For a different approach to understanding postwar German literature in relation to violence and the real, see Robert Buch's *The Pathos of the Real*, which focuses on 20th-century "aesthetics of violence" centered on "spectacles of suffering." Buch's study includes chapters on Peter Weiss and Heiner Müller but not Kluge. Langston characterizes his own analyses as "circuitous time travels" in post-fascist literature and visual culture (25). In "Kluge's *Auswege*" Stefanie Harris assesses formal narrative features of the author's prose in terms of "temporal asynchrony," which she casts in terms of both montage and counter-history (310 et passim), as discussed above.

165 For the phrasing cited here, see Anne McClintock, who links a crisis of futurity with "the collapse of both capitalist and communist teleologies of progress" in her postscript to *Imperial Leather* (391–396). Huyssen discusses the widespread "exhaustion of utopian energies vis-à-vis the future" at the end of the 20th century in terms of shifting emphases rather than a "radical turn" (*Twilight Memories* 87–88); see also Huyssen, *Present Pasts*.

166 Karsten Witte once observed that Kluge's overall style of writing should be considered a genre in its own right, one that melds "Science Fiction *mit* Social Fiction" (370). Presenting the enconium when Kluge was awarded the Büchner Prize for German literature, Jan Philipp Reemtsma opined that the author's texts belong to a literary genre all their own, which Reemtsma dubbed "Genre Kluge" [*Gattung Kluge*]. As I contend here and elsewhere, science fiction and utopianism are at least insufficient categories for considering the function of futurity in Kluge's prose (see Adelson, "Experiment Mars"). In an interview published in *Freitag* magazine in December 2009, Kluge is asked to talk about "the future." His reply commingles the rhetorical figure of futurity with allusions to Benjamin's angel. The future, Kluge says, "is *the potential we*

"Extraordinary voyages" through space, time, and technology are the crux of science fiction according to one historian of the genre, which portrays "alternative but self-consistent societies" (Adam Roberts vii–viii).[167] As readers of Kluge well know, nothing about the societal conditions we encounter in his texts is harmonious or self-consistent except perhaps the author's own preoccupation with inconsistency itself, the peculiar details that just don't seem to fit but belong in the text all the same. This preoccupation with inconsistency has most often been understood in terms of paradoxical logic or contingent ruptures in linear chains of causality, whereas I lay critical emphasis on futurity and future-making instead. The figure of the extraterrestrial for Kluge could be understood as an irritant or disturbance in linear or logical chains, a cipher of inconsistency. Yet Kluge's extraterrestrials cannot be fully grasped with recourse to a philosophy of contingency. Keen interest in all manner of things interplanetary, galactic, and cosmic arguably underwrites his entire oeuvre, and as noted, we find an intensified continuation of related motifs in many of his publications since 2000. These include, for example, time travel and philosophical discussions in Martian orbit in *Learning Processes with a Deadly Outcome*, the German version of which was first published in 1973 and reissued with slight modification in "Chronicle of

---

carry inside us. We would have perished long ago without some kind of guardian angel." For this reason, "there is no such thing as a future isolated from the subjunctive case," and the "evil wind blowing us from the past into the future [...] is also a wind [...] blowing towards us from the future because it has already been in the past so long" (Kluge, Michael Angele et al). The interview was conducted by Michael Angele, Ingo Arend, Jakob Augstein, and Philip Grassmann. Aside from figures of extraterrestrials and allusions to angels that crop up occasionally in Kluge's writing since 2000, the transmigration of souls is an additional though less frequent motif through which Kluge pursues the relationship between visible and invisible matter. Kluge's deep knowledge of Marxist theories of capitalist commodification, which renders social relations invisible, is well known.

167 The term "extraordinary voyages" stems from Jules Verne. Unlike Roberts, Darko Suvin defines science fiction as the literature of "cognitive estrangement" (*Metamorphoses of Science Fiction*). Although Kluge's writing does entail various strategies of both epistemological and aesthetic estrangement (*Verfremdung*) in relation to human histories of alienated labor (*Entfremdung* and *Verdinglichung*), Suvin's emphasis on cognitive estrangement would not do any more justice to Kluge's sense of time travel than Roberts's stress on "alternative but self-consistent societies." This is because Kluge's preferred forms of estrangement also entail a kind of desired habituation to that which is not yet familiar: in my reading, this notably applies to the future sense. This mode of habituation, which involves the cultivation of a long-distance organ of temporal sense perception, is different though from the kind of "naturalization" that Jonathan Culler analyzes as what readers do when they make what appears "strange" conform to the communicability they ascribe to literature (134–160). For Fludernik's discussion of the relative radicality of Culler, Genette, and Barthes vis-à-vis narratological concepts of verisimilitude, see *Towards a 'Natural' Narratology* (31–33).

Feelings" in 2000; an entire section of "Geschichten vom Weltall" ["Stories of the Cosmos"] in "The Gap the Devil Leaves Us" and other pieces referencing the 1912 work of French science fiction that Benjamin mentions in the *Arcades Project*; countless texts in "The Gap the Devil Leaves Us," "Door to Door with an Other Life" and elsewhere on the convoluted transnational history, science, technology, and politics of astrophysics and geobiology before, during, and after the cold war; the extraterrestrials that will demand our attention very soon; a DVD piece from 2007 on the loneliness and other sense organs of a long-distance astronaut; and much more.[168] However, something significant shifts for Kluge around the turn to the 21st century, and this goes beyond the historic changes to which he openly directs our attention.

In his preface to the German version of "The Gap the Devil Leaves Us" the author recalls a widespread sense of hopefulness that arose after 1989 when "the new century" seemed about to transform "the bitter experience of the 20th century" into something else.[169] In 2003 he asks whether the world is "falling back into the time of the Thirty Years' War" even though he himself does not believe in "apocalyptic scenarios" (7). The planetary shifts in political climate that

---

168 Kluge's text "Der Kosmos als Kino" ["The Cosmos as Cinema"] can be found in both *Geschichten vom Kino* (44–47), and *Glückliche Umstände, leihweise* ["Happy Circumstances, On Loan"] (36–40) within a larger section there titled "Our Ancestors, the Stars." An English translation of "The Cosmos as Cinema" is available in Kluge's *Cinema Stories* (91–94). For the DVD piece titled "Im Weltall braucht man keine Lesebrille: Helge Schneider und Peter Berling im Orbit" ["One Needs No Reading Glasses in the Cosmos: Helge Schneider and Peter Berling in Orbit"], see track 8 on the DVD that accompanies *Alexander Kluge: Magazin des Glücks* ["Alexander Kluge: Arsenal of Happiness"] (Sebastian Huber and Claus Philipp). There is no corresponding text in the book. Rainer Stollmann has written insightfully on the importance of significant early 20th-century physicists such as Fritz Zwicky and Ludwig Boltzmann for Kluge's *Learning Processes* in particular ("Schwarzer Krieg, endlos"). That is where Stollmann also alerts us to the text's puns on a "'quantum mechanics' [...] of history" (365). Theoretical physicist Kaku notes that Zwicky "coined the word 'supernova'" (71) and that Boltzmann was ridiculed for believing in atoms, which Mach said could not exist because they could not be seen (150–151).
169 Kluge diverges here ("The Gap the Devil Leaves Us" 7) from commentators such as McClintock and Jameson as cited above. For the English translation that appeared as *The Devil's Blind Spot* in 2004, Kluge altered the original temporal reference from "after 1989" (which connotes the fall of the Berlin Wall and other cold war boundaries) to "[a]fter 1991" instead, explicitly referencing in this case "the disintegration of the Russian imperium." The relevant sentence reads, in Martin Chalmers and Michael Hulse's translation: "After 1991, following the disintegration of the Russian imperium, as we looked forward to the year 2000, I had the feeling that the new century would take the bitter experience of the 20th century and turn it around into something hopeful" (*The Devil's Blind Spot* vii).

Kluge bookends with 1989 (the end of the cold war in Europe) and 2003 (the Iraq War cast as a response to the terrorist attacks of 9/11) were not the only changes afoot to affect his new writing in crucial ways. As one prominent scientist puts it, technological and cognitive advances in theoretical physics since the end of the 20th century mark the "third great revolution" in the field of cosmology after the invention of telescopes in the 1600s and the dramatic expansion of telescope capabilities in the 1900s (Kaku, *Parallel Worlds* xv–xvi). According to Michio Kaku, technological developments in telescopes, satellites, lasers, computers, and other arenas relevant to research in astrophysics have brought scientific theories of parallel universes and so-called dark or invisible matter closer than ever before "to experimental verification" (Kaku vi, 74, and 256).[170] While much remains unknown or unproven, scientists have "the most authoritative data yet on the nature of the universe, including its age, its composition, and perhaps even its future" (xvi). What scientists now know or surmise about the nature of the universe hinges on relationships between general relativity and quantum theory, between a "theory of the very large" (e. g., an expanding universe) and a "physics of the extremely small" (e. g., subatomic particles) (Kaku 79, 185). Ongoing scientific reflections on the relationship between classical physics through Einstein and quantum physics around 2000 thus probe ten or more dimensions linking our world of ordinary earthly matter with the extraordinary properties of the universe.[171] Kluge's "extraordinary voyages" through space and especially time must also be understood in this vein, and his literary writing since 2000 is riddled with the vocabulary if not the science of the new physics.

This becomes especially apparent in the language of "parallel worlds" with which "Door to Door with an Other Life" begins in 2006, but it is also evident in Kluge's multi-dimensional preoccupation with invisible matter, indirect means of detection and influence, distortions in perception, macrostructures in relation to microstructures, and so on.[172] For theoretical physicists and Kluge too, dark

---

170 Kaku notes that cosmology was long "more like a detective story" or "wild conjecture" than an "experimental science" (10, 54). New technological capabilities are tipping the scales in the other direction.
171 As Kaku observes, these are not mutually exclusive realms (266).
172 In Kluge's interview with *Freitag* magazine (Kluge, Angele et al.) the author links Einstein and quantum physics in the development of the Internet: "This is an incredible story! It stems from a tiny cell, from the curiosity about what connects the micro with the macro. It has given birth to a new public sphere." There are of course also other influences besides new physics on Kluge's interest in unseen forces and indirect influences on human history, including the material properties of hope (Critical Theory and Marxist theories of history among them). Kaku defines dimension as a "coordinate or parameter by which we measure space and time" and elaborates: "Our familiar universe has three dimensions of space (length, width, and depth) and one

matter indexes nothing sinister but a value-neutral physical substance that can be measured only "indirectly [...] because it bends starlight due to its gravity" (Kaku, *Parallel Worlds* 385). While this invisible substance of the universe is "usually found in a huge halo around galaxies," it might also be present in "your living room" (266).[173] The first numbered section of new stories in "Door to Door with an Other Life" also invokes the vocabulary of the new physics on the "curled" dimensional structure of reality, which might allow for parallel temporalities and "dimensional portals" (Kaku 118) between them. There Kluge writes, before the stories begin: "We live 'curled up' in the INSTANT and simultaneously in the STREAM OF TIME OF MILLIONS OF YEARS" [*Wir leben 'eingerollt' im AUGENBLICK und zugleich im ZEITSTROM VON MILLIONEN JAHREN*] (9).[174] If the new physics defines tunneling as "the process by which particles can penetrate barriers" in a way that defies the classical physics of time, and if the very "idea of tunneling is central to all of physics" today, as one string theorist claims (Kaku 54, 400), we should not be surprised to encounter heightened attention to "tunneling" motifs and extraordinary time travel in Kluge's new writing too. While Kluge's engagement with the history and terms of theoretical physics is by no means confined to the parallel-world stories published in 2006, I shall focus on three of them here to demonstrate how "extraordinary voyages" in time unfold in literary form not necessarily tied to a redemptive future in a deferred sense or even a self-consistent alternative to reality.[175]

The interlacing of "parallel worlds" in Kluge's literary reality is fundamentally different from the ostensibly impenetrable barrier keeping so-called parallel

---

dimension of time. In string and M-theory, we need ten (eleven) dimensions in which to describe the universe, only four of which can be observed in the laboratory" (386).

173 On quantum physics and its relationship to classical physics I rely largely on Kaku's formulations for a general educated readership. Langston is close to completing a major monograph on Kluge and Oskar Negt, tentatively titled *Dark Matter, In Defiance of Catastrophic Modernity*.

174 If "time was like an arrow" for Newton, Kaku tells us, Einstein saw time "more like a river" (128). Kluge's compound words for time here—"Augenblick" and "Zeitstrom"—draw on common German idioms but also implicitly reference key moments in the history of theoretical physics. Einstein saw time flowing like a river, and the relationship between an observable moment and a particle wave is key to quantum physics. Kluge is no doubt also drawing on Heideggerian commentary on time in the vocabulary of *Augenblick* ("moment of time") and *Zeitstrom* ("stream of time"). See Martin Heidegger, *Being and Time* (376, 478).

175 With its structuring principles of "human power" [*Menschenkraft*] and "devil's power" [*Teufelskraft*] "The Gap the Devil Leaves Us" entails stronger ties to traditions concerned with redemptive or at least radically improved futures. Even there, however, "Menschenkraft" at times has more to do with sheer survival than redemption. On "Teufelskraft" and "diabolical dialectics," see Matthew Miller. See also Martin Jay's discussion of Paul Connerton's account of Adorno's "'diabolisation' of history" (*Marxism and Totality* 263–264).

societies apart in 21ˢᵗ-century Germany. Even the OED lists divergent definitions of "parallel," which can mean "continuously equidistant" in Euclidean terms, "precisely [...] analogous," or "contemporary in duration," for example (Lesley Brown 2095). The "parallel worlds" with which "Door to Door with an Other Life" opens are not cast as separate worlds at all but as necessarily entwined realities.[176] "A reality that destroys human beings is 'real.' Human beings deny reality that shows them its inhuman side: this is also 'real.' Thus we live of necessity in parallel worlds: DOOR TO DOOR WITH AN OTHER LIFE" [*Eine Realität, die Menschen vernichtet, ist 'wirklich'. Eine Wirklichkeit, die sich gegenüber Menschen nicht-menschlich zeigt, wird von ihnen verleugnet: das ist ebenfalls 'wirklich'. So leben wir notwendig in Parallelwelten: TÜR AN TÜR MIT EINEM ANDEREN LEBEN*] (7). For the "A.K." who signs off on this wording from the book's preface, the parallel realities at stake are not earthly worlds in contradistinction to extraterrestrial ones but pivot jointly on what the preface characterizes as "a stock of hope in us" [*einen Hoffnungsvorrat in uns*], a "life force" [*Lebenskraft*] in the fiber of earthly human beings. This is a pre-human substance dating back 630 million years to "snowball-earth," we read, and the first warming of the planet much later gave rise to what the text designates the "First Globalization," the "children" of which "we" human beings become. The first of nine groupings of short "new stories" in "Door to Door with an Other Life" is thus titled "We Fortunate Children of the First Globalization" and features something that we might call a quirky physics of hope without an attendant utopian dream of redemption, though an intensified orientation in temporal sensibility to counterfactual realization does apply. Here I will focus on three entries in this section of Kluge's book, two in which extraterrestrials appear—"Besuch im Weißen Haus" ["Visitors in the White House"] and "Außerirdische unterwegs" ["Extraterrestrials on the Move"] (30–33)—and one in which they do not appear at all but nonetheless offer readers a key to understanding the temporal structure of the text's narration.

The long book section that bears the title "We Fortunate Children of the First Globalization" has embedded within it a subsection with the same title. This subsection consists of seven numbered pieces from which my three focal texts are drawn. "Visitors in the White House" and "Extraterrestrials on the Move" appear consecutively as numbered entries 2 and 3, and "Gesellschaftliche Prozesse als Erzählung" ["Social Processes as Narration"] concludes the series in this subset

---

[176] Physicists generally speak of time as one, but for Kluge the dimension of time operates in several temporalities.

as entry 7.[177] While "Door to Door with an Other Life" as a whole does contain occasional elements recalling the montage style more familiar to us from Kluge's earlier work—photographs, drawings, and maps, for example—it is striking that only two photographs are included in the larger section titled "We Fortunate Children" and virtually none of the usual elements associated with Kluge's montage in the subsection of the same title.[178] In this section of numbered entries we find instead a comparatively restrained mixture of narrative prose, marked dialogue, four footnotes, and two epigraphs in quotation marks. Entry 2—"Visitors in the White House"—consists of a single short paragraph following an epigraph taken from a poem by Clemens Brentano. While the Romantic epigraph figures a lame weaver dreaming "'he weaves'" ["*er webe*"], entry 2 in the Kluge text asserts the presence of extraterrestrials: "Once extraterrestrials were even in the White House" [*Einmal waren Außerirdische sogar im Weißen Hause*] (30).[179] The placement of the "even" in this sentence hints at a motif of endangerment and security that subsequent sentences introduce more directly, albeit in a perhaps surprising vein. "No one from the security personnel saw the aliens" [*Niemand vom Wachpersonal sah die Fremden*], because the extraterrestrials had arrived "in a 'curled up dimension'" [*in 'eingerollter Dimension'*] (30). Danger does not emanate from the extraterrestrials here, for as the narrative voice asserts with recourse to subjunctive mode, these creatures "would have known how to save the earth" [*die Rettungspläne für die Erde gewußt hätten*] (30–31), had they been able to perceive "our" ordinary realm of existence.

In these few sentences Kluge compactly conjures many themes from the new physics: parallel worlds, extraterrestrial intelligence, Earth's likely destruction in the cosmic scheme of things, reflections on future escape routes, "curled" dimensions of time, and the possibility of contact or portals between the dimensions of one universe and those of another (or between the visible and invisible dimensions of our universe). For our purposes, it is crucial that the extraterrestrials are presented as factually given but not seen, and not only by the security personnel. Because these visitors in the White House are not described in ways

---

[177] One should note, however, that the footnotes in the subsection "We Fortunate Children" begin with n. 3 on p. 30. This means that the numbered series for the footnotes is not contained within the subsection. This contrasts with the serial numbers used for the main entries in this subsection. That is to say, this section of "Door to Door with an Other Life" is structured according to two competing sets of ordinal numbers.

[178] See David Roberts ("Die Formenwelt des Zusammenhangs") for an especially helpful overview and critical assessment of montage elements in Kluge's early prose.

[179] One might say that entry 2 has a parallel text of sorts in Section 9 of "The Gap the Devil Leaves Us," where one entry is titled "The Devil in the White House" (903–905).

that would allow us to envision them—but only as "highly intelligent" and "at home in such an extremely small dimension" [*so extrem klein beheimatet*] (30–31)—they are in effect rendered figurally invisible to readers as well. Only the narrative voice serves as a gateway between parallel temporalities here, for the extraterrestrials given in the White House do not see our ordinary human universe either.[180] "Unrecognized and without cognition they traveled through the Oval Office" [*Unerkannt und ohne Kenntnis durchfuhren sie das Oval Office*] (31). Kant may be keeping these extraterrestrials company in spirit and visiting the White House with them when the extraterrestrials are described as attempting to exercise "their powers of judgment" [*dort ihre BEMÜHUNGEN UM URTEILSKRAFT ausübten*] (31). If these interplanetary travelers "without cognition" were part of a group tour through the White House, one can only wonder what they saw. This speculation is at the same time largely moot, since it is the narrator alone who places the extraterrestrials with certainty "in the White House." The narrative perspective is once again our potential portal through time. This may be true to varying degrees with classical forms of narration, but for Kluge access to different temporalities is pointedly tied to the voice of narration, which itself—as we have seen in the case of Kluge writing as Adorno's heir—is never firmly tethered to principles of self-identity.

Extraterrestrials in "Door to Door with an Other Life" are frequently the subject of speculation, and this appears to be their main function inasmuch as they do not otherwise appear in any recognizable material sense at all. If entry 2 asserts the certain presence of extraterrestrials that neither see humans nor are seen by them, entry 3 gives us "Extraterrestrials on the Move" that are presupposed to have appeared—as if in reference to "Visitors in the White House" in the preceding entry—without their appearance being "documented" in narration, at least not initially. The first-person plural voice that speaks in the opening lines of entry 3 is not necessarily conterminous with the narrative voice that refers to "our" universe [*das unsrige*] in entry 2. "How the extraterrestrials had arranged to cast an informative net such that we felt them, although they were looking for us in the wrong reality, we do not know" [*Wie es die Außerirdischen angstellt hatten, obwohl sie uns in der falschen Wirklichkeit suchten, ein informatives Netz auszuwerfen, so daß wir sie spürten, wissen wir nicht*] (31). The rest of entry 3 resonates with earthly issues of geopolitics and security, though perhaps in a different time frame from the one we encountered in entry 2.[181] In entry 3 the

---

180 This presumably distinguishes Kluge's extraterrestrials from ghosts, but an analysis of ghosts in his work would have to be undertaken before such a conclusion could be drawn.
181 This would be difficult to ascertain with certainty, since the time frame suggested in entry 2 is vague at best. We know only that there is a White House, one that has active security person-

time frame given is that of postcommunist Europe, where "a custodial couple and two researchers" occupy "an abandoned institute" in Siberia and something circulates, not as rumor, but as "the certainty" that extraterrestrials have landed on Earth, "the Blue Planet" (31). A competing model of futurity is invoked when we read that "this leftover institute of the great Soviet Union" specialized in the predictability of future tsunamis (31). Most of entry 3, however, consists of marked dialogue between interlocutors who are barely sketched with either minimal or no description. They are not rendered figurally in an embodied sense that readers are invited to picture, but they can be "heard" in dialogue.

This dialogue between unconvincing researchers and an unidentified participant or participants revolves around the invisible "signs" [*Zeichen*] that the tsunami specialists take as indirect evidence within themselves and other believers for the presence of extraterrestrials on earth (31). "Intelligence is contagious. In many places there was such a strong feeling that something supplementary had arrived on earth" [*Intelligenz ist ansteckend. Es wurde an vielen Stellen so empfunden, daß etwas Zusätzliches auf der Welt angekommen sei*], one of the Russians remarks. (32). Here the language of a supplement or *Zusatz* explicitly acquires extraterrestrial contours, which are invisible yet palpable. A skeptical interlocutor (in this case, in dialogical mode) asks whether the extraterrestrials had succeeded in disseminating information about their presence to humans (31). Do those who attest to the presence of extraterrestrials do so "as in a religious fervor" (32)? To this one of the researchers replies in the affirmative: "Yes, as if it came 'from above'" [*Ja, als wäre es 'von oben eingegeben'*] (32). In the language of counterfactuals this rhetorical allusion to the divine residing in heaven or to a secular authority on high is translated into the speaker's proof by indirection that creatures from outer space have landed on the planet and taken up residence "inside us" [*in unserem Innern*].[182] At this juncture the dialogue is interrupted and the voice of narration itself asserts the arrival of extraterrestrials as something factual. "In fact the extraterrestrials had landed in a 'dimension' or 'location' where the physics of gravity and the physics of quanta meet" [*Tatsächlich waren die Außerirdischen in einer 'Dimension' oder 'Örtlichkeit' gelandet, in der sich die Physik der Gravitation und die der Quanten begegnen*] (32). Despite the thematic allusion to a kind of "'location'" or emplacement here, the narrative intervention at this juncture is temporal.

---

nel some time after the 18th century, and that the voice of narration survives the past being narrated.

182 Here we see an obvious link to the quirky question that animated Kluge when he interviewed Yoko Tawada in 1993 (see Introduction for brief remarks on this moment of animation). For the full interview, see Kluge and Tawada.

This is not the voice of the uncertain "we" with which entry 3 begins, and not the voice of a cautiously questioning dialogic interlocutor either, but an assertive voice expressing sovereign command of scientific fact and citing the terms and technologies of quantum physics to do so. "Far beneath the scale of atoms or quarks, matter (or its equivalent from the beginnings, that is to say, in omega time from beginning to end) lingers here in a billionth of a billionth of a billionth of a millimeter. That was REALITY (as the intersection of natural constants)" [*Weit unterhalb der Größe von Atomen oder Quarks verweilt hier die Materie (oder ihr Äquivalent aus den Anfängen, d.h. in Omegazeit vom Anfang bis zum Ende) in einem Milliardstel von einem Milliardstel von einem milliardstel Millimeter. Das war DIE REALITÄT (als Kreuzungspunkt der Naturkonstanten)*] (32). Here we should note two features of this narrative scenario, the first of which is the heightened rhetoric of material miniaturization. The second is that the sovereign voice of factual narration, which interrupts but does not terminate the dialogue with believers, itself speaks as if "from above." Immediately following the researcher's dialogic affirmation that human belief in an extraterrestrial presence comes as if "'from above'," a "sign" that can be taken as evidence, the narrative intervention appears to provide in textual form just such an extraterrestrial sign. In this reading the narrator's voice aligns here with the extraterrestrials making their presence felt indirectly in Siberia through "signs."[183] Toying with naturalized conventions of authoritative third-person narration, this Kluge miniature gives us a seemingly authoritative voice of narration that is anything but affirmative, its positivistic content statement to the contrary. Here we see that, for Kluge, narrative forms of anti-realist realism can at times entail critical "strategies from above" too and not only "strategies from below." Enabled through Kluge's experiments in narrative form, this future-oriented perspective (on perspective as such) will elude us if we fail to consider the cosmic dimensions of his storytelling miniatures and focus only on those "strategies from above" that are destructive in social, political, military, and philosophical terms. In entry 7 we will encounter more miniaturization effects, this time without even the supposed appearance of extraterrestrials but in the service of parallel realities and temporal gateways between them.

---

183 Indirection as a trajectory of perception is not associated with extraterrestrials alone in "Door to Door with an Other Life," as we saw in "Hope at Sunrise," as discussed in the first section of Part One. In that miniature "the rosy dawn" is reflected in the "metallic sheen of medical equipment" in a hospital room that might not have any windows at all (27).

We should pause to note that the "mix-up of scales of time" [*Durcheinander der Zeitskalen*], for Kluge, does not necessarily serve the good.[184] How then does it operate in entry 7, "Social Processes as Narration," where important things happen when it is time for lunch, and where those important things are emphatically tied to narration itself as a social process? As far as we can see, no extraterrestrials visit "the German department at New York University," which marks the ostensible setting for this entry. The text presents a departmental chair wrestling with a widespread dilemma, namely, how to make the study of "German philology" popular with students in the United States. "How can the art of narration of Adam Smith, [David] Ricardo, Karl Marx, and Max Weber be continued under 21st-century conditions?" [*Wie setzt man die Erzählkunst von Adam Smith, Ricardo, Karl Marx und Max Weber unter den Prämissen des 21. Jahrhunderts fort?*] (37). This is the question posed in the voice of narration while the departmental chair opts to get sociologists involved in lecturing in the German department because social scientists tend to experience at least a different "crisis of expression" [*Ausdrucksnot*] (37) from literary scholars. Kluge's text then transitions into an account of a lecture given by Richard Sennett, a renowned sociologist in ordinary time who teaches at NYU and the London School of Economics and authored *The Culture of the New Capitalism* (2006), which is also the title of the NYU lecture featured in entry 7. "After a few sentences he began to tell his tale" [*Er geriet nach wenigen Sätzen ins Erzählen*] (37). Punctuated by several references to Sennett "continuing" his remarks, a verb harking back to the text's earlier question about a 21st-century "art of narration," the ensuing account of Sennett's lecture highlights relations between early and advanced capitalism, economic and military structures of labor and power, and Max Weber's use of "the metaphor of the pyramid" (37) to capture the top-down organizational form of bureaucracy. At this juncture the voice of narration intervenes to observe that most of the students in the audience expected "references to the pharaohs" [*Hinweise auf die Pharaonen*] (37), only to have Sennett explain that Weber's pyramid in the latter's essay on bureaucracy had nothing to do with Egypt. The social organization of metaphor is thus in play in Kluge's text but not at its counterfactual heart. Invoking other sorts of likenesses, Weber and Sennett in this account posit an analogy between hard-shelled insects, on the one hand, and military command structures and industrial organization, on the other. This is

---

184 See for example the dual reference to "a mix-up of scales of time" in "The Gap the Devil Leaves Us" (319, 379) and "Lunar Forces and Ultimate Victory" (292–293). In the latter an "SS-Obersturmführer" discusses "extraterrestrial light" [*außerirdisches Licht*] (292). In another miniature some members of the Nazi SS take up an ancient Roman cult of the "invincible sun" [*Sol invictus*] (see "Door to Door with an Other Life" 23).

where Sennett parts ways with Weber for reasons having to do with time. If hardshelled insects "must explode their static shell from time to time in order to grow" [*müssen von Zeit zu Zeit das statische Gehäuse sprengen, wenn sie wachsen sollen*] (38), Weber's mistake, according to Sennett, was to assume that hierarchies process "'commands from above'" in a static model of time. Alive with the dynamic participation of those in the lower echelons of hierarchy, hierarchical structures are constantly on the move instead (38). This suggests that they are also moving in time and—by dint of labor on social material—converting "'commands from above'" into something else. This also pertains to conversion as an operative form of narrative futurity in Kluge's cosmic miniatures, one that hinges on a sense of futurity that is not consistently deferred.

Entry 7 undergoes a temporal shift at this point when two literary scholars in the audience begin commenting on Sennett's lecture to each other in whispered tones [*tuschelten*], thus creating a parallel strand of activity that diverges from the lecture without "disturbing" it [*den Vortrag nicht störten*]. Sennett clearly stands at the top of the pyramid in this staging of academic hierarchies as he instructs the assembled audience how to read both a canonical figure of sociology such as Weber and the social reality of organized power. Kluge's text bestows greater interest but far less authority on the unnamed "philologists" in the audience, one specializing in French and the other in German literature. They appear both serious and clown-like in *sotto voce* dialogue as they find the sociologist's remarks "highly interesting" though "largely unintelligible" [*zum großen Teil unverständlich*] (38). Wondering to each other why literary authors other than Robert Musil and possibly Karl Aloys Schenzinger never seem to write about the decision-making processes that interest sociologists, the two colleagues agree: "If we had better words for it, we could deal with it" [*Wenn man bessere Worte dafür hätte, könnte man damit umgehen*] (39).[185] As Sennett lectures on, the whispered commentary of the two confused professors demonstrates involvement in hierarchical structures in exactly the dynamic sense that Sennett has just described. Although they barely have any words at all for what they mean, their verbal exchange represents a necessary intervention in Kluge's text, not because it exemplifies Sennett's case for hierarchical participation from below, but because the unauthorized exchange breaks away in narrative time from the hierarchical

---

185 Musil is mentioned by name in entry 7, while Schenzinger, the author of a 1937 novel set in colonial India about the German paint industry (*Anilin*), is not. Schenzinger, whose political sympathies lay with the Nazis, also authored a well-known propaganda novel about the Hitler Youth in 1932 (*Der Hitlerjunge Quex*). The earlier Schenzinger publication is not mentioned.

structure in which it participates. This is an intervention, however, that is immediately subject—in textual narration—to proliferating deviations.

Entry 7 in "We Fortunate Children of the First Globalization" switches here from marked dialogue to third-person narration, the voice of which reveals that the scholar of French literature understands a conversational remark (about the task of the literary author) in an illustrative vein.[186] Readers of the Kluge text at this point encounter two diverging paths of narration, one leading us into footnote 6 and the other continuing the account of the Sennett lecture from an unaccustomed temporal perspective. Typographically shrunken in size, the footnote is initially focalized through the scholar of German literature, who regards the relationship between literature and sociology as a disciplinary division of labor. Yet the division he posits between literary text and social content is immediately undermined by the perceptual simile invoked to liken the organization of disciplines to tunneling as "the breaking through of walls" [wie die Mauerdurchbrüche] (39). This "breaking through of walls" allowed victims of air raids to pass from one basement shelter to a neighboring cellar. Then the note concludes with a perspectival shift that belies its descriptive register: "The marked places on the wall were temporarily blocked and could be pushed in by hand" [Die markierten Stellen in der Wand waren provisorisch verschlossen und konnten von Hand eingedrückt werden] (39). While reference to World War II is not explicitly given in this piece, the dedication of the footnote to the professor of German literature and his disciplinary tradition, and Kluge's own involvement in writing about the Allied bombings of German cities, seem suddenly to conjure the 1940s as a temporality of endangerment (and the millennial turn around 2000 too, as a period of much public talk about wartime air raids on German cities) in the midst of the NYU lecture hall. The literal instantiation of a "tunneling" motif yields to a temporal "tunneling" between "parallel worlds" by virtue of this footnote, which itself appears as a "marked" place on a two-dimensional surface.[187] Rainer Stollmann alerts us to Kluge's punning on a "'quantum mechanics' [...] of history" in Learning Processes with a Deadly Outcome, where quanta can also be taken to mean "feet" ("Schwarzer Krieg, endlos" 365). Regarding the story collection explicitly situated "door to door with an other life," one might speak of a quantum narrative investment in futurity instead. However, the tunneling footnote in the lecture hall story functions in

---

[186] One of the interlocutors opines that "the author" must go to the seat of power and conduct research *in situ*, and the narrator explains that the professor of French literature was thinking of literate 12th-century messengers in that role.

[187] See David L. Pike for insights into the importance of tunneling motifs in cold war culture and a "flood" of representations of tunnels in German popular culture after 1989 (76 et passim).

this temporal mode only to the extent that the narrative voice comes to articulate what we might—with some hesitation—call a kind of perspective without focalization.

Hesitation is warranted because this would immediately have to be radically distinguished from what Gérard Genette in *Narrative Discourse* famously termed "zero focalization" (189), a seminal category in classical narratology that Monika Fludernik criticized twenty years ago as an illogical concept of "authorial aperspectivism" (*Towards a 'Natural' Narratology* 345; see also Fludernik, *An Introduction to Narratology* 153). From a broad range of critical standpoints, postclassical narratologists today continue to debate the usefulness and limits of focalization as a category, including the "zero focalization" that Genette associated with narrative omniscience (see for example Henrik Skov Nielsen, "Naturalizing and Unnaturalizing Reading Strategies: Focalization Revisited," and David Herman, "Beyond Voice and Vision: Cognitive Grammar and Focalization Theory"). For present purposes, it is important to note that the temporal perspective without focalization that Kluge's miniature makes available to us in the tunneling footnote is neither aperspectival nor predicated on any categorical relationship to logic, nature, visual orientation, or human form. The tunneling perspective here instead opens up a dimensional portal in time. The polysemy of the German word *Perspektive* is worth recalling here, since the more familiar visual perspective that Genette stressed in defining focalization also has a temporal double allowing for future life or "future chance." Adorno may be thinking of this second meaning too when he writes in "The Essay as Form" against the empirical presumptions of what he calls "mere 'perspectives'" (18). If the marked place on a two-dimensional surface is rendered accessible by "foot" rather than hand here, the foot or quantum of futurity in this instance is a function of a temporal perspective rather than beleaguered characters or anthropomorphic narrators in action.

This narrative perspective might be considered other-worldly but not entirely off-planet, since something not of this world has nonetheless entered it through the text's narration. Again we are reminded of Karsten Witte's fortuitous observation in 1990 that what may appear as science fiction in Kluge's prose must always be understood as social fictions of reality too. Kant's extraterrestrials are distant relations here (see discussion of Kant's extraterrestrials and Kluge's deviation from them in the Introduction). Footnote 6 becomes in one literal sense a "dimensional portal" from below—in contradistinction to dictates or bombs "'from above'"—but the access it provides to an other life simultaneously renders it a dimensional portal from above as well. This is a multidirectional portal through which a futurity of survival can be indirectly felt but not figurally presented or anthropomorphically embodied. In structural terms this miniaturized portal from below recalls for readers the feeling of encountering extraterrestrials in entries 2 and 3. Not all footnotes function in this way for Kluge, but this particular one offers a microscopic lens on the reading of differential temporalities in "Door to Door to Door with an Other Life." (Kaleidoscopic modes of narrative connectivity in relation to the future sense will be discussed in Part Two.) In my reading the "tunneling" at issue in entry 7 is partly a matter of montage (defined in Kluge's terms as a contrastive moment "between two perspectives," and just as crucially one of scale (as a dimensional coordinate). The movement involved is not from one dangerous place in time to a safe one or from a destructive past to a redemptive future, but a form of time travel in necessarily parallel or entwined worlds. If these worlds are necessarily entwined, they do not necessarily yield counter-histories in any positivist or merely imagined sense, though they do yield opportunities for future life. This future life is incrementally accessible to experience through Kluge's experiments in narrative form.

The second divergent path of narration mentioned above hews close to the concern for raw survival and comes in the main text when we read that Sennett's lecture runs into lunch time [*die Mittagszeit*] (39) by well over an hour. "At this point in time the cafeterias had no more nourishment to offer these desiccated bodies" [*Die Kantinen lieferten den ausgedörrten Körpern zu diesem Zeitpunkt keine Nahrung mehr*] (39). This is an extreme formulation for the effect of even a bad lecture on an academic audience, and the text gives us no reason to think that Sennett's presentation falls into this category. The threat of desiccation and the lack of nourishment are crucial, however, precisely as harboring the threat of destruction of human life. The entwined "parallel worlds" with which the book begins are defined by "A.K." as realities that destroy human beings and human life that denies such destruction.[188] Shifting from the content of Sennett's talk or even the whispered participation of the professors in the audience to a desperate need for sustenance, the voice of narration gives us the scene of the academic lecture as a staging ground for such parallel worlds. This disembodied voice likens the lecture to a literary genre beset by circumstances that deprive the instantiation of the form of a key aesthetic element—"pleasure" [*Genuß*] (39)—by threatening to destroy the very life of the audience members. Significantly this threat comes at the intersection of two different markings of time—the noon hour or "die Mittagszeit" (39)—and the hungry students either deny the reality that threatens their life force or defy the authorities that issue temporal "'commands from above'" by reporting to the departmental chair

---

[188] For some figures, there can be a fine line in these Kluge texts between denying and defying destructive realities.

that they found the lecture quite "'stimulating'" ['*anregend*'] and would love more history lectures about story-telling in the literature department (or more precisely: "*auch noch historische Vorlesungen über Geschichte*") (40). Entry 7 comes full circle here, since the enthusiastic response of thoughtful students hungry for more and different life would seem to resolve the German department's initial dilemma. Two strands of critical pedagogy come together in this miniature: a thematic motif of higher education as an institutional hierarchy, on the one hand, and a narrative apprenticeship in exercising the future sense, on the other. Yet the students do not quite have the last word. Constantly curling one dimension of temporal reality into another, entry 7 concludes its dizzying foray into multiple parallel worlds with an un-authorized sentence fragment: "Staging of Narration When Historical Processes Are Involved" [*Dramaturgie der Erzählung geschichtlicher Prozesse*] (40). Our disembodied narrator is perhaps out in search of some extraterrestrial lunch as entry 7 appears to describe its own formal trajectory. If Sennett's university lecture as staged here becomes a "marked" place where performance and narrative converge on the pages of Kluge's book, this piece requires no extraterrestrials for invisible "historical processes" to become sensible. "Door to door with an other life," they do so in parallel realities repeatedly converging and diverging in time. This alone will not guarantee a just society or a redemptive future, but Kluge's cosmic exercises in futurity require extraordinary time travel with or without visitors from other worlds. In this sense readers of Kluge's quirky but hardly idiosyncratic miniatures for the 21st century already are the extraterrestrials that Kant still imagined elsewhere. Kluge's cosmic miniatures and experiential horizons thus constitute animated interventions in the German tradition of critical theory and contemporary life alike, through narrative cultivation of the future sense.

Part Two
Global Miniatures and Marxist Horizons: Conjunctions in Narrative Time

1 Permanent Revolution

While Adorno's micrological orientation to counterfactual hope and the utopian dimension turns on the threat of "permanent catastrophe," Kluge writes his experimental miniatures in this vein too but—taking recourse to a contested Marxist term—explicitly foregrounds storytelling as "permanent revolution," with narration consisting, as he put it in his first Frankfurt poetics lecture in June 2012, "of temporal perspectives" ("Theory of Storytelling"). Part Two of *Cosmic Miniatures* asks what it might mean to consider permanent revolution, in this particular narrative sense, as something more than failure even in the generative critical sense that Kluge inherits from Adorno (see Geulen, Geuss, Pavsek, Erdle, and others as discussed in Part One for additional remarks on this well documented legacy of resistant "failure"). As argued in Part One, Kluge adapts from Adorno and Benjamin a core commitment to disjunctive temporalities as both a mark of social alienation and a promise of transformative liberation, while his writing also insists, in micrological kinship with Adorno, on conjunctive features of time as well as form. Kluge's ubiquitous and paradoxical trope of "relationality" or *Zusammenhang* would make no sense whatsoever without them, and neither would his storytelling. Yet as we have also seen in the discussion of Kluge's cosmic miniatures in Part One, the simultaneously disjunctive and conjunctive temporalities in play there are not differentially entangled in a merely telluric sense of future, past, and present. These disjunctive conjunctions in earthly time—and the narrative experiments in perspective and voice that Kluge uses to enliven them—are also vitally oriented to off-worldly temporalities of utopian dimension. The experimental relationality of human time and cosmic time in Kluge's 21st-century miniatures thus exceeds (in structural and not simply chronological terms)—even as it also bespeaks—the historical anachronism that underwrites Negt and Kluge's concept of a "proletarian public sphere" in 1972 (see *Öffentlichkeit und Erfahrung* or *Public Sphere and Experience* for the English translation, which first appeared two decades later).

At the time these Marxist social theorists countered Jürgen Habermas's seminal account of the "bourgeois public sphere" (*Strukturwandel der Öffentlichkeit* [1962] or *The Structural Transformation of the Public Sphere* [1989 in English translation]) by taking emphatic recourse to a critical language of time. They chose their distinctive descriptor *proletarian* only in part because the word "unambiguously" [*unzweideutig*] denotes class struggle and "the history of the emancipation of the working class" (*Public Sphere and Experience* xliv; *Öffentlichkeit und Erfahrung* 9).[1] Beyond this, they wrote:

> The other reason we have chosen this concept is because it is not at present susceptible to absorption into the ruling discourse [*das System der herrschenden Sprachregelungen*]; it resists being categorized into the symbolic spectrum of the bourgeois public sphere, which so readily accommodates the concept of a critical public sphere. There are objective reasons for this. Fifty years of counterrevolution and restoration have exhausted the labor movement's linguistic resources [*Ausdrucksmöglichkeiten*]. The word proletarian has, in the Federal Republic, taken on an attenuated, indeed an anachronistic sense. Yet the real conditions it denotes belong to the present, and there is no other word for them. (xliv–xlv)

> [*Wir wählen diesen Begriff auch deshalb, weil er in das System der herrschenden Sprachregelungen zur Zeit nicht integrierbar ist; er sperrt sich gegen die Einordnung in das Symbolspektrum der bürgerlichen Öffentlichkeit, in das der Begriff kritische Öffentlichkeit ohne weiteres paßt. Das hat objektive Gründe. Fünfzig Jahre Konterrevolution und Restauration haben die sprachlichen Ausdrucksmöglichkeiten der Arbeiterbewegung ausgetrocknet. Das Wort proletarisch hat in der Bundesrepublik eine verengte, ja anachronistische Bedeutung erhalten. Die wirklichen Verhältnisse, die es bezeichnet, sind aber gegenwärtig und besitzen keinen anderen Ausdruck.*] (9)

While the published English translation tells us, and accurately so, that the word "proletarian" is not susceptible to ideological discursive absorption "at present" [*zur Zeit*], one could conceivably also translate Negt and Kluge's German phrasing to signal ambiguously instead that their key term cannot be "integrated into the system of dominant regulations of language on time," with *zur Zeit* translated in the second instance as about or "on time." How we speak about language on time is in this reading also tied to the social experience of time in both empirical and metaphysical registers, which, as discussed in Part One, are for Kluge as well as Adorno inextricably entwined.

Part Two turns to what I propose, for three primary reasons, to call Kluge's "global miniatures" for the 21st century. First, in these experimental narratives, the scale of human relations to something that exceeds anthropocentric measure would at first glance appear to be pointedly earthly, geopolitical, and even plan-

---

[1] The published English translation at this juncture omits Negt and Kluge's references to both an unambiguous mode of signification and a conflictual "front" [*Frontstellung*] associated with class struggle. For overarching contrasts between *Public Sphere and Experience* and Negt and Kluge's later volume *History and Obstinacy* with regard to temporality and class struggle, see Fore's reflections under the rubric "The Anthropology of Capital" in his Introduction to *History and Obstinacy* (15–22).

etary, rather than cosmic in the both off-worldly and this-worldly sense discussed in Part One.² This includes global miniatures for example on the wars against Iraq launched by the United States in 1990–1991 and 2003, German scholars in post-revolutionary Iran, the European Union and a would-be immigrant's possible deportation to Dakar, the triple Fukushima disaster in Japan in 2011, various aspects of the French Revolution, Russian history, and contemporary China, and a Muslim scientist from Bangladesh (e.g. "Die Schnellsten werden die Letzten sein" ["The Fastest Will Be the Last"], "Ein deutscher Gelehrter in Persien" ["A German Scholar in Persia"], "Wie fängt man an der EU-Grenze das Böse ab?" ["How Does One Nab Evil at the EU-Border?"], "Tempus, Aevum, Aeternitas" ["Time, Age, Eternity"], and countless others scattered throughout "Door to Door with an Other Life," "The Gap the Devil Leaves Us," "The Fifth Book," "Kong's Great Hour," and more. Second, Kluge's "global" miniatures draw considerable breath (and breadth) from heightened degrees of earthbound connectivity widely associated with global finance capital, changing labor markets, digital media networks, and the geographic reach of contemporary globalization, even though Kluge's miniatures titled "We Fortunate Children of the First Globalization" date the phenomenon of globalization to 630 million years ago, long before the dawn of humankind ("Door to Door with an Other Life" 29). Readers will find all of these contemporary associations combined, for example, in a miniature titled "Die Revolution ist ein Lebewesen voller Überraschungen" ["The Revolution is an Organism Full of Surprises"], where two secret intelligence agents from China and Denmark discuss Berlin, Beijing, Cairo, Dresden, Munich, Tunis, and the relational status of commodities today ("The Fifth Book" 427–429). Third, Kluge's global miniatures also appear to underscore spatial connectivity rather than temporal variants by virtue of so many thematic appeals to global networks and the endangered planet we call Earth, as in one

---

2 The editors of *The Routledge Companion to Experimental Literature* define experimental literature in part as extending "the boundaries of knowledge" in competition with the "prestige" that modernity has "ceded [...] to science" (Joe Bray, Alison Gibbons, and Brian McHale 2). Along with Jan Alber, Henrik Skov Nielsen, and Brian Richardson, they consider "unnatural narratives" one "subset of experimental literature" (12), and the Routledge volume overall wants to restore a vibrant sense of "edginess, renovation and aesthetic adventure" to the term "experimental" as applied to literature (3). As Part One of the present volume has demonstrated, Kluge's literary miniatures in the tradition of critical theory resonate with narratological approaches to experimental literature and unnatural narrative in many respects, while also posing certain challenges to them in others. Kluge's sustained interests in scientific fields such as astrophysics, geology, quantum physics, mechanical engineering, and evolutionary biology would for example also unsettle the oppositional relationship that Bray, Gibbons, and McHale seem to posit between science and literature.

extended section of "Kong's Great Hour" devoted to Pangea (565–654), or in a storytelling section from "The Fifth Book" linking places as far afield as Australia, Uzbekistan, Istanbul, Haiti, Fukushima, Bad Säckingen, Chernobyl, Washington, Sparta, and the Schönefeld airport in Berlin, all under the rubric of real or possible catastrophe (see the twenty miniatures contained in the section "Uralte Freunde der Kernkraft" ["Age-Old Friends of Nuclear Power"] 49–68). In German one might be tempted to speak here of not *Sterndeutung* but *Ferndeutung*—not of reading the "stars" but of reading "distance" of a different spatial magnitude in relation to that which is near.

These global motifs in Kluge's storytelling prose for the 21st century might moreover, at least at first glance, seem entirely compatible with David Harvey's massively influential concept of "time-space compression" as indexing a conjoined effect of capitalist economies, communications technologies, environmental networks, and far-flung social relations associated with the millennial turn and globalization itself (see also Alexis Radisoglou 3–5). In 1990 this critical geographer famously remarked:

> As space appears to shrink to a 'global village' of telecommunications and a 'spaceship earth' of economic and ecological interdependencies—to use just two familiar and everyday images—and as time horizons shorten to the point where the present is all there is (the world of the schizophrenic), so we have to learn how to cope with an overwhelming sense of *compression* of our spatial and temporal worlds. (*The Condition of Postmodernity* 240)

Elsewhere Harvey elaborates on time-space compression as a historically evolving keystone of both "contemporary globalization" since the 1970s and Marx's theoretical legacy of conceptualizing capitalist accumulation and class struggle (see especially *Spaces of Hope* 53–72 as well as *Spaces of Capital* 122–124 and 237–266). On all counts, Harvey privileges space over time, with the "production of space" (*Spaces of Hope* 54) serving, for Harvey, as the dual-purpose key to understanding contemporary globalization and to unlocking what Marx meant when he wrote in the *Grundrisse* ["Foundations"] that capital always seeks at once to "'conquer the whole earth for its market'" and, with increasing speed, "'to annihilate this space with time'" (*Spaces of Capital* 244). Invoking both *The Communist Manifesto* and Kristin Ross's 1988 study of the Paris Commune, Harvey points to what he sees as an underlying problem in Marxist theory well into the 20th century.

> For while it is clear that the bourgeoisie's quest for class domination was (and is) a very geographical affair, the almost immediate reversion in the text [of the *Manifesto*] to a purely temporal and diachronic account is striking. It is hard, it seems, to be dialectical about space, leaving many Marxists in practice to follow Feuerbach in thinking that time is

"the privileged category of the dialectician, because it excludes and subordinates where space tolerates and coordinates." (*Spaces of Hope* 55)

To return to Kluge's literary experiments with globalization, which are not Harvey's concern, we must nonetheless pose one crucial question.

What if many of Kluge's global miniatures are also cosmic miniatures in disguise, and not even overly belabored disguise at that? Kluge is after all jointly committed to dialectics and dialogue in a Marxist tradition of disjunctive temporalities that he inherits from the likes of Benjamin and above all Adorno, and as already noted, he claims to follow the latter "faithfully" even as he deviates from him as well. There are conjunctive constellations here but no "compression" in the spatio-temporal sense that Harvey associates with globalization as a capitalist phenomenon. That is to say, if Kluge privileges time rather than space in his experimental miniatures for the 21st century—even in those we might rightly call "global"—these scalar experiments in narrative temporalities do not serve to lock globalization in place but to challenge its stranglehold on the dimension of time. In this regard his writing resists what Natalie Melas in other contexts has aptly diagnosed as a "terminal presentism" evident across the disciplines in even critical, postcolonial, and comparative work on the extensive contemporary reach of globalization as a form of capitalism ("Comparative Non-Contemporaneities" 73). Like his cosmic miniatures, Kluge's global miniatures also pivot, I shall suggest in Part Two, on narrative uses of futurity as experiential portals in time, and in this sense his experimental labors on telluric motifs share a greater affinity with what postcolonial theorist Gayatri Chakravorty Spivak envisions as transcendental "planetarity" in pointed critical challenge to capitalist globalization. "I propose the planet to overwrite the globe," she writes, for "[g]lobalization is the imposition of the same system of exchange everywhere" (*Death of a Discipline* 72–73). For Spivak writing in 2003, planetarity does not denote the planet Earth in an empirical sense but connotes instead a human intention "toward the other" and the human "effort required to figure the (im)possibility of this underived intuition" of what we are not yet but imagine we could or ought to be "as planetary subjects rather than global agents" (*Death of a Discipline* 72–73). Elaborating on this "imperative to re-imagine the planet" in 2012 (see Chapter Sixteen of *An Aesthetic Education in the Age of Globalization*), Spivak sounds very Kantian when she tells us that "[p]lanetary imaginings locate the imperative in a galactic and para-galactic alterity" (340)—and remarkably close to Kluge when she speaks of planetarity as "a catachresis" indexing "an experience of the impossible" (341).³

Kluge's global miniatures in my reading go even farther in their critical reach and anti-realist realism than either Harvey's account of contemporary globalization or Spivak's summons to planetary imperatives, precisely because Kluge's this-worldly and off-worldly labors on globalization and planetarity alike do more than index "something that stands outside the world and nevertheless extends into it" (to recall Philipp Weber's phrasing in reference to Benjamin's sidereal *Denkbilder*, as discussed in Part One).⁴ Kluge's narrative experiments with temporal perspectives in particular, as we have already seen with his cosmic miniatures, exceed the mere indexing of possibility by exercising the future sense and thus making futurity accessible to experience, however incrementally, through the legibility of form.⁵ How does this work in Kluge's global miniatures,

---

3 Some scholars see Kluge as aligned with Kant on other grounds. See for example Alexis Radisoglou on Kluge's cosmopolitanism (58–59) and Langston on Kluge's "Kantian dialogues" ("Toward an Ethics of Fantasy").

4 One might also contrast Kluge's narrative approach to globalization with Peter Sloterdijk's philosophical account of globalization in *In the World Interior of Capital*, especially with regard to temporality. For Brian Elliott, who juxtaposes Sloterdijk and Benjamin, "Sloterdijk's world interior of capital is a claustrophobic hothouse of irascible boredom" ("Revolution, History and Time" 111).

5 For other scholarly approaches to Kluge and contemporary globalization, see especially Chapter 3, "Democratic Poetics for the 21st Century: Globalization, Globality, and the Politics of Planetarity in the Later Fiction of Alexander Kluge," in Radisoglou's Columbia University dissertation in 2015. See also Miller, who remarks a "shift in focus" to "modernity's distinct historical trajectories in global comparison" in Negt and Kluge's English-language version of *Geschichte und Eigensinn*, published as *History and Obstinacy* in 2014 (Miller, "*Eigensinn* in Transit" 84–85, 101). Radisoglou notes that "[i]t is no exaggeration to say that the field of narration of Kluge's stories spans the entire globe" (1), a finding he then analyzes, drawing especially on Spivak as well as Rancière, in terms of "a 'politics of planetarity' in Kluge's later fiction" (33). As Radisoglou puts it: "It is precisely in a *heterological* relationship that planet and globe stand in Kluge's stories: the political aesthetics of planetarity disrupts and reconfigures the very distribution of the sensible that underlies the condition of globality" (33). For Radisoglou, who also stresses the importance of time for Kluge's approach to space, Kluge's aesthetics of planetarity is one of pointedly "chronotopic maximalism" (2, 19). Radisoglou casts this as a "radical counter-model" to "the reduction of the world to the globe," and planetary serves in his view as "an epistemological project," that is to say, "as an inquiry into the *conditions of possibility* for transformative practice" (34). Even though Radisoglou rightly stresses that Kluge rejects "the notion that politics is a mere art of the possible" (16), Radisoglou's analysis of Kluge's political aesthetic remains very much beholden to an epistemology of possibility, which Radisoglou considers politically transformative on epistemological grounds alone. By contrast, the present book argues that Kluge's narrative cultivation of the future sense as an experiential phenomenon in literary form is more than a merely epistemological exercise. *Cosmic Miniatures* furthermore aims to account for the

where so many global and earthly motifs at first blush seem so emphatically geocentric? To answer this question, we will need to consider that cosmic motifs also permeate many of these global miniatures, some more obviously than others. Furthermore, some of these global miniatures rise to the status of cosmic miniatures in ways that are historically acute for the early 21st century, though not empirically confined to the present. This is important because Kluge's micrological writing on worldly affairs, parallel worlds, and geocentric shifts at the crossroads of human catastrophe and planetary repair speaks to the heightened, not lessened relevance of German critical theory in the age of the Anthropocene.[6] Ador-

---

actual conversion in Kluge's prose, by narrative means, from empirical experience of historical catastrophe to metaphysical experience of counterfactual futurity as itself a social fact. Considering Kluge's mode of articulation as "contingent," "combinatory," or "connective" (see Radisoglou 41, 45, et passim, for example) does not go far enough to explain this formal relationship between Kluge's global miniatures and contemporary globalization. For additional commentary and other emphases regarding Kluge and globalization, see also Harro Müller, who notes both an increasing "globalization of the narrative field" in Kluge's prose and "great continuities" in his stylistic approach to anti-realist realism despite this thematic variation. As Müller astutely observes, these continuities and variations alike are "in the widest sense about orientation" ("Die authentische Methode" 112).

[6] This term has circulated with increasing frequency across the disciplines since 2000, when atmospheric chemist Paul Crutzen and aquatic biologist Eugene Stoermer proposed using it "for the current geological epoch" in order to "emphasize the central role of mankind in geology and ecology" on planet Earth (17). They date the beginning of the Anthropocene, partly in relation to the industrial revolution, to "the latter part of the 18th century" (17). Arguing in 2000 that, barring "major catastrophes," humankind is likely to "remain a major geological force for many millions of years to come," they concluded: "To develop a world-wide accepted strategy leading to sustainability of ecosystems against human induced stresses will be one of the great future tasks of mankind, requiring intensive research efforts and wise application of the knowledge thus acquired in the noösphere, better known as knowledge or information society" (18). The term Anthropocene has also been widely discussed in environmental studies, science and technology studies, media studies, and cultural philosophy, including by such notables as Bruno Latour and Jussi Parikka. For his geologically based approach to the deep history of media, Parikka additionally coins the term "the Anthrobscene" to underscore "what we knew but perhaps shied away from acting on: a horrific human-caused drive toward a sixth mass extinction of species" (6) in a "story of materials, metals, chemistry, and waste" (5). For Latour writing in 2011, "what we are now witnessing is anthropo*morphism* on steroids" ("Waiting for Gaia" 22), and the profound "disconnect" he describes between the limited parameters of human consciousness and the global magnitude of planetary effects we help to cause (whether we take responsibility for them or not) becomes, for Latour, a problematics of scale. "So what do we do when we are tackling a question that is simply too big for us? If not denial, then what?" (25). We might pause to note that the scalar "disconnect" Latour identifies between human perception and planetary endangerment in the 21st century sounds a bit like the alienation between human beings and the "starry sky" of the cosmos above that Lukács associated with the "transcendental homeless-

no's legacy pulsates vibrantly in Kluge's hands even as it is also necessarily historically transformed. To begin to understand, albeit with no pretense of comprehensiveness, how Kluge conjoins the cosmic and the global in his experimental miniatures for the 21st century, we will also need to bear in mind that these social fictions, as Karsten Witte would call them, work on both "1989" as a transnational signal event in real time and Kluge's "non-linear" narration as a celebrated marker of his unnatural writing style. We shall return to these two key nodes. For now, it is important to note that Kluge's narrative uses of futurity will shed light on both of them in ways that are not solely disjunctive but intensely conjunctive too.

On a thematic level alone, global and cosmic motifs are frequently interlaced in Kluge's 21st-century miniatures. The Muslim scientist from Bangladesh mentioned above is for example an astrophysicist ("The Gap the Devil Leaves Us" 325) in a longer section of miniatures titled "Stories of the Cosmos" (319–435). The express absence of a "'rosy-fingered dawn'" in war-torn Iraq in one miniature links the heliotropic poetics of Homer's *Odyssey*, the local devastation of

---

ness" of modernity. For Latour though, it is not so much the cosmos but the globe that we must struggle to engage. At the same time, as he is quick to point out: "It is a tenet of science studies and actor network theory that one should never suppose that differences of scale already exist but instead always look for how scale is produced" (25). This is beginning to sound a lot like Kluge, even more so when Latour writes: "things are not ordered by size as if they were boxes inside boxes. Rather they are ordered by connectedness as if they were nodes connected to other nodes" (25). Latour's emphasis on mediated acts of connectivity, composition, and "the assemblage of contradictory entities" (26 et passim) is also his point of entry for seeing Gaia—not merely as an empirically extant planet—but as both "a *scientific* concept" and a political project (29–31). For Latour, Gaia is "the perfect trickster," precisely because Gaia is characterized by a "total lack of unity" and "*continuity*" (30). What Latour begins by diagnosing as a historic "disconnect" is then celebrated in terms of "*politically* interesting" disjunctions (30). Kluge's "Pangea" is certainly a trickster too, though in good dialectical fashion hardly a "perfect" one. More to the point for present purposes, Kluge arguably differs from Latour in two key ways. First, in his experimental miniatures, which are among other things most certainly experiments in scale (see also Negt and Kluge's theoretical reflections on "relations of measure" in "Politics as Relations of Measure"), conjunctive constellations in time and form can be politically as interesting as figural disjunctions. Second, Kluge's narrative exercises in cultivating the future sense, in the spirit of his anti-realist realism, are always oriented to utopian dimensions, for which Latour's model of discontinuous composition does not account and expresses no interest. For especially insightful remarks on Negt and Kluge's co-authored "Politics as Relations of Measure" in critical relation to Hegel's ideas of "measure" and "essence," 1989 and "the dissolution of the high-contrast ideological binarisms of the Cold War," philosophies of latent and "emergent properties," and Marxist traditions of conceptualizing revolution as a "practice" and a "process" rather than "a radical historical caesura," see Fore's introduction to Negt and Kluge's *History and Obstinacy* (55–61).

contemporary global warfare, and a kind of "happiness" or "luck" one can speak of "when on this morning no shots are fired" [*man kann von Glück sagen, wenn an diesem Morgen nicht geschossen wird*] ("Door to Door with an Other Life" 24).[7] In "Kong's Great Hour" one miniature about the Russian Academy of Sciences, exploration in outer space, and Alexander Pushkin's personal ties to slavery and North Africa is titled "Nachricht an Außerirdische" ["News Item for Extraterrestrials"] (585). And more subtly, the opening entry in Kluge's "Chronik von Pangäa bis heute" ["Chronicle of Pangea till Today"] features a paleoclimatologist musing on the future-oriented movement of tectonic plates and the proper image for expressing this. That "reminds me of ships," he ponders before refining his poetic vision: "But then it would be ships trapped in icebergs or (that's an even better image) 'inclusions' in the rock that are moving closer toward the future, where we, the detecting agents, are waiting for them" [*Doch wären es dann in Eisbergen gefangene Schiffe oder (das ist ein noch besseres Bild) 'Einschlüsse' im Fels, die sich auf die Zukunft zu bewegen, wo wir, die Detektoren, auf sie warten*] (567). Trapped in an icy crag, this geological potential for future-oriented movement may also remind us intermittently of Benjamin's "secret index" of history or even what Adorno considered the "temporal core" of aesthetic form and social content (as discussed in Part One). Such temporal "inclusions" of history, latency, potential, and off-worldly futurity are also afoot in Kluge's global miniatures for the 21st century, but like the paleoclimatologist that appears in this one, these miniatures too are searching for "expressive possibilities" [*Ausdrucksmöglichkeiten*] that could rise to the lived circumstances they engage and the transformative challenges they pose. This involves future-making through narrative form in ways and degrees that neither Benjamin nor Adorno practiced, because they encountered structurally different times, which demanded different things of them. This socio-historical distinction is undoubtedly oversimplified but may nonetheless remind us in turn of Marx's own "epistemological grounds" for refusing to paint or accept too complete a portrait of "future society," since only "proletarian" inhabitants of that society would be historically positioned to articulate its shape (see Roger Paden 78, 89, who discusses a range of views on this contentious point in Marxist theory). To the degree that Kluge's increasingly global and geocentric miniatures are riddled with "inclusions" of sidereal motifs in and for the 21st century, this seemingly Earth-bound writing also invites us to ponder how futurity (beyond mere themes alone) becomes experientially acces-

---

[7] The German word *Glück* means both happiness and luck, a conjunction that animates Kluge's various projects in conceptually substantive ways.

sible as "something that stands outside the world and nevertheless extends into it" (to recall Philipp Weber on Benjamin).

"Global" and "cosmic" are clearly not mutually exclusive tropes in Kluge's experimental prose. See for example the miniature "Neue Erscheinungsform des Großen Drachen" ["New Manifestation Form of the Great Dragon"], which begins: "We Chinese were proud of the 'rising sun'" [*Stolz waren wir Chinesen auf die 'aufgehende Sonne'*], in reference to the Cultural Revolution ("Door to Door with an Other Life" 16). While one may readily find examples of global miniatures that are not explicitly tied to narratives of revolutionary horizons in communist histories or "proletarian" temporalities as Negt and Kluge conceive them, I shall focus in the remainder of Part Two on a subset of global miniatures that do revolve around conjunctions of contemporary globalization and revolutionary horizons in a Marxist vein in the aftermath of 1989. I do so precisely because Kluge, unlike many other leftist commentators at that multifaceted historic juncture, associated renewed hope with 1989 and 1991 respectively in his prefaces to "The Gap the Devil Leaves Us" (2003) and the book's abbreviated English translation, *The Devil's Blind Spot* (2004), without any obeisance to the ostensible triumph of capital or neoliberal "end of history" (Francis Fukuyama).[8] What kinds of revolutionary hopes and Marxist horizons do his global miniatures of communism entail, and how do they configure futurity as narrative form? Here too reading Kluge will prove to be, not a matter of interpreting the meaning of signs but rather an exercise in using futurity in particular ways. Whether the specter of 1989 connotes national unification in Germany and the downfall of state communism in Europe—as in "Waschleppas Atlas der Dampflokomotiven" ["Waschleppa's Atlas of Steam Locomotives"] in "Door to Door with an Other Life" (426–427)—or popular uprising and government suppression on Tiananmen Square in Beijing—as in "The Revolution is an Organism Full of Surprises" in "The Fifth Book" (427–429)—it is important to recall, as Fore reminds us more generally in his introduction to *History and Obstinacy*, that Kluge and Negt draw on Marxist traditions of conceptualizing revolution as a "practice" and a "process" (60). Historic dates, even those associated with revolutionary or communist horizons, signal no "punctual break with the past" for these theorists (58), no discrete dramatic events (see also Harro Müller, *Geschichte zwischen Kairos*

---

8 For sociological insights into conceptual relations between globalization and utopia with specific reference to "the anti-communist revolutions of 1989," see Larry Ray, who notes that "[t]he end of the Cold War and especially the Fall of the Berlin Wall were events symbiotically linked to globalization" (101, 103). For Ray, "although often pegged as 'anti-utopian' there were utopian moments to 1989 that reflected wider globalization utopias" across the political spectrum (103 et passim).

und Katastrophe 98, 112), but temporal thresholds of high-stakes connectivity. Revolution is a surprising "organism," we read in one global miniature from Kluge's "The Fifth Book," for revolution "never appears where we expect it" [*Nie tritt sie dort auf, wo wir sie erwarten*] (429).

The "permanent revolution" of "temporal perspectives" in Kluge's experimental miniatures is full of surprises, and some of them are very small. Harvey's seminal concept of time-space compression will not help us much in parsing the ones that Kluge's global miniatures afford, because these texts about contemporary globalization and communist horizons since 1989 are also narratively indebted to that off-worldly problem of futurity. Jacques Derrida's *Specters of Marx* might be helpful to a certain degree, inasmuch as Derrida in 1993 stressed the "non-contemporaneity with itself of the living present" and also distinguished between communist histories and Marxist thought (xix). Yet for Derrida too, like so many other modern thinkers before him (though he is so unlike them in many other brilliant ways), the future of what he calls a "heterodidactics between life and death" is always *"a-venir,"* a "future-to-come" (xvii, xix), which is to say, perennially deferred. The eponymous "communist horizon" of Jodi Dean's 2012 study in political theory since the demise of the Soviet Union would initially seem far more useful for reading Kluge's global miniatures, if only because she explicitly uses the rhetoric of horizon in the early 21st century "to designate a dimension of experience that we can never lose," in direct defiance of temporal horizons seen only as "converg[ing] with loss in a metaphor for privation and depletion" (1). Dean does so with the understanding, however, that the communist horizon of experience is "actual," by which she means both "Real," in an explicitly Lacanian sense of an "impossible" actuality, and not yet socially realized (2).[9] (On "all horizons being situational illusions" and Proust's rather different

---

[9] Kluge's "The Gap the Devil Leaves Us" also includes a miniature featuring discussion of Lacan and his concept of "Future Anterior" (221–222). One of the first-person interlocutors trying to understand this term is a Nazi delegate to "occupied Paris," to whom a dialogic partner responds: "Your grammatical future is cut off like a head by the guillotine" [*Ihr Futur ist abgeschnitten wie ein Kopf durch die Guillotine*] (221). Dean derives her book's title and key term "communist horizon" from Bruno Bosteels, whose own monograph focuses on Bolivian Marxism and its relevance for reconsidering the philosophy and politics of leftist ontologies today (*The Actuality of Communism*). Bosteels takes issue with Adorno's *Negative Dialectics* in his chapter on a 21st-century "ontological turn," partly on historical grounds. Bosteels writes: "if there is a common presupposition shared by all present-day political ontologies, it is that ontology is not, cannot be, or must not be a question of substance or of the Absolute. It presupposes neither the presence of being nor the identity of being and thinking as a guide for acting. On the contrary, ontology nowadays, in a well-nigh uniform fashion, tends to be qualified as spectral, nonidentical, and postfoundational. It tries to come to terms not with present beings, but with ghosts and

literary-critical significance for considering the effects of something we might call a "'real horizon'" nonetheless, see Claudia Brodsky's contribution to *Rethinking Emotion*.) For present purposes I would say that the communist horizon in Dean's usage is a horizon of orientation that remains structurally open in a traditional modern sense despite her invocations of Lacan. Beyond this, Dean overtly rejects any notion of micropolitics—especially those associated with "aesthetic disruptions" (11)—in favor of "large-scale organized collective struggle," by which she means formally instantiated communist parties (14, 19). For all of Kluge's wide-ranging interests in unalienated life and the large arcs of cosmic and global phenomena, the tiniest details of his literary practice are what matter most for our practice of reading them. Crucial among them are the temporal perspectives Kluge crafts on both globalization and communism at the crossroads of hope and despair.

Once again, we might want to reach for Fredric Jameson here, the Marxist theorist who has given us both "the geopolitical aesthetic" and "archaeologies of the future" in the wake of 1989 and linked them to artistic form, utopian horizons, and anti-capitalist critique.[10] As recently as 2015, he has also given us

---

phantasms; not with entities or things, but with events—whether with events in the plural, or, alternatively, with the singular event of the presencing of being as such, which should never be confounded with a given present, albeit a past or future one. Consequently, there can be no determinate politics, not even a democratic or radical-democratic one, not to mention communism, that would simply derive from ontology as a thoroughly desubstantialized field of investigation into being and/as event—even though most commentators are quick to add that democracy, often in the guise of direct democracy, radical democracy, or a democracy-to-come, rather than in any of its historical shapes, would be the only political formation or regime of power attuned to the horizon of ontology at the close of the metaphysical era" (42–43). While Kluge's miniatures often revolve around "spectral, nonidentical, and postfoundational" matters and time, his writing breaks with the "uniform" contemporary mold of leftist ontology that Bosteels describes, not least because Kluge, following Adorno though on different terms, continues to allow for metaphysical experience. His narrative use of futurity depends on it.

10 See also Jameson's "Notes on Globalization as a Philosophical Issue," which opens by mapping four positions "logically available" in 1998, one of which claims "nothing is new under the sun" (in the sense that "there is no such thing as globalization" because "national situations" still exist), another that "there has always been globalization," and a third "affirm[ing] the relationship between globalization and that world market which is the ultimate horizon of capitalism" (54). (The fourth position he describes at the outset of his essay sees globalization as an "intrinsic feature" of both "multinational" capitalism and the postmodern era.) Jameson then elaborates his own position, which is to consider globalization, among other things in relation to capitalism and philosophy, as "a communicational concept, which alternately masks and transmits cultural or economic meanings" (55). However, he "def[ies] anyone to try to think it in exclusively media or communicational terms." For Jameson, "one always finds other dimensions smuggled in" (56). The "dimensions" Jameson means here however are culture, economics,

"The Clocks of Dresden" and "Counterfactual Socialisms" (reprinted from 2011 and 2012 in turn)—the first an insightful essay about temporality and timelessness in an "'East German novel'" by Uwe Tellkamp from 2008, in a Germany that was once "the very heartland of Marxism," (*The Ancients and the Postmoderns* 255–268, here 255 and 256), and the second an especially incisive account of communism and genre in Francis Spufford's *Red Plenty* of 2012, a novel of "fairy-tale counterfactuality" about "the Soviet 1960s" (269–278, here 269 and 278). And yet, as we have already seen in Part One's discussion of Kluge's cosmic miniatures, Jameson's particular insistence on social "totality" in general and his focus on narrative impasses and absolute aporia in Kluge's earlier work on war prevent him from recognizing how Kluge extends Adorno's legacy of counterfactual hope beyond a mere index or distant horizon of possibility. Jameson does help us indirectly in one key way though when he bemoans "the way in which so much of Left politics today—unlike Marx's own passionate commitment to a streamlined technological future—seems to have adopted as its slogan Benjamin's odd idea that revolution means pulling the emergency brake on the runaway train of History, as though an admittedly runaway capitalism itself had the monopoly on change and futurity" (266).[11] Kluge's global miniatures in effect challenge that monopoly by narrative means, and part of this story to be told has a lot to do with trains. Turning now to global miniatures featuring German Marxists and toy trains in London, Soviet remnants relegated to academic invisibility at an elite university in the United States, and 21st-century "Fifth-Generation" cinema in the People's Republic of China, the close readings that follow are admittedly eclectic and not by any means exhaustive. They nonetheless aim to demonstrate how Kluge's global micrologies contribute to "permanent revolution" by narratively cultivating the future sense as a long-distance organ of temporal perception.[12]

---

and ideology. For a sampling of recent scholarship on Kluge and contemporary mediascapes, see *Glass Shards* (ed. Langston et al.), the second volume of the *Alexander Kluge-Jahrbuch* (2015), which also includes Lutz Koepnick's essay, "Inside Kluge's Cosmic Cinema: Critical Theory and Mobile Spectatorship Today."

11 Jameson alludes here to a famous line from Benjamin's reflective supplements to his philosophical theses "On the Concept of History" (1940). Benjamin himself takes issue with Marx's characterization of revolutions as "the locomotives of history" in his socio-historical account *The Class Struggles in France, 1848–1850*. As we shall see, Kluge engages the Marx quotation in terms of intensive narrative activation instead.

12 A prominent communist theorist of "permanent revolution" in early 20th-century Russia, Leon Trotsky also figures in Fore's analysis of heterogeneous but linked temporalities in Dziga Vertov's approach to Soviet filmmaking under and against the Stalinist "violence of monologization" (Fore, "The Metabiotic State" 19). Fore concludes by underscoring the renewed rele-

2 Global Connectivity

Recalling the double-jointed gesture of farewell and variation that has figured in so much of Kluge's critical work since *Yesterday Girl* or *Abschied von gestern* [literally: Farewell to Yesterday] in the 1960s (as discussed in Part One), one of the longer book sections in "Door to Door with an Other Life" is titled "Farewell to Locomotives" and subtitled in part "Abschied von einer Metapher des Fortschritts" ["Farewell to a Metaphor of Progress"] (409). One of the global miniatures in this section opens with a tagged Marx quotation—"'Revolutions are the locomotives of history'" [*Die Revolutionen sind die Lokomotiven der Geschichte*] (436; compare Marx, *The Class Struggles in France* 165)—and later features an unidentified time-traveling interlocutor asking, in the revolutionary St. Petersburg of late 1917: "What metaphor would we have for that in 2006?" [*Welche Metapher dafür hätten wir 2006?*] (438). This may remind us of the paleoclimatologist's tropic musings, in Kluge's "chronicle of Pangea," on "'inclusions' in the rock that are moving closer toward the future, where we, the detecting agents, are waiting for them." The time-traveling interlocutions that Kluge stages in quest of revolutionary metaphors in these global miniatures in any event have a temporal effect that tends to be kaleidoscopic rather than telescopic. These miniatures often favor intensified dispersion, permutation, and even approximation rather than forms of concentration in which relations of distance are collapsed.[13] Some prominent Kluge scholars—notably Thomas Combrink ("Zu Alexander Kluges Metaphernwelt") and Richard Langston ("'Windows are to a House...'")—alert us to key points of philosophical resonance between Hans Blu-

---

vance of both Vertov and Trotsky for 21st-century approaches to globalization: "parallels can again be seen between the fortunes of Vertov and those of Trotsky, whose theorization of structural nonsynchronicity and technical heterogeneity has become an important resource once again for critics of globalization seeking to understand a world system in which uneven development turns out increasingly to be the rule rather than the exception. Under such conditions, instead of the presentist rhetoric of eventhood and of messianic rupture proposed by neo-Stalinist currents within radical philosophy today, what is needed are strategies of persistence and obstinacy, a social attunement toward metabiotic relations, and a renewed commitment to permanent revolution" (37). Kluge's intensified investment in what he calls the "permanent revolution" of narrative practice arguably entails one important resource for the critical "strategies" that Fore has in mind.

13 See also Sigrid Weigel's critical approach to traumatic "télescopage in the unconscious" [*Télescopage im Unbewußten*]; she derives the term, as distinguished from "telescoping," from 19th-century terminology for what happens to railway cars in train accidents (65). As early as 1985, Erhard Schütz points to Kluge's "kaleidoscopic montage aesthetic" (61). 21st-century feuilleton reviews of Kluge's proliferating prose take increasing recourse to the adjective "kaleidoscopic" to describe it.

menberg and Kluge in their approaches to the radical "non-conceptuality" of metaphor (Blumenberg) and fundamental "ambivalence" of metaphor (as Combrink puts it with regard to Kluge). Although Blumenberg's name never appears in Kluge's oeuvre, Combrink argues, Kluge's extensive use of unruly metaphors establishes a certain "proximity" [*Nähe*] between these two critical thinkers (171; see also Langston).[14] We have already seen how even Kluge's metaphor of *Abschied* proves unfaithful to itself vis-à-vis "yesterday," in ways that allow this writer to follow his mentor Adorno "faithfully" and to deviate from him in his writing practice too, and we have good reason to suspect that the storytelling collection "Door to Door with an Other Life" is toying simultaneously with two historic metaphors: revolutions in Marxist parlance as "the locomotives of history" and networked connectivity as a "leading cultural metaphor" for contemporary globalization (see especially Alexander Friedrich; see also Hartmut Böhme for related reflections on networks of modernity).

Beyond this, in narrative terms, I suggest that the global miniatures gathered under the umbrella "Farewell to Locomotives" do not operate in the main metaphorically but metonymically instead, constantly mobilizing that which is "related" by virtue, not necessarily of being similar, but of being—or being made in Kluge's experimental storytelling associations—"proximate" or "aside" (see Gert Ueding and Bernd Steinbrink [294] on the rhetorical characteristics of metonymy). The term metonymy generally designates a mode of rhetorical figuration rather than narrative form, so it may seem outlandish to apply the term to the

---

[14] Combrink also observes a concern with sidereal metaphors (especially concerning the stars) that Kluge and Blumenberg share (175–176). According to Combrink, the main difference between the two lies in Blumenberg's attention to the philosophical problematic of "absolute metaphor" and Kluge's radical rejection of any aspiration to comprehend "the world as a whole" (177). Discussing Negt and Kluge's *History and Obstinacy*, for which he was the lead translator, Langston also focuses on Blumenberg's approach to metaphor as a point of comparison as well as contrast. For Langston, Blumenberg's reconsideration of the interiority and exteriority of Plato's cave helps us understand the "inherent ambiguity" of Negt and Kluge's metaphor of a "threshold" to a house. A significant difference Langston identifies lies in Blumenberg's rejection of Adorno's own "refusal to engage in philosophical dialogue." By contrast, Langston underscores a philosophical dialogue that Negt and Kluge cultivate with Marx by metaphorical and analogical means concerning built structures and bodily senses of human perception. According to Langston, Blumenberg's treatment of interiority, exteriority, and philosophical metaphor thus helps address an anthropological "gap" in German critical theory. For Blumenberg's own thoughts in English translation, see especially *Paradigms for a Metaphorology* and *Care Crosses the River*. For Kluge's extended reflections on what constitutes a metaphor, see the eponymous chapter in *Ferngespräche* ["Long-Distance Conversations"] (Kluge and Stollmann 19–23). These interviews also address digital technologies and new formats they have spawned, such as Skype, beyond the sensory experience of long-distance telephone calls.

narrative gesture of his global miniatures. I nonetheless think it applies because these miniatures literally activate endless chains of linguistic, temporal, and socio-historical associations through their storytelling maneuvers of syntax, sequence, and perspective. This cannot be a matter of what Bruno Bosteels might call "postfoundational ontology" alone (62). Many Kluge commentators and Kluge himself often speak of his intended "doubling of reality" [*Verdopplung der Realität*] (Kluge, "The Actuality of Adorno," *Personen und Reden* ["Persons and Speeches"] 70), and constant relational movement is arguably required for the intensified revolutionary doubling he intends. Kluge lends such narrative movement to metaphor and metonymy alike in his writing, and sometimes one finds figures of similitude and proximity concurrently—interacting, as it were—in his miniatures. This happens for example in Volume 1 of Kluge's "Chronicle of Feelings," in a miniature about two "'unknown soldiers of Critical Theory'" [*unbekannte Soldaten der Kritischen Theorie*], both named Müller, competing for a professorship in philosophy in Frankfurt and discussing over coffee the grammar of society and syntax ("Keine falsche Unmittelbarkeit" ["No False Immediacy"] 857–860). Forced by circumstance to hold their inaugural lecture jointly before the university discovers its clerical error, "[t]he two grammarians knew what they were talking about" [*Die beiden Grammatiker wußten, wovon sie sprachen*], but these dialogic interlocutors are soon "parted" [*getrennt*], and the university hires only one (860). We shall have occasion to return to these grammarians in section 3 below. Kluge's 21st-century stories of labor, locomotion, and revolution in section 6 of "Door to Door with an Other Life," however, yield all sorts of metonymic narrative constellations associated with trains and their tracks. Semantic and syntactical fields of "connections," "couplings," "linkings," derailings, junctions, and time are set in motion in one new story after another in this section, which bids "farewell" to locomotives as "a metaphor of progress" (in industrial as well as Marxist senses) while remaining narratively obsessed by this figure of revolution. How does this narrative obsession advance permanent revolution against ubiquitous catastrophe in the contemporary age of capitalist globalization? And how do the temporal perspectives of Kluge's global miniatures help generate a future sense that becomes accessible to revolutionary experience?

Here I suggest that Kluge's global miniatures in "Farewell to Locomotives" contributes to the field of experimental literature by reworking the very story of capitalist globalization. Liam Connell has argued that "[o]ne way to understand globalization is to see it as a particular way of narrating contemporary internationalism" (224). This reference to internationalism seems decidedly inaccurate, but Connell's emphasis on globalization as "a particular way of narrating" contemporary processes at work in the world is useful for considering the experimental futurity of Kluge's global miniatures. Connell identifies two narrative features common to stories of globalization as they circulate today. The first is "concatenation," whereby "'networks' that transcend their immediate locality" appear linked as in an overarching chain, and the second is "concentration," whereby "the local becomes the nodal point" where "'consciousness of the world as a whole'" appears to manifest as compression (224).[15] (This is different from Harvey's concept of time-space compression, in part, because the appearance of compression is not conflated with the reality of compression. Radisoglou, who seems to agree with Harvey and others on compression as one defining feature of neoliberal globalization, nonetheless and notably characterizes Kluge's formal literary approach to globalization in relation to "a paradoxical kind of shrinking" [8].) For Connell, many literary texts and scholarly narratives about globalization "reproduce the combination" of concatenation and concentration he has described, whereas experimental writing on globalization "trouble[s] this combination" instead by "disturbing the easy link between connectivity and proximity" (225).[16] Kluge's "farewell" to a particular revolutionary metaphor of progress advances this narrative disturbance by reconfiguring the temporal connectivity of revolutionary horizons on seemingly peripheral tracks of complex stories to be told.

One striking example of this is a "Marxist" miniature featuring two radical German socialists in London exile growing increasingly "excited" [*erregt*] (446) about real prospects for economic and political revolution. For the Karl Marx that Kluge gives us in "König Dampf, Kaiserin Elektrizität" ["King Steam, Empress Electricity"] (446–448), the miniature model of an electric train he has seen signals the "breakthrough" [*Durchbruch*]. "The problem is solved, the consequences are incalculable" [*Das Problem ist gelöst, die Folgen sind unabsehbar*], Kluge has him assert, using an adjective for "incalculable" that means both enormous and literally "unforeseeable" (446).[17] The friend and companion in this

---

15 On this latter point Connell cites Roland Robertson. The other exemplary study of globalization he cites—on "'complex connectivity'"—is by John Tomlinson (see Connell 224, Robertson 8, and Tomlinson 9).
16 For additional and wide-ranging approaches to literature and globalization, see the interdisciplinary reader edited by Liam Connell and Nicky Marsh. For a sampling of other approaches to globalization, narrative, and literary forms, see also Dominik Schreiber, Jernej Habjan and Fabienne Imlinger, and Gerald Prince.
17 Summarizing Darren Webb's discussion of Marx and Engels's critique of utopian socialism in favor of "scientific socialism," Paden recaps that "although Marx argued that Historical Materialism demonstrated that a communist society was inevitable, consistent with the epistemological limitations of scientific knowledge he also argued that it could not foretell the precise nature of that qualitatively different future society" (79; see Webb 90). Paden disagrees with Webb, in

narrated exchange is Wilhelm Liebknecht, who in empirical historical terms joined The Communist League before later helping to found the Social Democratic Party in Germany. In Kluge's rendition Marx is metonymically linked to and also dis-placed by Liebknecht, who eventually returns from Marx's flat to take some notes with an emphatically heliotropic orientation. We read:

> "That evening I never came home, we talked and laughed and drank until late the next morning, and the sun was already standing in the sky when I went to bed," he wrote in his journal. His claim was exaggerated: "the sun was already standing in the sky." More precisely, the cloud mass over London had not diminished, they just weren't the same as the evening before, though they had, to be sure, become markedly brighter to the extent that they were influenced (from high above) by the sun.

> [„Den Abend kam ich nicht mehr nach Hause, wir sprachen und lachten und tranken bis spät am anderen Morgen, und die Sonne stand schon am Himmel, als ich mich zu Bett legte", schrieb er in sein Tagebuch. Darin war die Behauptung übertrieben: „die Sonne stand schon am Himmel". Vielmehr hatte die Wolkenmasse über London sich nicht verringert, es waren nur nicht mehr dieselben wie am Vorabend; allerdings waren sie deutlich heller geworden, insofern (von ganz oben) von der Sonne beeinflußt.] (446)

Two things become especially clear here. First, the figure of Liebknecht is itself displaced by a narrative voice that cannot be located in time or space, though it assertively claims knowledge of both. Second and equally important, nothing at all becomes clear when this proximate voice troubles the relationship between near and far. This is partly because the barely embodied voice of narration and the agentially embodied figure of narration are in this instance at odds in their heliotropic orientations. Liebknecht excitedly sees the sun "already" standing in the sky after his lively dialogic exchange with Marx, and it is not too far fetched to read *this* sky in Liebknecht's "daybook" or journal as the "sky of history" in which the revolutionary sun of Benjamin's "secret heliotropism" is rising.

As discussed in Part One, Richardson defines the interlocutor in general terms, as a narratological category, as "a disembodied voice that poses questions which the narrative goes on to answer," and as we saw in Part One's discussion of Kluge's cosmic miniatures, Kluge frequently mobilizes this form of interlocution, as well as variations. Richardson's expanded characterization of the "unnatural" voice of the interlocutor as a protean narrative voice predicated on functional oscillation, I argued, is therefore even more useful for thinking about

---

part, because "Historical Materialism failed as a predictive science" and because it "rests on an implausible economic determinism" (79). As we saw in Part One One, Benjamin and Adorno too had strong objections to prognostic and predictive modes of futurity.

Kluge's diverse narrative figures of interlocution. As we saw in Part One, these narrative interlocutors help generate a productive oscillation between horizons of hope and conditions of despair. In the case of "King Steam, Empress Electricity," the narrative voice of interlocution does not itself bespeak a utopian inclination but rather seems to squash any such orientation by dismissing Liebknecht's excitement as exaggeration, asserting a corrective reality principle instead, and suggesting that it derives its authoritative knowledge "from high above." Here we may be reminded both of narrative interlocutors unsuccessfully asserting the reality principle in "Saturday in Utopia" and another one attesting to "extraterrestrials on the move" in a miniature with that title. Yet neither Liebknecht as figure nor the voice of narration can be said to represent proper perspective here. After all, we might just as easily say that Liebknecht traffics in cliché or that the interlocutor turns toward the unnatural sun of a revolutionary horizon in the final line of the quotation after all. Yet these sorts of mere position statements are decoys in this global miniature of communist horizons, which derives its revolutionary impulse from the contrast in temporal perspectives that the narrative relation between Liebknecht, already peripheral in relation to Marx, and the not quite disembodied voice of narration activates. The heliotropism of this miniature is in other words itself not self-identical. The contrastive conjunction of temporal perspectives it generates begins to animate the future sense. This inchoate animation of an off-worldly futurity of utopian dimension, "door to door with an other life" in 2006, is properly speaking not postcommunist but revolutionary in Kluge's narrative sense.

The proximate voice of interlocution in "King Steam, Empress Electricity" also troubles any easy relationship between near and far, and this disturbance echoes vaguely in the miniature's final paragraph, which in a narrative sense restores not Marx but Liebknecht to us, as a useful supplement in the history of communism. Here the one-time revolutionary reflects back on "the toy train in the London shop window," which now carries the "supplemental disadvantage" of moving "only in a circle" and not having been worked on or played with by a "public" that would be "connected" to it [*Die Spielzeugeisenbahn im Londoner Schaufenster, durch elektrischen Funken betrieben, schien ihm, nachträglich betrachtet, mit dem zusätzlichen Nachteil behaftet, daß sie nur im Kreise und nur in den Ausmaßen eines Fensters vor einem passiven, unterhaltungslüsternen, weder durch Arbeit noch durch Seelentätigkeit mit dem Spielzeug verbundenen Publikum ihre Bahn zog*] (448). This "supplemental disadvantage" should remind us however of the generative anachronism that Negt and Kluge associated with "expressive possibilities" for a radically "proletarian" public sphere in 1972. More than three decades later, our mysterious narrator in this global miniature reports via tagged indirect discourse: "the evening with Marx [...] remained [...]

something real [...] for Liebknecht, even if the bespiritedness of the two [...] could not be reproduced" [*Dennoch blieb für Liebknecht [...] der Abend mit Marx [...] etwas Reales, auch wenn sich die Begeisterung der beiden [...] nicht reproduzieren ließ*] (448). Here I translate the German word for enthusiasm [*Begeisterung*] literally as "bespiritedness," since a vague or—more precisely—oscillating spirit of revolutionary aspirations and counterfactual hope not only informs Kluge's weather reports but also enlivens his global miniatures *as* stories of usable futurities. These spirits are not the "ghosts" of which Derrida speaks in *Specters of Marx*, though the former are also responsible, in Derrida's sense of justice, to the latter. How could they be revolutionary otherwise? Yet the ghosts that Derrida means (past, present, and future) inhabit what he calls a "spectral moment, a moment that no longer belongs to time" (xviii–xix). Kluge has plenty to say about the ghosts of the dead and the disenfranchised throughout his multimedial oeuvre as well, but the "bespiritedness" at work in "King Steam, Empress Electricity" belongs, I argue here, to the experiential this-worldly and off-worldly temporality of the future sense. This temporality is disjunctive as well as conjoined.

The revolutionary connectivity of Kluge's global miniatures in the longer book section obsessively devoted to a "farewell to locomotives," including revolutions as "the locomotives of history," is the associative and experimental connectivity of *Zusammenhang* as discussed in Part One. For Adorno and Kluge too, albeit in different ways and to different degrees, this necessarily entails narrative and critical labor on especially capitalist but also communist histories of catastrophe—and on the experiential futurity of counterfactual hope. The relationality of "what hangs together" in Kluge's freewheeling prose marks both wound and chance in his aesthetics of the gap, which always cultivates, more than Adorno could, a "way out" of the permanent threat of catastrophe. This is not merely a matter of contingent disruptions of predictive causality, though Kluge's "Farewell to Locomotives" also includes several stories about horrific train accidents that are either averted or caused by something that could not have been foreseen (see for example two miniatures about World War I, "Eine schwer zu deutende Heldentat" ["A Heroic Deed That Is Hard to Interpret"] (416–417) and "Sechs Lokomotiven, Fahrlässigkeit und die Folgen" ["Six Locomotives, Recklessness, and the Consequences"] (420–425). Neither can the non-teleological sequentiality of these narratives be said to be consistently "non-linear," though Wolfgang Reichmann is correct in foregrounding non-linearity as a core characteristic of Kluge's poetics in general and his storytelling approach to time in "Door to

Door with an Other Life" in particular ("Tür an Tür mit einer anderen Zeit").[18] However, when Reichmann uses the term, he essentially means non-chronological (197 et passim). Addressing the temporal structure of many entries in Kluge's "Door to Door with an Other Life," beyond those that I have been able to accommodate here, Reichmann focuses on Kluge's stylistic proclivity to "palimpsestic overlappings" (196) and (in implicit allusion to Ernst Bloch and explicit reference to Reinhart Koselleck) "contemporaneities of non-contemporaneous historical layers" (193). Reichmann is right to do so, and his likening of Kluge's "non-linearity of narration" (193) to historical palimpsests, geological sedimentation, archaeological excavation, constellative "'cross-mapping,'" and especially digital "hypertext" is instructive (197, 199, 201; on Kluge and "hypertext," see also Georg Stanitzek, "Autorität im Hypertext"). For two reasons, this account of Kluge's non-linear narration in "Door to Door with an Other Life" is nonetheless not fully adequate to the global miniatures of communist horizons in "Farewell to Locomotives," which remains devoted to working on the narrative figure of revolution. First, the hyper-active figure of moving, stalled, abandoned, and toy trains on which this subset of global miniatures relies does occasionally feature linear elements in setting and sequence, linear elements without which a heightened sense of catastrophic danger on the tracks would not be felt. (This applies at least in some cases; see for example the opening miniature in this section, "Eisenroß um 2006" ["Iron Steed Around 2006"] (413), in which a Swiss train worker will or will not be crushed, depending on whether he has or has not moved off the linear track of a moving train.) The non-linear temporality of Kluge's experimental miniatures is usually but not exclusively tied to "non-linear narration." Second, and especially important, the reading presented here of "King Steam, Empress Electricity" shows us how something not yet of this earthly world begins to enter it anyway through Kluge's narrative exercising of "unnatural" temporal perspectives. The global connectivity of Kluge's global miniatures for the 21st century is enlivened by their cosmic and revolutionary orientations to the utopian dimension.

---

18 Kluge himself often speaks of a "non-linear" imperative to narrate by "gravitational" means (see for example his Frankfurt poetics lecture of 19 June 2012 in his series "Theory of Storytelling," or his explanation of his storytelling interest in Syria in "Corresponding to an Oasis"). For Kluge, "gravitational narration" involves both concentration and dispersion. For extended discussion of Kluge's "gravitational" style, see Langston ("'Windows are to a House'").

3 Revolutionary Subjectivity

If revolutionary futures manifest as narrative problems of linkage in Kluge's global miniatures, the storytelling status of revolutionary subjectivity is no less vexed. For how should we understand the relationship between what I earlier characterized as Kluge's anthropological investment in storytelling as somehow necessary for human survival now, on the one hand, and his frequent toying with or common disregard for anthropomorphism as a narrative device, on the other?[19] Thinking about this must color any analysis of voice, perspective, pronouns, character, affect, and mood. The German word for mood or atmosphere that Kluge uses to describe the feeling of conviviality shared by Liebknecht and Marx in a London apartment—*Stimmung* (446)—derives for example from the radical for voice.[20] When the narrative voice there intervenes to tell us that "they" are not what they were the evening before, the grammar of narration does not let us decide whether "they" refers to London clouds or to Marx and Liebknecht. This may remind us of Bruno Latour's discussion of "we" and "I" as forms of pronomial deixis in "Waiting for Gaia" in terms of "the total *disconnect* between the range, nature, and scale of the phenomena and the set of emotions, habits of thought, and feelings that would be necessary to handle those crises [of the Anthropocene]" (21). Yet the ambiguous pronomial deixis of Kluge's "they" in this miniature has more to do with Latour's emphasis on how scales of relation are "produced" rather than being simply given (25), and even more to do

---

19 Fotis Jannidis has argued contra Genette, who distinguished in the 1970s between voice and focalization to avoid then prevalent anthropomorphisms in narratology as a scholarly field, that narrotology needs more anthropomorphism after all to account for structural forms of narration (151 et passim). Kluge's phenomenological orientation to utopian dimensions and the future sense could conceivably both support and challenge this view. Jannidis for example lists the narrative "montage" of "linguistic material" as one of three forms entailing complete "loss of voice" (152), with loss of voice counting for Jannidis as an anthropomorphic register. Kluge's narrative interlocutors might be seen in terms of a gain in voice on similar grounds, and yet Kluge's modes of interlocution, as I have argued, are more properly speaking anthropocentric rather than anthropomorphic. The future sense his miniatures cultivate is both this-worldly and off-worldly too, which makes a world of difference.
20 For extended critical reflections on the many nuances and historical vicissitudes of *Stimmung* as a key aesthetic concept, see David E. Wellbery. Writing in 2003, Wellbery observed that a sharp decline in the conceptual relevance of *Stimmung* (which also means attunement) had taken place in the latter half of the 20th century, partly because of the reduced role that "musical metaphor," he surmised, has come to play in configuring subjective conditions (733). Kluge's longstanding though quirky interest in *Stimmung* and music alike, especially opera, could be one intriguing point of entry for reconsidering the status of *Stimmung* as an aesthetic concept today.

with the narrative production of revolutionary connectivity than the "total *disconnect*" that Latour ascribes to the Anthropocene.

The lingering and conjoined senses of disappointment and "bespiritedness" that seem literally to character-ize Liebknecht in "King Steam, Empress Electricity" play a similar role in a different global miniature, "Snowball-Earth" (Kluge uses the English term for this title), from "Door to Door with an Other Life" (29 – 30). This is the first entry in a subset of stories on what the text explicitly designates as "the first globalization." Typically for Kluge, ordinal sequentiality is invoked here too (as is often the case with Kluge's frequent references to historical calendar dates as well) and yet temporally toyed with by narrative means. Set after the end of the cold war in 20th-century Europe, "Snowball-Earth" gives us a geobiologist named David Imogen Kuhlke, who expounds on the relationship between "coldness" [*Kälte*] and "life" [*Leben*] in an ice age affecting earth's continental arrangement "630 million years ago" (29).[21] Unlike Liebknecht, who is narratively equipped in the miniature cited above with thick anthropomorphic description, Kuhlke is sketched with considerable narrative reserve. We learn that he is "the only one in his field" [*der einzige seines Faches*], a mere "leftover" [*übriggeblieben*] from the Soviet Academy of Sciences, now virtually off the academic radar screen as a hapless adjunct at Stanford, where his knowledge claims are given voice but entirely ignored. This figure—I would hesitate to call him a character, and he would undoubtedly fall under the rubric of what Fotis Jannidis discusses in "hybrid" narratological terms as "loss of voice" (152)—is a brooding presence in a tale of commingled pasts and futures.[22] With Kuhlke it is especially difficult to say whether this presence connotes hope or threat, or even communism in any substantive sense, though one would be hard pressed to argue that Kuhlke's presence connotes mere irrelevance, since Kluge devotes so much attention to it. A single sentence may help us think about this post-Soviet figure, at least in one narrative respect, in relation to futurity. Amidst his comments

---

21 Pavsek elaborates in his epilogue to *The Utopia of Film* on the importance of "cold in all of its dialectical richness" for Kluge and Adorno alike (239 et passim). On this motif, Adorno referred to coldness as "the basic principle of bourgeois subjectivity, without which there could have been no Auschwitz; this is the drastic guilt of him who was spared" (*Negative Dialectics* 363). For an extended section of Kluge's miniatures on "coldness hostile to human beings" [*menschenfeindliche Kälte*], including discussion of and with Adorno, see Kluge, "The Fifth Book" (223 – 271). As presented in his Frankfurt poetics lecture of 12 June 2012, Kluge's "theory of storytelling" also highlighted the non-sentimental importance of differentiating between "hot" and "cold" for thought as "concentrated feeling" [*verdichtetes Gefühl*].

22 Compare Alexander Hollenberg's astute narratological reflections on the importance of "thin characters" for what he calls "recalcitrant simplicity" in both Hemingway's fiction and theoretical accounts of narrative obstacles to hermeneutic reading.

on the earth's axis of orientation in "the first globalization," we read: "Toward both poles the oceans were, said Kuhlke, frozen" [*Zu beiden Polen hin waren die Meere, sagte Kuhlke, gefroren*] (29).

Syntactically this sentence says exactly what it means, and this tagged instance of indirect discourse recounts the content of Kuhlke's declaration. Separated from the proper name of this "leftover" only by a comma, however, the word "frozen" [*gefroren*] stands in apposition to "Kuhlke" and structurally positions the figure to which this name refers. The name "Kuhlke" thus simultaneously appears as a figure of arrested futurity while the relation of apposition indirectly unsettles any assertion of geobiological fact *and* splits the temporal frame of narration. This figure is certainly not dead, and the affective presence of Kuhlke as "leftover" would have to be understood as something other than nostalgia, for the orientation here is to a future horizon not lost but left over and moving anew, on peripheral revolutionary tracks as it were, in Kluge's prose.[23] The apposition that allows us to see this leftover horizon at this juncture is typographical rather than strictly speaking grammatical, and the narrative grammar of the sentence's textual reality is thus doubled, perhaps even unintentionally so in this instance. Kluge's bespirited "heterodidactics between life and death" nonetheless schools us to perceive this opening and proliferation of temporal perspective by dint of narrative experiment in writing. As Kluge notably stressed in his acceptance speech of the Kleist Prize for German literature in 1985, and as he has often repeated, writers are "guardians" of "the grammar of time," that is to say, "guardians of the difference" between past, present, and future ("Wächter der Differenz"). Especially in Kluge's adept storytelling hands, they are guardians of these conjunctive temporalities as well in the service of experiential futures beyond life's miseries. Commenting in *Maßverhältnisse des Politischen* ["Politics as Relations of Measure"] on "how much complexity it takes to read" [*wieviel Komplexität zum Lesen gehört*], Kluge underscores the importance of textual forms as a material "palimpsest" [*Übereinanderschreibung*], analogous to the "labor of historical relations" [*Arbeit geschichtlicher Verhältnisse*], and to the "labor of generations and their regulations of language" [*Arbeit der Generationen und ihrer Sprachregelungen*] (220). Even if a text does not change in its material details, he writes (though some of them do in his writing

---

23 Contrast this with Svetlana Bohm's *The Future of Nostalgia* and Charles Piot's *Nostalgia for the Future: West Africa After the Cold War*; see also Melas's discussion of Bloch and James as critical alternatives to nostalgia ("Comparative Non-Contemporaneities"). See as well Nahum Chandler's exposition of the renewed political and philosophical importance of W.E.B. DuBois for considering historical and contemporary globalization, "double consciousness," and critical orientation to counterfactual futurity.

practice, as many readers will note), these other relational elements are "vibrantly transformed" [*lebendig verändert*] (220) through use of them. For Kluge, every perspectival "change" [*Wechsel*] yields, not only a different constellation of relationality, but also the "ways out of history, that is to say, the texts we ought to be reading" [*Auswege der Geschichte, also die Texte, die es zu lesen gilt*] (221).

At this juncture we return to the storytelling constellation of the two "unknown soldiers of Critical Theory" discussed above, who are "grammarians." Their most interesting and excited conversation takes place over coffee before they enter the lecture hall. If syntax harbors the unknown, they ponder, where in a critical sentence does one look for a solution predicated on something unknown? One Müller says he looks "outside the sentence" [*Außerhalb des Satzes*], but then asks the other Müller where the "door of the sentence" [*Tür des Satzes*] might be, to which his dialogic interlocutor replies: "In the gap" [*In der Lücke*]. This creates a new problem for these conscientious critical theorists: "But we constructed sentences without any gaps" [*Wir haben aber lückenlose Sätze gebaut*]. One Müller then suggests: "Now I'll build a gap into the sentence" [*Jetzt baue ich eine Lücke in den Satz hinein*], which causes the other Müller to ask in consternation: "But how do you do that?" [*Aber wie machst du das?*]. The solution? "We have to look outside" [*Wir müssen nach draußen sehen*] (859). Although this exchange about a certain kind of doubling of reality in philosophical and syntactical form can be found in Volume I of Kluge's "Chronicle of Feelings" from 2000, it helps explain the off-worldly weight I am inclined to lend to a single comma placement in "Snowball-Earth," the global miniature featuring an adjunct Soviet geobiologist at Stanford after the ostensible erasure of communist horizons in Europe. The maverick but not ungrammatical apposition between "Kuhlke" and "frozen" opens up a "gap" in the textual syntax and in so doing creates a door in narration to an "other" future time. Kuhlke's revolutionary subjectivity lies, not in his indeterminate affect and brooding presence, but in the doubling of real temporal perspectives that Kluge's revolutionary storytelling about him affords. Whatever hybrid oral and textual elements of "talk fiction" and "secondary orality" (Irene Kacandes) do apply to Kluge's experimental prose, some formal features of his storytelling for the 21st century clearly rely on storytelling as a written rather than oral tradition. This too sets him further apart from—even if also in dialogue with—Benjamin's "The Storyteller" (*Illuminations* 83–110).

4 Counter-Catastrophic Futurity

If Kluge's storied "farewell to locomotives" reconfigures the futurity of globalization beyond 1989, beyond capitalist as well as communist catastrophes in empirical time, and if a narrative conceit of arrested futurity yields to vaguely persistent and oscillating horizons of revolutionary orientation in "Snowball-Earth," something at once grander and more emphatically diminutive takes place when Kluge's global miniatures turn to the People's Republic of China, where state-sponsored communism and global capital converge anew on the world stage.[24] Perhaps not surprisingly, the story collection that Kluge conjures "door to door with an other life" includes not one but two sections titled "We Fortunate Children of the First Globalization," one of which contains but also exceeds the second. The first four miniatures in the longer section bearing this title are all set in Shanghai, which might in some ways lend itself to being read as a "space of hope," as Harvey puts it in his account of a contemporary dialectic of the macro- and micro-dimensions of globalization and embodiment.[25] In his Frankfurt poetics lecture on 19 June 2012, the third in his series on "Theory of Storytelling," Kluge asks what revolution means in the 21st century [*Was bedeutet Revolution im 21. Jahrhundert?*] and at one point mentions Shanghai as "a promise for something that cannot be committed" [*ein Versprechen für etwas, was nicht begehbar ist*]. Kluge's phrasing *nicht begehbar* could also be translated literally as referring to "something that cannot be walked." The sensory organs of perception and proprioception required to realize this "something" in the temporal "promise" of Shanghai exceed the five human senses of embodiment familiar to Marx. In his aesthetics lecture of 12 June 2012 Kluge speaks of "approximately twenty-four" [*etwa vierundzwanzig*].

As argued throughout this book, the one Kluge's experimental miniatures work on is what I call the future sense.[26] The description in two of these "new

---

[24] This may help explain the reference to "Shakespeare's dramas about kings" in one of them (22).

[25] Kluge's Shanghai miniatures could be one important point of entry for reconsidering Kluge's relation to the German literary tradition of "metropolitan miniatures" (Huyssen), which in Huyssen's analysis ends with Adorno. On globalization and embodiment in sixth-generation cinema in the People's Republic of China, see Yan Haiping, "Intermedial Moments: An Embodied Turn in Contemporary Chinese Cinema."

[26] Kluge has also cultivated some degree of dialogic exchange with interlocutors from the People's Republic of China, notably in conversation with Wang Hui. A prominent public intellectual in Beijing and university professor specializing in Chinese literature, intellectual history, and social theory who has also held visiting appointments in Germany and the United States, Wang is author of several books including *China from Empire to Nation-State*, *China's New Order*, *The End*

stories" set in Shanghai of sorting out "found remnants of the technical world" [*Fundstücke der technischen Welt*] (14), "used up technical equipment" [*ausgedientes technisches Gerät*] (15) for sale or re-use, could assuredly be understood as indexing contemporary global economies of capital and labor.[27] However, the "stock of electrical cables, distributors, and switches" [*Vorrat an Elektrokabeln, Verteilern und Schaltern*] (13) conjured in one miniature is a figural decoy inasmuch as the "complex connectivity" at stake in Kluge's rendition of parallel worlds here is narrative in the main and not electrical or digital.[28] Another Shanghai story, which explicitly figures Niklas Luhmann "as sociologist and systems researcher in China" [*als Soziologe und Systemforscher in China*], highlights what the text calls the "forbidden" [*verboten*] poetics of sociological observation, and the voice of narration complains here that the prosthetic "'third eye'" [*(d)ieses 'dritte Auge'*] of the sociologist's computer can at best see "six to

---

of the Revolution: China and the Limits of Modernity, The Politics of Imagining Asia, and co-author of "Is the Public Sphere Unspeakable in Chinese?". Co-sponsored by the Goethe Institut China and Peking University in March 2012, a public screening in Beijing of Kluge's film "News from Ideological Antiquity: Marx—Eisenstein—Capital" was moderated by Wang and featured audience discussion with Kluge in Germany via Skype. The transcription of related Skype conversation between Kluge and Wang is included, in German translation by Ingrid Fischer-Schreiber, in "Long-Distance Conversations" (Kluge and Stollmann 35–52). "Politics as Relations of Measure," part of which Kluge co-authored with sociologist Oskar Negt, additionally includes a chapter written by Negt on contemporary China, with some commentary on the political significance of Tiananmen Square (153–170). Detailed analysis of intellectual exchange between Kluge and Wang in particular, especially concerning the temporal entanglements of Chinese and European modernities, would be productive ground for the growing field of Asian German Studies but would exceed the scope of the present study. For insights into uses of futurity in contemporary Chinese literature, see Paola Iovene, *Tales of Futures Past*.

27 Nathan Taylor noted this in a graduate seminar on Alexander Kluge at Cornell University in Spring 2012. One might additionally note a certain figural resemblance between Kluge's trash pickers "of the technical world" and Benjamin's description of the writer as "ragpicker, at daybreak" in his 1930s review of Siegfried Kracauer's book on "white-collar workers" in Weimar Germany (as cited in the editors' chronology in *Walter Benjamin: Selected Writings* [Vol. 2, Part 2] 838).

28 As noted above, Connell derives the term "complex connectivity" from Tomlinson's book on globalization (Connell 224, Tomlinson 9). See also n. 10 above on Jameson's discussion of globalization as a "communicational concept" beyond technological platforms alone. I adapt the term "complex connectivity" for different analytical purposes here and note further, as other scholars in digital humanities as well as German Studies have already done, that the narrative and the digital are not mutually exclusive (see for example N. Katherine Hayles [*My Mother was a Computer*], Madeleine Casad ["The Virtual Turn"], and Patrizia C. McBride [*The Chatter of the Visible*]). Here I underscore that Kluge's figuration of these trash pickers sorting through electronic refuse in Shanghai does much more than index the technological connectivity of global communications networks. See also Kluge and Stollmann's discussions of recent shifts in communications technologies in "Long-Distance Conversations."

eight years sharply into the future" [*blickt vielleicht sechs bis acht Jahre voraus scharf in die Zukunft*] This voice then continues: "That which is closer and that which is temporally farther away are unfocused" [*Das Nähere und das zeitlich weiter Entfernte sind unscharf*] (17–18). This lack of temporal focus could be related to what Erdle has analyzed in terms of Adorno's attention to "stupidity" as a critical mode of "thinking in times of danger" (265). Kluge's sustained narrative attention to lack of focus in his Shanghai miniatures is in any event clearly related to the pivotal oscillation of counterfactual hope that Kluge inherits from Adorno and expands on his own narrative terms, as discussed in Part One.

The "Chinese" miniature that interests me most is the fifth in this Shanghai series, and this fifth entry is titled "Schneller als das Schicksal" ["Faster than Fate"] (19–22). This global miniature focuses—in a very unfocused way—on Chen Kaige's "martial arts fantasy epic *The Promise* of 2005 and state censorship rather than street labor.[29] What begins as an apparent synopsis of the film effectively rewrites a key scene related to time. The slave Kunlun, who knows nothing of his origins as a prince but learns that he can run faster than time, is allowed in the film to look into the past to see his family and village eradicated by a cruel enemy in his absence. In Kluge's diction an "optical wall" makes these "realities diverge from each other" [*optische Wand, welche die Wirklichkeiten voneinander scheidet*] (19), and "the hero follows what happens, without being able to help, because he is after all on the side of the future" [*verfolgt der Held das Geschehen, ohne helfen zu können, denn er befindet sich ja auf der Seite der Zukunft*] (19). Yet Chen's cinematography does not honor the ascribed optical divide, as spectators watching the film are drawn into the past made visually present, and in terms of narrative diegesis Kunlun looks back from the present not the future in Chen's film. The "side of the future" is conjured only in Kluge's kaleidoscopic and synoptic narration, which both *un*does accelerated "time-space compression" in figural terms of the wall and constates the future in the present by use of the present tense.[30] In Marie-Laure Ryan's narratological terms, experimental literature that traffics in "impossible worlds"—in defiance of rules of logic—presents readers with oxymorons that are useful to readers

---

29 Here I cite Michael Berry's description of the film, which appeared in Mandarin under the title *Wuji* and in German as *Die Reiter der Winde* (85). Paul Clark characterizes *The Promise* as "a fantasy historical drama" (163).
30 For nuanced analysis of Kluge's varied use of the present tense in one narrative miniature from *Cinema Stories* in relation to critical reflections on film history, see Philipp Ekardt ("Film ohne Star").

in spite of making no logical sense ("Impossible Worlds" 369). We can understand Kluge's global miniatures of futurity as experimental in this vein as well.

Many more storytelling details in "Faster than Fate" would warrant analysis as uses and operations of futurity. In closing I shall mention just two. In Kluge's telling, Party censors had "a problem" [*ein Problem*] with Chen's film because of its status as an "ARTFUL FAIRY TALE" [*KUNSTMÄRCHEN*] (19). Aside from an allusion to the German Romantic tradition of artful fairy tales as distinguished from folk tales, the word "Märchen" and many motifs from German tales of fairies and folk occur with stunning frequency in Kluge's prose. Kluge frequently refers to the Grimm brothers' fairy tale of "The Obstinate Child" (Negt and Kluge, *History and Obstinacy* 292–293) as his favorite and at times likens "a real fairy tale" [*ein wirkliches Märchen*] to a form of montage (see Kluge's 2012 poetics lectures of 19 June and 12 June, respectively). Other fairy tales highlighted in *History and Obstinacy* alone range for example from "Hansel and Gretel," "Sleeping Beauty," "The Song of Blacksmith Volund," and "The Story of the Rejuvenated Little Old Man" to "The Wolf and the Seven Young Kids." One could understand such fairy tales as one form of "unnatural narration" that has become naturalized by convention.[31] One could also focus on an explicit comparative foil suggested in "Faster than Fate" when one unidentified dialogic partner mentions the Germanic folk legend of "Dwarf King Alberich, who renounces happiness in love in exchange for gold" [*Zwergenkönig Alberich, der für Gold seinem Liebesglück abschwört*] (20) in a plot that parallels the promise from which Chen's film derives its English title.

What I would stress, however, is not a crosscultural comparison of naturalized narration but the etymology of the word *Märchen* itself. In German the diminutive suffix –*chen* compounds by miniaturization premodern Germanic and Celtic designations for "report," "pronouncement" [*Kunde*], "news" [*Nachricht*], and "more" [*mehr*] (see the etymological entry on *Märchen* in Seebold 598). For Kluge, this diminutive suffix—which can operate linguistically only via conjunction—serves as a supplement (or in critical terminology that Kluge inherits from Marx: *Zusatz*) in both grammatical and temporal senses. This is not only a matter or problematics of scale (as Latour addresses the Anthropocene) but also, in its radical core, about experiential orientation to utopian dimensions of futurity in the doubled reality of this-worldly and off-worldly time. Here it behooves us moreover to recall that *The Communist Manifesto* of 1848 explicitly invokes,

---

[31] See Ryan on modes of unnatural narration that may become "popular" with frequent use ("Impossible Worlds" 368). On Kluge's use of "The Wolf and the Seven Young Kids" in terms of a dialectic of danger and safety in relation to interiority and exteriority, see Langston ("'Windows are to a House'").

not merely the "ghost of communism," but more precisely the "fairy tales of the ghost of communism" [*Märchen vom Gespenst des Kommunismus*] as that which the making "manifest" of the communist party is meant to counter (Marx and Engels, "Manifest der Kommunistischen Partei" 461; English versions based on Samuel Moore's authorized translation render *Märchen*, which Marx and Engels used in plural form, as "nursery tale" in the singular instead). What Kluge does with *Märchen* material in narrative form—as social labor on temporal perspective—is thus one crucial point of entry for reading the macro- and micro-dimensions of futurity, globalization, and communist horizons in the "permanent revolution" that his global miniatures encourage us to practice in the aftermath of 1989.

My final point about "Faster than Fate" is less a point than an oscillating question. This global miniature transitions after initial kaleidoscopic and synoptic narration to extended dialogue of a sort that recurs formally in much of Kluge's literary prose overall. This consists of dialogic sequencing and collaboration unmediated by character description, voice attribution, setting details, or narrative framing. We have already seen that narrative voices of interlocution in and beyond Richardson's narratological sense also sometimes sneak into such dialogic sequences and are themselves prone to functional oscillation. (This is why it is sometimes necessary to distinguish between dialogic interlocutors and narrative interlocutors in Kluge's writing, though his narrative interlocutors sometimes also take on dialogic roles.) In "Faster than Fate" the dialogic interlocution concerns the role and provenance of ghosts in Chen Kaige's film. One voice observes, "One of Marx and Engels' most important writings begins, after all, with a story about ghosts" [*Eine der wichtigsten Schriften von Marx und Engels beginnt ja mit einer Erzählung über Gespenster*] (20). "What are ghosts?" [*Was sind Gespenster?*], another voice asks. In apparent response we read: "Fateful predictions that join together into swarms" [*Schicksalhafte Vorhersagen, die sich zu Schwärmen zusammenschließen*] (20). "Swarms" here is another figure of indistinctness linked to a use of the future, and again, Derrida's discussion of what he calls "the non-finite process of spectralization" (193) in Marxist thought as an ethic of "responsibility" to ghosts who have been and those yet to come (viii) can surely be helpful in parsing the motif of ghosts and spirits in Kluge's global miniatures. A haunting question though is what to make of those "voices" of interlocution that manifest in his cosmic and global miniatures as ghosts, swarms, and masses, since, in Kluge's experimental miniatures, ghosts, swarms, and masses generally do not speak—though they could be said to write. This would be one way of reading Kluge's well-documented trope of a cautionary "writing on the wall" [*Menetekel*].[32]

Kluge's work is riddled with written dialogue that frequently manifests as floating, almost untethered, as if on currents of air. One Kluge scholar, who knows the author's extended multi-medial oeuvre better than most, argues in reference to some of Kluge's other writings that the author's insistent use of dialogue must be understood in terms of an intersubjective dialectic of Enlightened "autonomous" thought, albeit in a mode that favors ethical fantasy—"an unrealized potential of fantasy work"—over a Habermasian principle of rational communication (Langston, "Toward an Ethics of Fantasy" 285, 290–291; see Part One for additional remarks on dialogue and dialectics). For Langston, citing Volume 1 of Negt and Kluge's *Der unterschätzte Mensch* ["The Underestimated Human Being"] (274), this "unrealized potential" is always "to be found outside the immediate frame of dialogic exchange" (291). This is an astute observation on narrative grounds as well, but I would suggest that more than "unrealized" potential is at stake in Kluge's literary experiments. The Enlightenment thought-figure of perceptual and cognitive "intensity" that Erich Kleinschmidt discusses as an ambiguous threshold, "an excess, but also a vagueness with regard to a border value" (13), may prove more apt for wrestling with the oscillating intensity of counterfactual hope that Kluge reworks for the 21st century as heir to Adorno, Benjamin, Marx, and also Kant (on Benjamin's related critique of Enlightenment models of intensity, see Hamacher). But if we tend to Kluge's narrative forms with which futurity is enlivened and mobilized in his global miniatures, will his spirited voices of experimental dialogue always serve a dialectical model of futurity as a paradigm of progress and not merely critique?

I have argued here that Kluge's cosmic and global miniatures advance the cultivation of the future sense as something that becomes, however incrementally, phenomenologically accessible to social experience through reading. This advance is not linear or continuous, and neither are most of the storytelling forms on which it draws. And yet, the increasing claims to simultaneously social and off-worldly reality that the future sense of Kluge's writing can make are also not generically processual either (though they are certainly processual rather than conclusive). Something in the spirit of Marxist orientations to transformative horizons remains and continues to be worked on in Kluge's miniatures on contemporary globalization too. Pavsek writes in reference to Kluge's films

---

[32] Schulte has observed in a related vein that historical catastrophes, for Kluge, appear "as 'writings on the wall,' as advance messengers of further disasters in the future" ("Konstruktionen des Zusammenhangs" 47). See both Part Three and the discussion of "The Beautiful is Flawless" in Part One for different perspectives on futurity and narrative form in this regard.

that this artist's temporal "utopian imperative" is always "toward a redeemed future" (*The Utopia of Film* 23). This may be more true of the ethical imperative than the narrative orientation and storytelling forms of Kluge's actual writing practice.[33] These experimental miniatures arguably move us as readers—with stories we are invited to use in real time—toward a revolutionary future. If a redeemed future is always deferred, a revolutionary one becomes partially available to us through reading. To the degree that it becomes accessible to experience at all, this future is not permanently deferred but neither is it merely presentist. This is no longer about historical or dialectical failure alone, and neither does it guarantee any benchmarks of ethical or political success. The textual analyses proposed nonetheless suggest that something doubly real, something intangible though not in the least immaterial, does change in the process of reading Kluge's literary miniatures. That vague something is the lived and aspirational relationship linking anti-realist hope and real destruction. Kluge's cosmic miniatures as discussed in Part One help us understand how this process of conversion operates in narrative uses of futurity in Kluge's global miniatures too. The global connectivity at stake here is thoroughly entangled in earthly histories, planetary imperatives, and cosmic dimensions, all by means of micrological experimentation with poetics in print. The temporal perspectives and "ways out" of catastrophe and despair that Kluge's writing opens up for us do not rely on the future sense; they help to generate it as a long-distance sense organ of temporal perception.

---

33 In "The Utopia of Reading," Pavsek addresses key tropes of reading in Kluge's films. Several features he highlights—"non-places about which it may not be quite right to say that they reside 'in' the text" (104), a "bodily or affective impulse" that "might well be a transcendental" (104), and the importance of repeated "re-reading" for incremental learning processes (118–119)—are compatible with my discussion of Kluge's work on the future sense. However, these features alone cannot explain the importance of narrative form in Kluge's experimental writing as such.

Part Three
German Miniatures and Perspectival Horizons: Recalibrating Historical Voice

1 Persons One Can Lose and Those One Can Gain

The peripatetic series of experimental miniatures we encounter in "Door to Door with an Other Life" ends, however inconclusively, with an entry titled "The Six-Year-Old within Me and the Starry Sky above Me" (606–607). This rhetorical formulation is striking, first because Kluge chiastically inverts "the starry heavens above me and the moral law within me" from Kant's *Critique of Practical Reason* (see discussion of Kluge and Kant in my Introduction), and second because Kluge appears to displace "the moral law" with the six-year-old he conjures.[1] This shift in emphasis from "moral law" to "the six-year-old within me" merits additional note, since scholars often attribute the ethical force of Kluge's political counter-histories to their imaginative capacity to reflect critically on the failures, catastrophes, and crimes of German pasts. How could, should, and would such histories—especially the wars, dictatorships, genocide, and labor exploitation of the 20th century—have been averted? What cognitive insights and affective lessons about human agency can be gleaned from such counter-histories that would allow for more ethical futures and avert future disasters as well? These questions are entirely legitimate when brought to bear on Kluge's anti-realist realism, and scholars of varying methodological bents tie them in one way or another to horizons of possibility. Eshel explicitly links his crosscultural definition of literary "futurity" to the modern openness of possibility, and for him, Kluge's contributions to rewriting "history's book of calamities" for the sake of "one's own life" too (*Futurity* 185) pivots on "keep[ing] open the *possibility* of choice, the prospect of a less inhuman reality" (228).[2] As I have argued throughout

---

[1] Elsewhere Kluge plays with Kantian rhetoric in other ways when he titles another miniature "Dunsthimmel über mir und das Ding in mir" ["Hazy Sky above Me and the Thing inside Me"] ("Kong's Great Hour" 533–534), this time in reference to an adult narrator undergoing a cancer scare.

[2] Eshel specifically has Sebald's novel *Austerlitz* in mind when he refers to "not only a tale from history's book of calamities but also an opportunity to consider the past's value for one's own life" (185). For additional comparisons and contrasts between Sebald and Kluge, see Langston's approach to "feeling history" ("Affective Affinities") and Huyssen (*Present Pasts*). Omer Bartov by contrast discusses Kluge's filmic approach to World War II, the Holocaust, and the Third Reich in scathing terms as "a masterpiece of memory and repression" (140).

DOI 10.1515/9783110525649-004

this book, however, the mere indexing of possibility is insufficient to account for narrative forms of futurity in Kluge's miniaturized experiments in time. For these life-and-death experiments also turn, in their narrative orientation to the utopian dimension, on the actual revolutionary conversion of catastrophic time into what we might call, with phrasing borrowed from Adorno, a "future without life's miseries" (see Part One). The cultivation of the future sense in Kluge's 21st-century poetics makes this futurity incrementally and intermittently accessible to human experience through the legibility of counterfactual perspective in particular, as Parts One and Two have demonstrated, with the word *Perspektive* in German having both deictic and specifically future-oriented connotations.[3] The politics of Kluge's poetics are also "intimately" grounded, Kluge tells us, in his Frankfurt poetics lecture of 26 June 2012, in lived relations to both "persons that one can lose" and those "that one can gain" [*die man verlieren kann, die man gewinnen kann*] ("Theory of Storytelling"). What then are we to make of the seemingly personalized and certainly miniaturized figure of "the six-year-old within me," who does not replace but figurally displaces "the moral law" in orientation to "an other life"?

Is this six-year-old a reliable cipher of life writing in the spirit of self-oriented biography or autobiography? Many features of Kluge's oeuvre suggest such a reading, since real and fictional characters are sometimes given new life in his work, as we saw with the example of the Adornos in Part One, and since Kluge's own life and family history figure prominently in much of his documentary fiction as well. This applies in seminal ways to "The Air Raid on Halberstadt, 8 April 1945," which describes the Allied bombing of Kluge's home town and first appeared in his story collection *Neue Geschichten* ["New Stories/New Histories"] in 1977, though as Andrew Bowie noted in 1982, "Kluge does not write a personal account of his memories of that day" in that pivotal piece ("New Histories" 192). More and more autobiographical and biographical material concerning Kluge's life and family history makes its way into his newer writing. This includes for example an entire section of autobiographical miniatures under the rubric of "'Ich'" [I] in "Kong's Great Hour" (523–563), one long section in "The Fifth Book" titled "Die Lebensläufer und ihre Lebensgeschichten" ["The Course-of-

---

[3] These dual connotations of *Perspektive* are no doubt co-present when Adorno invokes the "standpoint of redemption" in the final entry of *Minima Moralia*: "Perspectives must be fashioned [*hergestellt*] that displace and estrange the world, reveal it to be, with its rifts and crevices, as indigent and distorted as it will appear one day in the messianic light" (Jephcott translation, 247). The Redmond translation renders Adorno's "hergestellt" more accurately as "produced" (274).

Lifers and Their Life Stories"] (9–160) plus one piece about a nasty fall that left Kluge badly bruised on the occasion of a visit to an elite research university in the United States (393–395), and several other multigenerational stories scattered throughout "Door to Door with an Other Life" (e.g. "Mein Großvater mütterlicherseits" ["My Maternal Grandfather"] 510–512, "Ein Streit mit meiner Mutter" ["A Fight with My Mother"] 587, and "Mein wahres Motiv" ["My True Motive"] 594–597) and other collections too.[4] Rather than approaching Kluge's German miniatures and their perspectival horizons through the life writing of human persons though, or even through their well established challenges to "linear" narration (see especially Wolfgang Reichmann, *Der Chronist Alexander Kluge* and "Tür an Tür mit einer anderen Zeit"), Part Three focuses on narrative forms that Kluge uses to engender the life writing of futurity as such, a long-distance sense organ of temporal perception that his storytelling actively cultivates.

This analytical lens will help sharpen our understanding of Kluge's ongoing interventions in the postwar German culture of *Vergangenheitsbewältigung*, most commonly understood as an ethically minded attempt to come to terms with a catastrophic or criminal national past, particularly in the wake of the Holocaust, and it will additionally shed light on the importance of Kluge's literary experiments for narratological considerations of collective voice. Like his cosmic and global miniatures too, Kluge's more emphatically German miniatures have many things to teach us about narrative oscillations between hope and despair. And yet the intimate intensity of the poetic miniatures discussed in Part Three remains deeply cultural in its German orientations too. The phenomenological futurity of the utopian dimension is no mere or ahistorical abstraction in thought for Kluge, though it does entail something off-worldly, non-empirical, and non-presentist entering into this-worldly time. How then do our readings of cosmic horizons and global revolution in Kluge's writing enrich our grasp of futurity as narrative form in his German miniatures too, and in what specific ways can we say that many of his German miniatures are also cosmic and global? To answer these questions, we will first take a closer look at the use of perspective and voice in "The Six-Year-Old within Me and the Starry Sky above Me" from "Door to Door with an Other Life," before turning to some of Kluge's seemingly straightforward scientific metanarratives about the long arc of cosmic formations resulting in stars, planets, and galaxies. These metanarratives represent one type of cosmic miniature in Kluge's prose that is oddly enough best explained in Part

---

[4] See also Kluge's fourth Frankfurt poetics lecture, which includes a story about his parents' marital discord and an incident in which he was publicly shamed for teenage drinking ("Theory of Storytelling," 26 June 2012).

Three, which focuses on German miniatures and collective voice in historical and utopian time. This will prepare the way for close readings of two final experiments, the first titled "Lebendigkeit von 1931" ["Liveness from 1931"] ("The Gap the Devil Leaves Us" 25–30), a bio-graphical miniature featuring the historical figure Werner Scholem, a German Jew and communist activist who was murdered in Buchenwald in 1940, and the second titled "Zeugen aus einer anderen Welt" ["Witnesses from an Other World"] ("'Whoever speaks a word of consolation is a traitor': 48 Stories for Fritz Bauer" 53–54), the only miniature to feature extraterrestrials in a collection devoted to the horrors of German anti-Semitism and the Nazi Holocaust.

2 The Six-Year-Old within Me, the Starry Sky above Me, and Narrative Voice

At first glance the miniature titled "The Six-Year-Old within Me and the Starry Sky above Me" eerily recalls textual themes and narrative elements from Kluge's cosmic miniature "Hope at Sunrise," as discussed in Part One of the present study. An unidentified third-person narrator introduces readers to a room for collective use that is "protectively closed off against the outside world" [*gegen die Außenwelt abgeschirmt*] (606). This room is not in a hospital but an office building in which the architectural need for sequential "meeting rooms" [*Sitzungsräume*] dictated "that not every room had windows that would guide the view outside" [*daß nicht jeder Raum Fenster besaß, die den Blick nach außen führten*]. Shades of Leibniz's windowless monads circulate here too, and like "Hope at Sunrise," this miniature also features a narrative disturbance in the field of epistemological certainty that the narrative voice seems to be creating. However, in this miniature, threats to life are only indirectly present, and the narrative disturbance in this case does not stem from perceptual ambiguity but from a literally heightened assertion of epistemological certainty instead. For as the third-person narrator of indeterminate standpoint goes on to observe in the form of an expansive qualification: "But even through windows one would not have been able to see the starry sky because of the milky midday light that filled the metropolis, although after all, at every point in time, the stars up there are guarding over us" [*Aber auch durch Fenster hätte man den gestirnten Himmel wegen des milchigen Mittagslichts, das die Großstadt erfüllte, nicht sehen können, obgleich doch die Sterne zu jedem Zeitpunkt dort oben über uns wachen*] (606).

The implied need for such sidereal watchmen suggests an amorphous threat of some kind, and readers will readily recognize Kluge's core constellation of relations between "above" and "below." Yet this narrative instance firmly asserts knowledge of cosmic-human relations that no mortal or "natural" observer could empirically possess. The narrative disturbance in the first paragraph of this cosmic German miniature thus comes in the diminutive first-person plural pronoun in its accusative form: "us." In linguistic terms the "us" in this context functions as an unmarked evidential, since we cannot resolve what kind of source information underwrites the assertion that the narrative voice has made. Sarah E. Murray's theory of evidentiality in speech acts more generally distinguishes between those evidential utterances that "contribute not-at-issue content, which cannot be directly challenged or denied" and those that put forth "at-issue content," which is "to be added to the common ground, up for negotiation" (4–5). The status of Kluge's "us" in this miniature arguably entails "at-issue content" that must be socially negotiated. Does the narrative voice that uses this pronoun belong to the world of windowless meeting rooms it has described, or does it belong to a world of sidereal perspectives, or does it rather oscillate—as counterfactual hope so often does in Kluge's writing—between otherwise opposing views? The "us" also interpellates the text's readers, who begin to oscillate between multiple perspectives as well. In the next step of analysis I argue that the remainder of Kluge's miniature shifts its narrative focus both from space to time and from the anonymity of office exchange to a polyphony of anthropocentric voices in which "the six-year-old within me" has a special role to play, though perhaps not the one readers might expect.[5]

The "us" is not repeated in this miniature, and no "we" ever makes an appearance at all. The text segues into a middle section consisting of three descriptive sentences narrated in a third-person voice now commenting on the "lovelessness" [*Lieblosigkeit*] (607) that prevailed among the disgruntled speakers in the meeting room. Nothing here indicates whether the narrative voice belongs to one of the people in the meeting room or not. The categorical status of the narrative voice shifts radically in the next and concluding paragraph though, when this voice now asserts in the present tense: "I am older than the others" [*Ich bin älter als die anderen*] (607). Suddenly the narrative voice appears to speak solidly from within the room, where readers can easily imagine the attendant anthropomorphic contours of a fully embodied participant even if such physical details

---

[5] Elsewhere Kluge refers to the "perspective of constellative narration" [*Perspektive des konstellativen Erzählens*] as serving the "revivification of POLYPHONY" [*Wiederbelebung der POLYPHONIE*] (Kluge and Stollmann, "Long-Distance Conversations" 190). To the extent that Kluge's approach to polyphonic narration is also tied to practices of "polychrony" in David Herman's narratological sense (*Story Logic* 217–220), we must remind ourselves that Kluge's storytelling practice is also riddled with a sense of "anachronism" that he inherits in part not from Genette but from Adorno (see Part One).

2 The Six-Year-Old within Me, the Starry Sky above Me, and Narrative Voice — 203

are not described. And yet the narrative voice that appears to consolidate its own contours as an "I" is immediately subject to a proliferating multiplicity.

> In me I hear the six-year-old that I once was AND THAT I ESSENTIALLY AM AT EVERY POINT IN TIME IN MY LIFE. The seventeen-year-old or the thirty-two-year old are also often speaking in me. But they seldom speak at the same time, whereas the interjections of the six-year-old seem to accord with each of the other voices.
>
> [*In mir höre ich den Sechsjährigen, der ich einmal war UND DER ICH AN SICH ZU JEDEM ZEITPUNKT MEINES LEBENS BIN. Oft sprechen in mir auch der Siebzehnjährige oder Zweiunddreißigjährige. Sie sprechen aber selten zur selben Zeit, während die Einwürfe des Sechsjährigen zu jeder der übrigen Stimmen zu passen scheinen.*] (607)

Elsewhere a narrative figure in the explicit guise of Alexander Kluge speaks, in conversation with a neurophysicist about how the brain recognizes multiple perceptions as cohering in an ostensibly single unit, of the "stubborn autonomy of my billions of interiorities" [*Eigensinnigkeit meiner Milliarden Innerlichkeiten*] (see "Durch Armut reich: das Ich" ["Rich from Poverty: the I"], "Kong's Great Hour" 528).

The "six-year-old within me" in the miniature under discussion notably countermands any consolidation of the self, even as the narrative voice speaks in the recognizable persona of an "I," and the figure of the six-year-old appears, not as an embodied person but solely as a persistent voice. Awarding Kluge the Federal Republic of Germany's Commander's Cross of Merit [*Großes Verdienstkreuz*] in 2007 on the occasion of Kluge's seventy-fifth birthday, then President Horst Köhler astutely remarked that Kluge's oeuvre is paradoxically self-biographical in its core construction but at the same time barely "centered in the self" [*ich-zentriert*] at all (2). Köhler's conjoined observations apply to the voices of this miniature too. All the voices "within me" and in dialogue with others in the meeting room are figured explicitly as figures in ordinal time—"the six-year-old," "the seventeen-year-old," "the thirty-two-year-old"—and the youngest of these (and simultaneously the oldest, if we focus on duration) presumably has special status in relation to all others precisely because it is available not only at its designated moment in a lifetime but "at every point in time." This is the only phrase used in the miniature to refer both to the six-year-old and to the stars watching "over us." This six-year-old within thus does not symbolize a child's idealized wonder, innocence, play, or even longevity. In narrative terms of perspective, voice, and figuration it rather marks a nexus in time at which access to futurity begins to be accessible to experience.

This sounds counterintuitive when we consider that the adult "I" in the meeting room necessarily represents a later developmental stage in ontogenetic terms and that the miniature itself invokes a register of memory in its conclusion, as we shall see. However, the narrative voice that speaks of its own multiplicity is the only instance to "hear" the six-year-old, for this miniaturized figure of a voice never actually speaks in the text. We are able to perceive this voice only to the degree that the text's narrative strategies make it available to us, and these narrative strategies are in effect running ahead of the figure of the six-year-old within "at every point in time." This miniature also devotes its final words to yet another leap in time, which demonstrates that the adult narrative voice is the most interesting one to track (and in this respect similar to what we observed in Adorno's "Heliotrope" miniature from *Minima Moralia*). The future horizon of the six-year-old in terms of development, this adult voice and its dimensional quality are themselves constantly oscillating in time.

> If I close my eyes for a moment, it can happen that I return to this room from an earlier time. I have the impression of having lived on one of the landed estates in ancient Syria. And if this is correct, I am also living now, while I am answering questions here in the conference, in this other time. Is this other time dear to me? Would I remember it if it weren't dear to me?
>
> [*Schließe ich einen Moment die Augen, so kann es sein, daß ich aus einer früheren Zeit in diesen Saal zurückkehre. Ich habe den Eindruck, auf einem der Landgüter im antiken Syrien gelebt zu haben. Und wenn dies zutrifft, lebe ich auch jetzt, während ich hier in der Konferenz Rede und Antwort stehe, in dieser anderen Zeit. Ist sie mir lieb? Würde ich mich an sie erinnern, wenn sie mir nicht lieb wäre?*] (607)

The miniature's temporal disjunctions and conjunctions at this point refuse any containment in the interiority of personhood or the exteriority of building or even in the ubiquitous voice of a six-year-old. Traveling in time, the concurrently self-dispersing and self-coalescing voice that narrates this piece underscores its liveness—"I am also living now"—in reference to an "other time."

This adult voice constates the existence of that other time and then asks two questions pertaining to its own affective orientation to that other time. Neither question is answered here, though one could conceivably interpret the second question as a rhetorical response to the first. A puzzle remains as to what binds this narrative voice affectively to "this other time" in Syria or to the stars watching over us or to the hyperactive six-year-old within. The fact that the thinly embodied narrative voice here raises questions that the narrative itself does not go on to answer would at first appear to disqualify it from Richardson's narratological definition of an interlocutor as an unnatural agent at "the very boundaries of narration" (79). And yet here too, similar to what we observed in Part One, Kluge's stylistic attention to dimensional oscillations in time suggests that the "I" of this miniature does function in narratological terms as an interlocutor despite its incipient embodiment, precisely because of its functional oscillation and because of its incipient embodiment. Primarily through narrative experimentation with unnatural perspective and voice, this cosmic German miniature allows for the future sense as an affective orientation of vital longing for an "other time" in which the six-year-old within and the starry sky above are constellated together for both the articulation of an "I" and the implied possibility of an articulated "we" beyond a constative "us."

3 Long Arcs of Cosmic Formation and the Narrative Trajectory of First-Person Pronouns

Among the most puzzling of Kluge's cosmic miniatures are his seemingly straightforward scientific metanarratives about the long arc of cosmic formations resulting in stars, planets, and galaxies. Such metanarratives either appear as freestanding miniatures, as in "Bauch der Milchstraße" ["Belly of the Milky Way"] in "The Gap the Devil Leaves Us" (332–333) and "Unser ständiger Begleiter, der Mond" ["Our Constant Companion, the Moon"] in "Door to Door with an Other Life" (544), or as embedded components of textually more varied miniatures such as "Our Ancestors, the Stars" ("Door to Door with an Other Life" 40–42) and "Sind Photonen individuell?" ["Are Photons Individual?"] ("The Gap the Devil Leaves Us" 505–506).[6] "Our Ancestors, the Stars," for example, begins with the following series of astrophysical or astrophysical-sounding assertions:

> Those zones in which much matter is already found, and that are therefore "hot," have no chance of clouds of molecules exerting reciprocal ATTRACTION such that they would compose themselves within eons into sun bodies. No, far from it, in cool, impoverished fields of the cosmos, those IRREGULARITIES IN HIGH VACUUM, from which the stars later develop, preserve themselves. BLUE GIANTS are formed that spend themselves. In three million years these massive balls of gas are burned out. Their particles disperse themselves into all horizons.

---

[6] "Our Ancestors, the Stars" and "Our Constant Companion, the Moon" belong to the few cosmic miniatures accompanied by graphic images, one simply labeled "Moon" ("Door to Door with an Other Life" 545) and the other designated as a photograph taken by the Hubble Space Telescope ("Door to Door with an Other Life" 41). Both images are explicitly assigned the textual status of *Abbildung* or "illustration," and yet neither image captures or illustrates the temporal complexity of what the accompanying narrative achieves. For an early analysis of Kluge's multimediality as a form of "montage" that challenges both coherent meaning and ideological domination of the senses, see Gerhard Bechtold.

[*Chance dazu, daß Molekülwolken ATTRAKTION aufeinander ausüben, so daß sie sich binnen Äonen zu Sonnenkörpern fügen, haben nicht jene Zonen, in denen sich viel Materie bereits befindet und die deshalb „heiß" sind. Nein, weit entfernt davon, in kühlen, armseligen Gefilden des Weltalls, erhalten sich jene UNREGELMÄSSIGKEITEN IM HOCHVAKUUM, aus denen sich später die Sterne entwickeln. Es bilden sich BLAUE RIESEN, die sich verschwenden. In drei Millionen Jahren sind diese gewaltigen Gasbälle ausgebrannt. Ihre Partikel zerstreuen sich in alle Horizonte.*] (40)

Or as we read about the moon, "our constant companion:"

Ten to the ninth power years ago, shortly after the accretion, the balling together of Earth, after its iron core had already developed, a large body must have collided with this conglomeration. This event slung out the material, from the Earth's mantle, for the moon that would take shape in the aftermath of this event.

[*Vor zehn hoch neun Jahren, kurz nach der Akkretion, der Zusammenballung der Erde, nachdem ihr Eisenkern schon entwickelt war, muß ein großer Körper mit diesem Konglomerat zusammengestoßen sein. Dieses Ereignis hat das Material für den sich daraufhin bildenden Mond aus dem Erdmantel herausgeschleudert.*] (544)

The miniature titled "Are Photons Individual?" similarly begins with a metanarrative linking temporality and the planet Earth to another sidereal body, in this case, the sun:

A particle of light that comes into existence in the sun's interior will be under way for a million years before it reaches the atmosphere of the sun. From there, at some point, when its turn comes to be radiated off, it will reach the Earth in eight minutes.

[*Ein Lichtpartikel, das im Inneren der Sonne entsteht, wird eine Million Jahre unterwegs sein, bis es in die Atmosphäre der Sonne gelangt und irgendwann dort, wenn die Reihe an es kommt, abgestrahlt zu werden, in acht Minuten die Erde erreichen.*]
("The Gap the Devil Leaves Us" 505)

In long-arc cosmic miniatures such as these, an explicitly measured temporal sequence colludes with linear narration to yield a causal and consequential cosmic event that is made perceptible through the storytelling horizon of indeterminate third-person perspective. Yet what makes these miniatures either revolutionary or useful for contemplating Kluge's more pointedly German miniatures too?[7]

---

7 Stressing more global effects of Kluge's 21st century writing, Radisoglou claims that "Kluge is no longer concerned with a predominantly German field of narration" (4). This is only partly true, and I would say that we still need to find ways to account for Kluge's evolving engagement with more emphatically German fields of narration too. For additional remarks on Radisoglou's insights into Kluge's narratives of globalization, see Part Two. On "the global resonance of Klug-

Two related answers have to do, first, with Kluge's narrative use of anthropomorphic figuration even in long-arc tales of cosmic development and, second, with his narrative deployment of personal pronouns. The moon is described as "tectonically dead, a 'premature birth'" [*tektonisch tot, eine "Frühgeburt"*] in one miniature for example ("Our Constant Companion," "Door to Door with an Other Life" 544), recalling motifs of birthing and midwifery that have circulated for decades throughout Kluge's oeuvre.[8] "Belly of the Milky Way" ultimately zeroes in surprisingly on the figure of a hat brim instead. Informing readers that the "belly" or "bulge" of the Milky Way contains "cool giant stars" [*kühle Riesensterne*] surrounded by a galactic disc that "contains most of the galaxy's stars" [*die Mehrzahl der Sterne der Galaxis enthält*] and is itself "embedded in a very thin and extremely hot gas" [*in ein sehr dünnes und extrem heißes Gas eingebettet*], this miniature concludes with the following paragraph:

> What the layer of gas is lacking in thickness, it makes up for in expansion. It extends out into a distance of 80,000 light years from the galactic center, while the stars already lose themselves at a radius of 50,000 light years. The outermost areas of the thin disc of gas are bent like a hat brim. Approximately 50% of spiral galaxies have this structure of a hat brim.
>
> [*Was der Gasschicht an Dicke fehlt, macht sie an Ausdehnung wett. Sie erstreckt sich hinaus in eine Ferne von 80000 Lichtjahren vom galaktischen Zentrum, während sich die Sterne schon bei einem Radius von 50000 Lichtjahren verlieren. Die äußersten Gebiete der dünnen Gasscheibe sind gebogen wie eine Hutkrempe. Etwa 50% der Spiralgalaxien besitzen diese Hutkrempenstruktur.*] ("The Gap the Devil Leaves Us" 332–333)

Anthropomorphic figuration of this sort has an arresting effect, but not merely because, on the most basic level, it once again underlines by narrative means a structural relationship between cosmic and human phenomena with special regard to time.

Beyond this, the narrative interjection of such anthropomorphic figuration is noteworthy because at first glance this figuration seems to recall what Fore incisively analyzes as a latent "structural anthropomorphism" informing deep technical relationships, rather than categorical oppositions, between modernism and realism in the interwar years in Europe (*Realism After Modernism* 2). Even where thematic references to human characters or personhood are wholly absent, Fore argues in reference to his interwar materials, "realism's humanist agenda" lives

---

e's aesthetic economy and its expanded [transnational] focus" since 2000, see also Miller ("*Eigensinn* in Transit" 101).

8 See for example related remarks by Christina Scherer (87). Kluge has often likened his artistic work to that of a midwife or alternately that of a "gardener."

on "at the level of artistic technique itself" (1). The "rehumanization of painting through the use of the easel," for example, was tied to "the return of linear one-point perspective," which was itself tied to an early modern conceptualization of an embodied human subject (1). As Fore elaborates concerning narrative technique:

> Like those developments in the visual arts, in prose the resurgence of great narrative forms such as the novel was buoyed by the latent figuration that is inherent to narrativity as such: even when absent of positive heroes and living figures, the contours of the plotline itself are 'inevitably anthropomorphous,' as Roland Barthes observed, since the causal sequences and notion of action that are fundamental to narrative always already presume human agency. (2)

When some of Kluge's cosmic miniatures give us long-arc origin stories of sidereal bodies and other cosmic matter, especially when those developmental narratives are abruptly set in relation to anthropomorphic figuration, it may therefore make sense to conclude that Kluge is subtly reminding us of the latent anthropomorphism of even anti-realist realism and narrative storytelling as such. However, I would suggest that the moon's "premature birth" and a sidereal "hat brim" in particular are also doing something rather different from the structural anthropomorphism of the interwar years for which Fore so ably accounts. For Kluge in a sense inverts the very perspective of narrative latency. Rather than projecting empirical human perspective into these stories of the stars, these seemingly straightforward metanarratives of cosmic formation above all bring something sidereal or off-worldly into the non-characterological figuration of the human as such. Once again, an indeterminate third-person voice grants readers access to this vague something, and we should therefore be careful not to assume that the cosmic key to these experimental miniatures lies in any implied analogies between developmental narratives of stars and developmental narratives of persons. Kluge's experiments in storytelling repeatedly draw our attention, however subtly, to functional oscillations in narrative voice instead.

We shall return to oscillating matters of narrative voice below when we return to one of Kluge's most complex cosmic metanarratives, "Our Ancestors, the Stars." Before doing so however, it will be helpful to discuss briefly one essay by Hans Blumenberg, a thinker of "non-conceptuality" who is not explicitly invoked in Kluge's work but whose approach to ambivalence, metaphor, and things sidereal shares at least some affinities with it, as Combrink and Langston have noted (see Part Two).[9] Dating to 1974, Blumenberg's English-language essay

---

[9] For extended commentary from various perspectives on Blumenberg in his own right, see

"On a Lineage of the Idea of Progress" tacitly bypasses Kantian modernity altogether in order to articulate a history of the idea of progress that is not predicated on Enlightenment reason, autonomy, or perfectability, but on a human relationship to observation of the stars. Here as elsewhere, Blumenberg's concomitant goal is to challenge the prevailing notion that modern progress must be conceived as the secularization of Christian faith in salvation (18). To make his case, Blumenberg traces the science and philosophy of astronomy from ancient Greece and Rome (notably in the work of Hipparchus, Pliny the Elder, and Seneca the Younger) to Galileo Galilei of Renaissance renown, with whom "the motion of progress" first became "recognizable as consisting in the production of problems by the solution of problems" (27).[10] For Blumenberg, astronomy is key to "a lineage of the idea of progress" in this emphatically future-generating sense, precisely because any "comparison between the course of history and that of an individual life" alone lacks both the temporal scale and the future life that the qualitative idea of progress demands (6). Blumenberg writes: "It is when the mere quantity of distance in time becomes the chief premise of new possibilities that the rationality of the idea of progress takes succinct form" (6), and in his assessment, the long-range "time basis" that the astronomical comparison of sidereal observations entails (7) is what ultimately comes to underwrite the modern idea of progress with Galileo. Prior to Galileo, "what happens in the sky" is in a sense "nothing; only very long time frames allow us to assume value changes large enough to cross the threshold of the empirical parameters" (8). Even if Blumenberg associates the astronomy of Pliny the Elder with "the Stoic dogma of a kinship between stars and men" (10), it is only with Galileo that combined factors of regularity and mutability affecting sidereal bodies and cosmic movements over very long periods of time are also seen as including the future too, one in which previously "unknown problems" will be not only latent but also "manifest themselves" *as* unknown problems for future astronomers to attempt to solve (27).

We might liken this in some limited respects to what James McFarland has to say about the word "constellation" as a "philosopheme" (472).

> The term constellation, which appears to be merely a synonym for a collection or arrangement, and whose meaning therefore seems to reside primarily in the relations among the

---

Telos 158 (2012), a special issue on Blumenberg co-edited by Paul Fleming, Rüdiger Campe, and Kirk Wetters.
10 As Blumenberg immediately explains: "Copernicus could never dream of this aspect; conclusively disposing of a problem was what he considered the 'normal' form of scientific achievement" (27).

elements constituting it, in the underdetermined unifying principle subsequent discourse intends to clarify, is already in fact the volatilization of any self-evident relation between the immediate observer and the objects at the limit that is observed. (474–475)

Yet for Blumenberg, "a logical tie between time quantum and achievement quality" is a necessary component in the idea of progress (7), and for this idea of progress, a temporal continuity rather than an agential one is key. "The gist of progress lies not in a continuity of actions; it lies in the continuity of the time which a tradition needs to pass them on. This is why the act of establishing this context must be realized not as a relic only, but as a future-oriented communication" (17). This is where Kluge and Blumenberg necessarily part ways though, for the astronomical temporal paradigm of cosmic-human progress Blumenberg articulates cannot allow for Kluge's disjunctive temporalities or the cultivation of a future sense that pierces and breaks any presumed temporal continuity of tradition.[11] Nonetheless, what Blumenberg's essay "On a Lineage of the Idea of Progress" does provide is a framework for understanding why Kluge's linear metanarratives of developmental macrocosmic formations are never cast as mere analogies of human lineages too—not even in a miniature titled "Our Ancestors, the Stars"—but as exercises in temporal perception. Narrative perspective and narrative voice trump whatever generational narrative they might otherwise appear to advance, and unnatural perspective as well as experimental voice serve the cultivation of futurity as an experiential portal in time. How does this work in "Our Ancestors, the Stars"? And how does something emphatically German become constellated in relation to these stars?

One of the earliest scholarly commentators on Kluge's "New Stories/New Histories" from the late 1970s, Andrew Bowie underscores the importance of Kluge's experimentation with storytelling form as a radical indictment of "the failure of 'Vergangenheitsbewältigung'" (Bowie, "New Histories" 193), by which Bowie mainly means those postwar German novels and short stories with which authors used moral suasion and above all human characters to attempt to come to terms honorably with the dishonor of the Nazi past. Yet it was precisely this reliance on human characters and anthropomorphic plot that doomed *Vergangenheitsbewältigung* to fail, according to Bowie, because the heightened abstraction of 20th-century social relations at every turn (in civilian life, military conflict, and industrialized killing) made individualized or even collective "personal experience" incapable of capturing or countering the forces of destruction at work ("'Sich rächen'" 81). To Bowie's mind, the brilliance of

---

[11] For an incisive sociological critique of conceptualizing modern traditions as in any way unbroken, see Andreas Langenohl.

Kluge's writing in the 1970s therefore lies in the author's insistence on abstract storytelling instead, meant "to heighten the capacity to experience" (in this case: to recognize) a deadly reality that "had become abstract" and otherwise inaccessible to experience and cognition (82). For Bowie, Kluge's literary work in particular effectively counters "an ever-growing disjunction between the way time is sensuously experienced and the way it works in historical developments" ("New Histories" 185). Kluge's stories are simultaneously "very German" in Bowie's assessment of the postwar era ("'Sich rächen'" 83). Citing the 1981 edition of Negt and Kluge's *Geschichte und Eigensinn*, David Roberts makes related points when he stresses that the Germany of 1945 was a unique "locus" for the articulation of Critical Theory, not for reasons of agency and guilt alone but on epistemological grounds ("Alexander Kluge und die deutsche Zeitgeschichte" 80; see also Negt and Kluge, *Geschichte und Eigensinn* 1122). And like Bowie, though for different formal reasons, Roberts also claims that Kluge's writing style in the 1970s precludes reliance on personalized figuration or anthropomorphic perspective (79).[12] The trajectory of these accounts does help us understand why Kluge's literary works have from the beginning been both deeply rooted in German crises of historical experience, conscience, and cognition, on the one hand, and at odds with the primary literary formations with which postwar German culture sought to address them, on the other.[13] Yet the trajectory of even very insightful accounts along these lines cannot help us address the specific functions of narrative voice as a formal device in Kluge's prose then or now. How are we to situate Kluge's 21st-century experiments with so-called unnatural voice in particular, in a narrative landscape where miniscule anthropomorphic turns are conjoined with macrocosmic tales of sidereal generation?

---

12 For Bowie, the deciding formal factor is abstraction; Roberts explicitly stresses montage instead. Another important early commentator on Kluge's approach to historical narrative characterizes his radical aesthetic as "entirely singular" in postwar German literature (Harro Müller, *Geschichte zwischen Kairos und Katastrophe* 115). Müller insightfully adds that the only other postwar German author who comes close to the radicality of Kluge's formal experiments is Manfred Franke in the novel *Mordverläufe: 9./10. XI. 1938, ein Protokoll von der Angst, von Misshandlung und Tod, vom Auffinden der Spuren und deren Wiederentdeckung* (1973), an experimental "protocol" of the murderous unfolding of events on the so-called Night of Broken Glass on 9 November 1938 in Nazi Germany.

13 For overviews of Kluge's approach to historical memory in German literary culture, see for example Rainer Stollmann ("Wovon man nicht reden kann"), Matthias Uecker, and Wilhelm Voßkamp ("Emblematik der Geschichte"); for a broader sampling of multimedial analyses, see Tara Forrest's edited volume, *Alexander Kluge*.

Eric L. Santner inadvertently gives us a helpful clue when he posits a sea change at the end of the 20th century in German cultural conditions for reflecting on *Vergangenheitsbewältigung* as a cultural formation:

> As the perpetrator generation dies out, more properly juridical issues of guilt and complicity yield to more inchoate questions of historical memory and of the mediation and transmittal of cultural traditions and identities. In the next stage the fundamental issue becomes, in a sense, what it means to say *"ich"* and *"wir"* in a Germany that still finds itself under the shadow of the Final Solution. What are the strategies and procedures by which a cultural identity may be reconstituted in post-Holocaust Germany? (xii–xiii)

For reasons that will become clear in the section of Part Three that deals with Kluge's German miniature featuring Werner Scholem, I am less interested in Santner's overt emphasis on cultural memory, tradition, and transmittal. What I wish to draw attention to instead is his equally explicit emphasis on the very German first-person pronouns for "I" and "we." I shall not discuss Kluge's experimental mobilization of first-person pronouns in terms of cultural identity though, but in relation to a radical use of narrative voice that serves the future sense, as a German bridge in time to the utopian dimension.

As we have already seen in "The Six-Year-Old within Me and the Starry Sky above Me," a narrative disturbance in sidereal narration manifests there in the form of "us," with this "us" functioning as an unmarked evidential, the social status of which must be negotiated. Something similar happens in "Our Ancestors, the Stars," the first paragraph of which begins with no "chance" of formation into "sun bodies" [*Sonnenkörper*] in the so-called hot zones of the cosmos, and concludes with the "particles" of giant stars that had formed in the "cool" zones being scattered into every horizon. The second paragraph of this cosmic miniature extends the narrative account of sidereal generation, exhaustion, and re-generation in the present tense, somehow culminating in the rather "average" formation of "OUR SUN."

> From the cool, unstressed margins, a star forms anew. This second generation of heavenly bodies already possesses HEAVY ELEMENTS. But even this star must live, die and explode in order to disperse, in the terrain of the universe, the rich mass of heavy and light atoms that pulls itself together to form OUR SUN. An average star. Few qualities that would charm the alchemists.
>
> [*Von den kühlen, unbetonten Rändern her bildet sich erneut ein Stern. Diese zweite Generation der Himmelskörper besitzt bereits gewisse SCHWERE ELEMENTE. Aber auch dieser Stern muß leben, sterben und explodieren, um im Gelände des Universums die reiche Masse von schweren und leichten Atomen zu zerstreuen, die sich dann zu UNSERER SONNE zusammenzieht. Ein durchschnittliches Gestirn. Wenig Eigenschaften, welche die Alchimisten entzücken.*]
> ("Door to Door with an Other Life" 40)

Narrative disturbance and unmarked evidential alike manifest here—subtly, almost but not quite "unstressed"—in the possessive pronoun "our" in social relation to "sun." An otherwise disembodied voice of sidereal narration suddenly appears here as an earthly figure steeped in the language of cosmic generation. And yet this voice hardly sounds a call to hope of any magnitude, since what it immediately stresses is mediocrity and the lack of any qualities that would charm an alchemist. If this narrative voice is an experiental portal in time, it would not appear to be an especially uplifting one. In what way can we say then that this narrative voice and something earthly—and even more specifically, something one might call "ours"—conspire to serve the future sense as a nonempirical experience to be had while reading Kluge's prose?

Unlike freestanding cosmic metanarratives such as "Belly of the Milky Way" and "Our Constant Companion, the Moon," "Our Ancestors, the Stars" proceeds to take readers on a wild telluric ride, the formal and perspectival trajectory of which seems to mimic the sidereal formations, explosions, implosions, and dispersals that the miniature's first two paragraphs have described. Overall this three-page miniature consists of a heliotropic epigraph from Voltaire's *Dictionnaire Philosophique* from the 18th century, the extended paragraphs of sidereal narration discussed above, a black-and-white photograph taken by the Hubble Space Telescope of a galactic spiral containing "a trillion suns" (which a narrative caption tells us "we see" as the spiral looked "25 million years ago"), free-floating dialogic exchange between initially unidentified human interlocutors about the rise and fall of stars as compared with an entertainment program broadcast by Radio Leipzig in 1939 in Nazi Germany, descriptions of two scholars from the Bauhaus University Weimar discussing Isaac Newton's account of a clockwork universe in 1704 and the mysteries of the cosmic genesis of the human race, and barely embodied narrative interjections featuring Peter Kreuder's hit song lyrics from 1939 "Auf dem Dach der Welt" ["On the Roof of the World"] from the German musical "Hallo Janine!," narrative interlocution (as opposed to the dialogic variety) concerning Newton's *Opticks* (on the distinction I draw between narrative and dialogic forms of interlocution in Kluge's writing, see Part One), and finally a modified excerpt from John Donne's very long poem "An Anatomy of the World" from 1611. Time travel is dizzying, as this list of topics alone suggests, but it is the functionally protean narrative voice and the experimental perspectives it affords that are most vital here.

The implied and generic earthly "we" that could claim orientation to "our sun" in the scientific-sounding metanarrative portion of the miniature is clearly also related, in some fashion, to the implied German "we" that seems to have direct knowledge of Radio Leipzig broadcasts "in 1939," German musicals from the Third Reich, and scholarly exchange at the Bauhaus University Weimar, originally founded in the mid 19th century and renamed by its director Walter Gropius in 1919. This temporal linkage of cosmic, human, and emphatically German spheres is narratively fostered by pronouns for collective voice. This linkage is also underscored thematically when the first line of dialogue by one of the German interlocutors yields an incredulous question: "Three stars must perish for the likes of us to come into existence?" [*Drei Sterne müssen vergehen, daß unsereins entsteht?*] (40). It is not clear here whether "the likes of us" refers to human beings in a generic sense or Germans in particular, and this ambiguity is no doubt both intended and partisan in its utopian orientation, for the "us" is both, though not merely in an empirical historical sense. Kluge's recurring motif of destruction is close at hand with the word "perish," and a few lines later the miniature has readers imaginatively listening to pop lyrics from Nazi Germany about procreation "on the roof of the world." Life and death appear eerily and threateningly conjoined here. What role does the inchoately embodied voice of narration play in this miniaturized scenario of time travel? This voice, which initially established itself in sidereal narration before aligning itself with collective expression in the first person, disturbs the very scene of narration four times beyond the assertion of an implied "we" in the idiom "our sun."

The first of these four disturbances is easily missed, because it reads like a mere illustration or detail description of the entertainment broadcast from Leipzig that the two dialogue partners have just mentioned. However, the narrative voice heightens the reality effect of Leipzig in 1939, by switching to the past tense and simultaneously providing the synaesthetic experience of hearing actual lyrics, which also creates an intensified effect of sensory intimacy. This temporal intervention on the part of the narrative voice is typographically rendered open rather than closed though by virtue of two elliptical dashes that Kluge adds, a marked "way out" to which we shall have cause to return.[14] The second

---

14 On the "poetics of punctuation," see especially the anthology edited by Nebrig and Spoerhase, which also includes Adorno's 1956 essay on the subject ("Satzzeichen"). Referring to Theodor Storm's use of dashes in particular, Adorno speaks of the "time" of the dash "between two sentences" as the time of a "weighty inheritance" [*eine des lastenden Erbes*] (57). Analyzing in the same volume Adalbert Stifter's use of the dash, Joseph Vogl notes that dashes paradoxically turn "the interruption, the break, and the gap into a moment of conjunction" [*die Unterbrechung, der Bruch und die Lücke zu einem verbindenden Moment*] (281). Turning to literary works by Ingeborg Bachmann, Nelly Sachs, and Paul Celan, Ulrike Vedder analyzes the "productivity of the dash" for textual dynamics "as well as the representation of breaking-off points and moments of re-orientation" [*Produktivität des Gedankenstrichs für den Fortgang bzw. die Dynamisierung eines Textes sowie für die Darstellung von Ab- und Umbrüchen*] (345). Especially for these writers, Vedder finds, real hope and doomed hope alike are conjoined in the dash (360–361).

disturbance comes when the narrative voice rather than one of the Weimar scholars implicitly asks what Newton could possibly mean when Newton himself asks: "What is there in places *almost empty of Matter*, and whence is it that the Sun and Planets gravitate towards one another, without dense Matter between them?" (Newton, *Opticks* 369; emphasis added). What could Newton have meant by a non-mechanical "very first Cause" (369)? The unnamed scholars talking in "Our Ancestors, the Stars" cite Newton's English text directly, whereas the narrative voice intervenes to ask in German: "What can 'spiritual nature' mean here?" [*Was heißt hier 'geistiger Natur'?*] (42). This voice does not cite Newton, who does not use the term "spiritual nature" in *Opticks*, but the fictional German conversation instead. As we saw in Part One, narratologist Brian Richardson defines the unnatural voice of a narrative interlocutor in the main as "a disembodied voice that poses questions which the narrative goes on to answer" (79; see Part One for discussion of ways in which Kluge's literary experiments suggest modifications to this experimental definition). In "Our Ancestors, the Stars" however, the narrative interlocutor poses the question without appearing to answer it, since no declarative statement responding to this question is uttered in this voice of interlocution. We must look elsewhere—to a subsequent narrative disturbance in the text—for an answer that comes in the voice of what Richardson would call "unnatural" interlocution. Let us recall though, as noted in Part One, that the unnatural narratives we encounter in Adorno's "Heliotrope" and Kluge's cosmic miniatures for the 21st century challenge real-world limits to off-world aspirations of futurity by expanding rather than accommodating the human sensorium of possible experience.

The third narrative disturbance is even more likely to escape detection than the first, since this one could be mistaken for self-reflection by one of the Weimar partners in dialogue. Yet it is clearly an other voice—that of the minimally embodied narrative interlocutor—that remarks in reference to one of the actual conversationalists: "It is not easy for an Enlightener to deal with a miracle" [*Es ist nicht leicht, als Aufklärer mit einem Wunder umzugehen*] (42). While this slight disturbance in the narrative field is less consequential than any of the others, it does suggest the lingering co-presence of an off-worldly voice from "an other life" amidst the dialogue in Weimar. The narrative then continues with focalization through the other German partner in dialogic exchange, who remarks that there is "no miracle anywhere" [*nirgends ein Wunder*] but "only a chance that is extremely extended in time" [*nur zeitlich eine extrem langgestreckte*

Kluge's use of dashes in "Our Ancestors, the Stars" bears traces of all the qualities listed here that Adorno, Vogl, and Vedder discuss.

Chance] (42). The emphasis on an opportunity in time is important to remark here, and so is the fact that the final word of this sentence in the German wording harkens back to the text's first word of narration, in a sentence asserting "no chance" of "sun bodies" being formed.

In this recursive temporal gesture the miniature "Our Ancestors, the Stars" undoes the thematic temporal dictates of its own sidereal metanarrative about what can and cannot take physical form. Another recursive temporal gesture takes shape when the miniature concludes with a marked quotation signing off with two more dashes. Signaling at once an absence and a presence too, this marked ellipsis harkens back in form to the hit song from Radio Leipzig in the Nazi Germany of 1939, as the song excerpt appears typographically higher up on the page. Yet something shifts in time, voice, and perspective here, in ways that do not apply to the Peter Kreuder song cited in reference to Radio Leipzig. For at the final juncture of this cosmic and also very German miniature, the dispersed particle that emerges here as a horizon of futurity manifests as a slight modification of one short excerpt from Donne's "An Anatomy of the World."

> Prince, subject, father, son, are things forgot,
> For every man alone thinks he hath got
> TO BE A PHOENIX – – (42)

Neither of the Newtonian discussants ever mentions this worldly "anatomy," and Donne's poetic lines must come to us from the at once off-worldly and this-worldly voice of narrative interlocution. The Donne citation appears on a stressed rather than an "unstressed" margin, we might say, and what is stressed is the temporal perspective of future rebirth from the ashes. This is ultimately Kluge's phoenix, not Donne's. The symbol or metaphor of a phoenix is not sufficient for an "other" future life to take shape though, and that is why the temporal perspective of this narrative voice also requires the paired dashes, a material mark of the futurity to be had in reading through the stars. The future sense that opens up to experience here bespeaks both catastrophic (Third Reich) and counter-catastrophic (Bauhaus University) German histories but is not confined to their empirical effects. Particles of sidereal sun bodies are dispersed into German horizons and double-track German perspectives too in this miniature, where real hope and doomed hope, as Ulrike Vedder writing on the German polysemy of the word *Verhoffen* might say (360), come together in the future as "the authentically human dimension," as Jean Améry once put it (128). Kluge's cosmically German miniature "Our Ancestors, the Stars" narratively cultivates this experiential utopian dimension in time as a chance, not a lineage.

4 Werner Scholem and the Life Writing of the Future Sense

This book's discussion of Kluge's narrative experiments with futurity as form aims to contribute in part to new impulses in narrative studies that challenge narratology's longstanding presumption of a default model of time understood as "linear and ubiquitously valid" (Weixler and Werner 9). As the editors of *Zeiten erzählen* ["Narrating Times"] underscore in their review of French, Russian, Anglophone, and German research on the subject, the spectrum of temporal forms in narrative arts is much more varied than the "relatively rigid notion" of Newtonian time that implicitly underwrites even many of the theoretical differentiations advanced by some postclassical narratologists (13). For this reason, Antonius Weixler and Lukas Werner speak ardently of an open-ended "plurality of temporal forms" for which narrative theory has yet to account (22). One of the many methodological questions they raise in this critical connection, without sharing the common presumption that figural and narrative perspective are categorically distinct, concerns the role that perspective itself plays in creating a given text's "temporal effects" (12, 18). Analysis of Kluge's cosmic and global miniatures in the present volume has already highlighted a range of ways in which this writer's literary experiments with perspective and voice help advance a narrative orientation to the utopian dimension as incrementally accessible to temporal experience, notably in the form of an emergent future sense. But what kind of life writing might we ascribe to this future sense as a historical phenomenon living door to door with an other or off-worldly life?

Reflecting on recent developments in narratological approaches to experimental life writing in particular, including her own experiments in *Daddy's War: Greek American Stories, A Paramemoir*, Irene Kacandes observes that all life writing, in "genres as diverse as blogs, diaries, hagiography, genealogy, letters, memoir, testimony, travel writing, and both biography and autobiography," for example, shares textual reference to real and necessarily relational worlds ("Experimental Life Writing" 380). Whatever referential, biographical, or autobiographical "pacts" prevail between readers and the life writing they encounter, however, Kacandes rightly accentuates a broad spectrum of formal and paratextual entanglements between reality and its various others (381).[15] Above all, she

---

[15] Kacandes cites Philippe Carrard's definition of "the biographical pact as 'the basic agreement through which biographers bind themselves to their readers, warranting to make true statements in the sense of 'statements whose accuracy can be verified in the archives''" (Kacandes, "Experimental Life Writing" 381; Carrard 299–300). On autobiographical and "'referential pacts'" more generally, Kacandes cites Philippe Lejeune's seminal formulations from *On Autobiography* (Kacandes, "Experimental Life Writing" 381; Lejeune 5, 22).

stresses the "high tolerance" that readers have for narrative "experimentation that might be construed as revealing or representing the complexity of reality" (381–382). With regard to Kluge's simultaneously anti-realist and realist experimentation with life writing, we might need to speak of *reworking* the temporal complexity of social reality instead. For Kacandes, even experimental life writing in an autobiographical register is beholden and bound to "the referential level" (382). These writing experiments are ultimately "for the sake of fact, not fiction," she claims (386). Kluge's life writing experiments in a biographical vein are by contrast, I suggest, for the sake of counterfactual hope and the future sense as revolutionary strategies of survival and contestation in catastrophic times. What kind of life writing or biographical experimentation is at stake then in "Liveness from 1931" ("The Gap the Devil Leaves Us" 25–30), Kluge's German miniature devoted to Werner Scholem, an assimilated German Jew and communist activist whom the Nazis imprisoned in several concentration camps before murdering him in Buchenwald in 1940?[16]

In the previous section of Part Three we saw how an experimental German miniature also functioned as a cosmic miniature, paradoxically making a non-empirical reality accessible to temporal experience by virtue of the future sense in narrative form. The present section considers how Kluge's "Liveness from 1931"—a German literary miniature with intensified textual reference to entangled German histories of Nazi dictatorship, communist revolution, military intelligence, and genocidal anti-Semitism—can and must be read as one of Kluge's global miniatures too. Ultimately I shall argue that "Liveness from 1931" is also a cosmic miniature in German and global guise, to the degree that its historical voice pivots on narrative uses of perspective and futurity as experiential portals in heliotropic time. For the moment however, it is more important to focus on this miniature's surprisingly global register, which manifests thematically both in the text's repeated allusions to China as a cipher of contemporary globalization, and in its concatenated probing of revolutionary horizons of futurity in a Marxist vein. As we shall see, these various story lines all appear concentrated (or more precisely: conjoined and not compressed) in the figure of life writing as bio-graphy itself. For Kluge's miniature on "liveness" constellates hope and

---

[16] For historical accounts of the life and death of Werner Scholem (1895–1940), I rely especially on publications by Ralf Hoffrogge, Mirjam Zadoff, Hermann Weber and Andreas Herbst, Michael Buckmiller and Pascal Nafe, and the Gedenkstätte Buchenwald. Relevant scholarship by Ralf Hoffrogge includes *Werner Scholem: Eine politische Biographie*, "Utopien am Abgrund," and "Emmy und Werner Scholem im Kampf zwischen Utopie und Gegenrevolution." See also Mirjam Zadoff, *Der rote Hiob: Das Leben des Werner Scholem*, and Mirjam Triendl-Zadoff, "Unter Brüdern."

catastrophe in the living and dead persona of Werner Scholem as a stressed figure of historical biography, while the text also assigns this real victim of Nazi brutality and possible Stalinist intrigue a fictional biographer in the form of Hong Tze-fei, "a Marxist from Peking University" [*ein Marxist an der Universität Peking*] (25). Ralf Hoffrogge, the German historian who has written most extensively on Werner Scholem and the four extant literary works about him, including Kluge's miniature, stresses the "fictive" nature of this Chinese professor, "author of a hefty Marxist biography about Werner Scholem, almost 5000 pages long" [*Autor einer fast 5000 Seiten starken marxistischen Biographie über Werner Scholem*] (*Werner Scholem* 389).[17] In his own "political biography" of Werner Scholem, one of three older brothers to Gershom Scholem—renowned German-Jewish expert on Kabbalistic mysticism, intellectual correspondent and friend to Walter Benjamin, and a Zionist immigrant to Palestine in 1923 who famously declared in 1964 that no "German-Jewish dialogue" had ever existed—Hoffrogge speaks of a general "Scholem boom" in scholarship since 1989 (*Werner Scholem* 12). He attributes this overall interest in the divergent political trajectories of the Scholem brothers to a contemporary crisis of "the great ideologies and utopias of modernity" (12), one that prompted communist politicians, Jewish Studies, and cultural historians alike to begin rediscovering the largely forgotten figure of Werner Scholem in the 1990s (12; see also Jay Howard Geller on the Scholem family and German-Jewish modernity).

According to Hoffrogge however, this Scholem figure has given rise to an unprecedented degree of "literary speculations," something that cannot be said of any other German Communist Party member who also served as a political representative in the German parliament or *Reichstag* of the early 20th century (11, 383). Hoffrogge is mainly concerned with setting the historical record straight re-

---

17 Hoffrogge additionally discusses a novel by Arkadi Maslow from the 1930s, a story by Franz Jung that was published posthumously in 1997, and prose by Hans Magnus Enzensberger from 2008 that Enzensberger himself termed a "'factography'" (Hoffrogge 391). As Christoph Zeller and many others have observed in similar spirit, "For Kluge, reality is a result of the power of imagination [*Einbildungskraft*] and not clearly distinguished from artistic imagination" (84; see also Kluge's often cited remarks on his approach to facts and fiction in his "realistic method," *Gelegenheitsarbeit einer Sklavin* ["Part-Time Work of a Domestic Slave"] 215). Hoffrogge seems to conflate Enzensberger's "factography" with western forms of documentary, without considering possible allusions to the factography of the Soviet avant-garde. On the latter, see especially Fore, "The Operative Word," "Die Emergenz," and *All the Graphs: Soviet Factography and the Emergence of Modernist Documentary*. Fore in particular alerts us to structural affinities between some aspects of Soviet factography and Kluge's theoretical approach to writing (for details, see Adelson "Experiment Mars" 39–41). At the conclusion of "Emergenz" Fore explicitly cites Kluge paraphrasing Lenin on the ubiquitous availability of a "way out" (402–403).

garding Scholem's communist, anti-fascist, and personal activities, and he devotes considerable attention to teasing fact and fiction apart (see his section on "novels and realities" with regard to Scholem's ties to a German general's daughters for example, 395–409). While the labyrinthine historical record does evidence good reason to consider Scholem's communist principles and his doubly disastrous political fate in Buchenwald in some relation to the family of *Reichswehr* Commander-in-Chief Kurt von Hammerstein-Equord and his adult daughters Marie-Luise and Helga (each of whom was opposed to Hitler, albeit for different reasons), Hoffrogge is understandably both amused and miffed when he observes that Kluge, who takes "the greatest poetic liberty" of all in his speculative portrait, turns Werner Scholem into a "communist James Bond" with a refined taste for wine and frequent patronage of Berlin bars "'in the service of world revolution'" (11).

Here I am especially interested in Hoffrogge's attempt to explain Kluge's fabrication of Werner Scholem's Chinese biographer with recourse to biography's own ostensible need for "red threads" of a person's development over time and the legibility of that linear trajectory (390). According to Hoffrogge, who writes as a professional historian, Kluge's inventive account gives us an "allegory of the complexity of life, with which historians in Beijing and Potsdam wrestle in equal measure" (389). The motif of a "'secret life'" in Kluge's Scholem miniature becomes, in this reckoning, a "metaphor for the contradictions of the human psyche," which in reality follows so many different paths (390). For Hoffrogge, Kluge's writing honors the "breaks" and "gaps" of human subjectivity in a general psychological sense, while the miniature also honors "a core problem of biographical work, namely, its imprecision [*Unschärferelation*], the fact that every reconstruction is an interpretation determined by the present" (390). For these reasons, Hoffrogge finds, Kluge "needs [...] a living storyteller who interprets the biography of the deceased," and the fictional Chinese historian Kluge assigns to Scholem fulfills this role in a generic sense too (390). To my mind, Hoffrogge is correct in surmising that Kluge is working on formal desiderata of life writing, but he is misguided in stressing generic precepts of either human subjectivity or biographical prose, and he underestimates the decidedly contemporary significance of Kluge's "Chinese" fabrication. My reading of narrative perspective and historical voice in Kluge's writing experiment with the life and death of Werner Scholem will instead assess the usefulness of this miniature for the life writing of the future sense, and re-consider the narrative function of Hong Tze-fei in relation to revolutionary horizons of contemporary globalization.[18]

---

[18] For more general and overarching narratological reflections on the controversial status of

4 Werner Scholem and the Life Writing of the Future Sense — 221

Kluge himself comments in another context on the "red thread" as "a form of narration in which the reader always knows what is at stake," even if the red thread manifests only "in the subtext" (see the author's critical glossary in Kluge and Stollmann, *Ferngespräche* ["Long-Distance Conversations"] 188). Yet in keeping with the constellative and associative storytelling practices illuminated in Parts One and Two, he underscores his "dramaturgical" preference "to tie everything to everything" in ways that work against the grain of red-thread storytelling, especially of the commonsensical variety (188). What he calls the "normal aggregate condition" of human relations is mixed in as a subtext into the "pseudo-relationality" his storytelling creates through "gluing and weaving threads" [*Das ist der normale Aggregationszustand aller Menschen, den ich unterschlage, wenn ich Pseudozusammenhänge durch Kleben und Fadenspinnen erzeuge*] (188), but none of these connecting threads are predicated on "unbroken connection" [*ununterbrochene Verbindung*]. The "free movement of 'narration'" he favors [*diese freie Bewegung des "Erzählens"*] is impeded by the "law of the Red Thread" [*Gesetz des Roten Fadens*], he warns, before cautioning us in the next sentence not to forget that some critical circumstances also "require the principle of the 'red thread'" [*das Prinzip des "roten Fadens" erfordern*]: "A lawyer in court and an emergency medical technician at an accident site will not express themselves in constellative montages" [*Ein Rechtsanwalt vor Gericht, ein Sanitäter an einem Unfallort werden sich nicht in konstellativen Montagen ausdrücken*] (188). Elements of life-threatening danger and turning points in catastrophe are thus close at hand in Kluge's thoughts on red-thread narration and its maverick relations, and at this juncture we might wish to recall that both Kluge and Scholem were professionally trained as lawyers. The "liveness" miniature

---

"voice" in relation to "perspective" since Gérard Genette's consequential distinction between voice functions ("who speaks?") and perceptual focalization ("who perceives?"), see especially Els Jongeneel, "Silencing the Voice in Narratology? A Synopsis," and Michael Scheffel, "Wer spricht? Überlegungen zur 'Stimme' in fiktionalen und faktualen Erzählungen," in *Stimme(n) im Text: Narratologische Positionsbestimmungen* (Andreas Blödorn, Daniela Langer, and Michael Scheffel 9–30 and 83–99). As Kluge's experimental miniatures for the 21st century repeatedly show, I argue, the perception of time is itself a conjoined narrative exercise in revolutionary perspective, historical voice, and the phenomenology of future-making. It is also worth noting that Oskar Negt, Kluge's longtime writing partner in the arena of social theory, has written extensively on modern and contemporary China in relation to public and political life in the world today. See Negt, *Modernisierung im Zeichen des Drachen* ["Modernization in the Sign of the Dragon"], and Negt's chapter titled "Chinesische Wundmale: Zur politischen Bedeutung von Trauer, Tod und Zeit" ["Open Chinese Wounds: On the Political Significance of Grief, Death, and Time"] in Negt and Kluge, "Politics as Relations of Measure" (151–170). Negt's book predates and his articles postdate the Tiananmen Square massacre of 1989.

published by Kluge in 2003 highlights "1931" as both the year in which Scholem passed his German bar exam and, in Hong Tze-fei's strong characterization, as "the year of multiple lives" [*das Jahr der multiplen Leben*]. As Scholem's fictional Chinese biographer elaborates, "If a human being leads 99 lives next to each other, and everyone else does this too, then that is the revolution" [*Wenn ein Mensch 99 Leben nebeneinander führt, und dies alle anderen auch tun, dann ist das die Revolution*] (27). 1931 also postdates the heyday of Scholem's leadership roles in the German Communist Party of the 1920s (including his far-left critique of over-dependency on Moscow and his subsequent exclusion from the Party by Stalinists in 1926) and predates the beginning of his fatal imprisonment by the Nazi regime, for political reasons, in 1933.[19] For Werner Scholem, 1931 was an especially liminal year. For a time in the late 1920s he had written for Leninist newspapers as well as a Trotsykist newspaper called *Permanent Revolution* (Weber and Herbst 821; Trotsky himself published extensively on "permanent revolution" between 1905 and 1929). As discussed in Part Two, "permanent revolution" is also a key term in Kluge's conceptual approach to storytelling and in our text-analytical understanding of his global miniatures in particular.

"Liveness from 1931" presents biography itself as a rhetorical figure of life writing just as much as it foregrounds Scholem as a biographical subject of historical importance (uncoupled here from overt stress on his far more famous brother or on Jewish identity as such).[20] However, the claim that life writing becomes a narrative figure in its own right in Kluge's miniature, even rivaling the red-thread figure of Werner Scholem as a puzzling story to be told, does not rest on Kluge's introduction of a fictional Chinese biographer alone. This claim largely rests instead on the narrative proliferation of biographical perspectives and historical voice as subtextual codes to be read in Kluge's miniature. The introjection of a fictional Chinese biographer is an important part of this, but rather than providing a linear red thread of interpretation as Hoffrogge contends, Hong Tze-fei is himself converted into a substantive object of biographical narration in one

---

19 Hoffrogge argues that the initial arrest in 1933 of both Werner Scholem and his wife Emmy, who was still an official member of the Communist Party, had nothing to do with the regime change early that year, but was instead part of the ongoing and "'entirely normal' persecution of communists" by authorities of the Weimar Republic. The investigative case against the Scholems "had begun in December 1932" and simply continued "without interruption" into 1933 (397–398).

20 For extended discussion of the Scholem brothers in relation to both Judaism and German anti-Semitism, see Mirjam Zadoff's biography of Werner Scholem, Mirjam Triendl-Zadoff on Jewish utopias in the interwar years, and Ralf Hoffrogge, "Utopien am Abgrund." On Werner Scholem's non-Jewish wife (Emmy Scholem née Wiechelt), see especially the Zadoff biography and Hoffrogge, "Emmy und Werner Scholem im Kampf zwischen Utopie und Gegenrevolution."

of the miniature's footnotes, where an incipiently embodied voice of temporal perception shifts our perspective to Hong Tze-fei's multidirectional familial and world-political orientations.

> Son of a Chinese brigade leader, who built the railway lines in East Africa, and a Spanish woman. The young Marxists at Peking University are searching for the lost concept of the political in China. Since Jürgen Habermas gave guest lectures there, they are taking in large quantities of European theory there. Hong Tze-fei was visiting the Federal Republic, Paris, and London for this purpose.
>
> [*Sohn eines chinesischen Brigadechefs, der Eisenbahnlinien im Osten Afrikas baute, und einer Spanierin. Die jungen Marxisten an der Universität Peking sind auf der Suche nach dem abhanden gekommenen Politischen in China. Seit Jürgen Habermas Gastvorlesungen hielt, rezipieren sie auf ihrer Suche große Mengen europäischer Theorie. Zu diesem Zweck besuchte Hong Tze-fei die Bundesrepublik, Paris und London.*] (25)[21]

This peripheral shift in biographical perspective appears even more complicated in structural terms when we realize that the barely embodied voice of textual narration is itself staking out various—and oscillating—claims to biographical, political, and temporal perspective.

This stake-claiming actually begins in the miniature's opening lines, first when the voice of narration introduces Werner Scholem as having gone to school, in his early years, with Ernst Jünger, and then when the voice of narration establishes a jarring temporal shift to the implied scene of Buchenwald (which the miniature never invokes by name). In reference to the biographical figure of Werner Scholem, who has just been introduced, we read that he is already dead. "He was shot on July 17, 1940, while attempting to escape. In a stone quarry. In the end he was a lawyer for fellow prisoners, although there was no court anywhere here. He had success" [*Er wurde am 17. Juli 1940 auf der Flucht erschossen. In einem Steinbruch. Zuletzt war er Anwalt der Mithäftlinge, obwohl es hier nirgends einen Gerichtshof gab. Er hatte Erfolg*] (25).[22] Several things are jarring about this string of formulations. First, what kind of "success" can be meant for someone viciously murdered in Buchenwald, and second, why stress Werner Scholem's status as a lawyer in a concentration camp? These irri-

---

[21] On Habermas's visit to China in 2001 and the overall intellectual reception of his work in China, see Gloria Davies.

[22] Jünger (1895–1998) is a historical figure who never resurfaces in Kluge's "liveness" miniature. A controversial German veteran of both world wars and a novelist, he is usually associated with militarism, nationalism, and a fiercely conservative critique of Hitler. On Jünger and futurity, see especially Peter Uwe Hohendahl, *Erfundene Welten*, and Wilhelm Voßkamp, *Emblematik der Zukunft* (296–304).

tations are addressed later in the text, in a middle section featuring dialogic exchange between Hong Tze-fei and a German journalist interviewing him for a leading German newspaper, the *Frankfurter Allgemeine Zeitung* (FAZ). There the Chinese biographer explains that Scholem, who did "nothing to save his life" [*nichts, um sein Leben zu retten*], was nonetheless successful in representing fellow prisoners and obtaining some favors for them from the camp commandant, whose "feeling of self" [*Selbstgefühl*] Scholem was able to "penetrate" [*eindringt*] (28). Here Kluge uses phrasing suggestive of military strategy, a rhetorical field that will figure more significantly in other aspects of the text as well. Hong Tze-fei in any event explains that Scholem's camp activities as a "lawyer" had nothing to do with legal justice or law-based representation. More to the point, the text's initial characterization of Scholem as a lawyer alerts us proleptically to what the miniature will reveal only later: The beginning of Scholem's functional status as a lawyer is 1931, "the year of multiple lives." Even more important in terms of narrative oscillations in the voice of life writing though, we should be doubly stunned to read that Scholem was shot "while attempting to escape." As professional historians of the Holocaust know, this is the bureaucratic language with which the Nazis at Buchenwald archived many sadistic murders at the arbitrary whim of SS guards presiding over life and death at the stone quarry there (Hoffrogge, *Werner Scholem* 441).[23] Yet Kluge's "Liveness from 1931" does not render this exculpatory formulaic turn as a marked citation, which effectively situates the voice of narration in this instance as a robotic voice of false archival record rather than a critical voice of historical interpretation. In this Kluge miniature too, we shall see that the voice of narration plays several different roles, a main one being to establish a field of contention in narrative perspective itself. The opening lines of this biographical miniature thus confront us with a hidden question of how to read perspective, and this also becomes a question of how to read life writing in a kill zone. Can this life writing be future-making too?

When the Chinese figure of Scholem's "biographer" is introduced in the text's second paragraph, Hong Tze-fei is cast as both a biographical object of narrative description—he is "himself under way on many tracks in the world" [*selber vielspurig in der Welt unterwegs*]—and a reading subject of the biograph-

---

[23] There is no question in the historical record that Scholem was murdered by SS guard Johannes Blank. Hoffrogge also discusses in detail one prisoner's later claim that Stalinists among the communist prisoners had conspired to facilitate this result given Scholem's support for Trotsky. Weighing all relevant factors with great care, Hoffrogge concludes however that the historical record does not support this claim (443–447). The Nazis destroyed his life because he was both "a Jew and a communist" (447).

ical "tracks" [*Spuren*] Scholem has left in history. The interpretation attributed to him as a reader of Scholem's tracks is at odds with that of historians in one particular sense, we learn: "An oddly activist pattern that lays out improbable connections between social strata for which historians presume there can be no connection" [*Ein merkwürdiges aktivistisches Muster, das unwahrscheinliche Verbindungen zwischen Gesellschaftsschichten legt, von denen die Historiker annehmen, daß die keine Verbindung haben könnten*] (25). This is how Hong Tze-fei explains how Emmy Scholem, who had been arrested with her husband, could escape Nazi clutches and emigrate to England with the aid of acquaintances in the Nazi *Sturmabteilung*.[24] When the narrative voice reports that this is "unthinkable" [*nicht denkbar*] unless Emmy's husband and her Nazi helper had known each other "before" [*vorher*], narrative voice and Hong Tze-fei's perspective appear to be perfectly aligned (25). This changes further down the page when the narrative voice of the miniature asserts its own referential authority and distinguishes its narrative perspective from that of the Chinese biographer, even as it avows that Hong Tze-fei shares the same focus in content. "In fact, and this is what Tze-fei's biography is concentrating on, since 1929 [Werner] Scholem belongs to the military-political apparatus of the German Communist Party" [*Tatsächlich, und hierauf konzentriert sich Tze-feis Biographie, gehört Scholem seit 1929 zum militärpolitischen Apparat der KPD*] (25). Precisely at this juncture of authoritative assertion, where the voice of narration more or less usurps Hong Tze-fei's status as biographer, Kluge's miniature paradoxically launches into the murkiest territory of political speculations about the historical record, which is riddled with gaps. Rather than marking this territory as speculative terrain though (about whether Scholem was ever gathering military-political intelligence or *Nachricht* for the Communist Party or not, to what degree he was romantically involved with one of the general's daughters, or what exactly lead to his arrest), the narrative voice concentrates our attention on what must be read "in fact" in terms of secret code. The political function the miniature ascribes to the rhetorical figure of Scholem here is "the detecting of illegal state secrets" [*die Ausspähung illegaler Staatsgeheimnisse*] (25).[25] And he is further depicted as a figure that cannot be easily or overtly read: "The Stalinists were suspicious of Werner Scholem" [*Bei den Stalinisten war Werner Scholem verdächtig*] (26). The biographical

---

[24] Kluge also takes some liberties with details of Emmy Scholem's release and emigration (including the date), but the historical record does indicate that she was assisted by Hans Hackebeil, an acquaintance in the SA who escaped Nazi Germany with her (see Hoffrogge, *Werner Scholem* 372–374, and Zadoff 224).

[25] Echoing the earlier allusion to Scholem as a lawyer without a court, a long footnote here elaborates on when such secrets may be considered legal or "illegal."

object of Hong Tze-fei's investigations thus becomes, quixotically so in the authoritative voice of textual narration, harder and harder (not easier) to decipher.

The first of the miniature's three main sections concludes with narrative commentary commingling Scholem's political and rhetorical status as a figure of biography in this miniature of "liveness from 1931." This commentary additionally re-introduces a rhetorical figure familiar to us from other sections of the present book: the inchoately embodied voice of narrative interlocution. The figure of Scholem that eludes Stalinist reading appears "politically ruined," the narrative voice tells us, because Scholem's long prison stints "signaled a zone of contact with state authorities, even if this was contact of hostile nature" [*Politisch ruinierte ihn der lange Aufenthalt in Polizeigefängnissen, der Berührungsfläche zu den staatlichen Behörden, wenn auch feindlicher Art, signalisierte*] (26). And now come two questions in the voice of narrative interlocution: "How can one differentiate collaboration and resistance if there is any zone of contact? Scholem's very characteristic, after his release, is to seek an unexpected zone of contact. Is he a curious person?" [*Wie kann man Zusammenarbeit und Widerstand unterscheiden, wenn überhaupt Berührungsfläche besteht? Es ist geradezu Charaktermerkmal Scholems, nach seiner Entlassung aus der Haft, unerwartete Berührungsfläche zu suchen. Ist er ein neugieriger Mensch?*] (26).[26] These questions are answered only with the perspectival collaboration of the textual figure of Hong Tze-fei though, as analysis will now show, and the revolutionary impulse of the future sense in this miniature derives precisely from this contrastive yet oscillating contact in temporal perspective.

The middle section of the miniature consists of direct dialogic exchange between Hong Tze-fei and the FAZ journalist who interviews him. They begin talking about Scholem in terms of life "'without pause'" [*ohne Pause*] because, as the Chinese biographer details, in every gap or "every pause that such a life leaves, a second and third life enters in" [*Weil in jede Pause, die ein solches Leben läßt, ein zweites und ein drittes Leben hineinragt*] (26). Social strata and ostensibly "impenetrable" [*undurchdringlich*] divisions in social relations are "unreal" [*unwirklich*] in this view, and Hong Tze-fei raises the specter of catachresis when he tries to find the right words to express Scholem's "affinity for living simultaneously on several levels" [*Affinität, in mehreren Etagen gleichzeitig zu leben*] (26). The German journalist immediately asks what this would sound like in Chinese translation or in the biographer's Spanish "'mother tongue'" [*Muttersprache*], but this Chi-

---

[26] Kluge alludes here to multiple politically motivated arrests beginning in 1917, when the historical Werner Scholem demonstrated against World War I while in military uniform. Arrested by the Nazis in 1933, he was eventually acquitted by a German court in 1935 on charges of high treason but never released (Hoffrogge 410–414).

nese persona rejects the requested gesture of translation into a foreign language and redirects the journalist's attention to German as a language of temporal translation, one that his Beijing colleagues are especially good at.

> Our experts at Peking University deal with the German entrusted to them much more carefully than the Germans. We have a *Privatdozent*, for example, who specializes in the German of Weimar Classicism and the Frankfurt idiom that was being spoken when Goethe was three years old. He speaks these languages of professional expertise as if they were colloquial. You don't have that here.
>
> [*Unsere Experten an der Pekinger Universität gehen mit dem ihnen anvertrauten Deutsch sorgfältiger um als die Deutschen. Wir haben einen Privatdozenten, der z. B. auf Weimarer Deutsch der Klassik und auf Frankfurter Mundart im dritten Lebensjahr Goethes spezialisiert ist. Er spricht diese Fachsprachen wie eine Umgangssprache. Das haben Sie hier nicht.*] (26)

To this the FAZ journalist halfheartedly replies: "Well, humankind's inheritance has to be preserved somewhere" [*Irgendwo muß das Erbe der Menschheit ja aufgehoben werden*], to which Hong Tze-fei rejoins: "Yes, that's what Peking University is there for" [*Ja, dafür ist die Universität Peking da*] (26).

Here and elsewhere in this lively dialogue, the fictional biographer repeatedly links the keen activist interest that he attributes to Scholem in "proletarian forces" [*proletarische Kräfte*] across political divisions and class-based categories to what we might call a cooperative narrative principle of proliferating temporal perspectives beyond social catastrophe. For Hong Tze-fei, this is "what we in Beijing are attempting to reconstruct" [*was wir in Peking zu rekonstruieren versuchen*] (27). For this biographer, Scholem is a product of bourgeois consciousness that thinks beyond its empirical historical constraints, a "'persona'" [*Person*] that behaves like an "urbanite" [*Städter*] in contrast to the party, which "behaves like a village" [*verhält sich dazu als Dorf*]. "What, [Scholem] asks, could we make of the bourgeois individual if it cooperated world-wide in fact?" [*Was, fragt er, wäre aus dem bürgerlichen Individuum zu machen, wenn es tatsächlich weltweit kooperiert?*] (27). This is a question about the very structure of life writing beyond the referential constraints of individual biography. The persona of the Chinese "biographer" in Kluge's miniature in effect marks a narrative rather than a figural investment in such global cooperation as an exercise in the making of revolutionary time.[27] This is why Hong Tze-fei also renders Marie-Luise von Hammerstein-

---

[27] For related remarks on Kluge's social concept of a "fusional group" as "an element of every revolution," see Kluge ("The Boring of Hard Boards" 138), Fore's substantive editorial introduction to Negt and Kluge (*History and Obstinacy* 57), and Radisoglou on the "collective imaginative labor" (48, 50) that transpires in what Kluge calls "the gaps that divide people from one anoth-

Equord as the more romantically inclined of the general's two daughters. In his account this daughter above all desires "the life next to her life" [*das Leben neben ihrem Leben*]. Door to door with an other life in this miniature, biographical objects and subjects alike are constantly set in relation to rifts, chances, and dangers in social time, or as Hong Tze-fei observes just before his reference to 1931 as the year of multiple lives: "always an abyss next to life, a second life so to speak, and next to that another abyss [...]. If a human being leads 99 lives next to each other, and everyone else does this too, then that is the revolution" [*immer ein Abgrund neben dem Leben, sozusagen ein zweites Leben und daneben wieder ein Abgrund [...]. Wenn ein Mensch 99 Leben nebeneinander führt, und dies alle anderen auch tun, dann ist das die Revolution*] (27). This is cooperative sequentiality with no red thread of biography or even teleology. Hong Tze-fei at one point portrays Scholem as a Marxist accelerationist who does not believe in the concept of class (28), but the simultaneously cooperative and disjunctive temporal principle of politics and narration that Kluge inscribes in this Chinese figure rivals any strategic content attributed to Scholem as a historical person, since the textual rhythm of "Liveness" is anything but accelerated.

Hong Tze-fei's functional significance as Scholem's ostensible biographer seems more akin to what Kluge discusses, in recorded public conversation via Skype, with Wang Hui, a prominent critical intellectual in the People's Republic of China who also participated in the Tiananmen Square protests in 1989, in terms of a cooperative temporal doubling of historical modernity and capitalist reality in relations between China and Europe. Kluge and Wang cast these relations as useful for rethinking the meaning of both communist histories and revolutionary politics today (for Kluge's remarks on the doubling this entails, see especially Kluge and Stollmann, "Long-Distance Conversations" 36, 183). In the public conversation that followed the Beijing screening of Kluge's film version of Marx's *Capital* in 2012, Wang Hui also lambastes a long dominant "model of class struggle" and argues that the contemporary "capitalist world" cannot be understood without consideration of global China (44–45). I cannot argue that Kluge's Scholem miniature instantiates such Chinese-European reciprocity in substance, though it certainly activates an orientation to such interlocution in narrative form. Wang Hui and Kluge alike are acutely interested in non-teleological practices of Marxist thought, and in their shared conversation in time despite the geographical distance between them (see 35, 40, and 44–45 for several references to this feature of the exchange), the Chinese philosopher highlights

---

er" (138). Here I cite Fore's translation of Kluge's phrasing in reference to "fusional" groups. The phrase "boring of hard boards" stems from Max Weber's 1919 lecture on "politics as a vocation."

"an intervention of documentary form into history"—an intervention into history "as such," as he puts it (37). Published nearly a decade before this conversation took place, Kluge's Scholem miniature narratively intervenes in the documentary form of historical life writing as biography, in part with the aid of Hong Tze-fei as a functional antidote to red-thread biography rather than its advocate.

The argument I wish to advance here goes even further, however, since I claimed above that the miniatures discussed in Part Three entail narrative experiments that engender the futurity of life writing, and that the figure of life writing at stake in Kluge's "Liveness" is ultimately not Werner Scholem as an empirical person but bio-graphy as a form of writing life itself in time. Even the functional role of Hong Tze-fei as a fictional character is insufficient to support such claims though, which will require us to revisit the oscillating functions of the voice of the text's narrative interlocutor, a partially embodied voice that resurfaces in the third and final section of the miniature. This follows on the heels of the text's only named reference to the Holocaust (in the middle section characterized by direct dialogue)—"The Holocaust is after all quite barbaric" [*Der Holocaust ist ja ziemlich barbarisch*], says Hong Tze-fei (29)—and the Chinese biographer's explicit assertion that he "can read tracks" [*Aber Sie wissen, ich kann Spuren lesen*] (29). When the journalist wants to know what kind, Hong Tze-fei answers in three steps: "written" tracks, those that Gershom Scholem as an expert in Jewish mysticism described as "powerful footprints left behind in the realm of ghosts" by his activist brother [*heftige Fußabdrücke im Reiche der Geister*], and those that index "a third existence" [*eine dritte Existenz*], much "quieter" [*ruhiger*] and perhaps more hidden than the obvious tracks of Werner Scholem's libidinal life and revolutionary activism (28–29). As in the early part of the miniature, Hong Tze-fei's role as a biographer who both reads tracks and leaves them in the world is stressed here, but this time the tracks he reads belong to the realm of ghosts not empiricism. "[Werner Scholem] was a prince of ghosts?" [*Er war ein Geisterfürst?*], the reporter asks incredulously, to which his Chinese exchange partner replies: "According to our findings at Peking University" [*Nach unseren Kenntnissen an der Universität Peking*] (29).

This is the precise juncture at which the narrative voice of interlocution quietly reappears. It does so to set and also expand the cooperative scene of dialogic exchange retroactively: "They were sitting in the cafeteria of the Frankfurt opera" [*Sie saßen in der Kantine der Oper Frankfurt*] (29). But this is hardly mere setting, for the voice of narration now introduces a secret cipher of cosmic orientation in the powerful "female singer of Montezuma" [*Sängerin des Montezuma*] appearing in the Frankfurt production of Wolfgang Rihm's late 20th-century opera, "Die Eroberung von Mexiko" ["The Conquest of Mexico"] (29). Colonialist catastrophe is thus close by in this seemingly innocuous setting. The doomed Aztec emperor was affiliated with Huitzilopochtli, a deity of war and "god of the sun" (Mark Cartwright), and the talented figure of the singer, most likely inspired by Annette Elster and "graced by the gods" [*von den Göttern begnadet*], always sings "hopeless destinies" or "fates without perspective" [*aussichtslose Schicksale*] (29). As she sips coffee too weak to awaken on its own the power she harbors in the form of transformative voice, "an urban climate" [*ein städtisches Klima*] arises in the cafeteria, a turn of phrase with which the narrative voice links this contemporary setting between hope and doom back to Hong Tze-fei's characterization of Werner Scholem's associative and conjunctive orientation to global cooperation in a revolutionary vein.

"Liveness from 1931" is thus a German and global miniature that is secretly cosmic too, and its secretly heliotropic voice of narration lays material tracks that quietly demand to be read in the service of realizing counterfactual hope and vital futures. "Is he a curious person?" this narrative interlocutor asks in a way that initially seems to go unanswered. But experimenting with the putative limits of "natural" narrative, this voice answers its own question in the end, by redirecting us to the biographical figure of Hong Tze-fei, who feels in 2001, "seventy years after" [*70 Jahre nach*] Scholem's year of multiple lives, "responsible for the human beings of China" [*verwantwortlich für die Menschen Chinas*] (29). This is where the text segues to an aggregate figure of "the Republic of China" [*die Republik China*], where "in contrast to the USA" [*im Gegensatz zu den USA*], social powers are "centralized" [*zentralisiert*] (29). In political terms this could yield good, indifferent, or bad results, we read. Yet narrative reference to a centralized power that as yet has "no concept" [*keinen Begriff*] rhetorically re-activates the gap of catechresis that Hong Tze-fei associated with Scholem's expressive possibilities for living "simultaneously on several levels," including a counterfactual future without life's catastrophic miseries. This is the sense in which "Liveness" ends by awakening our own temporal interest or curiosity in "the alert interest" [*das wache Interesse*] that Hong Tze-fei and his Chinese "comrades" [*Genossen*] bring to the "stocks of the Occident or any other continent" [*Vorräte des Abendlandes oder irgendeines anderen Kontinents*] where "something could be learned about the CONCEPT OF THE POLITICAL" [*etwas zu lernen wäre zum BEGRIFF DES POLITISCHEN*] (29–30). This is at least a narrative cipher of reciprocal curiosity about future expressive possibilities for revolutionary time in life writing as such.[28] The multiple lives, temporal perspectives, and non-em-

---

[28] In empirical biographical terms, Werner Scholem's hopes in 1939 for an exit visa to Shanghai were heightened when the Chinese consulate in Paris gave its consent, and then dashed when Nazi authorities refused to release him (see Hoffrogge 434–444, 462 for details).

pirical "ways out" of historical catastrophe and human despair that Kluge's German miniature about Werner Scholem opens up for readers do not rely on the future sense. They too help to generate it as a long-distance and global sense organ of temporal perception.

5 Making Time: *Zeit-Zeugen*, Holocaust History, and Co-Operative Voice

Like Werner Scholem, Fritz Bauer (1903–1968) was a 20th-century German-Jewish jurist whose course of life was radically altered by German anti-Semitism and the Nazi genocide of European Jews. Arrested and imprisoned in a concentration camp for nine months in 1933, the young Social Democrat was able to escape Nazi Germany in 1936 and survive in Scandinavian exile before returning to Germany in 1949, where he made it his mission to prosecute the perpetrators of genocide and reform German law from the inside out in the Federal Republic of Germany, which was the West German democratic successor state to the Third Reich and occupied Germany. As attorney general for the state of Hesse, Bauer is best known for the indispensable historical roles he played in initiating the two most prominent Holocaust-related trials to rivet German and global public spheres in the 1960s. For the Federal Republic of Germany, and in Bauer's official capacity as attorney general for Hesse, this included what would come to be known as Germany's own "Auschwitz trial," which took place in Frankfurt am Main from 1963 to 1965. Behind the scenes a few years earlier, Bauer had also communicated key information to the Israeli secret service about Adolf Eichmann's whereabouts in South America, which eventually lead in 1961 to the Eichmann trial in Jerusalem.[29] Despite his pivotal postwar influence on German and international law in response to genocide, "Germany's forgotten first Nazi hunter is being rediscovered and rehabilitated" by biographers and the arts only now, one British journalist claims (Tony Paterson).[30] A spate of feature "Bauer"

---

[29] For these and other biographical details, see publications by Irmtrud Wojak and Ronen Steinke, as well as the Web page of Frankfurt's interdisciplinary Fritz Bauer Institute, dedicated to researching the "history and consequences of the Holocaust" for the present.
[30] According to Paterson, Bauer was "ostracized by politicians" for being "gay, Jewish, and a high-profile German state prosecutor in 1960s West Germany," one who "feared denunciation as a 'criminal homosexual' and received constant death threats." Bauer's first biographer, Wojak speaks of a "second exile" for Bauer and other "political emigrants" more generally who had returned for the express purpose of building a new German "democratic republic" (243). Citing Kurt Sontheimer, Wojak argues forcefully against the notion of a clean break between Adenauer Germany and Nazi attitudes toward Jews, including in the justice system that Bauer was trying to

films appearing in German cinema and television since 2014 (*Labyrinth of Lies*, *The People Vs. Fritz Bauer*, and *Die Akte General* ["The General File"]) speaks to ongoing and evolving public interest in German cultural accountability for a genocidal past and democratic future alike. Kluge's publication in 2013 of a new collection of German miniatures under the title *"Wer ein Wort des Trostes spricht, ist ein Verräter": 48 Geschichten für Fritz Bauer* ["'Whoever speaks a word of consolation is a traitor': 48 Stories for Fritz Bauer"] is both a timely participant in this collective trend and yet oddly out of step with it in the collection's formal choices as well.[31]

As bewildered, historically well-informed reviewers have noted, the "brutally objective" tone and intensely minimalist writing style of Kluge's Holocaust stories for Fritz Bauer bring home a profound sense of sober despair without ever clarifying what factual lessons we might learn about this genocidal history, and without every telling us much about Fritz Bauer at all (see especially Gerrit Bartels, Reto Rössler, Hazel Rosenstrauch, Thomas Schmid, and Wolfram Schütte). These are "contingent stories" of mass murder on a transnational scale, with rare instances of ways out but no hint of real consolation or "saving principle" in sight (Rössler), most reviewers agree. One reader would like to know where the documentary "material" comes from (Rosenstrauch), while another resolves that sort of puzzle by observing that "Ein später Sieg des Spartakus" ["A Late Victory of Spartacus"] (40–42), a story about a partially successful (and historically documented) group escape from the Sobibor death camp, becomes an unduly "optimistic fantasy" that Kluge adapts from a passing comment by historian Saul Friedländer in *The Years of Extermination* about Alexander Pechersky, a Red Army officer and son of a Russian-Jewish Spartacist (Schütte; for Friedländer's comment, which Kluge provides as a marked albeit paraphrased citation from the German translation, see *Years of Extermination* 559). Taken together, Kluge's stories "for Fritz Bauer" signal his most concentrated storytelling

---

reform from within (243). "'When I leave my office,'" Bauer himself once said, "'I am in enemy territory'" (363).

31 The quotation in the title of the story collection "for Fritz Bauer" stems not from Bauer, but from a 1968 art installation by Bazon Brock, a radical art theorist and multimedial artist in postwar Germany who is also associated with the international experimental art movement known as Fluxus (see Bazon Brock, *Die Re-Dekade*, for a print version of the installation phrasing that Kluge uses for his title). Bauer himself makes a cameo appearance in *Yesterday Girl* (1965–1966), Kluge's first feature film and his internationally best known contribution to New German Cinema. More recently, documentary filmmaker Ilona Ziok (*Fritz Bauer—Tod auf Raten, Deutschland* ["Fritz Bauer—Death in Installments, Germany"]) and novelist Thomas Harlan (*Heldenfriedhof* ["Cemetery for Heroes"]) have contributed to the multifaceted 21st-century surge of interest in Bauer as well.

attention to date to the Nazi genocide of European Jews, while appearing to offer very little residual hope—counterfactual or otherwise—to be gleaned from this deadly and devastating tale.[32] Literary scholar Konstanze Hanitzsch notes the conjunction of documentary sobriety and "poetic style" in Kluge's prose and reaches the following conclusion regarding the structure of the story collection as a whole. "Historical facts and their narration are connected to each other through a nearly invisible core: This core is the address directed to Attorney General Fritz Bauer, who even in this book remains a blank spot [*Leerstelle*], which at best only begins to be filled by the title, the description of [Bauer's] funeral, and the dedication" (2). By referring to Bauer as a "blank spot" in the textual structure of these stories, which in my terms address and orient themselves apostrophically to both something missing and more pointedly *someone missing*, Hanitzsch effectively situates "'Whoever speaks a word of consolation is a traitor': 48 Stories for Fritz Bauer" in Kluge's disjunctive and conjunctive "aesthetics of the gap," as discussed in Parts One and Two concerning his cosmic and global experiments for the 21st century. This final section of Part Three examines how this disjunctive and conjunctive aesthetic pivots in the German miniatures of the Bauer collection on the production of counterfactual hope in the service of the future sense, despite the overwhelming tenor of profound despair and permanent catastrophe that permeates this book.

When Hanitzsch lists "the dedication" as one of the few textual elements to address Bauer directly, she refers to the book's final two paragraphs, set typographically against a still photo of Fritz Bauer taken from Kluge's 1960s film, *Yesterday Girl*. The first paragraph uses the grammatical voice of first-person singu-

---

[32] Schütte claims that Kluge had "largely avoided" the topic of the Holocaust in his previous work, and in the 1990s one Holocaust historian even indicted Kluge's writing as a thoroughgoing combination of "memory and repression" (Bartov 140). Contrasting Kluge and Sebald with regard to the poetics of historical representation, Mark Anderson finds Kluge's documentary style more generally "emotionally flat" (129, 137). Norbert Bolz once spoke of Kluge's writing style in terms of "the warm voice of the storyteller" instead (41). Most Kluge scholars would not agree that Kluge has "avoided" or "repressed" the Holocaust, since German accountability for life-and-death catastrophes of the mid 20th century has motivated most of his work from the 1960s on. The earliest Holocaust story for which he is best known is "Ein Liebesversuch" or "An Experiment in Love" in Leila Vennewitz's translation from Kluge's *Lebensläufe* (1962) or *Case Histories* (1988), respectively. For focused analysis of this story, see Ulrike Bosse, Manfred Durzak, Hans-Joachim Hahn, Michael Müller, Jürgen Nieraad, Ulrich Schmidt, Erhard Schütz ("Ein Liebesversuch oder Zeigen, was das Auge nicht sieht..."), Christian Schulte ("Alexander Kluge: 'Ein Liebesversuch'"), Rainer Stollmann (*Alexander Kluge zur Einführung* 29–42), and Veronika Zangl. In narrative terms "'Whoever speaks a word of consolation is a traitor': 48 Stories for Fritz Bauer" in any event does contain Kluge's most concentrated storytelling attention to the Holocaust to date.

lar narration—"I dedicate"—to describe Bauer as an especially "lonesome" [*einsam*] attorney general for the state of Hesse (113). Yet Kluge's subtle phrasing underscores both imaginative process and differential temporality when he writes: "I see him in front of me in the year 1962" [*Ich sehe ihn vor mir im Jahre 1962*] (113). This first paragraph of the dedication concludes by giving the apostrophic figure of Fritz Bauer some company in the form of Alfred Edel—a major German actor of the postwar era who also appeared in *Yesterday Girl* as well as many other films by Kluge, Herzog, Syberberg, and others, but whom Kluge's Bauer text describes only as a loner too who "lived nearby" [*in der Nähe wohnte*]. The tone shifts to a pedagogical register in the second paragraph when the grammatical voice of the first person yields to third-person narration in the guise of Fritz Bauer.

> Monstrous crimes have the characteristic, Fritz Bauer said, that as soon as they enter into the world, they arrange for their repetition. It is important, he opined, not to tire in observing and remembering them. There are namely "ghostly long-distance effects" and "noncausal networks" between the past and the present, between the attractors of evil and us. They must not be allowed to become more powerful than our experience.
>
> [*Monströse Verbrechen haben die Eigenschaft, sagte Fritz Bauer, daß die, sobald sie in die Welt treten, für ihre Wiederholung sorgen. Es ist wichtig, meinte er, in ihrer Beobachtung und der Erinnerung nicht zu erlahmen. Es gibt nämlich „gespenstische Fernwirkungen" und „nichtkausale Netze" zwischen Vergangenheit und Gegenwart, zwischen den Attraktoren des Bösen und uns. Sie dürfen nicht wirkmächtiger werden als unsere Erfahrung.*] (113)

Two things are especially striking in the final two sentences of this passage in terms of voice.

First, the voice of Bauer's pedagogical admonition never to forget seems to fuse with the third-person voice of narrated citation, except that the phrases set in quotation marks sound a lot more like Kluge than anyone else. And second, the voice of narration admonishes us in turn not to let seemingly immaterial "long-distance effects" of catastrophic danger and "monstrous crimes" in time become more powerful or more effective than "our experience." Empirical historical experience is precisely what gives rise to collective despair in these non-exculpatory stories of genocide though, and the collective but indeterminate personal pronoun "our" in the author's parting word recalls the non-empirical dimensions of Kluge's metanarratives of the long arcs of cosmic formation, as discussed in section 3 of Part Three. What are the cosmic stakes of collective voice in Kluge's concentrated German miniatures dedicated to Fritz Bauer? The rest of Part Three answers this question by analyzing "Witnesses from an Other World" (53–54), the only miniature in the Bauer volume with explicit reference to extraterrestrials, and by arguing that Kluge's extraterrestrials are key to

5 Making Time: *Zeit-Zeugen*, Holocaust History, and Co-Operative Voice — **235**

understanding his book's challenges to both the German culture of *Vergangenheitsbewältigung* and narratological conceptions of collective voice. Both challenges foster the revolutionary cultivation of the future sense in a counterfactual but experiential vein.

The textual figure of Fritz Bauer functions in this story collection paradoxically as a red thread that refuses to function as a red thread. As we saw in section 4 concerning the Scholem miniature, Kluge overtly rejects "the law of the Red Thread" (associated with linear or chronological narration) in favor of the associative "free movement" of constellative storytelling. And yet he also cautions us to recall that red threads can appear in subtextual mode and constitute "a form of narration in which the reader always knows what is at stake"—and some life-and-death circumstances even "require the principle of the 'red thread'" ("Long-Distance Conversations" 188). The apostrophic Bauer figure of "'Whoever speaks a word of consolation is a traitor': 48 Stories for Fritz Bauer" functions unambiguously as a red thread in this last crucial sense, by keeping readers on high alert regarding historic threats to human life caused by the Third Reich as a genocidal regime and by intersectional anti-Semitism in 20th-century Europe.[33] There is nothing the least bit ambiguous about the intensity, horror, and extent of the life-and-death-stakes involved here, or about Bauer's signal German-Jewish importance as an ethical lodestar lest such crimes be forgotten or repeated. This story collection is thus about historical catastrophe and about what Adorno termed "the permanent threat of catastrophe" as well ("The Position of the Narrator in the Contemporary Novel," *Notes to Literature* [Vol. 1] 34). The sly wit and subtle humor for which Kluge's writing is often also known—manifest in the cosmic miniatures about Adorno's love life or extraterrestrials touring the White House, for example—is notably entirely lacking in "'Whoever speaks a word of consolation is a traitor': 48 Stories for Fritz Bauer." Yet Kluge does not resort to red-thread narration of a linear sort to address or negotiate the *temporal* stakes of grievous loss and heightened danger that the Bauer stories convey. All appearances of overt emphasis to the contrary, like the cosmic and global experiments discussed in Parts One and Two, these German miniatures also work on future-making in narrative form, and they do so primarily through Kluge's microscopic perspective on historical but non-empirical dimensions of collective

---

[33] In this sense the story collection could be understood as the experimental missing address or "Ansprache" from Bauer's funeral service, from which—as the opening segment of the book's narrative frame reveals—Bauer had barred any eulogies in the conventional sense (7). Reading Kluge's text this way does not mean however that any gap is filled or circle closed. As the book's opening frame concludes, in reference to Bauer: "No one in the succeeding generation of the land replaced him" [*Niemand aus dem Nachwuchs des Landes ersetzte ihn*] (9).

voice. Characterized by temporal disjunction and conjunction alike, this voice should be understood as co-operative rather than simply plural or in any way uniform.

Witnessing is a major trope of memory culture and legal culture alike, especially so in the wake of the Holocaust and amidst evolving transnational cultures dedicated to bringing perpetrators of genocide to justice and preventing future genocidal catastrophes too. The experimental miniatures that Kluge dedicates to Fritz Bauer also draw on this familiar figure of witnessing, just as they repeatedly also draw on the historical figure of deportation trains taking Jewish victims en masse to Auschwitz. (One story for example turns on attempts by the Union of Orthodox Rabbis and others to persuade Washington to bomb relevant train tracks in 1944 to save the Jews of Budapest.) As with the global miniatures discussed in Part Two, even Kluge's emphatically German miniatures reveal many transnational dimensions as well, as the texts reference landscapes as European as Germany, Austria, Italy, France, Poland, Greece, Hungary, Spain, Latvia, Lithuania, Romania, Switzerland, England, Russia, and the Ukraine—or as far flung as Turkey, Argentina, Kenya, Morocco, India, and ancient Rome. Yet as we saw in Part Two, Kluge's global miniatures entail a revolutionary "farewell to locomotives" as narrative figures of either linear progress or certain doom. Can we say that Kluge's narrative use of witnessing takes a similar revolutionary turn in the ultimately very German miniatures of the Bauer collection? To answer this question, we will need to consider not only the eyewitnesses that Kluges's writing delineates as such (including the extraterrestrials who are coming soon), but also his storytelling use of narrative perspective and historical voice in the work of future-making.

The figure of witness is explicitly conjured in Kluge's prose, but hardly in a way that would bring any affective solace or ethical assurance to those concerned with historical justice or social futures without genocidal miseries. "Witnesses and guests" [*Zeugen und Gäste*] (59) are invited to one mass execution in Latvia for example, and in another entry a fascist eyewitness reporting mass murder of Jews and non-Jews in Hungary to a Portuguese diplomat is narratively displaced when a higher-ranking Hungarian fascist and anti-Semite summarily decides to avoid a "'second Katyn'" by not leaving any traces of the dead (33).[34] Even more acerbically, the narrative voice in "Das Schaf von Rom"

---

[34] In 1943 German Nazis reported finding mass graves of Poles murdered by Soviet secret police in Katyn in 1940. These events, the fascist slaughter of Hungarian Jews, and other mass murders that figure in Kluge's Bauer collection are based on the historical record, as are many of the named figures mentioned in passing, including Ferenc Orsós, the Hungarian forensics expert, and Carlos Branquinho, the Portuguese diplomat, mentioned above. My analysis of Kluge's

5 Making Time: *Zeit-Zeugen*, Holocaust History, and Co-Operative Voice — **237**

["The Sheep of Rome"] has this to say about the Third Reich's ambassador to the Vatican—easily identifiable in a historical register as Ernst von Weizsäcker (who served the German foreign office in this capacity from 1943 to 1945), even though von Weizsäcker, father of a future president of postwar Germany, is named only in a different miniature (45): "Before the eyes of the world, what happened was always the opposite of what he had spoken 'calmingly' about before" [*Vor den Augen der Welt war stets das Gegenteil dessen eingetreten, wovon er zuvor 'kalmierend' gesprochen hatte*] (51). Most crushingly of all, an entry titled "Wie in einer anderen Welt, durch eine unsichtbare Wand vom Übrigen getrennt" ["As in an Other World, Separated from the Rest by an Invisible Wall"] scenically recalls the "optical wall" separating divergent realities in Kluge's Chinese miniature "Faster than Fate" (discussed in Part Two), this time without constating any liveable "side of the future" by any narrative means of witnessing. To the contrary, the "invisible wall" of this Bauer miniature depicts a helpless Spanish diplomat, alerted to the Nazi deportation of Jewish victims being sent to Auschwitz from the Greek islands of Rhodes and Kos in 1944, a diplomat who feels his only ethical recourse under these circumstances is at least "to show himself" [*sich zu zeigen*] and to make his presence as an eyewitness known (84). The narrative voice in this miniature clearly and coolly judges this ethical stance as inadequate to the task of prevention. "This was supposed to mean: 'The world is watching what happens here.' That did not prevent the completion of the loading [of the deportation trains] and the departure" [*Das sollte heißen: 'Die Welt sieht zu, was hier geschieht.' Den Vollzug der Verladung und die Abfahrt verhinderte das nicht*] (84).

The miniature bearing the title "Witnesses from an Other World" both resonates with the hopeful counterfactual doubling of reality that readers encounter in Kluge's cosmic configurations "door to door with an other life" and disappoints these hopes when "extraterrestrials" [*Außerirdische*] are introduced to the Bauer collection as witnesses who, similar to the Spanish diplomat who stands by helplessly as Greek Jews are deported to Auschwitz, see danger to human life and do nothing to thwart catastrophe. The head of British maritime radio surveillance in the wartime Mediterranean likens himself to these extraterrestrial witnesses in this sense.

> Just as I read in a science-fiction novel that extraterrestrials spy on humankind, but that their professional ethos nonetheless forbids them from intervening anywhere (in order not to betray themselves but above all not to be exposed to contamination), so too are

---

Bauer stories as experimental literary miniatures focuses on their narrative production of counterfactual hope and the future sense under conditions of historical catastrophe.

we bound to keep our knowledge in our storage attics and not give rise to any interventions down there, for example in Rome, that would betray our perfect surveillance.

[*Wie ich es in einem Science-fiction-Roman gelesen habe, daß Außerirdische die Menschheit abhorchen, jedoch ihrem Berufsethos nach nirgends eingreifen dürfen (um sich nicht zu verraten, vor allem aber, damit sie sich nicht kontaminieren), so sind auch wir gehalten, unser Wissen in unseren Speichern zu verwahren und keine Eingriffe dort unten, zum Beispiel in Rom, zu veranlassen, die unsere perfekte Überwachung verraten würden.*] (53)

This passage reads like a strange mixture of Star Trek's prime directive not to intervene in the catastrophic events of interstellar worlds and a failure of the Kantian imperative to consider extraterrestrial perspectives so that we humans may act more ethically on Earth (see discussion of Kant and extraterrestrials in my Introduction). Kluge's core constellation of "above" and "below" also reverberates in this passage though, and attentive readers of the German phrasing will additionally note that the witnessing and spying at stake here, for the extraterrestrials and the radio surveillance expert alike, are cast in terms of listening ("abhorchen" or listening intently and secretly for things one is not meant to hear) rather than seeing. If witnessing has some sort of hopeful valence in "'Whoever speaks a word of consolation is a traitor': 48 Stories for Fritz Bauer," we will need to look or listen for it in narrative functions for which trauma-based concepts of interpersonal "cowitnessing" (Irene Kacandes, *Talk Fiction* 107) and "secondary witness" (Aleida Assmann, "The Empathetic Listener") cannot fully account, even though the functions that Kluge's storytelling activates also pivot on social relations in their imaginative and historical dimensions.[35]

---

[35] Kacandes illuminates "interpersonal witnessing" as a means by which "'listening' to trauma narratives can transform the listener" (107). Assmann highlights the importance of a "secondary witness" in terms of empathetic dialogue that reinforces truth claims. Both theorists address commingled forms of history and fiction. Kluge's writing on Holocaust memory does evidence many features that Michael Rothberg analyzes in terms of transcultural "multidirectional memory" more generally. His widely cited study of memory cultures concerning the Holocaust and decolonization describes "multidirectional" memory for example "as subject to ongoing negotiation, cross-referencing, and borrowing: as productive and not privative" (3). Building on the work of Richard Terdiman, Jonathan Boyarin, and others, he also argues that multidirectional memory is "a contemporary phenomenon, something that, while concerned with the past, happens in the present; and […] that memory is a form of work, working through, labor, or action" (3–4). To the degree that Rothberg's incisive work on multidirectional memory cultures is focused both on trauma though and on cultural relationships between past and present, his seminal concept is of limited value for addressing Kluge's narrative work on historical catastrophe, counterfactual hope, and the cultivation of the future sense. The same caveat applies to Marianne Hirsch's influential concept of "postmemory" as a transgenerational cultural phenomenon in response to historical trauma (see especially *Family Frames* and *The Generation of Postme-*

5 Making Time: *Zeit-Zeugen*, Holocaust History, and Co-Operative Voice — **239**

One of the most prolific commentators on 20th-century critical debates about "history and memory after Auschwitz," Dominick LaCapra has argued that "just as history should not be conflated with testimony, so agency should not simply be conflated with, or limited to, witnessing" (12). If Kluge's Holocaust stories in the Bauer collection conjure a marked figure of witnessing only to draw our attention to the agential inadequacy of this trope, where else might we look or listen for their narrative uses of counterfactual futurity as experiential portals in time? To pose this question is to ask again how these German miniatures of 20th-century catastrophe can be read as cosmic miniatures too. The text's lone reference to extraterrestrials becomes a crux of temporal conversion after all, not as an overt cipher of ineffectual witnessing but as an indexical figure of differential temporalities in cosmic-human relations. They point us in the direction of far more subtle turns of narrative perspective and historical voice in this miniature, turns that will allow us to orient ourselves more effectively to the book's counterfactually and counter-intuitively productive work on the utopian dimension in time.

Almost all of the miniatures in the Bauer collection are presented in a largely disembodied voice of third-person narration and sobering reportage, although it is also clear that this voice always expresses narrative alignment with a non-focalized desire to save murdered Jews and other victims of the Nazis from their factual ends. For example, in one story about Jacques Helbronner, a decorated and well connected World War I veteran and "the most French of all Jews" [*der allerfranzösischste aller Juden*] (19), who was arrested by the Gestapo in 1943 and murdered in Auschwitz, the voice of narration contemplates temporal opportunities and social associations that could have saved him, ultimately finding it "puzzling that nothing happened" [*rätselhaft, daß nichts geschah*] (20). A different story presents an engineering inventor and his "'bone mill'" [*"die Knochenmühle"*], designed to eliminate any traces of the dead, something that the narrative voice considers under the rubric of "a principle of extreme destruction that corresponds to modernity" [*ein Vernichtungsprinzip, das der Moderne entspricht*] (62). The third-person voice of narration thus seems to offer our best

---

mory). However, like Rothberg, Hirsch also characterizes postmemory in some ways that resonate with Kluge's writing, for example, when she highlights "imaginative investment, projection, and creation" and "an uneasy oscillation between continuity and rupture" (*The Generation of Postmemory* 5, 6). Huyssen, who has written with great insight on transnational dimensions of the cultural memory of historical trauma (see especially *Present Pasts*), has also written incisively about critical tensions in Kluge's German writing between "an aesthetic redemption of history" and "the methods of analytic writing" ("An Analytic Storyteller in the Course of Time," *Twilight Memories* 155).

hope in this book of critical perspective and counterfactual futures, and this voice also travels in historical time, not only in the 20th and 21st centuries but also to a Salamancan sage trying to orient himself and others in 1492 "in the tunnels of the future" [*in den Tunneln der Zukunft*] (21). The extraterrestrials seem flat-footed in comparison. And yet the time-traveling narrative voice in the Salamancan miniature tells us that the sage's "prophetic" views of the future were also "imprecise" [*unscharf*] or vague (21). These critical and temporal features of the otherwise disembodied voice of narration in the Bauer stories are important, first because they evidence multidirectional arcs of historical perspective, and second because they stand in formal contrast to the narrative voice of "Witnesses from an Other World."

This miniature is one of the very few in this collection to be directly narrated in first-person voices of "I" and "we" (as opposed to many instances of first-person voices in reported speech)—which may recall the discussion in section 3 of Kluge's radical use of pronouns in the service of the future sense—and "Witnesses from an Other World" is the only entry in the volume to set narrating voices of first-person articulation in relation to invisible extraterrestrials. This is a cosmic-human constellation that Kluge intensifies in the two framing narratives of "'Whoever speaks a word of consolation is a traitor': 48 Stories for Fritz Bauer"—the opening description of the day of Bauer's funeral and the closing dedication to the German-Jewish jurist—two miniatures that are not counted among the "48 stories for Fritz Bauer" but that nonetheless establish their oscillating temporal stakes for us as readers through the medium of voice.[36] "Witnesses from an Other World" sets a preliminary stage for this, first by introducing the extraterrestrials (more or less mid way into the volume) and then by conjoining their introduction to disruption of third-person narration by the "I" and "we" of a British naval officer in command of listening surveillance or *Horchdienst*. The determinate qualities of this "I" include this assignment for military intelligence, in addition to a joint position as "mathematician and Assyriologist at the University of Oxford" [*Mathematiker und Assyriologe an der Universität Oxford*] (53). The determinate "we" of the radio surveillance service to which he belongs shares certain metaphysical attributes with the extraterrestrials: "We are active like angels or gods" [*Wir sind wie Engel oder Götter tätig*] (53). But this metaphysical activity, readers are told in a critical vein, stops short of preventing disaster. The first-person narrator in this instance then concludes the miniature with a puz-

---

[36] Technically what is depicted is not a funeral but a memorial service without any eulogizing speeches. Because the text also refers to Bauer, among other designations, as "the one who was buried today" [*der heute Beerdigte*] (9), I will nonetheless refer to the scene of this first miniature as a funeral.

5 Making Time: *Zeit-Zeugen*, Holocaust History, and Co-Operative Voice — 241

zling comparison, one that reasserts both historical perspective and Kluge's aesthetics of the gap.

> I compare the cartographic, comprehensive, and collecting attitude that we take on, and that prevents us from saving human lives, with the city god of Ashur, "who withdrew from human beings." That was in the late phase of the northern Mesopotamian city. Before the "time of the great silence."
>
> [*Ich vergleiche die kartographierende, übergeordnete, sammelnde Haltung, die wir einnehmen und die uns daran hindert, Menschenleben zu retten, mit der des Stadtgottes von Assur, „der sich von den Menschen zurückgezogen hat." Das war in der Spätphase der nordmesopotamischen Stadt. Vor der „Zeit des großen Schweigens."*] (54)

While one might associate these references in thematic terms with the rise and fall of empire, the geographic area today known as northern Iraq, or in more obvious ways to the world's "great silence" as the Holocaust was under way, in textual terms what is most important about this passage is that the miniature concludes by referring us back in time to Kluge's opening frame.

For the "time of the great silence" in the Bauer collection is the day of Bauer's funeral, from which the deceased had banned eulogizing speech. Kluge underscores this gap in speech with recourse to the figure of Adorno, who had arranged for three full string quartets by Beethoven to be played at the funeral—"at government expense" [*auf Regierungskosten*] (7)—and who "would like to see the event repeated" [*gern die Veranstaltung wiederholt sähe*] (8). The funeral scene of "silence" or "speechlessness" [*Sprachlosigkeit*] (8) that serves as the book's opening frame thus also includes sound, and this scene is furthermore narrated by a German voice that does bespeak loss, in the first person of "I" though not yet in any declarative "we." The figure of the extraterrestrials in "Witnesses from an Other World" reminds us (all ascribed inactivity to the contrary) that unseen forces of sound are operative in Kluge's prose as it labors on the production of hope under conditions of catastrophe. As detailed in the Introduction and Part One, extraterrestrial perspectives on human life matter less in Kluge's experimental writing than what non-empirical human perspective oriented to "an other life" affords. That "other life" is both counterfactual and real, as are the voices that help create it. The analysis now turns to what Kluge's narrative fictions allow in the Bauer collection rather than what an "extraterrestrial" witnessing perspective would prohibit.

Many German nouns are compound forms derived from other substantives. The compound noun deriving from the words for "time" [*Zeit*] and "witnesses" [*Zeugen*] yields *Zeitzeugen*, which denotes those who witness not discrete events per se but something we might call "historical time" as lived time. The first-person voice of narration in the opening salvo of the Bauer collection—an entry that

I propose to read as an experimental miniature in its own right—could be understood as a *Zeitzeuge* in this standard sense, since this "I" attends and describes Bauer's funeral, and in the mode of apparent recollection also "see[s] the dead man" [*Ich sehe den Toten*] addressing others while he was alive (8). This narrative gesture of eyewitness accounting is echoed in the concluding dedication: "I see him in front of me in the year 1962." And the centrifugal proliferation of empirical historical perspectives in the overall book (where we encounter not only Jewish victims of the Holocaust but also Nazi perpetrators, frustrated diplomats, forced laborers, prisoners of war and prison guards, communists, and mindful as well as unwitting rescuers) could be understood as a polyphony of *Zeitzeugen* in this generic sense too. And yet in terms of narrative form, Kluge's framing entries of funeral and dedication activate an altogether different functional valence of conjoining *Zeit* and *zeugen*, which as a verb can mean to bear witness, indicate, create, or produce. Elsewhere Kluge remarks that social transformation has "an extraordinary need for time" [*einen ungeheuren Bedarf an Zeit*] ("Long-Distance Conversations" 51). My argument is that Kluge's experimental miniatures literally make or produce time, and the time that even his Bauer stories of Holocaust memory make in social terms—this-worldly and off-worldly alike—is the future sense of temporal perception.

In narrative terms this makes Kluge's Bauer kin to Werner Scholem and his fictional Chinese biographer too, and the global stakes of this stylistic constellation come into even sharper view when we consider what Oskar Negt, Kluge's longtime partner in social theory, wrote about the "political significance of grief, death, and time" in "Politics as Relations of Measure" in the section prompted by the events of Tiananmen Square and titled "Open Chinese Wounds" (151– 170). As the final essay in that "Chinese" section begins, Negt effectively comments on temporal privation as a worsening symptom of capitalist globalization. "*Death* is taboo in our society, not *killing*" [*Der Tod ist in unserer Gesellschaft ein Tabu, nicht das* Töten] (166). For Negt, "Wherever life stands in desperate need of time, no time remains for dealing with death. The inner lack of calm to use time is itself already an element of what is dead, of the *process of becoming an object*" [*Wo das Leben unter Zeitnot steht, da bleibt für die Beschäftigung mit dem Tod keine Zeit. Die innere Unruhe, Zeit zu nutzen, ist selber schon ein Element des Toten, des zum* Gegenstand-Werdens] (166). The attentive lingering over Bauer's funeral in Kluge's opening miniature thus stands in critical contrast to the temporal attitude of the Hungarian fascist and forensics expert who says to his dinner companions, "'Throw the dead Jews into the Danube'" [*"Werft die toten Juden in die Donau"*], because he wants to leave no traces behind (33). The capacity for grief "begins" with time, Negt contends, and bombarded by "medial perspectives on catastrophes" [*Medienblick auf Katastrophen*], "people must take time to create expressive possibilities for their own desires and their own distress" [*Die Menschen müssen sich Zeit nehmen, um ihren eigenen Triebregungen und ihrer Bestürzung Ausdrucksmöglichkeiten zu verschaffen*] (170). Kluge's narrative experiments with perspective and voice in the Bauer miniatures are therefore not only about a historical imperative not to forget, but also about the expressive capabilities of the future sense as a counterfactual voice of hope in time.

As we have already seen, the narrative "I" in "Witnesses from an Other World" is set in relation to both distant extraterrestrials and the determinate "we" of the British radio surveillance service in wartime. The narrative "I" in the opening funeral entry is relational in multiple directions too. He knows the deceased, he knows the Adornos (both of whom are present, with Adorno lingering over the music), he knows the prison director who leaves "quickly" [*rasch*], and he knows a high-ranking judge in attendance as well as the judge's wife, who makes arrangements for a group gathering over drinks that follows the memorial service. However, in terms of narrative attention the relationship that matters most is to the figure of Bauer, who is otherwise a "blank spot" (Hanitzsch) in the collection of stories dedicated to him. The narrating "I" of the funeral miniature presents him by contrast in two extended anecdotes as "the dead man" [*den Toten*] and "the one who was buried today" [*der heute Beerdigte*] (8, 9). Paradoxically in Kluge's diction the dead man speaks in both anecdotes, while at his memorial service as such all others are admonished to silence. With one minor exception the voice of narration and Bauer are the only figures who do speak in first-person singular voice, and though they do not speak to each other directly anywhere in the text, the tone and duration of narrative attention establish a narrative intimacy of sorts. The only figures to assert the collective voice of "we" as if shared identity were self-understood and given come across as distasteful and suspect instead. This is significant because "the dead man" who speaks in the first Bauer anecdote invokes an entirely different form of collective address, and this address could also be seen as the otherwise missing address or "Ansprache" of the funeral scene.

"I see the dead man as he has all the cells unlocked at the Butzbach prison and addresses the prisoners with 'comrades'" [*Ich sehe den Toten, wie er im Zuchthaus Butzbach alle Zellen aufschließen läßt, die Gefangenen mit 'Kameraden' anspricht*] (8). Bauer's use of this collective address and the complete avoidance of any recourse to "we" in the textual figuration of both Bauer and the framing voice of narration in Kluge's story collection together suggest that something especially important is happening here in the articulation of historical voice. Problematic relationships between "I" and "we" are also a very German concern because of the socio-political history of the Third Reich, as Santner tells us (see section 3), and the articulation of plural subjects is at the same time a contemporary narratological concern. Building on Alan Palmer's concepts of "social mind" and "intermental thought" in fictional narratives, Fludernik, one of the leading voices in postclassical narratology, combines narratological analysis and New Historicist readings to probe textual relationships between hegemony and subversion in early modern narrative ("Collective Minds" 695, 699, 723 et passim). In doing so she also addresses what she sees as a larger conceptual lacuna in narrative studies, namely, a "narratological neglect of collectives" in both fiction and fact (694). As she puts it:

> Collective experience is rarely consistent or uniform; at close range, groups tend to split up into smaller units and even into individuals who have their own agendas and views. Though historiographic narrative may require the construction of seemingly unproblematic agency and thus attributes appropriate intentionality and motivation to group members, the communality of collective experience is a fiction, that is, an invention or stipulation. (695)

With reference to widely varying modes of representing thought and perception through narrative form, Fludernik's analyses of collective-subject formation ask "whether the multitude is referred to by means of a singular noun or plural noun phrases or whether these alternate" (723). Her conceptual approach to the narratological parameters of collective subjects is also instructive for considering what Kluge calls "fusional" groups in storytelling form, and for considering Bauer's use of the group plural "comrades" and the framing narrative distaste for "we." As previously noted, Kluge posits a social concept of a "fusional group" as "an element of every revolution," with permanent revolution entailing, among other things, variegated work on "the gaps that divide people from one another" (*Das Bohren harter Bretter* ["The Boring of Hard Boards"] 138).[37] However, in order to account for Kluge's experiments with perspectival horizons and historical voice in the Bauer collection, we must once again orient ourselves to the text's utopian dimension, however unsettling and counterintuitive that may initially seem in the context of Holocaust memory in Germany.

When the first-person voice of narration sees (and by implication also hears) Bauer as a dead man speaking to the prisoners of Butzbach as "comrades," this is presented as a perlocutionary speech act in the sense that Bauer is not addressing an existing collective but a future collective he would like to call into

---

[37] See also Radisoglou 51–61 (on Kluge in relation to Paolo Virno's "grammar of the multitude"). An English translation of this Kluge collection by Wieland Hoban is forthcoming under the title *Drilling through Hard Boards: 133 Political Stories*. The translation provided here is my own, with page reference to the German publication.

being. Kluge's text tells us nothing about the nature of the crimes for which these persons have been imprisoned in postwar Germany, only that Bauer is empowered "to unlock all the cells" and that his colleagues in the justice department consider him a "fool" [*Narren*] for expressing himself this way (8). Historian Claudia Fröhlich elaborates on the empirical Bauer's use of "comrades" in his own autobiographical writings on human rights and in a controversial address to inmates in Butzbach on the occasion of a prison concert in 1956. According to the historical record as cited by Fröhlich, the attorney general "justified his word choice by saying that, with the address, he wanted to build 'a bridge to social life [*Gemeinschaft*]' for the imprisoned in particular," that is to say, by using address as one form of "re-socialization" in democratic Germany (250). Kluge's narrative use of historical voice as a call to re-socialization is both slyer and shyer than this, and his bridge-building to new dimensions of social life is moreover a matter of time. The gap between the future collective subject that the textual Bauer addresses in the present tense as "comrades," on the one hand, and either the self-complacent "we" of government representatives or the fascist implications of what the text terms "the old camaraderie" [*die alte Kameraderie*] (8), on the other (as something that Bauer does everything in his power to prevent from resurfacing in postwar Germany), is political but also temporal. This is a revolutionary portal in time where the future sense slips in, as a German bridge in time to the utopian dimension of a "future without life's miseries," as Adorno put it. The historical voices of Kluge's conjunctive cultivation of differential temporalities in narrative perspective are not simply plural, collective, or even collaborative but co-operative instead. Something revolutionary happens here in the narrative use of co-operative voice, but historical differences are not erased.

The "dedication" with which Kluge's collection of Holocaust stories concludes honors Bauer, as a "lonesome" person one has lost and as a co-operative voice one must work to gain, with a kind of intimate respect. This is also where the narrating "I" of the dedication performs its own perlocutionary speech act by speaking, for the first time, of "us."

> Monstrous crimes have the characteristic, Fritz Bauer said, that as soon as they enter into the world, they arrange for their repetition. It is important, he opined, not to tire in observing and remembering them. There are namely "ghostly long-distance effects" and "non-causal networks" between the past and the present, between the attractors of evil and us. They must not be allowed to become more powerful than our experience.
>
> [*Monströse Verbrechen haben die Eigenschaft, sagte Fritz Bauer, daß die, sobald sie in die Welt treten, für ihre Wiederholung sorgen. Es ist wichtig, meinte er, in ihrer Beobachtung und der Erinnerung nicht zu erlahmen. Es gibt nämlich „gespenstische Fernwirkungen" und „nicht-kausale Netze" zwischen Vergangenheit und Gegenwart, zwischen den Attraktoren des Bösen und uns. Sie dürfen nicht wirkmächtiger werden als unsere Erfahrung.*] (113)

At this juncture the voice of narration co-operates with both Bauer and readers eager to be released from what imprisons them. The real forces of catastrophe and despair must not be allowed to become more powerful than "our experience," including the real counterfactual force of hope that Kluge's German miniatures, even the Holocaust stories among them, help us experience with the aid of the future sense.

Postscript
Futurity as Fairy Tale? From *Flaschenpost* to *Nachricht* and More

The most important 20th-century figure of interlocution for Kluge as a writer of experimental literary miniatures is Theodor W. Adorno, as Kluge in many overt and covert ways indefatigably reminds us. When Kluge delivered the oral version of his acceptance speech upon receiving Frankfurt's Adorno Prize in 2009, he characterized Adorno as a "partisan" bringer of "unshakeable hope that, if necessary in the form of a message in a bottle, somewhere on our shores fragments or pebbles of true aliveness will arrive" [*unbeirrbare Hoffnung, dass notfalls in Form einer Flaschenpost, an irgendeiner Stelle unserer Strände Fragmente oder Kieselsteine von wahrer Lebendigkeit ankommen*] ("The Actuality of Adorno," Web version).[1] Here Kluge invokes the rhetorical figure of *Flaschenpost* or "a message in a bottle" most commonly associated with both Adorno and the Frankfurt School of critical theory more generally during their years of exile from Nazi Germany in the 1930s and 1940s. As Richard Langston recapitulates in his editorial introduction to the second issue of the *Alexander Kluge-Jahrbuch*—the first journal to be devoted to Kluge's polyphonic and multimedial projects from the 1960s on, with this second issue bearing the title *Glass Shards: Echoes of a Message in a Bottle*—the trope of a message in a bottle used to describe the conceptual work of the Frankfurt School under lived conditions of historical catastrophe "dates back to a fundraising letter written by Max Horkheimer in late June 1940 during his Californian exile" (Richard Langston, Gunther Martens, Vincent Pauval, Christian Schulte, and Rainer Stollmann, *Glass Shards* 9). The epigraph to Kerstin Stolt's study of what she calls "Teddy's *Flaschenpost*" recounts an anecdote attributed to Leo Löwenthal situating Adorno and other émigré friends standing at the edge of the Pacific Ocean, with Adorno sighing and wishing he could cast his thoughts in catastrophic times inside a bottle into the sea. "'Then some person, one distant day on a distant island, will find and open the bottle and read...'" (Stolt n.p.). Langston notes that in intellectual terms Adorno "explicitly incorporated the concept only once in his entire oeuvre" (in an essay on Arnold Schönberg and "'advanced music'"), and as countless other scholars of the Frankfurt School tradition and legacy have observed, that the figure of *Flaschenpost* is most succinctly captured though not named in Horkheimer and

---

[1] This passage does not appear in the print version of Kluge's acceptance speech in *Personen und Reden* (67–75, see especially 74–75).

Adorno's *Dialectic of Enlightenment* (*Glass Shards* 9): "If there is anyone today to whom we can pass the responsibilities for the message, we bequeath it not to the 'masses,' and not to the individual (who is powerless), but to an imaginary witness—lest it perish with us" (Horkheimer and Adorno 256). Yet as the close readings of *Cosmic Miniatures* have shown, Kluge's narrative figuration of visiting extraterrestrials complicates the operative function of even imagined witnesses, and communicative models of narrative transmission and philosophical legacy could only bypass the vital work on and with the future sense that these literary miniatures engender. Kluge himself now speaks polyphonically of his perspectival optic in relation to a broken bottle, the "shards" of which yield an "inverted message in a bottle, the echo of the bottle, so to speak" (Langston, "'Das ist die umgekehrte Flaschenpost': Ein montiertes Interview mit Oskar Negt und Alexander Kluge" 50). Kluge is clearly conjuring the spirits of both Benjamin and Adorno in this strange phrasing, even as his experimental writing, as we have seen and heard, breaks with them on the matter of futurity. If Kluge's 21st-century miniatures cannot be understood as sending "a message in a bottle," what else should we call whatever his experimental writing uses to call out to us as readers?[2]

The term that comes to mind and lies at our fingertips is ubiquitous in Kluge's prose and many other works from the early 1960s on, from his outsized attempt to come to grips with World War II's Battle of Stalingrad in narrative form (*Schlachtbeschreibung* [literally: battle description], 1964) to his daring effort to do his part to realize Sergei Eisenstein's project of bringing Marx's *Capital* to life on cinematic screens (*Nachrichten aus der ideologischen Antike* ["News from Ideological Antiquity"], 2008), and resounds as well in one of his favored television programming formats called News & Stories. This term is *Nachricht* (a singular noun usually and somewhat clumsily translated as *news*), which Kluge however explicitly sets in differentiated relationship to "news."

> For me, News are *Nachrichten* that are already so worked up that they can be sold on a market. Even News consist of life-world and experience, however the other half is already system, a medium that publishes the report. Life-world and system now stand in a reciprocal relationship to each other. There are News that concern one directly, and then there are News that must first be "grounded," reinterpreted by the person reading or hearing them. The result is that the front between life-world and system is shifted to a different place. First a human being flees the life-world, lets himself be seduced, checks his own ex-

---

[2] Huyssen astutely observes that the legacy of post-exilic critical theory in postwar Germany after the defeat of German fascism could "no longer" be conceived as "a message in a bottle" for Adorno and others (*Miniature Metropolis* 293; see also 278). See also Max Pensky, "Beyond the Message in a Bottle."

periences at the coatroom, but then he recollects them again. It's like at the stock market: bankruptcy ends the boom.

[News sind für mich Nachrichten, die bereits so aufbereitet sind, dass sie auf einem Markt verkauft werden können. Auch News bestehen aus Lebenswelt, aus Erfahrung, die andere Hälfte ist jedoch bereits System, ein Medium, das die Meldung publiziert. Lebenswelt und System stehen nun in einer Wechselwirkung zueinander. Es gibt News, die einen unmittelbar etwas angehen, und dann gibt es News, die müssen zuerst 'geerdet', umgedeutet werden von dem, der sie liest oder hört, so dass immer eine Frontverschiebung stattfindet zwischen Lebenswelt und System: Einmal flüchtet der Mensch aus der Lebenswelt, lässt sich verführen, gibt seine eigenen Erfahrungen an der Garderobe ab; dann wieder besinnt er sich aber auf sie. Das ist wie an der Börse: Der Bankrott beendet den Boom.] (Kluge, Binzegger, and Heller 22)[3]

In this quotation one recognizes familiar motifs of social tensions arising between capital's systemic expropriation of the senses and the anachronistic resistance to such expropriation that *Eigensinn* or "obstinacy" entails, as discussed in the Introduction. And Andreas Huyssen has illuminated the many ways in which Adorno's micrological writing practice both draws on and marks a coda to the literary tradition of modernist and metropolitan miniatures that began with European newspapers around 1900 and the urban snapshot-narratives that their cultural pages and miscellaneous reports afforded (*Miniature Metropolis*). *Cosmic Miniatures* has demonstrated how Kluge's own writing practice for the 21st century both draws on and deviates from the critical and narrative legacies he inherits from Adorno (as well as Benjamin, Marx, and Kant), specifically with regard to uses of futurity and cultivation of the future sense. *Nachricht* has a role to play here too, albeit in heliotropic and extraterrestrial aspects that most discussions of the term tend not to address.

The first of these is address itself, which Kluge explicitly cites as one of the core elements of News that are always infused or infiltrated with the doggedness of *Nachricht* too. Insisting that he speaks as a literary author, even in an interview about news and experience in television, Kluge discusses a mode of "address" [*Adressierung*] that "concerns me" [*mich angeht*] and is also a form of "intensification" [*Zuspitzung*] (Kluge, Binzegger, and Heller 22; see also 26).

---

3 Readers will note that in this passage Kluge uses the plural form of *Nachricht* and the English word "news," which he capitalizes. See also Huyssen, who discusses Kluge as "an analytic storyteller in the course of time" in the 20th century and observes the following: "Many stories focus on events and situations in the lives of individuals, but instead of traditional heroes or modernist antiheroes, Kluge offers what looks at first sight like narrative chaos, a series of unrelated accounts of events as one might find them on the local news page of the daily paper" (*Twilight Memories* 146). See also Langston, Martens, Pauval, Schulte, and Stollmann on Kluge's multimedial *Nachrichten* as a nexus of narration and montage (10).

However, the intensification of temporal sense perception that Kluge's experimental literary miniatures for the 21st century foster must additionally be understood as this-worldly and off-worldly at the same time and in the very dimensionality of time. The experiential conversion of catastrophic histories into partisan horizons of counterfactual hope with real effect depends on this differential conjunction in time. Regardless of the medium in which he operates, hope and fear are always linked affects of futurity for Kluge (23), and an element of conversion and not legacy alone attaches to *Nachricht* in particular:

> Half of all news [*Nachrichten*] could be characterized [...] as trash. But human beings are well-meaning and want to re-interpret the News in keeping with their experience, in order to supplement their experience and in this way to make good news [*Nachrichten*] out of bad ones.
>
> [*Die Hälfte aller Nachrichten könnte man [...] als Schrott bezeichnen. Es gibt aber ein Wohlwollen im Menschen, die News nach seiner Erfahrung umzudeuten, um seine Erfahrung zu ergänzen und dadurch aus schlechten Nachrichten gute zu machen.*] (24)

Whatever else it entails, *Nachricht* thus also entails a literal en-couragement to a supplemental temporality of conversion. This becomes especially evident in the close readings of Kluge's cosmic, global, and German miniatures that have been advanced here in relation to the future sense and narrative form. Throughout Kluge's oeuvre though, *Nachricht* should also be understood as military intelligence to the degree that life-and-death stakes of happiness and survival are involved. This explains for example why Kluge's outsized writing about the Battle of Stalingrad begins paradoxically enough—in the revised version published in 2000—with a miniature titled "Nachricht" ["News Item/Military Intelligence"], which opens by avowing that the adage "'A boy doesn't cry'" ["*Ein Junge weint nicht*"] is itself a news item or *Nachricht* meant to muster a "sense of reality" [*Wirklichkeitssinn*], one that Kluge's "Nachricht" textually undermines (see "Chronicle of Feelings," Vol. I, 513–514; for the original phrasing in Kluge's Stalingrad opus of 1964, see *Schlachtbeschreibung* 549). The use of *Nachricht* as military intelligence also helps explain frequent references or allusions to Carl von Clausewitz throughout Kluge's work, or even his designation of Adorno as a "partisan" bringer of hope in times of despair.

If the future sense of Kluge's literary experiments of more recent vintage also multi-tasks as military intelligence and intensified address, this long-distance sense organ of temporal perception is able to do so only with heightened attention to the sensory valence of narrative form. While the composite noun *Nachricht* also conjures associations with both temporal "afterness" [*nach*] and legal "judgment" [*richten*] (on the importance of "afterness" as a figure of modern thought, see especially Gerhard Richter), the futurity of Kluge's 21st-century miniatures pivots more pointedly on tropes of directionality [*nach*] and orientation [*sich richten nach*]. The orientation at stake in Kluge's storytelling is to the intensified reality of the utopian dimension in lived social time, and this intensified reality is something that Kluge's narrative experiments in temporal perspective and historical voice allow and encourage us to make through the work of reading. It is important to recall however that this affective longing or lived orientation to the utopian dimension (as a temporal structure) in Kluge's literary work is made experiential without ever being merely empirical or presentist alone. The narrative operations of social labor on perspective and voice in Kluge's cosmic, global, and German experiments also turn on a linkage in Kluge's writing practice between *Nachricht* and *Märchen* or fairy tale.[4] As Part Two's discussion of revolutionary horizons details, this has to do in part with the etymology of the word *Märchen* itself, which compounds miniaturization with "pronouncement" [*Kunde*], "news" [*Nachricht*], and "more" [*mehr*] (Seebold 598). For Kluge, multidimensional news items in narrative form are also *Märchen* creating the "more" of temporal supplementation. Even when fairy tales are not explicitly invoked as thematic motif, these miniature literary experiments in cosmic relations, catastrophic histories, and transformative horizons bring something off-worldly and "unnatural" into the temporal dimension of human experience. This is future-making in Kluge's heliotropic and sidereal key. The 20th century was riddled with the philosophical and anthropological refrain of something missing, and as critical social theorists of the Frankfurt School well knew, in catastrophic histories there is always someone missing too. This much applies to the catastrophic histories of the 21st century as well. Kluge's intensified investment in experimental storytelling with real claims to futures without life's miseries is addressed to us, readers whom hope will not abandon and who are called upon to make more and better times. Pay attention to the small things that matter. That missing someone could be the extraterrestrial in you.

---

4 On the importance of fairy tales for Negt and Kluge's social theory more generally, see Fore's introduction to *History and Obstinacy* (21). Negt and Kluge themselves write: "fairy tales reverse real experiences" (283), thus stressing what I would speak of not in terms of negation or resistance alone but actual conversion in time.

Works Cited

Adelson, Leslie A. "Experiment Mars: Contemporary German Literature, Imaginative Ethnoscapes, and the New Futurism." *Über Gegenwartsliteratur: Interpretationen und Interventionen*. Ed. Mark W. Rectanus. Bielefeld: Aisthesis, 2008. 23–49.
Adelson, Leslie A. "The Future of Futurity: Alexander Kluge and Yoko Tawada." *The Germanic Review* 86.3 (2011): 153–184.
Adelson, Leslie A. "Futurity Now: An Introduction." *Futurity Now*. Ed. Leslie A. Adelson and Devin Fore. Spec. issue of *The Germanic Review* 88.3 (2013): 213–218.
Adelson, Leslie A. "Horizons of Hope: Alexander Kluge's Cosmic Miniatures and Walter Benjamin." *Gegenwartsliteratur: Ein germanistisches Jahrbuch* 13 (2014): 203–225.
Adelson, Leslie A., and Devin Fore, eds. *Futurity Now*. Spec. issue of *The Germanic Review* 88.3 (2013).
Adolf, Heinrich. "Adornos verkaufte Braut——Rekonstruktion einer Beziehung, *Die vergessene Geliebte*." *Adorno-Portraits: Erinnerungen von Zeitgenossen*. Ed. Stefan Müller-Doohm. Frankfurt am Main: Suhrkamp, 2007. 309–334.
Adorno, Theodor W. *Aesthetic Theory*. Trans. and ed. Robert Hullot-Kentor. London: Athlone, 1997.
Adorno, Theodor W. *Ästhetische Theorie*. 2nd ed. Frankfurt am Main: Suhrkamp, 1974.
Adorno, Theodor W. *Critical Models: Interventions and Catchwords*. Trans. Henry W. Pickford. New York: Columbia University Press, 2005.
Adorno, Theodor W. "Ernst Bloch's *Spuren:* On the Revised Edition of 1959." *Notes to Literature*. Vol. 1. Trans. Shierry Weber Nicholsen. New York: Columbia University Press, 1991. 200–215.
Adorno, Theodor W. *Erziehung zur Mündigkeit: Vorträge und Gespräche mit Hellmut Becker 1959–1969*. Ed. Gerd Kadelbach. Frankfurt am Main: Suhrkamp, 1971.
Adorno, Theodor W. *Minima Moralia: Reflections from Damaged Life*. Trans. Edmund Jephcott. London: Verso, 2005.
Adorno, Theodor W. *Minima Moralia: Reflections from the Damaged Life*. Trans. Dennis Redmond. Lexington, KY: Prism Key Press, 2011.
Adorno, Theodor W. *Minima Moralia: Reflexionen aus dem beschädigten Leben*. Ed. Rolf Tiedemann. 8th ed. Frankfurt am Main: Suhrkamp, 2012.
Adorno, Theodor W. *Negative Dialectics*. Trans. E.B. Ashton. New York: Seabury, 1973.
Adorno, Theodor W. *Negative Dialektik*. 5th ed. Frankfurt am Main: Suhrkamp, 1988.
Adorno, Theodor W. *Noten zur Literatur*. Ed. Rolf Tiedemann. Frankfurt am Main: Suhrkamp, 1981.
Adorno, Theodor W. *Notes to Literature*. Vol. 1. Trans. Shierry Weber Nicholsen. New York: Columbia University Press, 1991.
Adorno, Theodor W. *The Stars Down to Earth and Other Essays on the Irrational in Culture*. Ed. Stephen Crook. London: Routledge, 2002.
Adorno, Theodor W., Ernst Bloch, and Horst Krüger. "Something's Missing: A Discussion between Ernst Bloch and Theodor W. Adorno on the Contradictions of Utopian Longing." Ernst Bloch. *The Utopian Function of Art and Literature: Selected Essays*. Trans. Jack Zipes and Frank Mecklenburg. Cambridge, MA: MIT Press, 1988. 1–17.
Adorno, Theodor W. and Arnold Gehlen. "Ist die Soziologie eine Wissenschaft vom Menschen? Ein Streitgespräch zwischen Theodor W. Adorno und Arnold Gehlen."

Friedemann Grenz. *Adornos Philosophie in Grundbegriffen: Auflösung einiger Deutungsprobleme*. Frankfurt am Main: Suhrkamp, 1974. 224–251. Print supplement.
Adorno, Theodor W., Hans Albert, Ralf Dahrendorf, Jürgen Habermas, Harald Pilot, Karl R. Popper. *The Positivist Dispute in German Sociology*. Trans. Glyn Adey and David Frisby. London: Heinemann, 1976.
Alber, Jan. "Impossible Storyworlds—and What to Do with Them." *Storyworlds: A Journal of Narrative Studies* 1.1 (2009): 79–96.
Alber, Jan, Henrik Skov Nielsen, and Brian Richardson. "Unnatural Voices, Minds, and Narration." *The Routledge Companion to Experimental Literature*. Ed. Joe Bray, Alison Gibbons, and Brian McHale. New York: Routledge, 2012. 351–367.
Alber, Jan, and Monika Fludernik, eds. *Postclassical Narratology: Approaches and Analyses*. Columbus, OH: Ohio State University Press, 2010.
Alexander, Bryan N. "Jameson's Adorno and the Problem of Utopia." *Utopian Studies* 9.2 (1998): 51–57.
Althaus, Thomas, Wolfgang Bunzel, and Dirk Göttsche. *Kleine Prosa: Theorie und Geschichte eines Textfeldes im Literatursystem der Moderne*. Tübingen: Niemeyer, 2007.
Améry, Jean. "Ressentiments." *Jean Améry: Werke*. Ed. Irene Heidelberger-Leonard, Vol. 2. *Jenseits von Schuld und Sühne, Unmeisterliche Wanderjahre, Örtlichkeiten*. Ed. Gerhard Scheit. Stuttgart: Klett-Cotta, 2002. 118–148.
Anderson, Mark. "Documents, Photography, Postmemory: Alexander Kluge, W.G. Sebald, and the German Family." *Poetics Today* 29.1 (2008): 129–153.
Anz, Thomas. "Adorno, Luhmann und die Liebe in Frankfurts Zeiten der Studentenrevolte: Fragmentarische Fortsetzung einer abgebrochenen Recherche und eine halbwahre Geschichte Alexander Kluges über das Wintersemester 1968/69." *literaturkritik.de: rezensionsforum*. C.H. Beck. 6 May 2010. Web. 7 October 2015.
Appadurai, Arjun. *The Future as Cultural Fact: Essays on the Global Condition*. London: Verso, 2013.
Assmann, Aleida. "The Empathetic Listener and the Ethics of Storytelling." *Storytelling and Ethics: Historical Imagination in Contemporary Literature, Media, and Visual Arts*. Ed. Hanna Meretoja and Colin Davis. London: Routledge, forthcoming.
Assmann, Aleida. "Transformations of the Modern Time Regime." *Breaking Up Time: Negotiating the Borders between Past, Present, and Future*. Ed. Chris Lorenz and Berber Bevernage. Göttingen: Vandenhoeck & Ruprecht, 2013. 39–56.
Baecker, Dirk, and Alexander Kluge. *Vom Nutzten ungelöster Probleme*. Berlin: Merve, 2003.
Bartels, Gerrit. "Mechanik des Bösen." *Der Tagesspiegel*. 4 August 2013. Web. 14 July 2016.
Bartov, Omer. "War, Memory, and Repression: Alexander Kluge and the Politics of Representation in Postwar Germany." *Murder in Our Midst: The Holocaust, Industrial Killing, and Representation*. New York: Oxford University Press, 1996. 139–152.
Bechtold, Gerhard. "Die Sinne entspannen: Zur Multimedialität in Alexander Kluges Texten." *Alexander Kluge*. Ed. Thomas Böhm-Christel. Frankfurt am Main: Suhrkamp, 1983. 212–232.
Behrens, Roger. "Mathematik." *Adorno-ABC*. Leipzig: Reclam, 2003. 148–149.
Benhabib, Seyla. *Critique, Norm, and Utopia: A Study of the Foundations of Critical Theory*. New York: Columbia University Press, 1986.
Benjamin, Walter. *The Arcades Project*. Trans. Howard Eiland and Kevin McLaughlin. Cambridge, MA: Belknap Press, 1999.

Benjamin, Walter. *Berlin Childhood around 1900*. Trans. Howard Eiland. Cambridge, MA: Harvard University Press, 2006.
Benjamin, Walter. *Einbahnstraße*. Frankfurt am Main: Suhrkamp, 1955.
Benjamin, Walter. "Der Erzähler: Betrachtungen zum Werk Nikolai Lesskows." *Illuminationen: Ausgewählte Schriften*. Ed. Siegfried Unseld. 2nd ed. Frankfurt am Main: Suhrkamp, 1980. 385–410.
Benjamin, Walter. "Goethe's Elective Affinities." Trans. Stanley Corngold. *Walter Benjamin: Selected Writings, Volume 1, 1913–1926*. Ed. Marcus Bullock and Michael W. Jennings. Cambridge, MA: Belknap Press, 1996. 297–360.
Benjamin, Walter. *Illuminationen: Ausgewählte Schriften*. Ed. Siegfried Unseld. 2nd ed. Frankfurt am Main: Suhrkamp, 1980.
Benjamin, Walter. *Illuminations*. Trans. Harry Zohn. New York: Harcourt, Brace & World, 1968.
Benjamin, Walter. "One-Way Street." Trans. Edmund Jephcott. *Walter Benjamin: Selected Writings*. Vol. 1: 1913–1926. Ed. Marcus Bullock and Michael W. Jennings. Cambridge, MA, and London, England: Belknap Press, 1996. 444–488.
Benjamin, Walter. *Das Passagen-Werk*. 2 Vols. Ed. Rolf Tiedemann. Frankfurt am Main: Suhrkamp, 1982.
Benjamin, Walter. *The Storyteller: Short Stories*. Trans. and ed. Sam Dolbear, Esther Leslie, and Sebastian Truskolaski. London: Verso, 2016.
Benjamin, Walter. "Theses on the Philosophy of History." *Illuminations*. Trans. Harry Zohn. New York: Harcourt, Brace & World, 1968. 255–266.
Benjamin, Walter. "Über den Begriff der Geschichte." *Illuminationen: Ausgewählte Schriften*. Ed. Siegfried Unseld. 2nd ed. Frankfurt am Main: Suhrkamp, 1980. 251–261.
Benjamin, Walter. *Walter Benjamin: Selected Writings*. Vol. 2, Part 2: 1931–1934. Trans. Rodney Livingstone and Others. Ed. Michael W. Jennings, Howard Eiland, and Gary Smith. Cambridge, MA, and London, England: Belknap Press, 1999.
Bennington, Geoffrey. *Frontières kantiennes*. Paris: Galilée, 2000.
Benzaquén, Adriana S. "Thought and Utopia in the Writings of Adorno, Horkheimer, and Benjamin." *Utopian Studies* 9.2 (1998): 149–161.
Berry, Michael. "Chen Kaige: Historical Revolution and Cinematic Rebellion." *Speaking in Images: Interviews with Contemporary Chinese Filmmakers*. New York: Columbia University Press, 2005. 82–106.
Birkmeyer, Jens. "Eigensinn und Anerkennung: Anthropologische Phantasie bei Alexander Kluge und Peter Weiss." *Diese bebende, zähe, kühne Hoffnung: 25 Jahre Peter Weiss, die Ästhetik des Widerstands*. Ed. Arnd Beise, Jens Birkmeyer, and Michael Hofmann. St. Ingbert: Röhrig Universitätsverlag, 2008. 115–142.
Birkmeyer, Jens, Torsten Pflugmacher, and Ulrike Weymann. *"Man kann nicht lernen, nicht zu lernen": Alexander Kluge im Unterricht*. Spec. issue of *Der Deutschunterricht: Beiträge zu seiner Praxis und wissenschaftlicher Grundlegung* 64.3 (2012).
Bloch, Ernst. *Heritage of Our Times*. Trans. Neville and Stephen Plaice. Berkeley, CA: University of California Press, 1991.
Bloch, Ernst. *The Principle of Hope*. 3 Vols. Trans. Neville Plaice, Stephen Plaice, and Paul Knight. Cambridge, MA: MIT Press, 1986.
Bloch, Ernst. *Das Prinzip Hoffnung*. 3 Vols. 1938–1947. Frankfurt am Main: Suhrkamp, 1959.
Bloch, Ernst. *The Spirit of Utopia*. Trans. Anthony A. Nassar. Stanford, CA: Stanford University Press, 2000.
Bloch, Ernst. *Traces*. Trans. Anthony A. Nassar. Stanford, CA: Stanford University Press, 2006.

Bloch, Ernst. "Zur Ontologie des Noch-Nicht-Seins." 1960. *Ernst Bloch—Auswahl aus seinen Schriften*. Ed. Hans Heinz Holz. Frankfurt am Main: Fischer, 1967. 41–66.
Blödorn, Andreas, Daniela Langer, and Michael Scheffel, eds. *Stimme(n) im Text: Narratologische Positionsbestimmungen*. Berlin: De Gruyter, 2006.
Blumenberg, Hans. *Care Crosses the River*. Trans. Paul Fleming. Stanford, CA: Stanford University Press, 2010.
Blumenberg, Hans. "On a Lineage of the Idea of Progress." Trans. E.B. Ashton. *Social Research* 41.1 (1974): 5–27.
Blumenberg, Hans. *Paradigms for a Metaphorology*. Trans. Robert Savage. Ithaca, NY: Cornell University Press and Cornell University Library, 2010. Signale: Modern German Letters, Cultures, and Thought.
Bode, Christoph, and Rainer Dietrich. *Future Narratives: Theory, Poetics, and Media-Historical Moment*. Berlin: De Gruyter, 2013.
Böhm-Christel, Thomas, ed. *Alexander Kluge*. Frankfurt am Main: Suhrkamp, 1983.
Böhme, Hartmut. "Netzwerke: Zur Theorie und Geschichte einer Konstruktion." *Netzwerke: Eine Kulturtechnik der Moderne*. Ed. Jürgen Barkhoff, Hartmut Böhme, and Jeanne Riou. Cologne: Böhlau, 2004. 17–36.
Bohm, Svetlana. *The Future of Nostalgia*. New York: Basic Books, 2001.
Bohn, Carolin. "Zur Ästhetik der Abwesenheit: Die Denk-Figur der Lücke (Adorno, Kluge, Boltanski)." *Comparative Arts: Universelle Ästhetik im Fokus der vergleichenden Literaturwissenschaft*. Ed. Achim Hölter. Heidelberg: Synchron, 2011. 311–321.
Bolz, Norbert. "Eigensinn: Zur politisch-theologischen Poetik Hans Magnus Enzensbergers und Alexander Kluges." *Das schnelle Altern der neuesten Literatur: Essays zu deutschsprachigen Texten 1968–1984*. Ed. Jochen Hörisch and Hubert Winkels. Düsseldorf: Claaassen, 1985. 40–59.
Bosse, Ulrike. "Ein Liebesversuch—Der Mensch als Objekt der Geschichte." *Alexander Kluge: Formen literarischer Darstellung von Geschichte*. Frankfurt am Main: Peter Lang, 1989. 43–47.
Bosteels, Bruno. *The Actuality of Communism*. London: Verso, 2014.
Bowie, Andrew. "Kluge and Negt 30 Years On: A Brief Reflection." *Glass Shards: Echoes of a Message in a Bottle*. Ed. Richard Langston, Gunther Martens, Vincent Pauval, Christian Schulte, and Rainer Stollmann. *Alexander Kluge-Jahrbuch* 2 (2015): 77–82.
Bowie, Andrew. "New Histories: Aspects of the Prose of Alexander Kluge." *Journal of European Studies* 12 (1982): 180–208.
Bowie, Andrew. Rev. of *Geschichte und Eigensinn*, by Oskar Negt and Alexander Kluge. *Telos: A Quarterly Journal of Critical Thought* 66 (1985): 183–190.
Bowie, Andrew. "Sich rächen ist eine komplizierte Arbeitsleistung: Überlegungen zur Vergangenheitsbewältigung am Beispiel Alexander Kluges." *Literatur und Erfahrung* 6 (1981): 69–84.
Brandstetter, Gabriele, Sibylle Peters, and Kai van Eikels, eds. *Prognosen über Bewegungen*. Berlin: B-Books, 2009.
Brauers, Claudia. "An sich ein Lernprozess ohne tödlichen Ausgang: Alexander Kluges Ästhetik der Lücke." *Klassik, modern: Für Norbert Oellers zum 60. Geburtstag*. Ed. Georg Guntermann. Spec. issue of *Zeitschrift für deutsche Philologie* 115 (1996): 169–178.
Braunstein, Dirk, and Stefan Müller-Doohm. "Zeitdiagnose." *Adorno-Handbuch: Leben – Werk – Wirkung*. Ed. Richard Klein, Johann Kreuzer, and Stefan Müller-Doohm. Stuttgart: Metzler, 2011. 248–253.

Bray, Joe, Alison Gibbons, and Brian McHale, eds. *The Routledge Companion to Experimental Literature*. New York: Routledge, 2012.

Bray, Michael. "Openness as a Form of Closure: Public Sphere, Social Class and Alexander Kluge's Counterproducts." *Telos: A Quarterly Journal of Politics, Philosophy, Critical Theory, Culture, and the Arts* 159 (2012): 144–171.

Breithaupt, Fritz. "History as the Delayed Integration of Phenomena." *Benjamin's Ghosts: Interventions in Contemporary Literary and Cultural Theory*. Ed. Gerhard Richter, Stanford, CA: Stanford University Press, 2002. 191–203 and 334–338.

Brock, Bazon. *Die Re-Dekade: Kunst und Kultur der achtziger Jahre (Zeit, Zeuge, Kunst)*. Munich: Klinkhardt & Biermann, 1990.

Brodsky, Claudia. "'The Real Horizon' (beyond Emotions): What Proust (Wordsworth, Rousseau, Diderot, and Hegel) Had 'in' Mind." *Rethinking Emotion: Interiority and Exteriority in Premodern, Modern, and Contemporary Thought*. Ed. Rüdiger Campe and Julia Weber. Berlin: De Gruyter, 2014. 219–242.

Brown, Lesley, ed. *The New Shorter Oxford English Dictionary on Historical Principles*. Vol. 2. Oxford: Clarendon, 1993.

Brumlik, Micha. "Theologie und Messianismus." *Adorno-Handbuch: Leben – Werk – Wirkung*. Ed. Richard Klein, Johann Kreuzer, and Stefan Müller-Doohm. Stuttgart: Metzler, 2011. 295–309.

Buch, Robert. *The Pathos of the Real: On the Aesthetics of Violence in the Twentieth Century*. Baltimore: Johns Hopkins UP, 2010.

Buck-Morss, Susan. *Dreamworld and Catastrophe: The Passing of Mass Utopia in East and West*. Cambridge, MA: MIT Press, 2000.

Buck-Morss, Susan. *The Origin of Negative Dialectics: Theodor W. Adorno, Walter Benjamin, and the Frankfurt Institute*. New York: The Free Press, 1977.

Buckmiller, Michael, and Pascal Nafe. "Die Naherwartung des Kommunismus—Werner Scholem." *Judentum und politische Existenz: Siebzehn Porträts deutsch-jüdischer Intellektueller*. Ed. Michael Buckmiller, Dietrich Heimann, and Joachim Perels. Hannover: Offizin, 2000. 61–81.

Buden, Boris. *Zone des Übergangs: Vom Ende des Postkommunismus*. Frankfurt am Main: Suhrkamp, 2009.

Bühler, Benjamin, and Stefan Willer, eds. *Futurologien: Ordnungen des Zukunftswissens*. Munich: Wilhelm Fink, 2016.

Burdick, Anne, Johanna Drucker, Peter Lunenfeld, Todd Pressner, and Jeffrey Schnapp. *Digital_Humanities*. Cambridge, MA: MIT Press, 2012.

Burger, Rudolf. "Die Mikrophysik des Widerstandes." *Ästhetik und Kommunikation* 48 (1982): 110–124.

Burke, Kenneth. *A Grammar of Motives*. Berkeley: University of California Press, 1953.

Busche, Hubertus. "Fensterlosigkeit—Leibniz' Kritik des Cartesianischen 'Influxus Physicus' und sein Gedanke der energetischen Eigenkausalität." *Leibniz' Auseinandersetzung mit Vorgängern und Zeitgenossen*. Ed. Ingrid Marchlewitz and Albert Heinekamp. Stuttgart: Steiner, 1990. 100–115.

Campe, Rüdiger. *The Game of Probability: Literature and Calculation from Pascal to Kleist*. Trans. Ellwood H. Wiggins Jr. Stanford, CA: Stanford University Press, 2012.

Campe, Rüdiger. "How to Use the Future: The Old European and the Modern Form of Life." *Prognosen über Bewegungen*. Ed. Gabriele Brandstetter, Sibylle Peters, and Kai van Eikels. Berlin: b-books, 2009. 107–120.

Caracciolo, Marco. "Experientiality." *The Living Handbook of Narratology.* Interdisciplinary Center for Narratology (University of Hamburg, Germany). Revised 1 July 2014. Web. 9 September 2015.

Caracciolo, Marco. *The Experientiality of Narrative: An Enactivist Approach.* Berlin: De Gruyter, 2014. Print.

Caroti, Simone. "Defining Astrosociology from a Science Fiction Perspective." *Astropolitics: The International Journal of Space Politics and Policy* 9.1 (2011): 39–49.

Carrard, Philippe. "Biography and the Representation of Consciousness." *Narrative* 5 (1997): 287–305.

Cartwright, Mark. "Huitzilopochtli." *Ancient History Encyclopedia.* 27 August 2013. Web. http://www.ancient.eu/Huitzilopochtli/. 10 July 2016.

Casad, Madeleine. "The Virtual Turn: Narrative, Identity, and German Media Art Practice in the Digital Age." Diss. Cornell University, 2012.

Chandler, Nahum Dimitri. *Toward an African Future—of the Limit of World.* London: Living Commons Collective, 2013.

Chaudhary, Zahid R. *Afterimage of Empire: Photography in Nineteenth-Century India.* Minneapolis, MN: University of Minnesota Press, 2012.

Chaudhary, Zahid R. "Subjects in Difference: Walter Benjamin, Frantz Fanon, and Postcolonial Theory." *differences: A Journal of Feminist Cultural Studies* 23.1 (2012): 151–183.

Chignell, Andrew. *What May I Hope? Kant's Questions.* London: Routledge, forthcoming.

Chrostowska, S.D. "Thought Woken by Memory: Adorno's Circuitous Path to Utopia." *New German Critique* 118 [Vol. 40, Nr. 1] (2013): 93–117.

Cicovacki, Predrag. "Pure Reason and Metaphors: A Reflection on the Significance of Kant's Philosophy." *Annales Philosophici* 1.2 (2011): 9–19.

Clark, Paul. *Reinventing China: A Generation and its Films.* Hong Kong: The Chinese University Press, 2005.

Claussen, Detlev. *Theodor W. Adorno: One Last Genius.* Trans. Rodney Livingstone. Cambridge, Massachusetts: Belknap Press, 2008.

Cobley, Paul. *Narrative.* London: Routledge, 2001.

Combrink, Thomas. "Zu Alexander Kluges Metaphernwelt: Mit Blick auf die Überlegungen Hans Blumenbergs." *Glass Shards: Echoes of a Message in a Bottle.* Ed. Richard Langston, Gunther Martens, Vincent Pauval, Christian Schulte, and Rainer Stollmann. *Alexander Kluge Jahrbuch* 2 (2015): 171–178.

Connell, Liam. "Globalization and Transnationalism." *The Routledge Companion to Experimental Literature.* Ed. Joe Bray, Alison Gibbons, and Brian McHale. New York: Routledge, 2012. 224–237.

Connell, Liam, and Nicky Marsh, eds. *Literature and Globalization: A Reader.* London: Routledge, 2011.

Connell, Matt F. "Body, Mimesis and Childhood in Adorno, Kafka and Freud." *Body & Society* 4.4 (1998): 67–90.

Connell, Matt F. "Childhood Experience and the Image of Utopia—The Broken Promise of Adorno's Proustian Sublimations." *Radical Philosophy* 99 (2000): 19–30.

Crary, Jonathan. *24/7: Late Capitalism and the Ends of Sleep.* London: Verso, 2013.

Crowe, Michael J. *The Extraterrestrial Life Debate, 1750–1900.* New York: Dover, 1999.

Crutzen, Paul J., and Eugene F. Stoermer. "The 'Anthropocene'." *IGBP [International Geosphere-Biosphere Programme] Global Change Newsletter* 41 (2000): 17–18.

Culler, Jonathan. *Structuralist Poetics: Structuralism, Linguistics and the Study of Literature*. London: Routledge & Kegan Paul, 1975.
Dannenberg, Hilary P. *Coincidence and Counterfactuality: Plotting Time and Space in Narrative Fiction*. Lincoln, NE: University of Nebraska Press, 2008.
Davies, Gloria. "Habermas in China: Theory as Catalyst." *The China Journal* 57 (2007): 61–85.
Dean, Jodi. *The Communist Horizon*. London: Verso, 2012.
Demirović, Alex. *Der nonkonformistische Intellektuelle: Die Entwicklung der Kritischen Theorie zur Frankfurter Schule*. Frankfurt am Main: Suhrkamp, 1999.
Derrida, Jacques. *Specters of Marx: The State of the Debt, the Work of Mourning and the New International*. Trans. Peggy Kamuf. New York/London: Routledge, 1994.
Derrida, Jacques. "White Mythology: Metaphor in the Text of Philosophy." *Margins of Philosophy*. Trans. Alan Bass. Chicago, IL: University of Chicago Press, 1982. 207–271.
Dick, Steven J. *The Plurality of Worlds: The Extraterrestrial Life Debate from Democritus to Kant*. Cambridge, UK: Cambridge University Press, 1984.
Downing, Eric. *The Chain of Things: Magic, Reading, Sympathy, and the Future in German Literature and Thought 1850–1940*. Ithaca, NY: Cornell University Press, forthcoming.
Downing, Eric. "Magic Reading." *Literary Studies and the Pursuits of Reading*. Ed. Jonathan M. Hess and Richard V. Benson. Rochester, NY: Camden House, 2012. 190–215.
Drews, Jörg. "Leseprozesse mit paradoxem Ausgang: Elf Kurz-Essays über Alexander Kluge." *Alexander Kluge*. Ed. Heinz Ludwig Arnold. *text + kritik* 85/86 (1985): 22–32.
Düttmann, Alexander. *So ist es: Ein philosophischer Kommentar zu Adornos 'Minima Moralia'*. Frankfurt am Main: Suhrkamp, 2004.
Durzak, Manfred. "Anpassung bis zum Untergang: Deutschland im Dritten Reich." *Die deutsche Kurzgeschichte der Gegenwart: Autorenporträts, Werkstattgespräche, Interpretationen*. Würzburg: Königshausen & Neumann, 2002. 330–349.
Eder, Klaus, and Alexander Kluge. *Ulmer Dramaturgien: Reibungsverluste*. Arbeitshefte Film 2/3. Ed. Klaus Eder. Munich: Hanser, 1980.
Eiland, Howard, and Michael W. Jennings. *Walter Benjamin: A Critical Life*. Cambridge, MA: Belknap Press, 2014.
Ekardt, Philipp. "Film ohne Star: Alexander Kluges Präsensgeschichte über Asta Nielsen." *Der Präsensroman*. Ed. Armen Avanessian and Anke Henning. Berlin: De Gruyter, 2013. 237–247.
Ekardt, Philipp. "Starry Skies and Frozen Lakes: Alexander Kluge's Digital Constellations." *October* 138 (2011): 107–119.
Elliott, Brian. "Revolution, History and Time in Benjamin and Sloterdijk." *Critical Time in Modern German Literature and Culture*. Ed. Dirk Göttsche. Oxford: Peter Lang, 2016. 101–125.
Elsaesser, Thomas. *German Cinema: Terror and Trauma, Cultural Memory Since 1945*. New York: Routledge, 2014.
Erdle, Birgit R. *Literarische Epistemologie der Zeit: Lektüren zu Kant, Kleist, Heine und Kafka*. Paderborn: Fink, 2015.
Erdle, Birgit R. "'Sticking to our language'/'an unserer Sprache festhalten': Adorno in NYC." *'Escape to Life': German Intellectuals in New York, A Compendium on Exile after 1933*. Ed. Eckart Goebel and Sigrid Weigel. Berlin: De Gruyter, 2012. 9–26.
Erdle, Birgit R. "Thinking in Times of Danger: Adorno on Stupidity." Trans. Gabriele Rahaman. *Futurity Now*. Ed. Leslie A. Adelson and Devin Fore. Spec. issue of *The Germanic Review* 88.3 (2013): 260–270.

Eshel, Amir. *Futurity: Contemporary Literature and the Quest for the Past.* Chicago, IL: University of Chicago Press, 2013.
Eshel, Amir. "The Past Recaptured? Günter Grass's *Mein Jahrhundert* and Alexander Kluge's *Chronik der Gefühle.*" *Gegenwartsliteratur* 1 (2002): 63–86.
Eshel, Amir. *Zukünftigkeit: Die zeitgenössische Literatur und die Vergangenheit.* Trans. Irmgard Hölscher. Berlin: Jüdischer Verlag im Suhrkamp Verlag, 2012.
Esposito, Elena. *Die Fiktion der wahrscheinlichen Realität.* Trans. Nicole Reinhardt. Frankfurt am Main: Suhrkamp, 2007.
Esposito, Elena. *The Future of Futures: The Time of Money in Financing and Society.* Trans. Elena Esposito and Andrew K. Whitehead. Northampton, MA: Edward Elgar, 2011.
Ette, Ottmar, ed. *Nanophilologie: Literarische Kurz- und Kürzestformen in der Romania.* Tübingen: Niemeyer, 2008.
Falke, Gustav. "Neoklassizismus als andere Moderne: Strawinsky und Ravel." *Adorno-Handbuch: Leben – Werk – Wirkung.* Ed. Richard Klein, Johann Kreuzer, and Stefan Müller-Doohm. Stuttgart: Metzler, 2011. 138–145.
Fischer, Kai Lars. *Geschichtsmontagen: Zum Zusammenhang von Geschichtskonzeption und Text-Modell bei Walter Benjamin und Alexander Kluge.* Hildesheim: Olms, 2013.
Fisher, Jaimey. "Adorno's Lesson Plans? The Ethics of (Re)education In 'The Meaning of "Working through the Past"'." *Language Without Soil: Adorno and Late Philosophical Modernity.* Ed. Gerhard Richter. New York: Fordham University Press, 2009. 76–98.
Fleming, Paul. "On the Edge of Non-Contingency: Anecdotes and the Lifeworld." *Telos: A Quarterly Journal of Politics, Philosophy, Critical Theory, Culture, and the Arts* 158 (Spring 2012): 21–35.
Fludernik, Monika. "Collective Minds in Fact and Fiction: Intermental Thought and Group Consciousness in Early Modern Narrative." *Poetics Today* 35.4 (2014): 689–730.
Fludernik, Monika. "How Natural is 'Unnatural Narratology'; or, What is Unnatural about Unnatural Narratology?" *Narrative* 20 (2012): 357–370.
Fludernik, Monika. *An Introduction to Narratology.* Trans. Patricia Häusler-Greenfield and Monika Fludernik. London: Routledge, 2009.
Fludernik, Monika. "Natural Narratology and Cognitive Parameters." *Narrative Theory and the Cognitive Sciences.* Ed. David Herman. Stanford, CA: CSLI Publications, 2003. 243–267.
Fludernik, Monika. "New Wine in Old Bottles? Voice, Focalization, and New Writing." *New Literary History* 32 (2001): 619–638.
Fludernik, Monika. *Towards a 'Natural' Narratology.* London: Routledge, 1996.
Flug, Noach. Untitled address. *Holocaust Era Assets: Conference Proceedings, Prague, June 26–30, 2009.* Ed. Jiří Schneider, Jakub Klepal, and Irena Kalhousová. Prague: Forum 2000 Foundation, 2009 [ISBN 978–80–254–6406–9]. 268–270. Web. http://www.holocausteraassets.eu. 24 September 2015.
Fontenelle, Bernard le Bovier de. *Conversations on the Plurality of Worlds.* Trans. H.A. Hargreaves. Berkeley, CA: University of California Press, 1990.
Fore, Devin. *All the Graphs: Soviet Factography and the Emergence of Modernist Documentary.* Chicago: Universotu of Chicago Press, 2016.
Fore, Devin. "Die Emergenz der sowjetischen Faktographie." *Deutsche Vierteljahrsschrift für Literaturwissenschaft und Geistesgeschichte* 89.3 (2015): 376–403.
Fore, Devin. "The Metabiotic State: Dziga Vertov's *The Eleventh Year.*" *October* 145 (2013): 3–37.

Fore, Devin. "The Old, the New, and the Now: Points of Orientation at the End of the Cold War." German Studies Association Annual Convention. Washington, D.C. 4 October 2015. Conference presentation.

Fore, Devin. "The Operative Word in Soviet Factography". *October* 118 (Fall 2006): 95–131.

Fore, Devin. *Realism After Modernism: The Rehumanization of Art and Literature*. Cambridge, MA: MIT Press, 2012.

Forrest, Tara, ed. *Alexander Kluge: Raw Materials for the Imagination*. Amsterdam: Amsterdam University Press, 2012.

Forrest, Tara. *The Politics of Imagination: Benjamin, Kracauer, Kluge*. Bielefeld: transcript, 2007.

Friedländer, Saul. *The Years of Extermination: Nazi Germany and the Jews, 1939–1945*. New York: Harper Collins, 2009.

Friedrich, Alexander. *Metaphorologie der Vernetzung: Zur Theorie kultureller Leitmetaphern*. Paderborn: Wilhelm Fink, 2015.

Fröhlich, Claudia. *"Wider die Tabuisierung des Ungehorsams": Fritz Bauers Widerstandsbegriff und die Aufarbeitung von NS-Verbrechen*. Frankfurt am Main: Campus, 2006.

Fuchs, Anne, and Jonathan Long, eds. *Time in German Literature and Culture, 1900–2015: Between Acceleration and Slowness*. New York: Palgrave Macmillan, 2015.

Fukuyama, Francis. *The End of History and the Last Man*. 1992. With a New Afterword. New York: Free Press, 2006.

Gabriel, Nicole. "Unbehagen in der Kultur und Glücksversprechen." *Sigmund Freud: Immer noch Unbehagen in der Kultur?*. Ed. Franz Kaltenbeck and Peter Weibel. Zurich: Diaphanes, 2009. 207–219.

Gagnebin, Jeanne Marie. *Geschichte und Erzählung bei Walter Benjamin*. Trans. Judith Klein. Würzburg: Königshausen & Neumann, 2001.

Galli, Matteo. "Wirklichkeitsentzug—Krieg und Medien bei Alexander Kluge." *Amsterdamer Beiträge zur neueren Germanistik* 57.1 (2005): 313–328.

Gedenkstätte Buchenwald, ed. *Buchenwald Concentration Camp 1937–1945: A Guide to the Permanent Historical Exhibition*. Frankfurt am Main: Wallstein, 2006.

Geller, Jay Howard. "The Scholem Brothers and the Paths of German Jewry, 1914–1939." *Shofar* 30.2 (2012): 52–73.

Genette, Gérard. *Narrative Discourse: An Essay in Method*. Trans. Jane E. Lewin. Ithaca, NY: Cornell University Press, 1980.

Genette, Gérard. *Narrative Discourse Revisited*. Trans. Jane E. Lewin. Ithaca, NY: Cornell University Press, 1988.

Geulen, Eva. "A Matter of Tradition." *Telos: A Quarterly Journal of Critical Thought* 89 (1991): 155–166.

Geulen, Eva. "Mega Melancholia: Adorno's *Minima Moralia*." *Critical Theory: Current State and Future Prospects*. Ed. Peter Hohendahl and Jaimey Fisher. New York: Berghahn Books, 2001. 49–68.

Geulen, Eva. "'No Happiness Without Fetishism': *Minima Moralia* as Ars Amandi." *Feminist Interpretations of Theodor Adorno*. Ed. Renée Heberle and Nancy Tuana. University Park, PA: Pennsylvania State University Press, 2006. 97–112.

Geuss, Raymond. "Adorno's Gaps." *Arion: A Journal of Humanities and the Classics* 12.2 (2004): 161–180.

Gibson, Nigel, and Andrew Rubin, eds. *Adorno: A Critical Reader*. Malden, MA: Blackwell, 2002.
Giles, Steve. "Realism after Modernism: Representation and Modernity in Brecht, Lukács and Adorno." *Aesthetics and Modernity from Schiller to the Frankfurt School*. Ed. Jerome Carroll, Steve Giles, and Maike Oergel. Oxford: Peter Lang, 2012. 275–296.
Gilgen, Peter. "Structures, But in Ruins Only: On Kant's History of Reason and the University." *New Centennial Review* 9.2 (2009): 165–194.
Giroux, Henry A. "Critical Theory and Educational Practice." *The Critical Pedagogy Reader*. Ed. Antonia Darder, Marta P. Baltodano, and Rodolfo D. Torres. 2nd ed. New York: Routledge, 2008. 27–51.
Göttsche, Dirk. *Kleine Prosa in Moderne und Gegenwart*. Münster: Aschendorff, 2006.
Göttsche, Dirk. "Zeitpoetik in kleiner Prosa der Gegenwart." *Critical Time in Modern German Literature and Culture*. Ed. Dirk Göttsche. Oxford: Peter Lang, 2016. 249–270.
Gregersen, Erik. "Coma Berenices: Constellation." *Encyclopaedia Britannica Online*. Encyclopaedia Britannica Inc. Revised 29 September 2013. Web. 21 September 2015.
Grice, Paul. *Studies in the Way of Words*. Cambridge, MA: Harvard University Press, 1989.
Groys, Boris. *Das kommunistische Postskriptum*. Frankfurt am Main: Suhrkamp, 2006.
Groys, Boris, Anne von der Heiden, and Peter Weibel, eds. *Zurück aus der Zukunft: Osteuropäische Kulturen im Zeitalter des Postkommunismus*. Frankfurt am Main: Suhrkamp, 2005.
Gumbrecht, Hans Ulrich. *Nach 1945—Latenz als Ursprung der Gegenwart*. Trans. Frank Born. Berlin: Suhrkamp, 2012.
Guyer, Paul. "18th Century German Aesthetics." *The Stanford Encyclopedia of Philosophy*. Ed. Edward N. Zalta. Revised 3 March 2014. Web. 17 September 2015.
Guyer, Paul. "Introduction: The Starry Heavens and the Moral Law." *The Cambridge Companion to Kant*. Cambridge, UK: Cambridge University Press, 1992. 1–27.
Habermas, Jürgen. *Autonomy and Solidarity: Interviews with Jürgen Habermas*. Ed. Peter Dews. Rev. and enlarged edition. London: Verso, 1992.
Habermas, Jürgen. *Structural Transformation of the Public Sphere: An Inquiry into a Category of Bourgeois Society*. Trans. Thomas Burger, with the assistance of Frederick Lawrence. Cambridge, MA: MIT Press, 1989.
Habermas, Jürgen. *Strukturwandel der Öffentlichkeit: Untersuchungen zu einer Kategorie der bürgerlichen Gesellschaft*. Frankfurt am Main: Suhrkamp, 1962.
Habjan, Jernej, and Fabienne Imlinger, eds. *Globalizing Literary Genres: Literature, History, Modernity*. London: Routledge, 2016.
Haenni, Sabine. "Intellectual Promiscuity: Cultural History in the Age of the Cinema, the Network, and the Database." *New German Critique* 122 [Vol. 41. Nr. 2] (2014): 189–202.
Hahn, Barbara. "'Gemeinsame Philosophie': Ein Projekt von Oskar Negt und Alexander Kluge." *Der Maulwurf kennt kein System: Beiträge zur gemeinsamen Philosophie von Oskar Negt und Alexander Kluge*. Ed. Christian Schulte and Rainer Stollmann. Bielefeld: transcript, 2005. 103–106.
Hahn, Hans-Joachim. "NS-Mediziner in Peter Weiss' Die Ermittlung und Alexander Kluges 'Ein Liebesversuch'." *NS-Medizin und Öffentlichkeit: Formen der Aufarbeitung nach 1945*. Ed. Stephan Braese. Frankfurt am Main: Campus, 2015. 215–232.
Hamacher, Werner. "Intensive Sprachen." *Übersetzen: Walter Benjamin*. Ed. Christiaan L. Hart Nibbrig. Frankfurt am Main: Suhrkamp, 2001. 174–235.

Hanitzsch, Konstanze. "Ein Buch des Nicht-Trostes für den Generalstaatsanwalt Fritz Bauer." *Literaryundercurrents—Forum für Literaturwissenschaft*. 30 May 2013. Web. 20 January 2016.
Hansen, Miriam Bratu. "Alexander Kluge, Cinema and the Public Sphere: The Construction Site of Counter-History." *Discourse* 6 (1983): 53–74.
Hansen, Miriam Bratu. "Alexander Kluge: Crossings between Film, Literature, Critical Theory." *Film und Literatur: Literarische Texte und der neue deutsche Film*. Ed. Sigrid Bauschinger, Susan L. Cocalis, and Henry A. Lea. The Thirteenth Amherst Colloquium on German Literature. Bern: Francke, 1984. 169–196.
Hansen, Miriam Bratu. *Cinema and Experience: Siegfried Kracauer, Walter Benjamin, and Theodor W. Adorno*. Berkeley, CA: University of California Press, 2012.
Hansen, Miriam Bratu. "Introduction to Adorno: 'Transparencies on Film'." *New German Cinema*. Spec. double issue of *New German Critique* 24/25 (1981–1982). 186–198.
Hansen, Miriam Bratu. "Reinventing the Nickelodeon: Notes on Kluge and Early Cinema" [1988]. *Alexander Kluge: Raw Materials for the Imagination*. Ed. Tara Forrest. Amsterdam: Amsterdam University Press, 2012. 389–408.
Hansen, Miriam Bratu. "The Stubborn Discourse: History and Story-Telling in the Films of Alexander Kluge." *Die Schrift an der Wand/Alexander Kluge: Rohstoffe und Materialien*. Ed. Christian Schulte. Osnabrück: Universitätsverlag Rasch, 2000.119–131.
Hansen, Miriam Bratu. "'With Skin and Hair': Kracauer's Theory of Film, Marseille 1940." *Critical Inquiry* 19.3 (1993): 437–469.
Hansen, Per Krogh, Stefan Iversen, Henrik Skov Nielsen, and Rolf Reitan, eds. *Strange Voices in Narrative Fiction*. Berlin: De Gruyter, 2011.
Harris, Stefanie. "Kluge's *Auswege*." *The Germanic Review* 85.4 (2010): 294–317.
Harris, Stefanie. *Mediating Modernity: German Literature and the 'New' Media, 1895–1930*. University Park, PA: Pennsylvania State University Press, 2009.
Hartmann, Heinrich, and Jakob Vogel. eds. *Zukunftswissen: Prognosen in Wirtschaft, Politik und Gesellschaft seit 1900*. Frankfurt am Main: Campus, 2010.
Hartwig, Ina. "Arlette und ihr Adorno: Die Geliebte und der Philosoph: Eine alte Geschichte, neu erzählt." *Zeit Online* 41. 4 October 2012. Web. 24 Sepstember 2015.
Harvey, David. *The Condition of Postmodernity: An Enquiry into the Conditions of Cultural Change*. Cambridge, MA: Blackwell, 1990.
Harvey, David. *Spaces of Capital: Toward a Critical Geography*. New York: Routledge, 2001.
Harvey, David. *Spaces of Hope*. Berkeley, CA: University of California Press, 2000.
Hayles, N. Katherine. *My Mother Was a Computer: Digital Subjects and Literary Texts*. Chicago: University of Chicago Press, 2005.
Heidegger, Martin. *Being and Time*. Trans. John Macquarrie and Edward Robinson. New York: Harper Perennial Modern Thought, 2008.
Heißenbüttel, Helmut. "Rede auf Alexander Kluge zur Verleihung des Kleist-Preises." *Kleist-Jahrbuch 1986*. Ed. Hans-Joachim Kreutzer. Berlin: Erich Schmidt, 1986. 19–24.
Heitmeyer, Wilhelm, Joachim Müller, and Helmut Schröder, eds. *Verlockender Fundamentalismus: Türkische Jugendliche in Deutschland*. Frankfurt am Main: Suhrkamp, 1997.
Hell, Julia. "Eyes Wide Shut: German Post-Holocaust Authorship." *New German Critique* 88 (2003): 9–36.
Helmling, Steven. "Constellation and Critique: Adorno's Constellation, Benjamin's Dialectical Image." *Postmodern Culture* 14.1 (2003): n.p. Web. Accessed 22 July 2015.

Herman, David. *Basic Elements of Narrative*. Oxford: Wiley-Blackwell, 2009.
Herman, David. "Beyond Voice and Vision: Cognitive Grammar and Focalization Theory." *Point of View, Perspective and Focalization: Modeling Mediation in Narrative*. Ed. Peter Hühn, Wolf Schmid, and Jörg Schönert. Berlin: De Gruyter, 2009. 119–142.
Herman, David. *Story Logic: Problems and Possibilities of Narrative*. Lincoln, NE: University of Nebraska Press, 2002.
Herman, David, James Phelan, Peter J. Rabinowitz, Brian Richardson, and Robyn Warhol. *Narrative Theory: Core Concepts of Critical Debates*. Columbus, OH: Ohio State University Press, 2012.
Hirsch, Marianne. *Family Frames: Photography, Narrative, and Postmemory*. Cambridge, MA: Harvard University Press, 1997.
Hirsch, Marianne. *The Generation of Postmemory: Writing and Visual Culture After the Holocaust*. New York: Columbia University Press, 2012.
Hoffrogge, Ralf. "Emmy und Werner Scholem im Kampf zwischen Utopie und Gegenrevolution." *Hannoversche Geschichtsblätter* 65 (2011): 157–176.
Hoffrogge, Ralf. "Utopien am Abgrund: Der Briefwechsel Werner Scholem-Gershom Scholem in den Jahren 1914–1919." *Schreiben im Krieg—Schreiben vom Krieg: Feldpost im Zeitalter der Weltkriege*. Ed. Veit Didczuneit, Jens Ebert, and Thomas Jander. Essen: Klartext, 2011. 429–440.
Hoffrogge, Ralf. *Werner Scholem: Eine politische Biographie (1895–1940)*. Constance and Munich: UVK Verlagsgesellschaft, 2014.
Hohendahl, Peter Uwe. *Erfundene Welten: Relektüren zu Form und Zeitstruktur in Ernst Jüngers erzählender Prosa*. Paderborn: Wilhelm Fink, 2013.
Hohendahl, Peter Uwe. *The Fleeting Promise of Art: Adorno's Aesthetic Theory Revisited*. Ithaca, NY: Cornell University Press, 2013.
Hohendahl, Peter Uwe. *Prismatic Thought: Theodor W. Adorno*. Lincoln, NE: University of Nebraska Press, 1995.
Hohendahl, Peter Uwe. "Progress Revisited: Adorno's Dialogue with Augustine, Kant, and Benjamin." *Critical Inquiry* 40.1 (2013): 242–260.
Holl, Herbert. "Die Gewalt des Zusammenhangs." *Der Maulwurf kennt kein System: Beiträge zur gemeinsamen Philosophie von Oskar Negt und Alexander Kluge*. Ed. Christian Schulte and Rainer Stollmann. Bielefeld: transcript, 2005. 131–152.
Hollenberg, Alexander. "Recalcitrant Simplicity: Thin Characters and Thick Narration in *A Farewell to Arms*." *Narrative* 20.3 (2012): 301–321.
Honold, Alexander. "Erzählen." *Benjamins Begriffe*. Ed. Michael Opitz and Erdmut Wizisla. Vol. 1. Frankfurt am Main: Suhrkamp, 2000. 363–398.
Hoppe, Vinzenz, and Kaspar Renner. "'Eigensinnige Kinder'—Jacob Grimm and Alexander Kluge als Gründerfiguren einer neuen Geschichtspädagogik." *Mythen, Märchen und moderne Zeit: Beiträge zur Kinder- und Jugendliteratur*. Ed. Alfred Clemens Baumgärtner. Würzburg: Königshausen & Neumann, 1987. 459–472.
Horkheimer, Max, and Theodor W. Adorno. *Dialectic of Enlightenment*. Trans. Edmund Jephcott. Ed. Gunzelin Schmid Noerr. Stanford, CA: Stanford University Press, 2007.
Horkheimer, Max, and Theodor W. Adorno. *Dialectic of Enlightenment*. Trans. John Cumming. New York: Herder & Herder, 1972.
Horkheimer, Max, and Theodor W. Adorno. *Dialektik der Aufklärung*. Amsterdam: Querido, 1947.

Hoy, David Couzens. *The Time of Our Lives: A Critical History of Temporality.* Cambridge, MA: MIT Press, 2009.
Huber, Sebastian, and Claus Philipp, eds. *Alexander Kluge: Magazin des Glücks.* Vienna: Springer, 2007.
Huff, Micha. "Relational Poetics of Novel and Novella in J.W. Goethe's *Die Wahlverwandtschaften* (1809)." German Studies Association Annual Convention. Washington, D.C. 3 October 2015. Conference presentation.
Huyssen, Andreas. "An Analytic Storyteller in the Course of Time." *Twilight Memories: Marking Time in a Culture of Amnesia.* NY: Routledge, 1995. 145–155.
Huyssen, Andreas. *Miniature Metropolis: Literature in an Age of Photography and Film.* Cambridge, MA: Harvard University Press, 2015.
Huyssen, Andreas. "Modernist Miniatures: Literary Snapshots of Urban Spaces." *PMLA* 122.1 (2007): 27–42.
Huyssen, Andreas. *Present Pasts: Urban Palimpsests and the Politics of Memory.* Stanford, CA: Stanford University Press, 2003.
Huyssen, Andreas. *Twilight Memories: Marking Time in a Culture of Amnesia.* New York: Routledge, 1995.
Huyssen, Andreas. "The Urban Miniature and the Feuilleton in Kracauer and Benjamin." *Culture in the Anteroom: The Legacies of Siegfried Kracauer.* Ed. Gerd Gemünden and Johannes von Moltke. Ann Arbor: University of Michigan Press, 2012. 213–225.
Iovene, Paola. *Tales of Futures Past: Anticpation and the Ends of Literature in Contemporary China.* Stanford, CA: Stanford University Press, 2014.
Jäger, Christian. "Zonenrandgebiet: Zu Oskar Negts und Alexander Kluges *Geschichte und Eigensinn.*" *Jahrbuch für internationale Germanistik* 31.1 (2000): 104–125.
Jäger, Lorenz. *Adorno: Eine politische Biographie.* Munich: Deutsche Verlags-Anstalt, 2003.
Jäger, Ludwig. "Das Flüssige und das Feste: Bemerkungen zur Verfahrenslogik des kulturellen Gedächtnisses." *Eloquentia copiosus: Festschrift für Max Kerner zum 65. Gerburtstag.* Ed. Lotte Kéry. Aachen: Thouet, 2006. 265–282.
Jameson, Fredric. *The Ancients and the Postmoderns: On the Historicity of Forms.* London: Verso, 2015.
Jameson, Fredric. *The Antinomies of Realism.* London: Verso, 2013.
Jameson, Fredric. *Archaeologies of the Future: The Desire Called Utopia and Other Science Fictions.* London: Verso, 2005.
Jameson, Fredric. *The Geopolitical Aesthetic: Cinema and Space in the World System.* Bloomington, IN: Indiana University Press, 1992.
Jameson, Fredric. *Late Marxism: Adorno or the Persistence of the Dialectic.* London: Verso, 1990.
Jameson, Fredric. *Marxism and Form: Twentieth-Century Dialectical Theories of Literature.* Princeton, NJ: Princeton University Press, 1971.
Jameson, Fredric. "Notes on Globalization as a Philosophical Issue." *The Cultures of Globalization.* Ed. Fredric Jameson and Masao Miyoshi. Durham and London: Duke University Press, 1998. 54–77.
Jameson, Fredric. "On Negt and Kluge." *October* 46 (1988): 151–177.
Jameson, Fredric. *The Seeds of Time.* New York: Columbia University Press, 1994.
Jameson, Fredric. "War and Representation." *PMLA* 124.5 (2009): 1532–1547.

Jannidis, Fotis. "Wer sagt das? Erzählen mit Stimmverlust." *Stimme(n) im Text: Narratologische Positionsbestimmungen*. Ed. Andreas Blödorn, Daniela Langer, and Michael Scheffel. Berlin: De Gruyter, 2006. 151–164.

Jay, Martin. *The Dialectical Imagination: A History of the Frankfurt School and the Institute of Social Research, 1923–1950*. Boston: Little, Brown and Company, 1973.

Jay, Martin. "Experience without a Subject: Walter Benjamin and the Novel." *New Formations* 20 (1993): 145–155.

Jay, Martin. *Marxism and Totality: The Adventures of a Concept from Lukács to Habermas*. Berkeley, CA: University of California Press, 1982.

Jay, Martin. "Theodor Adorno and Max Horkheimer: Towards a New Manifesto." Book review. *Philosophical Reviews: An Electronic Journal*. University of Notre Dame. February 2012. Web. 21 September 2015. http://ndpr.nd.edu/news/29021-towards-a-new-manifesto/.

Kacandes, Irene. *Daddy's War: Greek American Stories, A Paramemoir*. Lincoln, NE: University of Nebraska Press, 2009.

Kacandes, Irene. "Experimental Life Writing." *The Routledge Companion to Experimental Literature*. Ed. Joe Bray, Alison Gibbons, and Brian McHale. New York: Routledge, 2012. 380–392.

Kacandes, Irene. *Talk Fiction: Literature and the Talk Explosion*. Lincoln, NE: University of Nebraska Press, 2001.

Kaku, Michio. *Parallel Worlds: The Science of Alternative Universes and our Future in the Cosmos*. London: Penguin, 2006.

Kampa, Daniel, ed. *Kurz und bündig: Die schnellsten Geschichten der Welt*. Zurich: Diogenes, 2007.

Kant, Immanuel. *Critique of Practical Reason*. Trans. Werner S. Pluhar. Intro. Stephen Engstrom. Indianapolis, IN: Hackett, 2002.

Kant, Immanuel. *Kants gesammelte Schriften*. Ed. Königliche Preussische Akademie der Wissenschaften. Berlin and Leipzig: De Gruyter, 1902 ff.

Karpat, Berkan, and Zafer Şenocak. *nâzım hikmet: auf dem schiff zum mars*. Munich: Babel, 1998.

Kittler, Friedrich. "'Alles steuert der Blitz'." *Alexander Kluge*. Ed. Thomas Combrink. New edition of *text + kritik* 85/86 (November 2011): 11–14.

Klein, Naomi. *The Shock Doctrine: The Rise of Disaster Capitalism*. New York: Metropolitan Books, 2007.

Klein, Richard, Johann Kreuzer, and Stefan Müller-Doohm, eds. *Adorno-Handbuch: Leben – Werk – Wirkung*. Stuttgart: Metzler, 2011.

Kleinschmidt, Erich. *Die Entdeckung der Intensität: Geschichte einer Denkfigur im 18. Jahrhundert*. Göttingen: Wallstein, 2004.

Kluge, Alexander. *Air Raid*. Trans. Martin Chalmers. Chicago, IL: Seagull Books, 2014.

Kluge, Alexander. "The Air Raid on Halberstadt, 8 April 1945." Trans. Reinhard Mayer. *Semiotext(e)* 4.2 (1982): 306–315.

Kluge, Alexander. "Die Aktualität Adornos: Dankesrede zur Verleihung des Adorno Preises, 11.09.2009, Frankfurt." www.kluge-alexander.de. Alexander Kluge, Kairos Film (Munich). 25 May 2010. Web. 28 April 2014. http://www.kluge-alexander.de/zur-person/reden/2009-adorno-preis.html.

Kluge, Alexander. *Attendance List for a Funeral*. Trans. Leila Vennewitz. New York: McGraw-Hill, 1966.

Kluge, Alexander. *Das Bohren harter Bretter: 133 politische Geschichten*. Mit einem Gastbeitrag von Reinhard Jirgl. Berlin: Suhrkamp, 2011.
Kluge, Alexander. *Case Histories: Stories*. Trans. Leila Vennewitz. New York: Holmes & Meier, 1988.
Kluge, Alexander. *Chronik der Gefühle*. Vol. 1: *Basisgeschichten* and Vol. 2: *Lebensläufe*. Frankfurt am Main: Suhrkamp, 2000.
Kluge, Alexander. *Cinema Stories*. Trans. Martin Brady and Helen Hughes. New York: New Directions, 2007.
Kluge, Alexander. *The Devil's Blind Spot: Tales from the New Century*. Trans. Martin Chalmers and Michael Hulse. New York: New Directions, 2004.
Kluge, Alexander. *Drilling through Hard Boards: 133 Political Stories*. Trans. Wieland Hoban. With a contribution by Reinhard Jirgl. Chicago, IL: Seagull Books, 2017.
Kluge, Alexander. "Die Entsprechung einer Oase: Essay für die digitale Generation." Berlin: Mikrotext, 2013. Digital file.
Kluge, Alexander. *Fontane—Kleist—Deutschland—Büchner: Zur Grammatik der Zeit*. 1987. Berlin: Wagenbach, 2004.
Kluge, Alexander. *Das fünfte Buch: Neue Lebensläufe, 402 Geschichten*. Berlin: Suhrkamp, 2012.
Kluge, Alexander. *Gelegenheitsarbeit einer Sklavin: Zur realistischen Methode*. Frankfurt am Main: Suhrkamp, 1975.
Kluge, Alexander. *Geschichten vom Kino*. Frankfurt am Main: Suhrkamp, 2007.
Kluge, Alexander. "Glück." *Die Grimmwelt: Vom Ärschlein bis Zettel*. Ed. Stadt Kassel [City of Kassel], in cooperation with Annemarie Hürlimann and Nicola Lepp. Munich: Sieveking, 2015. 99–107.
Kluge, Alexander. *Glückliche Umstände, leihweise*. Ed. Thomas Combrink. Frankfurt am Main: Suhrkamp, 2008.
Kluge, Alexander. "Der große Sammler der Wahrheit." Interview by Sven Siedenberg. *Süddeutsche Zeitung* Nr. 274 (Nov. 28, 2000): 18.
Kluge, Alexander. "'Ich liebe das Lakonische.'" Interview by Mathias Schreiber and Volker Hage. *Der Spiegel* 45 (Nov. 6, 2000): 336–340.
Kluge, Alexander. "Kein Abschied von gestern: Der neue deutsche Film von 1962 bis 1981 – gesehen von 2011." *Personen und Reden*. Berlin: Wagenbach, 2012. 108–115.
Kluge, Alexander. *Kongs große Stunde: Chronik des Zusammenhangs*. Berlin: Suhrkamp, 2015.
Kluge, Alexander. *Das Labyrinth der zärtlichen Kraft: 166 Liebesgeschichten*. Frankfurt am Main: Suhrkamp, 2009. Print with DVD.
Kluge, Alexander. "Landkarte der Begriffe: Ein Glossar zu *Geschichte und Eigensinn*." *Glass Shards: Echoes of a Message in a Bottle*. Ed. Richard Langston, Gunther Martens, Vincent Pauval, Christian Schulte, and Rainer Stollmann. *Alexander Kluge-Jahrbuch* 2 (2015): 21–46.
Kluge, Alexander. *Learning Processes with a Deadly Outcome*. Trans. Christopher Pavsek. Durham, NC: Duke University Press, 1996.
Kluge, Alexander. *Lebensläufe*. 2nd ed. Stuttgart: Henry Goverts Verlag, 1962.
Kluge, Alexander. "Lernprozesse mit tödlichem Ausgang" [1973]. *Chronik der Gefühle*. Vol. 2. Frankfurt am Main: Suhrkamp, 2000. 827–920.
Kluge, Alexander. *Die Lücke, die der Teufel läßt: Im Umfeld des neuen Jahrhunderts*. Frankfurt am Main: Suhrkamp, 2003.

Kluge, Alexander. *Der Luftangriff auf Halberstadt am 8. April 1945*. Frankfurt am Main: Suhrkamp, 2008.
Kluge, Alexander. *Nachrichten aus der ideologischen Antike: Marx–Eisenstein–Kapital*. 3 DVDs with an Essay by Alexander Kluge. Berlin: Suhrkamp, 2008.
Kluge, Alexander. *Neue Geschichten: Hefte 1–18, ›Unheimlichkeit der Zeit‹*. Frankfurt am Main: Suhrkamp, 1977.
Kluge, Alexander. *Personen und Reden: Lessing–Böll–Huch–Schiller–Adorno–Habermas–Müller–Augstein–Gaus–Schlingensief–Ad me ipsum*. Berlin: Wagenbach, 2012.
Kluge, Alexander. "The Political as Intensity of Everyday Feelings." Trans. Andrew Bowie. *Alexander Kluge: Raw Materials for the Imagination*. Ed. Tara Forrest. Amsterdam: Amsterdam University Press, 2012. 283–290.
Kluge, Alexander. "The Sharpest Ideology: That Reality Appeals to Its Realistic Character." Trans. David Roberts. *Alexander Kluge: Raw Materials for the Imagination*. Ed. Tara Forrest. Amsterdam: Amsterdam University Press, 2012. 191–196.
Kluge, Alexander. *Theodor Fontane, Heinrich von Kleist und Anna Wilde: Zur Grammatik der Zeit*. Berlin: Wagenbach, 1987.
Kluge, Alexander. *Theorie der Erzählung: Frankfurter Poetikvorlesungen*. Berlin: Filmedition Suhrkamp, 2013. DVD-ROM with booklet ed. by Thomas Combrink.
Kluge, Alexander. *Tür an Tür mit einem anderen Leben: 350 neue Geschichten*. Frankfurt am Main: Suhrkamp, 2006.
Kluge, Alexander. "Wächter der Differenz: Rede zur Verleihung des Kleist-Preises." *Kleist-Jahrbuch 1986*. Ed. Hans Joachim Kreutzer. Berlin: Erich Schmidt, 1986. 25–37.
Kluge, Alexander. *"Wer ein Wort des Trostes spricht, ist ein Verräter": 48 Geschichten für Fritz Bauer*. Berlin: Suhrkamp, 2013.
Kluge, Alexander, Christian Schulte, and Rainer Stollmann. *Verdeckte Ermittlung: Ein Gespräch*. Berlin: Merve, 2001.
Kluge, Alexander, and Gerhard Richter. *Nachricht von ruhigen Momenten*. Berlin: Suhrkamp, 2013.
Kluge, Alexander, and Gertrud Koch. "Undercurrents of Capital: An Interview with Alexander Kluge." Trans. Gerrit Jackson. *The Germanic Review* 85.4 (2010): 359–367.
Kluge, Alexander, and Jochen Rack. "Erzählung ist die Darstellung von Differenzen: Alexander Kluge im Gespräch mit Jochen Rack," *Neue Rundschau* 112.1 (2001): 73–91.
Kluge, Alexander, and Joseph Vogl. "Zeit ohne Raum." *Soll und Haben: Fernsehgespräche*. Zurich: Diaphanes, 2009. 261–283.
Kluge, Alexander, Lilli Binzegger, and Andreas Heller. "'Kolonisatoren, die in die Schwäche eindringen': Ein Gespräch über Nachrichten und Erfahrung." *Neue Rundschau* 2 (1995): 22–28.
Kluge, Alexander, Michael Angele, Ingo Arend, Jakob Augstein, and Philip Grassmann. "The Attack of the 13th Fairy: *Freitag* magazine talks to Alexander Kluge about the Internet, dragonfly intelligence and why he likes 'gardener' as a job description." *Freitag* Magazine. 24 December 2009. Web. 13 August 2010. http://www.signandsight.com/features/1990.html.
Kluge, Alexander, and Rainer Stollmann. *Ferngespräche: Über Eisenstein, Marx, das Kapital, die Liebe und die Macht der zärtlichen Kraft*. Berlin: Vorwerk 8, 2016.
Kluge, Alexander, and Stuart Liebman. "On New German Cinema, Art, Enlightenment, and the Public Sphere: An Interview with Alexander Kluge." *October* 46 (1988): 23–59.

Kluge, Alexander, and Yoko Tawada. "'Roher Fisch und Rinderzunge führen ein Telefongespräch': Zu einer Gedichtzeile der japanischen Autorin Yoko Tawada." Dir. Alexander Kluge. News & Stories 20 September 1993. Development Company for Television Program GmbH [Düsseldorf] http://www.dctp.de. Videocassette.

Koch, Gertrud. "Between Fear of Contact and Self-Preservation: Taboo and Its Relation to the Dead." Trans. Rachel Leah Magshamhrain. *New German Critique* 90 (2003): 71–83.

Koch, Gertrud. "Mimesis and the Ban on Graven Images." *Religion and Media*. Ed. Hent de Vries and Samuel Weber. Stanford, CA: Stanford University Press, 2001. 151–162.

Köhler, Horst. "Laudatio von Bundespräsident Horst Köhler auf Alexander Kluge anlässlich seines 75. Geburtstages und der Verleihung des Großen Verdienstkreuzes des Verdienstordens der Bundesrepublik Deutschland am 26. April 2007, in Schloss Bellevue." 26 April 2007. Web. http://www.bundespraesident.de/SharedDocs/Reden/DE/Horst-Koehler/Reden/2007/04/20070426_Rede.html. 30 March 2016.

Koepnick, Lutz. "Inside Kluge's Cosmic Cinema: Critical Theory and Mobile Spectatorship Today." *Glass Shards: Echoes of a Message in a Bottle*. Ed. Richard Langston, Gunther Martens, Vincent Pauval, Christian Schulte, and Rainer Stollmann. *Alexander Kluge-Jahrbuch* 2 (2015): 125–142.

Köster, Werner, ed. *Parallelgesellschaften: Diskursanalysen zur Dramatisierung von Migration*. Essen: klartext, 2009.

Kohler, Georg, and Stefan Müller-Doohm, eds. *Wozu Adorno? Beiträge zur Kritik und dem Fortbestand einer Schlüsseltheorie des 20. Jahrhunderts*. Weilerswist: Velbrück Wissenschaft, 2008.

Koselleck, Reinhart. *Futures Past: On the Semantics of Historical Time*. Trans. Keith Tribe. New York: Columbia University Press, 2004.

Koselleck, Reinhart. *The Practice of Conceptual History: Timing History, Spacing Concepts*. Trans. Todd Samuel Presner and Others. Stanford, CA: Stanford University Press, 2002.

Koselleck, Reinhart. *Vergangene Zukunft: Zur Semantik geschichtlicher Zeiten*. Frankfurt am Main: Suhrkamp, 1979.

Koselleck, Reinhart. "Die Verzeitlichung der Utopie." *Zeitschichten: Studien der Historik*. Frankfurt am Main: Suhrkamp, 2003. 131–149.

Koschorke, Albrecht. *Wahrheit und Erfindung: Grundzüge einer Allgemeinen Erzähltheorie*. 2nd ed. Frankfurt am Main: Fischer, 2012.

Kracauer, Sigfried. *Theory of Film: The Redemption of Physical Reality*. 1960. With introduction by Miriam Bratu Hansen. Princeton, NJ: Princeton University Press, 1997.

LaCapra, Dominick. *History and Memory After Auschwitz*. Ithaca, NY: Cornell University Press, 1998.

Langenohl, Andreas. *Tradition und Gesellschaftskritik: Eine Rekonstruktion der Modernisierungstheorie*. Frankfurt am Main: Campus, 2007.

Langston, Richard. "Affective Affinities: Sebald and Kluge on Feeling History." *Gegenwartsliteratur: A German Studies Yearbook* 6 (2007): 44–68.

Langston, Richard. "'Das ist die umgekehrte Flaschenpost': Ein montiertes Interview mit Oskar Negt und Alexander Kluge." *Glass Shards: Echoes of a Message in a Bottle*. Ed. Richard Langston, Gunther Martens, Vincent Pauval, Christian Schulte, and Rainer Stollmann. *Alexander Kluge-Jahrbuch* 2 (2015): 47–75.

Langston, Richard. "Permanent Catastrophe and Everyday Life: Remediation of the Political in Kluge's *Vermischte Nachrichten* and Chernobyl Broadcasts." *Vermischte Nachrichten*. Ed.

Richard Langston, Gunther Martens, Vincent Pauval, Christian Schulte, and Rainer Stollmann. *Alexander Kluge-Jahrbuch* 1 (2014): 101–123.
Langston, Richard. "Toward an Ethics of Fantasy: The Kantian Dialogues of Oskar Negt and Alexander Kluge." *The Germanic Review* 85.4 (2010): 271–293.
Langston, Richard. *Visions of Violence: German Avant-Gardes After Fascism*. Evanston, IL: Northwestern University Press, 2008.
Langston, Richard. "'Windows are to a House...': Marx, Blumenberg, Negt and Kluge." German Studies Association Annual Convention. Washington, D.C. 4 October 2015. Conference presentation.
Langston, Richard, Gunther Martens, Vincent Pauval, Christian Schulte, and Rainer Stollmann, eds. *Glass Shards: Echoes of a Message in a Bottle. Alexander Kluge-Jahrbuch* 2 (2015).
Langston, Richard, Gunther Martens, Vincent Pauval, Christian Schulte, and Rainer Stollmann, eds. *Vermischte Nachrichten. Alexander Kluge-Jahrbuch* 1 (2014).
Latour, Bruno. "Waiting for Gaia: Composing the Common World through Arts and Politics." Lecture presented at the French Institute, London (November 2011). *What is Cosmopolitical Design?*. Ed. Albena Yaneva and Alejandro Zaero-Polo. Farnham, Surrey: Ashgate, 2015. 21–32.
League, Kathleen. *Adorno, Radical Negativity, and Cultural Critique: Utopia in The Map of the World*. Lanham, MD: Rowman & Littlefield, 2011.
Lehr, A. *Kleine Formen: Konstellation/Konfiguration, Montage und Essay bei Theodor W. Adorno, Walter Benjamin und anderen*. Norderstedt: Books on Demand GmbH, 2007.
Lejeune, Philippe. *On Autobiography*. Foreword by Paul John Eakin. Trans. Katherine Leary. Minneapolis, MN: University of Minnesota Press, 1989.
Leopold, David. "The Structure of Marx and Engels' Considered Account of Utopian Socialism." *History of Political Thought* 26.3 (2005): 443–466.
Levitas, Ruth. *The Concept of Utopia*. 2nd ed. Oxford: Peter Lang, 2010.
Lewandowski, Rainer. *Alexander Kluge*. Munich: C.H. Beck, 1980.
Lewis, Michael. "In Nature's Casino." *The New York Times Magazine*. 26 August 2007. Web. 25 September 2016.
Liisberg, Sune, Esther Oluffa Pedersen, and Anne Line Dalsgård, eds. *Anthropology and Philosophy: Dialogues on Trust and Hope*. New York: Berghahn, 2015.
Lotman, Yuri. *Kul'tura i vzryv*. Moscow: Gnozis, 1992.
Lovell, David W. "Marx's Utopian Legacy." *European Legacy: Toward New Paradigms* 9.5 (2004): 629–640.
Luhmann, Niklas. "Describing the Future," *Observations on Modernity*. Trans. William Whobrey. Stanford, CA: Stanford University Press, 1998. 63–74.
Luhmann, Niklas. "The Future Cannot Begin: Temporal Structures in Modern Society." *Social Research* 43.1 (Spring 1976): 130–152.
Lukács, Georg. *The Theory of the Novel: A Historico-Philosophical Essay on the Forms of Great Epic Literature*. Trans. Anna Bostock. Cambridge, MA: MIT Press, 1971.
Lukes, Steven. "Marxism and Utopianism." *Utopias*. Ed. Peter Alexander and Roger Gill. London: Duckworth, 1984. 153–167.
Lutze, Peter C. *Alexander Kluge: The Last Modernist*. Detroit: Wayne State University Press, 1998.
Maler, Henri. "An Apocryphal Testament: Socialism, Utopian and Scientific." *Science & Society* 62.1 (1998): 48–61.

Malkmus, Bernard. "Intermediality and the Topography of Memory in Alexander Kluge." *New German Critique* 107 (2009): 231–252.

Marasco, Robyn. "'I would rather wait for you than believe that you are not coming at all': Revolutionary Love in a Post-Revolutionary Time." *Philosophy and Social Criticism* 36.6 (2010): 643–662.

Marten, Susanne. "Unterirdisch, außerirdisch: Paris, Juni 1940, Alexander Kluges Auseinandersetzung mit der deutschen Besatzung Frankreichs." *Vermischte Nachrichten*. Ed. Richard Langston, Gunther Martens, Vincent Pauval, Christian Schulte, and Rainer Stollmann. *Alexander Kluge-Jahrbuch* 1 (2014): 179–192.

Martens, Gunther. "Distant(ly) Reading Alexander Kluge's Distant Writing." *Vermischte Nachrichten*. Ed. Richard Langston, Gunther Martens, Vincent Pauval, Christian Schulte, and Rainer Stollmann. *Alexander Kluge-Jahrbuch* 1 (2014): 29–42

Martens, Gunther. "'Wann wird man soweit sein, Bücher wie Kataloge zu schreiben?' Alexander Kuge und die enzyklopädische Literatur." *Alexander Kluge*. Ed. Thomas Combrink. *text + kritik* 85/86 [New edition] (2011): 128–136.

Marx, Karl. *Capital: A Critique of Political Economy*. Vol. 1. Introduced by Ernest Mandel. Trans. Ben Fowkes. London: Penguin Classics, 1990.

Marx, Karl. *Class Struggles in France, 1848–1850*. Trans. Henry Kuhn. With an Introduction by Frederick Engels. New York: Labor News, 1924.

Marx, Karl. *Das Kapital: Kritik der politischen Oekonomie*. Vol. 1. 2nd rev. ed. Hamburg: Otto Meissner, 1872.

Marx, Karl, and Friedrich Engels. "Manifest der Kommunistischen Partei." *Marx-Engels Werke [MEW]*. Vol. 4. Berlin: Dietz, 1959. 461–493.

Maxwell, Barry. "The Paths in the Midst of Collapse: Utopian Direction in Ernst Bloch and Walter Benjamin." *Viaggi in utopia*. Ed. Raffaella Baccolini, Vita Fortunati, and Nadia Minerva. Ravenna: Longo Editore, 1996. 217–230.

McBride, Patrizia C. *The Chatter of the Visible: Montage and Narrative in Weimar Germany*. Ann Arbor: University of Michigan Press, 2016.

McBride, Patrizia C. "*Konstruktion als Bildung:* Refashioning the Human in German Constructivism." *Futurity Now*. Ed. Leslie A. Adelson and Devin Fore. Spec. issue of *The Germanic Review* 88.3 (2013): 233–247.

McClintock, Anne. *Imperial Leather: Race, Gender, and Sexuality in the Colonial Contest*. New York: Routledge, 1995.

McFarland, James. "Sailing by the Stars: Constellations in the Space of Thought." *Modern Language Notes* 126.3 (2011): 471–485.

McGettigan, Andrew. "As Flowers Turn Towards the Sun: Walter Benjamin's Bergsonian Image of the Past." *Radical Philosophy* 158 (2009): 25–35.

McLuhan, Marshall. *Essential McLuhan*. Ed. Eric McLuhan and Frank Zingrone. New York: Basic Books, 1996.

Melas, Natalie. "Comparative Non-Contemporaneities: C.L.R. James and Ernst Bloch." *Theory Aside*. Ed. Jason Potts and Daniel Stout. Durham, NC: Duke University Press, 2014. 56–77.

Menke, Christoph. *The Sovereignty of Art: Aesthetic Negativity in Adorno and Derrida*. Trans. Neil Solomon. Cambridge, MA: MIT Press, 1998.

Menninghaus, Winfried. "Geschichte und Eigensinn: Hermeneutik-Kritik und Poetik Alexander Kluges." *Geschichte als Literatur: Formen und Grenzen der Repräsentation von*

Vergangenheit. Ed. Hartmut Eggert, Ulrich Profitlich, and Klaus R. Scherpe. Stuttgart: Metzler, 1990. 258–272.

Meretoja, Hanna. *The Narrative Turn in Fiction and Theory: The Crisis and Return of Storytelling from Robbe-Grillet to Tournier*. New York: Palgrave Macmillan, 2014.

Mertes, Valentin. "'Beweis dessen, daß auch unzulängliche, ja kindische Mittel zur Rettung dienen können': Eigensinn und Verfahren der Distanzierung in Alexander Kluges Film *Vermischte Nachrichten*." *Vermischte Nachrichten*. Ed. Richard Langston, Gunther Martens, Vincent Pauval, Christian Schulte, and Rainer Stollmann. *Alexander Kluge-Jahrbuch* 1 (2014): 125–142.

Michel, Sascha. "Inszenierte Kontingenz: Zur Kleinen Prosa von Thomas Bernhard, Alexander Kluge und Ror Wolf." *Kleine Prosa: Theorie und Geschichte eines Textfeldes im Literatursystem der Moderne*. Ed. Thomas Althaus, Wolfgang Bunzel, and Dirk Göttsche. Tübingen: Niemeyer, 2007. 328–340.

Mieth, Corinna. "Die utopische Dimension von Anthropologie und Geschichte bei Oskar Negt und Alexander Kluge." *Der Maulwurf kennt kein System: Beiträge zur gemeinsamen Philosophie von Oskar Negt und Alexander Kluge*. Ed. Christian Schulte and Rainer Stollmann. Bielefeld: transcript, 2005. 181–200.

Mieth, Corinna. *Das Utopische in Literatur und Philosophie: Zur Ästhetik Heiner Müllers und Alexander Kluges*. Tübingen: Francke, 2003.

Milfull, John. "Short Stories? Brecht, Adorno, Grass and the Child's Eye View." *Australian Humanities Review* 43 (December 2007): n.p. Web. 14 August 2016.

Miller, Matthew. "Atlantic Transfers of Critical Theory: Alexander Kluge and the U.S. in Fiction." *Different Germans, Many Germanies*. Ed. Konrad Jarausch, Harald Wenzel, and Karin Goihl. New York: Berghahn, forthcoming.

Miller, Matthew. "Critical Storytelling and Diabolical Dialectics: Alexander Kluge and the Devil's Blind Spots." *The Germanic Review* 85.4 (2010): 318–339.

Miller, Matthew. "*Eigensinn* in Transit: Re-Examining a Concept for the Twenty-First Century." *Glass Shards: Echoes of a Message in a Bottle*. Ed. Richard Langston, Gunther Martens, Vincent Pauval, Christian Schulte, and Rainer Stollmann. *Alexander Kluge-Jahrbuch* 2 (2015): 83–102.

Moretti, Franco. *Distant Reading*. London: Verso, 2013.

Müller, Harro. "Die authentische Methode: Alexander Kluges antirealistisches Realismusprojekt." *Gegengifte: Essays zu Theorie und Literatur der Moderne*. Bielefeld: Aisthesis, 2009. 97–121.

Müller, Harro. *Geschichte zwischen Kairos und Katastrophe: Historische Romane im 20. Jahrhundert*. Frankfurt am Main: Athenäum, 1988.

Müller, Harro. "'In solche Not kann nicht die Natur bringen': Stichworte zu Alexander Kluges *Schlachtbeschreibung*." *Merkur* 36.9 (1982): 889–897.

Müller, Harro. "Kritische Theorie und Realismusbegriff: Horkheimer, Adorno, Kluge." *Realitätsbegriffe in der Moderne: Beiträge zu Literatur, Kunst, Philosophie und Wissenschaft*. Ed. Susanne Knaller and Harro Müller. Paderborn: Fink, 2011. 229–246.

Müller, Harro. "Verwendungsweisen des Authentizitätsbegriffs bei Theodor W. Adorno und Alexander Kluge." *Die Frage des Zusammenhangs: Alexander Kluge im Kontext*. Ed. Christian Schulte. Vorwerk 8: Berlin, 2012. 50–63.

Müller, Michael. "Gefangen vom Text: Überlegungen zur Lesersteuerung am Beispiel eines Textes von Alexander Kluge." *Der Deutschunterricht: Beiträge zu seiner Praxis und wissenschaftlichen Grundlegung* 40.4 (1988): 59–67.

Müller-Doohm, Stefan. *Adorno: A Biography.* Trans. Rodney Livingstone. Cambridge, UK: Polity, 2005.
Murray, Sarah E. "Evidentiality and the Structure of Speech Acts." Diss. Rutgers University, 2010.
Nägele, Rainer. "Body Politics: Benjamin's Dialectical Materialism Between Brecht and the Frankfurt School." *The Cambridge Companion to Walter Benjamin.* Ed. David Ferris. Cambridge, UK: Cambridge University Press, 2004. 152–176.
Nebrig, Alexander, and Carlos Spoerhase, eds. *Die Poesie der Zeichensetzung: Studien zur Stilistik der Interpunktion.* Bern: Peter Lang, 2012.
Negt, Oskar. *Modernisierung im Zeichen des Drachen: China und der europäische Mythos der Moderne—Reisetagebuch und Gedankenexperimente.* Frankfurt am Main: Fischer, 1988.
Negt, Oskar, and Alexander Kluge. *Geschichte und Eigensinn: Geschichtliche Organisation der Arbeitsvermögen, Deutschland als Produktionsöffentlichkeit, Gewalt des Zusammenhangs.* Frankfurt am Main: Zweitausendeins, 1981.
Negt, Oskar, and Alexander Kluge. *History and Obstinacy.* Ed. Devin Fore. Trans. Richard Langston, Cyrus Shahan, Martin Brady, Helen Hughes, and Joel Golb. New York: Zone Books, 2014.
Negt, Oskar, and Alexander Kluge. *Maßverhältnisse des Politischen: 15 Vorschläge zum Unterscheidungsvermögen.* Frankfurt am Main: Fischer, 1992.
Negt, Oskar, and Alexander Kluge. *Öffentlichkeit und Erfahrung: Zur Organisationsanalyse von bürgerlicher und proletarischer Öffentlichkeit.* Frankfurt am Main: Suhrkamp, 1972.
Negt, Oskar, and Alexander Kluge. *Public Sphere and Experience: Toward an Analysis of the Bourgeois and Proletarian Public Sphere.* Foreword by Miriam Hansen. Trans. Peter Labanyi, Jamie Owen Daniel, and Assenka Oksiloff. Minnepolis, MN: University of Minnesota Press, 1993.
Negt, Oskar, and Alexander Kluge. *Der unterschätzte Mensch: Gemeinsame Philosophie in zwei Bänden.* Frankfurt am Main: Zweitausendeins, 2001.
Neumann, Klaus. *Shifting Memories: The Nazi Past in the New Germany.* Ann Arbor, MI: University of Michigan Press, 2000.
Newton, Isaac. *Opticks: Or, a Treatise of the Reflections, Refractions, Inflections and Colours of Light.* 4th ed. London: William Innys, 1730. The Project Gutenberg EBook of Opticks. 23 August 2010. Web. 3 May 2016.
Nielsen, Henrik Skov. "Naturalizing and Unnaturalizing Reading Strategies: Focalization Revisited." *A Poetics of Unnatural Narrative.* Ed. Jan Alber, Henrik Skov Nielsen, and Brian Richardson. Columbus, OH: Ohio State University Press, 2013. 67–93.
Nieraad, Jürgen. "Shoah-Literatur: Weder Fiktion noch Dokument—Alexander Kluges 'Liebesversuch' und Heimrad Bäckers 'nachschrift'." *In der Sprache der Täter.* Ed. Stephan Braese. Wiesbaden: VS Verlag für Sozialwissenschaften, 1998. 137–148.
Nikulin, Dmitri. *Dialectic and Dialogue.* Stanford, CA: Stanford University Press, 2010.
Nousek, Katrina Louise. "Pasts with Futures: Temporality, Subjectivity, and Postcommunism in Contemporary German Literature by Herta Müller, Zsuzsa Bánk, and Terézia Mora." Diss. Cornell University, 2015.
Overy, Richard. *The Bombers and the Bombed: Allied Air War over Europe, 1940–1945.* New York: Viking, 2013.
Pabst, Reinhard. "Ein Sohn aus gutem Hause: Theodor W. Adornos Kindheit in Frankfurt." *Forschung Frankfurt* 3–4 (2003): 44–47.

Pabst, Reinhard, ed. *Theodor W. Adorno: Kindheit in Amorbach, Bilder und Erinnerungen.* Frankfurt am Main and Leipzig: Insel, 2003.
Paden, Roger. "Marx's Critique of the Utopian Socialists." *Utopian Studies* 13.2 (2002): 67–91.
Palmer, Alan. *Social Minds in the Novel.* Columbus, OH: Ohio State University Press, 2010.
Parikka, Jussi. *The Anthrobscene.* Minneapolis, MN: University of Minnesota Press, 2014.
Parkinson, Anna. "Adorno on the Air Waves: Feeling Reason, Educating Emotion." *West Germany's Cold War Radio: The Crucible of the Transatlantic Century.* Ed. Yuliya Komska. Spec. issue of *German Politics and Society* 32.1 (2014): 43–59.
Parkinson, Anna. *An Emotional State: The Politics of Emotion in West German Culture.* Ann Arbor, MI: University of Michigan Press, 2015.
Paterson, Tony. "Germany Finally Pays Tribute to First Nazi Hunter Fritz Bauer." *Independent.* 28 February 2016. Web. http://www.independent.co.uk/news/world/europe/germany-finally-pays-tribute-to-the-first-nazi-hunter-fritz-bauer-auschwitz-nazism-adolf-eichmann-6901756.html. 13 July 2016.
Pavsek, Christopher. "History and Obstinacy: Negt and Kluge's Redemption of Labor." *New German Critique* 68 (1996): 137–163.
Pavsek, Christopher. "The Storyteller in the Age of Mechanical Reproduction: Alexander Kluge's Reworking of Walter Benjamin." *Found Object* 2 (1993): 83–92.
Pavsek, Christopher. *The Utopia of Film: Cinema and Its Futures in Godard, Kluge, and Tahimik.* New York: Columbia University Press, 2013.
Pavsek, Christopher. "The Utopia of Reading." *Glass Shards: Echoes of a Message in a Bottle.* Ed. Richard Langston, Gunther Martens, Vincent Pauval, Christian Schulte, and Rainer Stollmann. *Alexander Kluge-Jahrbuch* 2 (2015): 103–119.
Pensky, Max. *The Actuality of Adorno: Critical Essays on Adorno and the Postmodern.* Albany: State University of New York Press, 1997.
Pensky, Max. "Beyond the Message in a Bottle: The Other Critical Theory." *Constellations* 10.1 (2003): 135–144.
Phelan, James. "Estranging Unreliability, Bonding Unreliability, and the Ethics of *Lolita.*" *Narrative* 15.2 (2007): 222–238.
Phelan, James. "Implausibilities, Crossovers, and Impossibilities: A Rhetorical Approach to Breaks in the Code of Mimetic Character Narration." *A Poetics of Unnatural Narrative.* Ed. Jan Alber, Henrik Skov Nielsen, and Brian Richardson. Columbus, OH: Ohio State University Press, 2013. 167–184.
Phelan, James. *Living to Tell about It: A Rhetoric and Ethics of Character Narration.* Ithaca, NY: Cornell University Press, 2005.
Pike, David. "Wall and Tunnel: The Spatial Metaphorics of Cold War Berlin," *New German Critique* 110 [Vol. 37, Nr. 2] (Summer 2010): 73–94.
Piot, Charles. *Nostalgia for the Future: West Africa After the Cold War.* Chicago, IL: University of Chicago Press, 2010.
Plass, Ulrich. "Dialectic of Regression: Theodor W. Adorno and Fritz Lang." *Telos: A Quarterly Journal of Politics, Philosophy, Critical Theory, Culture, and the Arts* 149 (2009): 127–150.
Plass, Ulrich. *Language and History in Theodor W. Adorno's Notes to Literature.* New York: Routledge, 2007.
Pollmanns, Marion. *Didaktik und Eigensinn: Zu Alexander Kluges Praxis und Theorie der Vermittlung.* Wetzlar: Büchse der Pandora, 2006.

Prince, Gerald. "On A Postcolonial Narratology." *A Companion to Narrative Theory*. Ed. James Phelan and Peter J. Rabinowitz. Oxford: Blackwell, 2005. 372–381.

Radisoglou, Alexis. "Keeping Time in Place: Modernism, Political Aesthetics, and the Transformation of Chronotopes in Late Modernity." Diss. Columbia University, 2015.

Rancière, Jacques. *The Politics of Aesthetics: The Distribution of the Sensible*. Trans. Gabriel Rockhill. London: Continuum, 2004.

Ray, Larry. "After 1989: Globalization, Normalization, and Utopia." *Globalization and Utopia: Critical Essays*. Ed. Patrick Hayden and Chamsy el-Ojeilli. New York: Palgrave Macmillan, 2009. 101–116.

Reemtsma, Jan Philipp. "Laudatio zur Verleihung des Georg-Büchner-Preises." Alexander Kluge Homepage. 25 October 2003. Web. http://www.kluge-alexander.de/zur-person/laudatio/2003-buechnerpreis.html. 12 November 2015.

Reichmann, Wolfgang. *Der Chronist Alexander Kluge: Poetik und Erzählstrategien*. Bielefeld: Aisthesis, 2009.

Reichmann, Wolfgang. "Tür an Tür mit einer anderen Zeit: Zeitschichten und nichtlineares Erzählen bei Alexander Kluge." *Die Frage des Zusammenhangs: Alexander Kluge im Kontext*. Ed. Christian Schulte. Vorwerk 8: Berlin, 2012. 192–207.

Rentschler, Eric. "Kluge, Film History, and *Eigensinn*: A Taking of Stock from the Distance." *New German Critique* 31 (1984): 109–124.

Richardson, Brian. *Unnatural Voices: Extreme Narration in Modern and Contemporary Fiction*. Columbus, OH: Ohio State University Press, 2006.

Richter, Gerhard. *Afterness: Figures of Following in Modern Thought and Aesthetics*. New York: Columbia University Press, 2011.

Ricoeur, Paul. *Time and Narrative*. 3 Vols. Trans. Kathleen McLaughlin, David Pellauer, and Kathleen Blamey. Chicago, IL: University of Chicago Press, 1984–1988.

Roberts, Adam. *The History of Science Fiction*. New York: Palgrave Macmillan, 2006.

Roberts, David. "Alexander Kluge und die deutsche Zeitgeschichte: Der Luftangriff auf Halberstadt am 8.4.1945." *Alexander Kluge*. Ed. Thomas Böhm-Christel. Frankfurt am Main: Suhrkamp, 1983. 77–116.

Roberts, David. "Die Formenwelt des Zusammenhangs: Zur Theorie und Funktion der Montage bei Alexander Kluge." *Montage*. Ed. Helmut Kreuzer. *LiLi: Zeitschrift für Literaturwissenschaft und Linguistik* 46 (1982): 104–119.

Robertson, Roland. *Globalization: Social Theory and Global Culture*. London: Sage, 1992.

Rössler, Reto. "Kein Trostbuch—Alexander Kluge erzählt '48 Geschichten für Fritz Bauer.'" *literaturkritik.de: rezensionsforum*. 8 August 2013. Web. 21 January 2016.

Rosenfeld, Gavriel D. *Hi Hitler! How the Nazi Past is Being Normalized in Contemporary Culture*. Cambridge, UK: Cambridge University Press, 2015.

Rosenfeld, Gavriel D. *The World Hitler Never Made: Alternate History and the Memory of Nazism*. Cambridge, UK: Cambridge University Press, 2005.

Rosenstrauch, Hazel. "Woher ist das Material?" *Der Freitag*. 4 November 2013. Web. 21 January 2016.

Rothberg, Michael. *Multidirectional Memory: Remembering the Holocaust in the Age of Decolonization*. Stanford, CA: Stanford University Press, 2009.

Rüsen, Jörn, Michael Fehr, and Thomas W. Rieger. *Thinking Utopia: Steps into Other Worlds*. New York: Berghahn, 2005.

Ruschig, Ulrich. "Materialismus: Kritische Theorie nach Marx." *Adorno-Handbuch: Leben – Werk – Wirkung*. Ed. Richard Klein, Johann Kreuzer, and Stefan Müller-Doohm. Stuttgart: Metzler, 2011. 335–345.
Ryan, Marie-Laure. "Impossible Worlds." *The Routledge Companion to Experimental Literature*. Ed. Joe Bray, Alison Gibbons, and Brian McHale. New York: Routledge, 2012. 368–379.
Ryan, Marie-Laure. *Narrative as Virtual Reality: Immersion and Interactivity in Literature and Electronic Media*. Baltimore, MD: Johns Hopkins University Press, 2001.
Ryan, Marie-Laure. "Temporal Paradoxes in Narrative." *Style* 43 (2009): 142–164.
Santner, Eric L. *Stranded Objects: Mourning, Memory, and Film in Postwar Germany*. Ithaca, NY: Cornell University Press, 1990.
Sargent, Lyman Tower. "The Necessity of Utopian Thinking: A Cross-National Perspective." *Thinking Utopia: Steps into Other Worlds*. Ed. Jörn Rüsen, Michael Fehr, and Thomas W. Rieger. New York: Berghahn, 2005. 1–14.
Scherer, Christina. "Alexander Kluge und Jean-Luc Godard: Ein Vergleich anhand einiger filmtheoretischer 'Grundannahmen'." *Die Schrift an der Wand/Alexander Kluge: Rohstoffe und Materialien*. Ed. Christian Schulte. Osnabrück: Universitätsverlag Rasch, 2000. 79–102.
Scherpe, Klaus. "Literatur nach der Kritischen Theorie: Hans Magnus Enzensberger und Alexander Kluge." *Stadt.Krieg.Fremde: Literatur und Kultur nach den Katastrophen*. Tübingen: Francke, 2002. 315–334.
Scherpe, Klaus. "Dem Realen auf der Spur: Exerzitien der Beschreibung in der deutschen Nachkriegsliteratur." *Realismus nach den europäischen Avantgarden: Ästhetik, Poetologie und Kognition in Film und Literatur der Nachkriegszeit*. Ed. Claudia Ohlschläger, Lucia Perrone Capano, and Vittoria Borsò. Bielefeld: transcript, 2012. 141–161.
Schiesser, Giaco. "Arbeit am und mit EigenSinn." *netzspannung.org*. 2 December 2004. Web. 29 January 2016.
Schiffauer, Werner. *Parallelgesellschaften: Wie viel Wertekonsens braucht unsere Gesellschaft? Für eine kluge Politik der Differenz*. Bielefeld: transcript, 2008.
Schiller, Hans-Ernst. "Tod und Utopie: Ernst Bloch, Georg Lukács." *Adorno-Handbuch: Leben – Werk – Wirkung*. Ed. Richard Klein, Johann Kreuzer, and Stefan Müller-Doohm. Stuttgart: Metzler, 2011. 25–35.
Schlüpmann, Heide. "'What is Different is Good': Women and Femininity in the Films of Alexander Kluge." *Alexander Kluge: Raw Materials for the Imagination*. Ed. Tara Forrest. Amsterdam: Amsterdam University Press, 2012. 72–92.
Schmid, Thomas. "Der krumme Weg des Guten." *Die Welt am Sonntag*. 22 April 2013: 22. Web. 1 February 2016.
Schmidt, Ulrich. "Täter und Ermittler oder: Verhöhnung der Opfer." *Zwischen Aufbruch und Wende: Lebensgeschichten der sechziger und siebziger Jahre*. Tübingen: Niemeyer, 1993. 112–114.
Schmitt, Carl. "Die legale Weltrevolution: Politischer Mehrwert als Prämie auf juristische Legalität und Superlegalität." *Der Staat* [Berlin] 17 (1978): 321–339.
Schmitt, Carl. *The Nomos of the Earth*. Trans. G.L. Ulmen. 1950. New York: Telos, 2003.
Schmitt, Carl. "El orden del mundo después de la segunda guerra mondiale." *Revista de Estudios Politicos* 122 (1962): 19–38.

Schönfeld, Martin. "Kant's Philosophical Development." *The Stanford Encyclopedia of Philosophy*. Ed. Edward N. Zalta. Winter 2012 Edition. http://plato.stanford.edu/archives/win2012/entries/kant-development. PDF.

Schreiber, Dominik. *Narrative der Globalisierung: Gerechtigkeit und Konkurrenz in faktualen und fiktionalen Erzählungen*. Wiesbaden: Spring, 2015.

Schütte, Wolfram. "Alexander Kluge: '48 Geschichten für Fritz Bauer'—Respektvolle Erinnerung an einen Humanisten." *Deutschlandfunk*. 31 January 2014. Web. 21 January 2016.

Schütz, Erhard. "Ein Liebesversuch oder Zeigen, was das Auge nicht sieht…: Der 'kalte Blick' in Alexander Kluges Prosa." *Alexander Kluge*. Ed. Heinz Ludwig Arnold. text + kritik 85/86 (1985): 50–62.

Schuh, Franz. "Über den Eigensinn der Philosophie: Zum Philosophiebegriff in Negt/Kluges *Geschichte und Eigensinn*." *Alexander Kluge*. Ed. Thomas Böhm-Christel. Frankfurt am Main: Suhrkamp, 1983. 153–166.

Schulte, Christian. "Alexander Kluge: *Ein Liebesversuch*." *Klassische deutsche Kurzgeschichten*. Ed. Werner Bellmann. Stuttgart: Reclam, 2004. 247–258.

Schulte, Christian, ed. *Die Frage des Zusammenhangs: Alexander Kluge im Kontext*. Berlin: Vorwerk 8, 2012.

Schulte, Christian. "Kairos und Aura: Spuren Benjamins im Werk Alexander Kluges." *Schrift.Bilder.Denken: Walter Benjamin und die Kunst der Gegenwart*. Ed. Detlev Schöttker. Frankfurt am Main: Suhrkamp, 2004. 220–233.

Schulte, Christian. "Konstruktionen des Zusammenhangs: Motiv, Zeugenschaft und Wiedererkennung bei Alexander Kluge." *Die Schrift an der Wand/Alexander Kluge: Rohstoffe und Materialien*. Ed. Christian Schulte. Osnabrück: Universitätsverlag Rasch, 2000. 45–67.

Schulte, Christian. "Kritische Theorie als Gegenproduktion: Zum Projekt Alexander Kluges." *gift: zeitschrift für freies theater* 3 (2010): 37–44.

Schulte, Christian, Winfried Siebers, Valentin Mertes, and Stefanie Schmitt, eds. *Formenwelt des Dialogs. Alexander Kluge-Jahrbuch* 3 (2016).

Sebald, W.G. *Luftkrieg und Literatur* [1999]. 4th ed. Frankfurt am Main: Fischer, 2003.

Sebald, W.G. *On the Natural History of Destruction*. Trans. Anthea Bell. New York: Random House, 2003.

Seebold, Elmar, ed. *Kluge: Etymologisches Wörterbuch der deutschen Sprache*. 24th rev. ed. Berlin: De Gruyter, 2002.

Sennett, Richard. *The Culture of the New Capitalism*. New Haven: Yale University Press, 2006.

Siegert, Bernhard. *Cultural Techniques: Grids, Filters, Doors, and Other Articulations of the Real*. Trans. Geoffrey Winthrop-Young. New York: Fordham University Press, 2015.

Singles, Kathleen. *Alternate History: Playing with Contingency and Necessity*. Berlin: De Gruyter, 2013.

Sloterdijk, Peter. *In the World Interior of Capital: For a Philosophical Theory of Globalization*. Trans. Wieland Hoban. London: Polity, 2014.

Smith, Eric D. *Globalization, Utopia, and Postcolonial Science Fiction: New Maps of Hope*. New York: Palgrave Macmillan, 2012.

Smith, Nicholas H. "Hope and Critical Theory." *Critical Horizons: A Journal of Philosophy and Social Theory* 6 (2005): 45–61.

Spivak, Gayatri Chakravorty. *An Aesthetic Education in the Era of Globalization*. Cambridge, MA: Harvard University Press, 2012.

Spivak, Gayatri Chakravorty. *Death of a Discipline*. New York: Columbia University Press, 2003.
Stanitzek, Georg. "Autorität im Hypertext: 'Der Kommentar ist die Grundform der Texte' (Alexander Kluge)." *Internationales Archiv für Sozialgeschichte der deutschen Literatur* 23.2 (1998): 1–46.
Stanitzek, Georg. "Massenmedium Kluge." *Die Schrift an der Wand/Alexander Kluge: Rohstoffe und Materialien*. Ed. Christian Schulte. Osnabrück: Universitätsverlag Rasch, 2000. 241–251.
Steinke, Ronen. *Fritz Bauer, oder Auschwitz vor Gericht*. Munich: Piper, 2013.
Stiegler, Bernd. "Die Realität ist nicht genug: Alexander Kluges praktische Theorie und theoretische Praxis der Montage." *Alexander Kluge*. Ed. Thomas Combrink. *text + kritik* 85/86 [New edition] (2011): 52–58.
Stollmann, Rainer. *Alexander Kluge zur Einführung*. Hamburg: Junius, 1988.
Stollmann, Rainer. "Das Private und die verwaltete Welt: Oder wie Politik verschwindet." *Der Deutschunterricht* 64.3 (2012): 48–57.
Stollmann, Rainer. "Schwarzer Krieg, endlos: Erfahrung und Selbsterhaltung in Alexander Kluges 'Lernprozesse mit tödlichem Ausgang'." *Text und Kontext* 12.2 (1984). Spec. issue on *Zukunftsbilder in der deutschen Literatur des 20. Jahrhunderts*. 349–369.
Stollmann, Rainer. "Wovon man nicht reden kann, das ist gemeinsame Sache aller Teilsprachen: KZ, Krieg, politisches Verbrechen im Werk Alexander Kluges." *Rechenschaften: juristischer und literarischer Diskurs in der Auseinandersetzung mit den NS-Massenverbrechen*. Ed. Stephan Braese. Göttingen: Wallstein, 2004. 146–164.
Stollmann, Rainer. "Zusammenhang, Motiv, Krieg: Ein Holzschnitt zu Negt/Kluges Theoriearbeit." *Alexander Kluge*. Ed. Heinz Ludwig Arnold. *text + kritik* 85/86 (1985): 82–102.
Stolt, Kerstin. "Teddys Flaschenpost: Die Figur der Verdinglichung in Adornos Kritik der Massenkultur." Berlin: John F. Kennedy-Institut für Nordamerikastudien der Freien Universität Berlin [Working Paper Series], 1997. PDF.
Suvin, Darko. *Metamorphoses of Science Fiction: On the Poetics and History of a Literary Genre*. New Haven, CT: Yale University Press, 1979.
Szendy, Peter. *Kant in the Land of Extraterrestrials: Cosmopolitical Philosofictions*. Trans. Will Bishop. New York: Fordham University Press, 2013.
Szondi, Peter. "Hoffnung im Vergangenen: Walter Benjamin und die Suche nach der verlorenen Zeit." *Zeugnisse: Theodor W. Adorno zum sechzigsten Geburtstag*. Ed. Max Horkheimer. Frankfurt am Main: Europäische Verlagsanstalt, 1963. 241–256.
Szondi, Peter. "Hope in the Past: On Walter Benjamin." Trans. Harvey Mendelsohn. *Critical Inquiry* 4.3 (1978): 491–506.
Thompson, William. *An Inquiry into the Principles of the Distribution of Wealth Most Conducive to Human Happiness; Applied to the Newly Proposed System of Voluntary Equality of Wealth*. London: Longman, 1824.
Thorne, Christian. "The Antinomy of Antinomies." *Boundary 2* 32.3 (2005): 81–96.
Tiedemann, Rolf. *Mythos und Utopie: Aspekte der Adornschen Philosophie*. Munich: edition text + kritik, 2009.
Tomlinson, John. *Globalization and Culture*. Cambridge, UK: Polity, 1999.
Traverso, Enzo. *L'histoire comme champ de bataille: interpréter les violences du xxe siècle*. Paris: La Découverte, 2010.

Triendl-Zadoff, Mirjam. "Unter Brüdern—Gershom und Werner Scholem: Von den Utopien der Jugend zum jüdischen Alltag zwischen den Kriegen." *Münchner Beiträge zur jüdischen Geschichte und Kultur* 1.2 (2007): 56–66.
Trotsky, Leon. *The Permanent Revolution*. Trans. Max Shachtman. New York: Pioneer Publishers, 1931.
Uecker, Matthias. "Wiederholungszwang und Veränderungswunsch: Zu einem Motiv in Alexander Kluges Prosa." *Keiner kommt davon: Zeitgeschichte in der Literatur nach 1945*. Ed. Erhard Schütz and Wolfgang Hardtwig. Göttingen: Vandenhoeck & Ruprecht, 2008. 115–129.
Ueding, Gert, and Bernd Steinbrink. *Grundriß der Rhetorik: Geschichte, Technik, Methode*. 3rd rev. and expanded edition. Stuttgart: Metzler, 1994.
Vázquez-Arroyo, Antonio Y. "Minima Humana: Adorno, Exile, and the Dialectic." *Telos: A Quarterly Journal of Politics, Philosophy, Critical Theory, Culture, and the Arts* 149 (2009): 105–125.
Vedder, Ulrike. "'Verhoffen': Gedankenstriche in der Lyrik von Ingeborg Bachmann, Nelly Sachs und Paul Celan." *Die Poesie der Zeichensetzung: Studien zur Stilistik der Interpunktion*. Ed. Alexander Nebrig and Carlos Spoerhase. Bern: Peter Lang, 2012. 345–361.
Villarejo, Amy. *Ethereal Queer: Television, Historicity, Desire*. Durham and London: Duke University Press, 2014.
Visch, Marijke. "Zur Funktion von Dokumenten im historischen Roman: Eine exemplarische Untersuchung anhand von Alexander Kluges *Schlachtbeschreibung*." *Alexander Kluge*. Ed. Thomas Böhm-Christel. Frankfurt am Main: Suhrkamp, 1983. 26–49.
Vogl, Joseph. "Woher der Storch die Kinder bringt." *Theodor W. Adorno: 'Minima Moralia' neu gelesen*. Ed. Andreas Bernard and Ulrich Raulff. Frankfurt am Main: Suhrkamp, 2003. 43–46.
Von Boeckmann, Staci. "The Life and Work of Gretel Karplus/Adorno: Her Contributions to Frankfurt School Theory." Diss. University of Oklahoma, 2004.
Von Boeckmann, Staci. "Trachodon und Teddie: Über Gretel Adorno." *Adorno-Portraits: Erinnerungen von Zeitgenossen*. Ed. Stefan Müller-Doohm. Frankfurt am Main: Suhrkamp, 2007. 335–352.
Von Wussow, Philipp. *Logik der Deutung: Adorno und die Philosophie*. Würzburg: Königshausen & Neumann, 2007.
Voßkamp, Wilhelm. "Emblematik der Geschichte: Alexander Kluges literarische und filmische Geschichtsschreibung." *Internationales Archiv für Sozialgeschichte der deutschen Literatur* 36.2 (2011): 361–372.
Voßkamp, Wilhelm. *Emblematik der Zukunft: Poetik und Geschichte literarischer Utopien*. Berlin: De Gruyter, 2016.
Voßkamp, Wilhelm. "Literatur als Geschichte: Überlegungen zu dokumentarischen Prosatexten von Alexander Kluge, Klaus Stiller und Dieter Kuhn." *Basis: Jahrbuch für deutsche Gegenwartsliteratur* 4 (1973): 235–250.
Wang, Hui. *China from Empire to Nation-State*. Trans. Michael Gibbs Hill. Cambridge, MA: Harvard University Press, 2014.
Wang, Hui. *China's New Order: Society, Politics, and Economy in Transition*. Ed. Theodore Huters. Cambridge, MA: Harvard University Press, 2003.
Wang, Hui. *The End of the Revolution: China and the Limits of Modernity*. Trans. Rebecca E. Karl, Christopher Connery, Audrea Lim, and Hongmei Yu. London: Verso, 2011.

Wang, Hui. *The Politics of Imagining Asia.* Ed. Theodore Huters. Trans. Matthew A. Hale, Wang Yang, Chris Berry, Theodore Huters, and Zhang Yongle. Cambridge, MA: Harvard University Press, 2011.
Wang, Hui, Leo Ou-fan Lee, and Michael M.J. Fischer. "Is the Public Sphere Unspeakable in Chinese? Can Public Spaces (*gonggong kongjian*) Lead to Public Spheres?" *Public Culture* 6.3 (1994): 597–605.
Wankhammer, Johannes. "Cultures of Sense: Science, Aesthetics, and the Art of Attention in the Eighteenth Century." Diss. Cornell University, 2016.
Webb, Darren. *Marx, Marxism, and Utopia.* Aldershot, UK: Ashgate, 2000.
Weber, Hermann, and Andreas Herbst. "Scholem, Werner." *Deutsche Kommunisten: Biographisches Handbuch 1918 bis 1945.* 2nd edition. Berlin: Karl Dietz, 2008. 820–822.
Weber, Max. "Bureaucracy." *Max Weber: Essays in Sociology.* Ed. and trans. H.H. Gerth and C. Wright Mills. New York: Oxford University Press, 1973. 196–244.
Weber, Philipp. *Stern.Bilder.Denken: Aspekte einer Denkfigur bei Walter Benjamin.* Frankfurt am Main: Peter Lang, 2010.
Weidner, Daniel, and Stefan Willer, eds. *Prophetie und Prognostik: Verfügungen über Zukunft in Wissenschaften, Religionen und Künsten.* Munich: Wilhelm Fink, 2013.
Weigel, Sigrid. *Body- and Image-Space: Re-Reading Walter Benjamin.* Trans. Georgina Paul with Rachel McNicholl and Jeremy Gaines. London: Routledge, 1996.
Weigel, Sigrid. *Entstellte Ähnlichkeit: Walter Benjamins theoretische Schreibweise.* Frankfurt am Main: Fischer, 1997.
Weigel, Sigrid. "Télescopage im Unbewußten: Zum Verhältnis von Trauma, Geschichtsbegriff und Literatur." *Trauma: Zwischen Psychoanalyse und kulturellem Deutungsmuster.* Ed. Elisabeth Bronfen, Birgit R. Erdle, and Sigrid Weigel. Cologne: Böhlau, 1999. 51–76.
Weixler, Antonius, and Lukas Werner. "Zeit und Erzählen—eine Skizze." *Zeiten erzählen: Ansätze—Aspekte—Analysen.* Ed. Antonius Weixler and Lukas Werner. Berlin: De Gruyter, 2015. 1–24.
Wellbery, David E. "Stimmung." *Ästhetische Grundbegriffe: Historisches Wörterbuch in sieben Bänden.* Vol. 5. *Postmoderne—Synästhesie.* Ed. Karlheinz Barck, Martin Fontius, Dieter Schlenstedt, Burkhart Steinwachs, and Friedrich Wolfzettel. Stuttgart: Metzler, 2003. 703–733.
Wellmer, Albrecht. *The Persistence of Modernity: Essays on Aesthetics, Ethics, and Postmodernism.* Trans. David Midgley. Cambridge, MA: MIT Press, 1991.
Wentzer, Thomas Schwarz. "The Eternal Recurrence of the New." *Anthropology and Philosophy: Dialogues on Trust and Hope.* Ed. Sune Liisberg, Esther Oluffa Pedersen, and Anne Line Dalsgård. New York: Berghahn, 2015. 76–89.
Wesche, Tilo. "Moral und Glück: Hoffnung bei Kant und Adorno." *Deutsche Zeitschrift für Philosophie* [Akademie Verlag] 60.1 (2012): 49–71.
Whitebook, Joel. *Perversion and Utopia: A Study in Psychoanalysis and Critical Theory.* Cambridge, MA: MIT Press, 1995.
Willer, Stefan. *Erbfälle: Theorie und Praxis kultureller Übertragung in der Moderne.* Munich: Fink, 2014.
Willer, Stefan. "Nachhaltige Zukunft: Kommende Generationen und ihr kulturelles Erbe." *Zukunftswissen: Prognosen in Wirtschaft, Politik und Gesellschaft seit 1900.* Ed. Heinrich Hartmann und Jakob Vogel. Frankfurt am Main: Campus, 2010. 267–283.
Willer, Stefan. "Prognose." *Historisches Wörterbuch der Rhetorik.* Vol. 10. *Nachträge A-Z.* Ed. Gert Ueding. Berlin: Walter de Gruyter, 2012. 958–966.

Willer, Stefan. "Vom Nicht-Wissen der Zukunft: Prognostik und Literatur um 1800 und um 1900." *Literatur und Nicht-Wissen: Historische Konstellationen in Literatur und Wissenschaft, 1750–1930*. Ed. Michael Bies and Michael Gamper. Berlin: Diaphanes, 2012. 171–196.
Willer, Stefan. "Zur literarischen Epistemologie der Zukunft." *Wissens-Ordnungen: Zu einer historischen Epistemologie der Literatur*. Ed. Nicola Gess and Sandra Janßen. Berlin: De Gruyter, 2014. 224–260.
Willer, Stefan. "Zurück in die Zukunft, vorwärts in die Vergangenheit: Zeitreisen in Literatur und Film." *Interjekte* 5 (2014): 34–51.
Willer, Stefan. "Zwischen Futur Eins und Futur Zwei: Georg Kleins Grammatik der Zukunft." *'Wie in luzidem Schlaf': Zum Werk Georg Kleins*. Ed. Christoph Jürgensen and Tom Kindt. Berlin: Erich Schmidt, 2013. 131–141.
Wirt, Candace. "'I Am a Patriot of the 20s': An Interview with Alexander Kluge." *Notebook* [Digital Magazine of International Cinema and Film Culture]. MUBI. 20 February 2012. Web. https://mubi.com/notebook/posts/i-am-a-partriot-of-the-20s-an-interview-with-alexander-kluge. 5 November 2015.
Witte, Karsten. "Alexander Kluge." *Neues Handbuch der deutschsprachigen Gegenwartsliteratur seit 1945*. Ed. Dietz-Rüdiger Moser. Munich: Nymphenburger, 1990. 369–370.
Wojak, Irmtrud. *Fritz Bauer 1903–1968: Eine Biographie*. 2nd ed. Munich: Beck, 2009.
Wolf, Fred Alan. *Parallel Universes: The Search for Other Worlds*. New York: Simon & Schuster, 1990.
Wolin, Richard. "Utopia, Mimesis, and Reconciliation: A Redemptive Critique of Adorno's Aesthetic Theory." *Representations* 32 (1990): 33–49.
Yan, Haiping. "Intermedial Moments: An Embodied Turn in Contemporary Chinese Cinema." *Journal of Chinese Cinema* 7.1 (2013). 6 January 2014. Web. 24 December 2015.
Yildiz, Yasemin. *Beyond the Mother Tongue: The Postmonolingual Condition*. New York: Fordham University Press, 2012.
Zadoff, Mirjam. *Der rote Hiob: Das Leben des Werner Scholem*. Munich: Hanser, 2014.
Zangl, Veronika. "Zum Eigensinn der Faktizität in Alexander Kluges 'Ein Liebesversuch'." *Die Frage des Zusammenhangs: Alexander Kluge im Kontext*. Ed. Christian Schulte. Berlin: Vorwerk, 2012. 169–180.
Zeller, Christoph. *Ästhetik des Authentischen: Literatur und Kunst um 1970*. Berlin: De Gruyter, 2010.
Žižek, Slavoj. "From Revolutionary to Catastrophic Utopia." *Thinking Utopia: Steps into Other Worlds*. Ed. Jörn Rüsen, Michael Fehr, and Thomas W. Rieger. New York: Berghahn, 2005. 247–262.
Zuidervaart, Lambert. "Theodor W. Adorno." *The Stanford Encyclopedia of Philosophy* (Winter 2011 Edition). Ed. Edward N. Zalta. Web. http://plato.stanford.edu/archives/win2011/entries/adorno/. 3 August 2015.

Alphabetical List of Kluge Titles Discussed, in German and English

"Abschied von den Lokomotiven" ["Farewell to Locomotives"]
"Abschied von einer Metapher des Fortschritts" ["Farewell to a Metaphor of Progress"]
Abschied von gestern [*Yesterday Girl*]
Air Raid
"Die Aktualität Adornos" ["The Actuality of Adorno"]
Der Angriff der Gegenwart auf die übrige Zeit [*The Assault of the Present on the Rest of Time*]
"Außerirdische unterwegs" ["Extraterrestrials on the Move"]
"Bauch der Milchstraße" ["Belly of the Milky Way"]
"Begegnung mit dem Unbekannten" ["Encounter with the Unknown"]
"Besuch im Weißen Haus" ["Visitors in the White House"]
"Die blaue Gefahr" ["The Blue Peril"]
Das Bohren harter Bretter ["The Boring of Hard Boards"]
Chronik der Gefühle ["Chronicle of Feelings"]
"Chronik von Pangäa bis heute" ["Chronicle of Pangea till Today"]
The Devil's Blind Spot
"Dunsthimmel über mir und das Ding in mir" ["Hazy Sky above Me and the Thing inside Me"]
"Durch Armut reich: das Ich" ["Rich from Poverty: the I"]
"Ein deutscher Gelehrter in Persien" ["A German Scholar in Persia"]
"Ein später Sieg des Spartakus" ["A Late Victory of Spartacus"]
"Ein Streit mit meiner Mutter" ["A Fight with My Mother"]
"Eine schwer zu deutende Heldentat" ["A Heroic Deed That Is Hard to Interpret"]
"Einen Ausweg muß es geben" ["There Has to Be A Way Out"]
"Eisenroß um 2006" ["Iron Steed Around 2006"]
"Die Entsprechung einer Oase" ["Corresponding to an Oasis"]
Ferngespräche ["Long-Distance Conversations"]
Das fünfte Buch ["The Fifth Book"]
"Futur antérieur" ["Future Anterior"]
"Geister, wie Walter Benjamin sie beschreibt" ["Ghosts as Walter Benjamin Describes Them"]
Gelegenheitsarbeit einer Sklavin ["Part-Time Work of a Domestic Slave"]
Geschichten vom Kino [*Cinema Stories*]
"Geschichten vom Weltall" ["Stories of the Cosmos"]
"Gesellschaftliche Prozesse als Erzählung" ["Social Processes as Narration"]
Glückliche Umstände, leihweise ["Happy Circumstances, On Loan"]
"'Grausam wie ein Mongole'" ["'Cruel As a Mongolian'"]
"Gußeiserne Balkons als Saturnring oder Saturnring aus Gußeisen"
    ["Cast Iron Balconies as Saturnian Ring or Saturn's Ring out of Cast Iron"]
"Hoffnung bei Sonnenaufgang" ["Hope at Sunrise"]
"Hündchen Laika" ["Little Dog Laika"]
"Hybride Formen des Zirkus" ["Hybrid Forms of the Circus"]
"Im Weltall braucht man keine Lesebrille: Helge Schneider und Peter Berling im Orbit"
    ["One Needs No Reading Glasses in the Cosmos: Helge Schneider and Peter Berling in Orbit"]

"Intelligenz zweiten Grades" ["Second-Order Intelligence"]
"Katzen im Weltraum" ["Cats in Outer Space"]
"Keine falsche Unmittelbarkeit" ["No False Immediacy"]
"König Dampf, Kaiserin Elektrizität" ["King Steam, Empress Electricity"]
Kongs große Stunde ["Kong's Great Hour"]
"Der Kosmos als Kino" ["The Cosmos as Cinema"]
"Kot von Außerirdischen" ["Extraterrestrials' Shit"]
"Die Küche des Glücks" ["The Kitchen of Happiness"]
Das Labyrinth der zärtlichen Kraft ["The Labyrinth of Tender Power"]
"Lebendigkeit von 1931" ["Liveness from 1931"]
Lebensläufe [*Case Histories* and *Attendance List for a Funeral*]
"Die Lebensläufer und ihre Lebensgeschichten" ["The Course-of-Lifers and Their Life Stories"]
Lernprozesse mit tödlichem Ausgang [*Learning Processes with a Deadly Outcome*]
Die Lücke, die der Teufel läßt ["The Gap the Devil Leaves Us"]
Der Luftangriff auf Halberstadt am 8. April 1945
 ["The Attack by Air on Halberstadt on April 8, 1945"]
"Mein Großvater mütterlicherseits" ["My Maternal Grandfather"]
"Mein wahres Motiv" ["My True Motive"]
"Mentalesisch" ["Mentalese"]
"Die Mondkräfte und der Endsieg" ["Lunar Forces and Ultimate Victory"]
"Nachricht" ["News Item/Military Intelligence"]
"Nachricht an Außerirdische" ["News Item for Extraterrestrials"]
Nachrichten aus der ideologischen Antike ["News from Ideological Antiquity"]
"Neue Erscheinungsform des Großen Drachen"
 ["New Manifestation Form of the Great Dragon"]
Neue Geschichten ["New Stories/New Histories"]
Personen und Reden ["Persons and Speeches"]
"Das Politische als Intensität alltäglicher Gefühle"
 ["The Political as Intensity of Everyday Feelings"]
"Die Revolution ist ein Lebewesen voller Überraschungen"
 ["The Revolution is an Organism Full of Surprises"]
"Samstag in Utopia" ["Saturday in Utopia"]
"Das Schaf von Rom" ["The Sheep of Rome"]
Schlachtbeschreibung [*The Battle*]
"Schneller als das Schicksal" ["Faster than Fate"]
"Die Schnellsten werden die Letzten sein" ["The Fastest Will Be the Last"]
"Das Schöne ist fehlerfrei" ["The Beautiful is Flawless"]
"Schwarzer Tropfen/Bailyscher Tropfen" ["Black Drop/Baily's Beads"]
"Sechs Lokomotiven, Fahrlässigkeit und die Folgen"
 ["Six Locomotives, Recklessness, and the Consequences"]
"Der Sechsjährige in mir und der gestirnte Himmel über mir"
 ["The Six-Year-Old within Me and the Starry Sky above Me"]
"The Sharpest Ideology: That Reality Appeals to Its Realistic Character"
"Sind Photonen individuell?" ["Are Photons Individual?"]
"Snowball-Earth"
"Tempus, Aevum, Aeternitas" ["Time, Age, Eternity"]
"Der Teufel im Weißen Haus" ["The Devil in the White House"]

Theorie der Erzählung ["Theory of Storytelling"]
Tür an Tür mit einem anderen Leben ["Door to Door with an Other Life"]
"Unser ständiger Begleiter, der Mond" ["Our Constant Companion, the Moon"]
"Unsere Vorfahren, die Sterne" ["Our Ancestors, the Stars"]
"Uralte Freunde der Kernkraft" ["Age-Old Friends of Nuclear Power"]
"Walter Benjamin kommt bis Halberstadt" ["Walter Benjamin Comes As Far As Halberstadt"]
"Waschleppas Atlas der Dampflokomotiven" ["Waschleppa's Atlas of Steam Locomotives"]
"Weltzeit" ["World Time"]
"Wer ein Wort des Trostes spricht, ist ein Verräter": 48 Geschichten für Fritz Bauer
    ["'Whoever speaks a word of consolation is a traitor': 48 Stories for Fritz Bauer"]
"Wie fängt man an der EU-Grenze das Böse ab?"
    ["How Does One Nab Evil at the EU-Border?"]
"Wie in einer anderen Welt, durch eine unsichtbare Wand vom Übrigen getrennt"
    ["As in an Other World, Separated from the Rest by an Invisible Wall"]
"Wir Glückskinder der Ersten Globalisierung"
    ["We Fortunate Children of the First Globalization"]
"Zeugen aus einer anderen Welt" ["Witnesses from an Other World"]
"Zustöpseln eines Kinderhirns" ["Plugging Up a Child's Brain"]

Index of Persons

Adolf, Heinrich 127
Adorno, Gretel 91, 93, 127, 132, 139, 143, 199
Adorno, Theodor W. 1–4, 15, 17, 21, 26, 31f., 37, 43, 45, 48, 50–147, 154, 157, 163, 166f., 170, 173f., 176–178, 180f., 183, 185, 188, 191, 193, 196, 199, 202, 204, 214f., 235, 241, 243, 245, 247–250
Alber, Jan 29, 103f., 109, 168
Alexander, Bryan N. 72f.
Althaus, Thomas 48
Améry, Jean 216
Anderson, Benedict 144
Anderson, Mark 233
Angele, Michael 151, 153
Anz, Thomas 56
Appadurai, Arjun 33, 41, 61
Aragon, Louis 101
Arend, Ingo 151
Arendt, Hannah 14, 67
Ashton, E.B. 52, 75, 80
Assmann, Aleida 32, 148, 238
Augstein, Jakob 151
Augustine 66

Bachmann, Ingeborg 214
Bacon, Francis 94
Badiou, Alain 98
Bakhtin, Mikhail Mikhailovich 54
Balibar, Étienne 54
Bartels, Gerrit 232
Barthes, Roland 104, 151, 208
Bartov, Omer 198, 233
Baudelaire, Charles 48, 89, 91, 128
Bauer, Fritz 7, 201, 231–246
Baumgarten, Alexander Gottlieb 114
Beals, Kurt 7
Beauvoir, Simone de 98
Bechtold, Gerhard 205
Beckett, Samuel 75
Beethoven, Ludwig van 241
Behrens, Roger 112
Bell, Anthea 2
Benhabib, Seyla 28, 57

Benjamin, Walter 2f., 6, 8, 17, 22, 25, 28, 30–50, 52f., 56, 58, 63, 66–68, 71–75, 78, 81, 83, 90, 93, 95, 97f., 100–102, 109, 112, 128, 150, 152, 166, 170f., 174f., 178, 183, 190, 192, 196, 219, 248
Bennington, Geoffrey 10
Bense, Max 89
Benzaquén, Adriana S. 62, 73
Bergson, Henri 36
Bernard, Andreas 92
Berry, Michael 193
Binzegger, Lilli 3
Birkmeyer, Jens 24, 113
Blank, Johannes 224
Bloch, Ernst 28, 31, 42, 52, 58–63, 67f., 83, 140, 186, 189
Blumenberg, Hans 70, 180, 208–210
Bock, Wolfgang 34
Bode, Christoph 26f., 65, 145f.
Boeckmann, Staci von 127, 143
Böhme, Hartmut 180
Böhme, Jakob 41
Bohm, Svetlana 189
Bohn, Carolin 57
Bolter, Jay David 74
Boltzmann, Ludwig 152
Bolz, Norbert 24f., 233
Born, Erik 96
Bosse, Ulrike 233
Bosteels, Bruno 176f., 181
Bostock, Anna 34
Bowie, Andrew 4, 23f., 45, 85, 199, 210f.
Boyarin, Jonathan 238
Brandstetter, Gabriele 33
Branquinho, Alberto Carlos de Liz Texeira 236
Brauers, Claudia 57
Braunstein, Dirk 75
Bray, Joe 168
Bray, Michael 143
Brecht, Bertolt 31, 56, 60
Breithaupt, Fritz 36f.
Brentano, Clemens 156
Brock, Bazon 232

Brodsky, Claudia   177
Brown, Lesley   155
Brumlik, Micha   64, 66
Buch, Robert   150
Buck-Morss, Susan   53, 55 f., 58, 62, 72, 129
Buckmiller, Michael   218
Buden, Boris   62
Bühler, Benjamin   27, 148
Burdick, Anne   71
Burger, Rudolf   24, 45
Burke, Kenneth   3
Busche, Hubertus   41

Campe, Rüdiger   27, 38, 61, 68, 209
Caracciolo, Marco   110
Caroti, Simone   11
Carrard, Philippe   217
Cartwright, Mark   230
Casad, Madeleine   192
Casanova, Giacomo   129
Celan, Paul   214
Chalmers, Martin   2, 7 f., 33, 152
Chandler, Nahum D.   189
Chaudhary, Zahid R.   72
Chen Kaige   193–195
Chignell, Andrew   64
Chrostowska, S.D.   60
Cicovacki, Predrag   19 f.
Clark, Paul   193
Clary, Jonathan   60
Clausewitz, Carl von   4, 31
Claussen, Detlev   1, 95, 99
Cobley, Paul   40
Combrink, Thomas   179 f., 208
Connell, Liam   181 f., 192
Connell, Matt F.   107
Connerton, Paul   154
Crowe, Michael J.   10
Crutzen, Paul J.   172
Culler, Jonathan   151

Dannenberg, Hilary P.   27 f., 78
Davies, Gloria   223
Dean, Jodi   176 f.
Demirović, Alex   113
Democritus   10
Derrida, Jacques   12, 58, 98, 176, 185, 195

Descartes, René   17, 94
Dick, Philip K.   123
Dick, Steven J.   10
Dietrich, Rainer   26 f., 65, 145 f.
Donne, John   18, 213, 216
Downing, Eric   49
Drews, Jörg   77
DuBois, W.E.B.   189
Durzak, Manfred   233
Düttmann, Alexander   91

Eagleton, Terry   98
Edel, Alfred   234
Eder, Klaus   83
Eichmann, Adolf   231
Eikels, Kai van   33
Eiland, Howard   8, 36, 93
Einstein, Albert   70, 153 f.
Eisenstein, Sergei Mikhailovich   2, 31
Ekardt, Philipp   22 f., 193
Elliott, Brian   171
Elsaesser, Thomas   51
Elster, Annette   230
Engels, Friedrich   59, 182, 195
Enzensberger, Hans Magnus   219
Erdle, Birgit R.   27, 75, 118, 148, 166, 193
Eshel, Amir   27, 31, 37 f., 57, 65, 77, 145, 148, 198
Esposito, Elena   33
Ette, Ottmar   48

Falke, Gustav   84
Feuerbach, Ludwig   62, 169
Fischer, Kai Lars   30, 53, 81, 84
Fischer-Schreiber, Ingrid   192
Fisher, Jaimey   113
Fleming, Paul   70, 209
Fludernik, Monika   82, 104 f., 109 f., 151, 163, 244
Flug, Noach   141 f.
Fontane, Theodor   81, 85
Fontenelle, Bernard le Bovier de   15
Fore, Devin   3, 5, 25, 31, 41–43, 45, 53 f., 67, 79, 82, 148, 167, 173, 175, 178 f., 207 f., 219, 227 f.
Forrest, Tara   1, 7, 56, 81, 211
Foucault, Michel   45

Fourier, Charles 31
Fowkes, Ben 136
Franke, Manfred 211
Freud, Sigmund 59
Friedländer, Saul 232
Friedrich, Alexander 180
Fröhlich, Claudia 245
Fuchs, Anne 27
Fujita Hirose, Jun 33
Fukuyama, Francis 175

Gadamer, Hans-Georg 123
Gagnebin, Jeanne Marie 43
Galilei, Galileo 70, 209
Galli, Matteo 4
Gehlen, Arnold 53f., 67
Geller, Jay Howard 219
Genette, Gérard 104f., 151, 163, 187, 202, 221
Geulen, Eva 69, 96, 98f., 129f., 166
Geuss, Raymond 53, 112, 114, 166
Gibbons, Alison 168
Gibson, Nigel 57
Gibson, William 145
Gilbert, Joanna 143
Giles, Steve 31
Gilgen, Peter 20
Giroux, Henry A. 113
Goethe, Johann Wolfgang von 66, 227
Göttsche, Dirk 44
Grassmann, Philip 151
Gregersen, Erik 122
Grice, Paul 131
Grimm, Jacob 24f., 194
Grimm, Wilhelm 24f., 194
Grimmelshausen, Hans Jakob Christoffel von 3
Gropius, Walter 214
Grossman, David 65
Groys, Boris 62
Grusin, Richard 74
Gumbrecht, Hans Ulrich 33
Guyer, Paul 16–21, 114

Habermas, Jürgen 58, 113, 119, 166, 196, 223
Habjan, Jernej 182

Hackebeil, Hans 225
Haenni, Sabine 71
Hahn, Barbara 87
Hahn, Hans-Joachim 233
Hamacher, Werner 6, 196
Hammerstein-Equord, Helga von 220
Hammerstein-Equord, Kurt von 220
Hammerstein-Equord, Marie-Luise von 220, 228
Hanitzsch, Konstanze 233, 243
Hansen, Miriam 1, 23, 33, 42, 51, 71, 83–85, 87, 137, 143f.
Hansen, Per Krogh 105, 110
Hardt, Michael 98
Harlan, Thomas 232
Harris, Stefanie 77, 82, 90, 150
Hartmann, Heinrich 33
Hartwig, Ina 127
Harvey, David 169–171, 176, 182, 191
Hayles, N. Katherine 192
Hegel, Georg Wilhelm Friedrich 11, 19, 25, 55, 71f., 123, 125, 173
Heidegger, Martin 66, 140, 154
Heißenbüttel, Helmut 150
Heitmeyer, Wilhelm 149
Helbronner, Jacques 239
Hell, Julia 2
Heller, Andreas 3
Helmling, Steven 66
Hemingway, Ernest 188
Heraclitus 6
Herbst, Andreas 218, 222
Herman, David 49, 116, 118, 121, 131, 163, 202
Herodotus 43
Herzberger, Else 95
Herzog, Werner 234
Hetzel, Andreas 55f.
Hipparchus 70, 209
Hirsch, Marianne 238f.
Hitler, Adolf 93, 220, 223
Hoban, Wieland 244
Hölderlin, Friedrich 6, 53
Hoffrogge, Ralf 218–220, 222, 224–226, 230
Hohendahl, Peter Uwe 54f., 57f., 60, 66–69, 72f., 80, 84, 223

Holl, Herbert   75
Hollenberg, Alexander   188
Holzhey, Helmut   64
Homer   173
Hoppe, Vinzenz   24
Horkheimer, Max   1f., 55, 73, 99, 107f., 113
Hoy, David Couzens   39
Huff, Micha   116
Hullot-Kentor, Robert   61
Hulse, Michael   7f., 33, 152
Hume, David   55
Huyssen, Andreas   2f., 32, 39, 47f., 71, 82, 89–93, 99–101, 148, 150, 191, 198, 239

Imlinger, Fabienne   182
Iovene, Paola   192
Iversen, Stefan   105, 110

Jäger, Christian   24
Jäger, Lorenz   34, 59, 95, 99
James, C.L.R.   72, 189
Jameson, Fredric   3f., 24, 38, 57, 59, 68f., 72f., 79, 147–149, 152, 177f., 192
Jannidis, Fotis   187f.
Jay, Martin   25, 59, 67, 72, 127, 154
Jennings, Michael W.   93
Jephcott, Edmund   26, 56, 73, 80, 91–95, 97, 102, 105f., 111f., 128, 199
Jongeneel, Els   221
Joyce, James   88, 118f.
Jünger, Ernst   223
Jung, Franz   219

Kacandes, Irene   132, 190, 217f., 238
Kafka, Franz   48, 65, 88, 90
Kaku, Michio   149, 152–154
Kampa, Daniel   48
Kant, Immanuel   3, 10–23, 31, 55, 58, 60, 63–67, 70, 75, 94, 114, 119, 126, 147, 157, 163, 165, 170f., 196, 198, 238
Karpat, Berkan   148f.
Kittler, Friedrich   4
Klein, Naomi   61
Klein, Richard   55–58, 64, 67
Kleinschmidt, Erich   6, 196
Koch, Getrud   1, 51, 62, 73
Koepnick, Lutz   178

Kohler, Georg   64
Köhler, Horst   203
Korsch, Karl   31
Koschorke, Albrecht   26, 144f.
Koselleck, Reinhart   20, 22, 27, 41, 46f., 49f., 52, 61–63, 72, 98, 123, 126, 144, 186
Köster, Werner   149
Kracauer, Siegfried   31, 48, 71, 90, 136f., 192
Kreuder, Peter   213, 216
Kreuzer, Johann   56f., 64, 67
Krüger, Horst   60

Lacan, Jacques   79, 176f.
LaCapra, Dominick   239
Lang, Fritz   1, 97, 107
Langenohl, Andreas   210
Langston, Richard   1–3, 9, 23–25, 38, 45, 67, 70, 72, 74–76, 81, 84, 87, 105, 119f., 150, 154, 171, 178–180, 186, 194, 196, 198, 208
Latour, Bruno   172f., 187f., 194
League, Kathleen   57
Lehr, Andreas   48, 85
Leibniz, Gottfried Wilhelm   17, 41f., 129, 201
Lejeune, Philippe   217
Lenin, Vladimir Ilyich   85, 219
Leopold, David   59, 143
Leskov, Nikolai Semyonovich   43
Levitas, Ruth   59, 62
Lewandowski, Rainer   1
Lewis, Michael   61
Liebknecht, Wilhelm   183–185, 187f.
Liebman, Stuart   1, 15
Löwenthal, Leo   1
Long, Jonathan   27
Lotman, Yuri Mikhailovich   45
Lovell, David W.   59
Luhmann, Niklas   27, 31, 34, 37, 46, 56, 67, 74, 144, 192
Lukács, Georg   8, 24, 31, 34, 40, 57, 68, 88, 172
Lukes, Steven   59
Lutze, Peter C.   9

Index of Persons

Mach, Ernst 152
Maler, Henri 59
Malkmus, Bernard 31, 81
Mann, Thomas 88
Marasco, Robyn 97–99
Marcuse, Herbert 113
Marsh, Nicky 182
Marten, Susanne 84
Martens, Gunther 1, 3, 22, 45, 74, 84
Marx, Karl 2f., 17, 23, 31, 54–56, 59f., 62, 66f., 71–73, 94, 135f., 160, 169, 174, 176, 178–180, 182–185, 187, 191, 194–196, 228
Maslow, Arkadi 219
Maxwell, Barry 28, 52, 63
McBride, Patrizia C. 31, 43, 82f., 192
McClintock, Anne 150, 152
McFarland, James 209
McGettigan, Andrew 31, 36
McHale, Brian 168
McLaughlin, Kevin 8, 36
McLuhan, Marshall 77
Melas, Natalie 170, 189
Méliès, Georges 14
Menke, Bettine 34
Menke, Christoph 57f.
Menninghaus, Winfried 24, 34
Meretoja, Hanna 27
Mertes, Valentin 25, 124
Michel, Sascha 44
Mieth, Corinna 63, 87
Milfull, John 107
Miller, Matthew 23, 25, 48, 67, 71, 154, 171, 207
Montezuma II 229
Moore, Samuel 195
More, Thomas 125f., 143
Moretti, Franco 22
Mörike, Eduard 97, 102
Mosès, Stéphane 34
Müller, Harro 31, 56, 76f., 80, 83, 87, 172, 175, 211
Müller, Heiner 150
Müller, Joachim 149
Müller, Michael 233
Müller-Doohm, Stefan 1, 54–57, 59, 64, 67, 75, 95, 103, 127, 139

Murray, Sarah E. 202
Musil, Robert 23, 48, 90, 161

Nafe, Pascal 218
Nägele, Rainer 42f., 67
Nebrig, Alexander 214
Negri, Antonio 98
Negt, Oskar 2, 5, 22–25, 40f., 43, 45, 54, 57, 63, 67, 71, 74f., 79, 86f., 105, 119, 154, 166f., 171, 173, 175, 180, 184, 192, 194, 196, 211, 221, 227, 242
Nell, Renée 139
Neumann, Klaus 148
Newton, Isaac 18f., 154, 213, 215
Nicholsen, Shierry Weber 88
Nielsen, Henrik Skov 29, 104f., 109f., 163, 168
Nieraad, Jürgen 233
Niffenegger, Audrey 123
Nikulin, Dmitri 117, 120, 123–125
Nousek, Katrina Louise 62

Orsós, Ferenc 236
Overy, Richard 2
Ovid 117

Pabst, Reinhard 97, 107
Paden, Roger 59, 174, 182
Palmer, Alan 244
Parikka, Jussi 172
Parkinson, Anna 63, 113
Paterson, Tony 231
Pauval, Vincent 1, 3, 45, 84
Pavsek, Christopher 9, 15, 23f., 30, 33, 48, 50, 52f., 81, 87, 96, 114, 130, 166, 188, 196f.
Pechersky, Alexander Aronovich 232
Pensky, Max 2, 86, 113
Peters, Sibylle 33
Pflugmacher, Torsten 113
Phelan, James 115–117, 120, 122, 144
Piccone, Paul 55
Pickford, Henry 66, 113
Pielmann, Arlette 127
Pike, David L. 162
Piot, Charles 189
Plass, Ulrich 68, 85, 94, 97, 100, 107f.

Plato 19, 104, 123, 180
Pliny the Elder 209
Pluhar, Werner S. 17
Pollmanns, Marion 24
Prince, Gerald 182
Prior, Arthur Norman 123
Proust, Marcel 88, 101, 176
Pushkin, Alexander Sergeyevich 174

Rabinowitz, Peter J. 115 f.
Rack, Jochen 86
Radisoglou, Alexis 132, 169, 171 f., 182, 206, 227, 244
Rancière, Jacques 14, 69, 171
Raulff, Ulrich 92
Ray, Larry 175
Redmond, Dennis 26, 71, 93–95, 97, 102 f., 105, 199
Reemtsma, Jan Philipp 150
Reichmann, Wolfgang 49, 81, 185 f., 200
Reitan, Rolf 105, 110
Renard, Maurice 8
Renner, Kaspar 24
Rentschler, Eric 24
Ricardo, David 160
Richardson, Brian 29, 103 f., 106, 109, 116–120, 130, 168, 183, 195, 204, 215
Richter, Gerhard 5, 61, 63
Ricœur, Paul 40
Rihm, Wolfgang 229
Rilke, Rainer Maria 47, 90
Roberts, Adam 151
Roberts, David 80, 83, 156, 211
Robertson, Roland 182
Robinson, Kim Stanley 148
Rössler, Reto 232
Rosenfeld, Gavriel 65
Rosenstrauch, Hazel 232
Ross, Kristin 169
Rothberg, Michael 238 f.
Rubin, Andrew 57
Ruschig, Ulrich 72
Ryan, Marie-Laure 77, 110, 122 f., 193 f.

Sachs, Nelly 214
Santner, Eric L. 212, 243
Sargent, Lyman Tower 62

Scheffel, Michael 221
Schenzinger, Karl Aloys 161
Scherer, Christina 83, 207
Scherpe, Klaus 1, 80
Schiesser, Giaco 24
Schiffauer, Werner 149
Schiller, Friedrich 6
Schiller, Hans-Ernst 58–60, 62 f.
Schlüpmann, Heide 51, 143
Schmid, Thomas 232
Schmidt, Ulrich 233
Schmitt, Carl 11–13, 110
Schmitt, Stefanie 124
Scholem, Emmy 222, 225
Scholem, Gershom 219, 222, 229
Scholem, Werner 201, 212, 217–231, 235, 242
Schönberg, Arnold 1
Schönfeld, Martin 10, 18 f.
Schreiber, Dominik 182
Schröder, Helmut 149
Schroer, Markus 67
Schütte, Wolfram 232 f.
Schütz, Erhard 84, 179, 233
Schuh, Franz 24
Schulte, Christian 1, 3, 23 f., 45, 49, 73 f., 77, 84 f., 113 f., 116, 124, 126, 196, 233
Sebald, W.G. 2–4, 31, 45, 79, 150, 198, 233
Seebold, Elmar 5, 75, 126, 194
Seneca the Younger 209
Sennett, Richard 160–162, 164 f.
Şenocak, Zafer 148 f.
Shahan, Cyrus 23
Siebers, Winfried 124
Siegel, Don 14
Siegert, Bernhard 78 f.
Singles, Kathleen 65
Sloterdijk, Peter 171
Smith, Adam 160
Smith, Eric D. 147 f.
Smith, Nicholas H. 64
Sohn-Rethel, Alfred 31
Sonnenfeld, Barry 14
Sontheimer, Kurt 231
Spivak, Gayatri Chakravorty 170 f.
Spoerhase, Carlos 214
Spufford, Francis 178

Stanitzek, Georg 80, 186
Stanzel, Franz Karl 105
Steinbrink, Bernd 180
Steinke, Ronen 231
Stiegler, Bernard 54
Stiegler, Bernd-Alexander 81
Stifter, Adalbert 214
Stoermer, Eugene F. 172
Stollmann, Rainer 1–3, 45, 74, 84 f., 94, 152, 162, 180, 192, 202, 211, 221, 228, 233
Stolt, Kerstin 1
Storm, Theodor 214
Suvin, Darko 151
Syberberg, Hans-Jürgen 234
Szendy, Peter 10–16, 110, 125 f.
Szondi, Peter 101 f.

Tawada, Yoko 5 f., 8, 158
Taylor, Nathan 192
Teichert, Gabi 144
Tellkamp, Uwe 178
Terdiman, Richard 238
Thomas, D.M. 123
Thompson, William 135
Thorne, Christian 92
Tiedemann, Rolf 55, 57, 66
Tomlinson, John 182, 192
Traverso, Enzo 72
Tretyakov, Sergei Mikhailovich 31
Trotsky, Leon 178 f., 222, 224

Uecker, Matthias 211
Ueding, Gert 180

Vázquez-Arroyo, Antonio Y. 72
Vedder, Ulrike 214–216
Vennewitz, Leila 1, 233
Verne, Jules 151
Vertov, Dziga 178 f.
Villarejo, Amy 63
Virno, Paolo 33, 244
Visch, Marijke 80
Vogel, Jakob 33
Vogl, Joseph 40, 53, 214 f.

Voltaire 56, 213
Voßkamp, Wilhelm 81, 211, 223

Walsh, Richard 104, 106, 109
Wang Hui 191 f., 228
Wankhammer, Johannes 116
Warhol, Robyn 116
Webb, Darren 182
Weber, Hermann 218, 222
Weber, Max 160 f., 228
Weber, Philipp 34–36, 171, 175
Weidner, Daniel 27, 33, 61
Weigel, Sigrid 35, 42, 179
Weiss, Peter 150
Weixler, Antonius 217
Weizsäcker, Ernst von 237
Wellbery, David E. 187
Wellmer, Albrecht 58
Wentzer, Thomas Schwarz 67
Werner, Lukas 217
Wesche, Tilo 63–66, 73, 92
Wetters, Kirk 209
Weymann, Ulrike 113
Whitebook, Joel 57
Willer, Stefan 27, 33, 61, 148
Wirt, Candace 67
Witte, Karsten 5, 150, 163, 173
Wojak, Irmtrud 231
Wolf, Fred Alan 149
Wolff, Christian 17, 114
Wolin, Richard 57, 60, 63
Wussow, Philipp von 60, 100

Yan Haiping 191
Yildiz, Yasemin 93

Zadoff, Mirjam 218, 222, 225
Zangl, Veronika 233
Zeller, Christoph 30, 219
Ziok, Ilona 232
Zipes, Jack 24
Žižek, Slavoj 57 f., 98
Zohn, Harry 36 f.
Zuidervaart, Lambert 54
Zwicky, Fritz 152

Index of Works

1 Works by Alexander Kluge

Abschied von den Lokomotiven [Farewell to Locomotives]   52, 179–181, 185f.
Abschied von einer Metapher des Fortschritts [Farewell to a Metaphor of Progress]   179
Abschied von gestern [*Yesterday Girl*]   50f., 179, 232–234
Air Raid   2
Außerirdische unterwegs [Extraterrestrials on the Move]   7, 155, 157, 184

Bauch der Milchstraße [Belly of the Milky Way]   205, 207, 213
Begegnung mit dem Unbekannten [Encounter with the Unknown]   7
Besuch im Weißen Haus [Visitors in the White House]   7, 10, 155–157

Chronik der Gefühle [Chronicle of Feelings]   1f., 4, 6, 37, 51, 148, 152, 181, 190
Chronik von Pangäa bis heute [Chronicle of Pangea till Today]   174, 179

Das Bohren harter Bretter [The Boring of Hard Boards]   227, 244
Das fünfte Buch [The Fifth Book]   7, 168f., 175f., 188, 199
Das Labyrinth der zärtlichen Kraft [The Labyrinth of Tender Power]   56
Das Politische als Intensität alltäglicher Gefühle [The Political as Intensity of Everyday Feelings]   85
Das Schaf von Rom [The Sheep of Rome]   237
Das Schöne ist fehlerfrei [The Beautiful is Flawless]   113, 116, 118, 120f., 123, 125, 128, 144, 149, 196
Der Angriff der Gegenwart auf die übrige Zeit [*The Assault of the Present on the Rest of Time*]   33
Der Kosmos als Kino [The Cosmos as Cinema]   44, 152
Der Luftangriff auf Halberstadt am 8. April 1945 [The Attack by Air on Halberstadt on April 8, 1945]   1–3
Der Sechsjährige in mir und der gestirnte Himmel über mir [The Six-Year-Old within Me and the Starry Sky above Me]   17, 198, 200–205, 212
Der Teufel im Weißen Haus [The Devil in the White House]   8, 156
Die Aktualität Adornos [The Actuality of Adorno]   1, 84, 86, 181
Die blaue Gefahr [The Blue Peril]   8
Die Entsprechung einer Oase [Corresponding to an Oasis]   44, 186
Die Küche des Glücks [The Kitchen of Happiness]   56
Die Lebensläufer und ihre Lebensgeschichten [The Course-of-Lifers and Their Life Stories]   200
Die Lücke, die der Teufel läßt [The Gap the Devil Leaves Us]   7f., 10, 31, 33, 48, 56, 70, 79, 84f., 94, 125, 132, 152, 154, 156, 160, 168, 173, 175f., 201, 205, 206f., 218
Die Mondkräfte und der Endsieg [Lunar Forces and Ultimate Victory]   7, 160
Die Revolution ist ein Organismus voller Überraschungen [The Revolution is an Organism Full of Surprises]   168, 175f.
Die Schnellsten werden die Letzten sein [The Fastest Will Be the Last]   168
Dunsthimmel über mir und das Ding in mir [Hazy Sky above Me and the Thing inside Me]   198
Durch Armut reich, das Ich [Rich from Poverty, the I]   203

Ein deutscher Gelehrter in Persien [A German Scholar in Persia]   168
Ein später Sieg des Spartakus [A Late Victory of Spartacus]   232
Ein Streit mit meiner Mutter [A Fight with My Mother]   200
Eine schwer zu deutende Heldentat [A Heroic Deed That Is Hard to Interpret]   185
Einen Ausweg muß es geben [There Has to Be A Way Out]   7
Eisenroß um 2006 [Iron Steed Around 2006]   186

Ferngespräche [Long-Distance Conversations]   180, 192, 202, 221, 228, 235, 242
Futur antérieur [Future Anterior]   79, 176

Geister, wie Walter Benjamin sie beschreibt [Ghosts as Walter Benjamin Describes Them]   31
Gelegenheitsarbeit einer Sklavin [Part-Time Work of a Domestic Slave]   81, 219
Geschichten vom Kino [*Cinema Stories*]   7f., 44, 152, 193
Geschichten vom Weltall [Stories of the Cosmos]   152, 173
Gesellschaftliche Prozesse als Erzählung [Social Processes as Narration]   155, 160
Glückliche Umstände, leihweise [Happy Circumstances, On Loan]   152
'Grausam wie ein Mongole' ['Cruel As a Mongolian']   7, 10
Gußeiserne Balkons als Saturnring oder Saturnring aus Gußeisen [Cast Iron Balconies as Saturnian Ring or Saturn's Ring out of Cast Iron]   56

Hoffnung bei Sonnenaufgang [Hope at Sunrise]   32, 37–43, 47, 49, 149, 159, 201
Hündchen Laika [Little Dog Laika]   94
Hybride Formen des Zirkus [Hybrid Forms of the Circus]   8

Im Weltall braucht man keine Lesebrille, Helge Schneider und Peter Berling im Orbit [One Needs No Reading Glasses in the Cosmos, Helge Schneider and Peter Berling in Orbit]   152
Intelligenz zweiten Grades [Second-Order Intelligence]   7

Katzen im Weltraum [Cats in Outer Space]   95
Keine falsche Unmittelbarkeit [No False Immediacy]   181
Kongs große Stunde [Kong's Great Hour]   7, 95, 128, 168f., 174, 198f., 203
König Dampf, Kaiserin Elektrizität [King Steam, Empress Electricity]   182, 184–186, 188
Kot von Außerirdischen [Extraterrestrials' Shit]   7, 84

Lebendigkeit von 1931 [Liveness from 1931]   201, 218, 221–224, 226, 228–230
Lebensläufe [*Case Histories* and *Attendance List for a Funeral*]   1, 51, 53, 233
Lernprozesse mit tödlichem Ausgang [Learning Processes with a Deadly Outcome]   20, 44, 57, 62, 113, 148, 151, 152, 162

Mein Großvater mütterlicherseits [My Maternal Grandfather]   200
Mein wahres Motiv [My True Motive]   200
Mentalesisch [Mentalese]   8

Nachricht an Außerirdische [News Item for Extraterrestrials]   174
Nachricht [News Item/Military Intelligence]   4
Nachrichten aus der ideologischen Antike [News from Ideological Antiquity]   2, 67, 192

Neue Erscheinungsform des Großen Drachen [New Manifestation Form of the Great Dragon]   175
Neue Geschichten [New Stories/New Histories]   1 f., 199, 210

Personen und Reden [Persons and Speeches]   1, 86 f., 181

Samstag in Utopia [Saturday in Utopia]   56, 60, 125–146, 184
Schlachtbeschreibung [The Battle]   2–4, 9
Schneller als das Schicksal [Faster than Fate]   193–195, 237
Schwarzer Tropfen/Bailyscher Tropfen [Black Drop/Baily's Beads]   7
Sechs Lokomotiven, Fahrlässigkeit und die Folgen [Six Locomotives, Recklessness, and the Consequences]   185
Sind Photonen individuell? [Are Photons Individual?]   205 f.
Snowball-Earth   7, 188, 190 f.

Tempus, Aevum, Aeternitas [Time, Age, Eternity]   168
The Devil's Blind Spot   175
The Devil's Blind Spot   7 f., 33, 56, 113, 152
The Sharpest Ideology – That Reality Appeals to Its Realistic Character   27, 80 f.
Theorie der Erzählung [Theory of Storytelling]   17, 30, 75, 83, 166, 186, 188, 191, 199 f.
Tür an Tür mit einem anderen Leben [Door to Door with an Other Life]   212
Tür an Tür mit einem anderen Leben [Door to Door with an Other Life]   7–10, 17 f., 31 f., 37 f., 43, 49, 52, 57, 70, 91, 113, 149, 152–157, 159 f., 164, 168, 174 f., 179–181, 186, 188, 191, 198, 200, 205, 207

Unser ständiger Begleiter, der Mond [Our Constant Companion, the Moon]   205–207, 213
Unsere Vorfahren, die Sterne [Our Ancestors, the Stars]   18, 49, 152, 205, 208, 210, 212 f., 215 f.
Uralte Freunde der Kernkraft [Age-Old Friends of Nuclear Power]   169

Walter Benjamin kommt bis Halberstadt [Walter Benjamin Comes As Far As Halberstadt]   31
Waschleppas Atlas der Dampflokomotiven [Waschleppa's Atlas of Steam Locomotives]   175
Weltzeit [World Time]   6
"Wer ein Wort des Trostes spricht, ist ein Verräter". 48 Geschichten für Fritz Bauer ["Whoever speaks a word of consolation is a traitor". 48 Stories for Fritz Bauer]   7, 201, 232–244
Wie fängt man an der EU-Grenze das Böse ab? [How Does One Nab Evil at the EU-Border?]   168
Wie in einer anderen Welt, durch eine unsichtbare Wand vom Übrigen getrennt [As in an Other World, Separated from the Rest by an Invisible Wall]   237
Wir Glückskinder der Ersten Globalisierung [We Fortunate Children of the First Globalization]   8, 38, 113, 149, 155 f., 162, 168, 191

Zeugen aus einer anderen Welt [Witnesses from an Other World]   201, 234, 237, 240 f., 243

2 Works co-authored by Oskar Negt and Alexander Kluge

Der unterschätzte Mensch [The Underestimated Human Being]   87, 196
Geschichte und Eigensinn [*History and Obstinacy*]   5, 23–26, 40 f., 45, 54, 57, 67, 71, 74 f., 79, 113, 167, 171, 173, 175, 180, 194, 211, 227
Maßverhältnisse des Politischen [Politics as Relations of Measure]   45, 173, 189, 192, 221, 242
Öffentlichkeit und Erfahrung [*Public Sphere and Experience*]   74, 86, 166 f.

3 Selected Works by Other Authors

Adorno, Theodor W.
  Ästhetische Theorie [*Aesthetic Theory*]   57, 61, 63, 75
  Der böse Kamerad [The bad comrade]   95
  Der Essay als Form [The Essay as Form]   88, 100, 163
  Groß und klein [Great and small]   26, 91, 94
  Heliotrop [Heliotrope]   76, 95–110, 112, 128, 130, 204, 215
  Lücken [Gaps]   111 f., 114, 116, 129
  Minima Moralia   26, 32, 53, 56, 60 f., 70–73, 75 f., 78 f., 85, 88, 91–96, 98–101, 103, 107, 109, 111, 114, 127–130, 138, 143, 146, 199, 204
  Ne cherchez plus mon coeur [Look for my heart no longer]   128 f., 138
  Negative Dialektik [*Negative Dialectics*]   26, 52, 54, 56–59, 66–69, 72, 75, 79 f., 102, 141, 176, 188
  Standort des Erzählers im zeitgenössischen Roman [The Position of the Narrator in the Contemporary Novel]   75, 88, 235
  Zum Ende [Finale]   95, 101

Adorno, Theodor W., Ernst Bloch, and Horst Krüger
  Something's Missing   60

Benjamin, Walter
  Das Passagen-Werk [*The Arcades Project*]   8, 30 f., 35–37, 152
  Der Erzähler [The Storyteller]   32, 43, 190
  Einbahnstraße [*One-Way Street*]   31–34, 68, 97
  Goethes Wahlverwandtschaften [Goethe's Elective Affinities]   66, 102
  The Storyteller. Short Stories   32
  Über den Begriff der Geschichte [Theses on the Philosophy of History]   36, 93

Bloch, Ernst
  Heritage of Our Times   58
  The Principle of Hope   58, 62, 68
  The Spirit of Utopia   58
  Traces   58
  Zur Ontologie des Noch-Nicht-Seins [On the Ontology of Not-Yet-Being]   42

Blumenberg, Hans
    On a Lineage of the Idea of Progress   70, 209f.

Grimmelshausen, Hans Jakob Christoffel von
    Der abentheuerliche Simplicissimus Teutsch [The Adventures of Simplicissimus]   3f.

Horkheimer, Max, and Theodor W. Adorno
    Dialectic of Enlightenment   2, 55–57, 59, 107

Jameson, Fredric
    Archaeologies of the Future   59, 147f., 177
    Late Marxism   57, 68f., 72f.
    Marxism and Form   68
    Notes on Globalization as a Philosophical Issue   177
    On Negt and Kluge   24, 38
    The Ancients and the Postmoderns   178
    The Antinomies of Realism   3
    The Geopolitical Aesthetic   147, 177
    The Seeds of Time   57
    War and Representation   3f.

Kant, Immanuel
    Anthropology from a Pragmatic Point of View   11
    Critique of Practical Reason   16f., 21, 198
    Critique of Pure Reason   15, 19
    Critique of the Power of Judgment   11
    Groundwork for the Metaphysics of Morals   20
    The Conflict of the Faculties   11, 13
    Thoughts on the True Estimation of Living Forces   19
    Universal Natural History and Theory of the Heavens   11, 18f.

Lukács, Georg
    The Theory of the Novel   8, 34

Marx, Karl
    Das Kapital [Capital]   2, 135f., 228
    Grundrisse [Foundations]   169
    The Class Struggles in France, 1848–1850   178f.

Marx, Karl, and Friedrich Engels
    Manifest der Kommunistischen Partei [The Communist Manifesto]   169, 194f.

Negt, Oskar
    Modernisierung im Zeichen des Drachens [Modernization in the Sign of the Dragon]   221

Sebald, W.G.
    Luftkrieg und Literatur [On the Natural History of Destruction]   2f., 31

Szendy, Peter
　Kant in the Land of Extraterrestrials　10, 14

Index of Terms

9/11 149, 153
1989 33, 45, 62, 77, 147, 152f., 162, 173, 175–177, 191, 195, 219, 221, 228

above and below 1, 5, 10, 17, 20, 45, 76, 133, 163, 201, 238
– strategies from above 1, 4f., 45f., 147, 159
– strategies from below 1, 4f., 45f., 147, 159
Adorno Prize 1, 4, 7, 86
adult 96, 99, 101, 105, 107–109, 112, 128, 130, 198, 203f., 220
aesthetics 30, 57f., 68–70, 72, 74, 79–85, 90, 92, 110, 113f., 116, 150, 171, 185, 191, 233, 241
alienation 8, 22, 33, 40, 43, 57–59, 68, 73, 88, 166, 172
allosensus 124
Allotria 99f.
anachronism 9, 89, 95, 116, 166, 184, 202
angel 73, 92, 150f., 240
– angel of history 3, 31, 45, 73, 150
– rescuing angel 96f., 106
Anthropocene 29, 172, 187f., 194
anthropology 5, 11, 34, 38, 41–43, 54, 63, 67, 86, 128, 180, 187
– anthropological materialism 42f., 67
– materialist anthropology 43, 54, 67f.
– philosophical anthropology 53f., 60, 67f.
anthropomorphism 3f., 43, 46, 49, 78, 102, 163, 172, 187f., 202, 207f., 210f.
anti-Semitism 66, 91, 100, 201, 218, 222, 231, 235f.
apprenticeship 111f., 165
associative networks 86
astrology 56
astrophysics 10, 16, 18, 32, 44, 46, 70, 114f., 117, 121–123, 149, 152f., 168, 173, 205
astrosociology 11
asynchrony 77, 150
Auschwitz 51, 55, 57, 64, 66, 87, 112, 188, 231, 236f., 239

Ausweg (see also way out) 7, 52, 57, 70, 76f., 79, 85, 111, 127, 190
avant-garde 3, 9, 76, 82, 103, 149f., 219

Bauhaus University 213, 216
beauty 110–126, 128, 134, 137, 144, 149, 194, 196
bespiritedness 185, 188f.
biography 1, 33, 97, 102, 127, 138f., 199, 203, 217–220, 222–227, 229–231, 245
– bio-graphy 201, 218, 229
– red-thread biography 228f.
birth 18, 124, 153, 207f.
blank spot 64, 69, 233, 243
bombing 1f., 4, 45, 150, 162f., 199, 236
books 1, 5, 7, 17, 87, 130, 198
Buchenwald 201, 218, 220, 223f.

capital, capitalism 2f., 9, 20, 23, 53–55, 59–61, 66, 69, 72f., 75, 89, 92, 107, 109, 135f., 138, 141, 148, 150f., 160, 167–171, 175, 177f., 181, 185, 191f., 228, 242
catastrophe 1, 3, 22, 26f., 29, 31, 42, 51, 61, 63, 65, 70, 73–77, 88, 92–94, 97, 111, 113f., 116, 120, 126f., 141, 146, 150, 169, 172, 181, 185, 191, 196–198, 219, 221, 227, 231, 233, 235–239, 241f., 246
– colonialist catastrophe 229
– permanent catastrophe 72, 75f., 78, 87, 92, 134, 142, 166, 233
– total catastrophe 75, 85
causality 18, 44, 72, 82, 151, 185
chance 16, 49, 59, 72, 77, 163, 185, 205f., 212, 215f., 228
Chernobyl 72, 75f., 169
child 9, 24, 26, 38, 95–103, 105–109, 112f., 128–131, 149, 155f., 162, 168, 191, 194, 203
China 44, 168, 178, 191f., 218, 221, 223, 228, 230
cinema 1f., 7, 15, 30, 33, 43f., 48, 50f., 57, 71, 81, 96, 114, 136, 144, 178, 191, 193, 232

class struggle   36, 167, 169, 179, 228
clouds   183, 187, 205 f.
coherence   18, 74–76, 87, 114 f., 131
coldness   188
color   41, 68, 96 f., 102, 106, 132, 187
commodity   53, 68, 71, 136, 168
communism   33, 59, 62, 147, 150, 169, 175–178, 182, 184–186, 188, 190 f., 194 f., 218, 220, 228
Communist Party   177, 195, 219, 222, 225, 227
complexity   18, 189, 205, 218, 220
concatenation   82, 182
concentration   179, 182, 186
concentration camps   93, 141, 218, 223, 231
conjunction   4, 22 f., 28, 42, 61, 66, 86, 105, 121, 140, 166, 174 f., 184, 194, 204, 214, 233, 236
connectivity   164, 168, 173, 176, 179–186, 188, 192, 197
constellation   4, 22, 34, 52, 56 f., 66, 75, 78, 80, 85, 87, 91, 94, 111, 113, 121 f., 127, 170, 173, 181, 190, 201, 209, 238, 240, 242
contingency   28, 44, 57, 70, 72, 151
conversion   4 f., 27 f., 45, 78, 99, 117, 120, 143, 161, 172, 197, 199, 239
cooperation, co-operation   19, 21, 85, 131 f., 227–230, 236, 245 f.
cosmic motifs, cosmos, cosmology   9–14, 16–19, 32, 35, 41, 43 f., 69, 82, 97, 99, 110, 114 f., 149, 152 f., 172 f., 205 f., 212
cosmopolitanism   10, 12 f., 99, 171
crisis   47 f., 66, 90, 93, 150, 160, 187, 211, 219
critical theory   1 f., 5, 10, 21, 28–31, 50, 52, 54 f., 63, 72 f., 76, 78, 89 f., 98 f., 114, 125, 127, 134, 143, 145–148, 153, 165, 168, 172, 180 f., 190, 211
Cross of Merit   203

dash   214–216
death   3 f., 18, 24, 26, 39, 43, 60, 66, 94, 101, 117, 121, 125, 140, 142–144, 176, 189, 199, 214, 218, 220 f., 224, 231–233, 235, 242
deportation   168, 236 f.

despair   4, 29, 64–67, 70, 73, 76, 80, 97 f., 100–102, 109, 111, 119, 144, 177, 184, 197, 200, 231–234, 246
dialectics   2, 23, 25, 35 f., 42, 55 f., 61 f., 69–72, 83, 86, 93 f., 98, 107, 123–125, 143, 148, 169 f., 173, 188, 191, 194, 196 f.
– diabolical dialectics (see also Miller)   48, 71, 154
– negative dialectics (see also Adorno)   26, 53, 55 f., 58 f., 62, 64, 66 f., 69, 72 f., 75, 78 f., 87, 97, 99, 102, 104, 106–108, 111, 115, 117 f., 125, 128 f., 140 f., 145
dialogue   10, 15, 39, 47, 66 f., 80, 87, 109, 115 f., 118–125, 131, 156, 158 f., 161 f., 170 f., 176, 180 f., 183, 190 f., 194–196, 203, 213–215, 219, 224, 226 f., 229, 238
dictatorship   20, 30, 42, 198, 218
digital humanities   22, 71, 192
disjunction   28, 173, 204, 211, 236
documentary   5, 80, 144, 199, 219, 229, 232 f.
dogs, doggedness   3, 26, 91, 94 f., 100
door logic (see also Siegert)   78 f.

Earth   6, 8, 13 f., 38 f., 45, 49, 56, 85, 94, 155 f., 158, 168–170, 172, 174, 188–191, 206, 238
Eigensinn (see also obstinacy)   3, 22–25, 67, 203, 211
– "Das eigensinnige Kind" ["The Obstinate Child"]   24
embodiment   25, 76, 82, 120, 125, 132, 136, 150, 191, 204 f.
equivalence   111, 115, 122, 142 f., 159
evidentiality   202
exile   1, 55, 72, 91, 128, 182, 231
expectation   39, 42, 46 f., 63, 102 f., 132
experience   1–5, 9, 13, 15, 17, 20, 23, 25–27, 29, 33, 36, 38, 40, 43, 46–50, 52, 57, 59, 62 f., 66, 68, 70, 72–74, 77–83, 85, 88–91, 96, 98, 100–102, 105–110, 112, 116, 119 f., 123, 126, 128, 130, 134, 143, 145 f., 152, 160, 164, 166 f., 171 f., 176 f., 180 f., 196 f., 199, 203, 210 f., 213–218, 234, 244–246
experiment   3–5, 21 f., 25 f., 28, 30, 32, 43 f., 52, 57, 60, 62, 65, 67, 71, 82, 89, 110,

Index of Terms — 299

119f., 123, 125, 130, 133, 139, 141, 143–146, 150, 159, 164, 166–168, 170f., 173, 181, 189, 193, 196f., 199–201, 205, 208, 210f., 215, 217f., 220f., 229, 232f., 235, 237, 243f.
extraterrestrials 2, 5–18, 20, 22, 32, 46, 48, 69, 73, 84, 126, 147–165, 174, 184, 201, 234–241, 243

factography 219
failure, imperfection 2, 4, 48, 61, 68, 70, 93, 96, 114, 119, 129, 166, 197f., 210, 238
fairy tale 1, 5, 24f., 59, 68, 93, 96, 178, 194f.
fantasy 9, 64, 105, 119, 125f., 140, 145, 148, 193, 196, 232
farewell 50–52, 179–182, 185f., 191, 236
fascism 2, 20, 30, 78, 91–93, 95f., 150, 236, 242, 245
Federal Republic of Germany 4, 141, 167, 203, 223, 231
Flaschenpost (see also message in a bottle) 1f., 87
flawlessness 114–118
focalization 115, 117, 128–131, 134, 137, 139f., 162f., 187, 215, 221
folk legend 194
Frankfurt School 1, 5, 63, 67, 113, 127, 134, 143
Frankfurter Allgemeine Zeitung 224, 226f.
Fukushima 168f.
fusional groups 227f., 244
futurity 1–5, 9f., 17, 21f., 26–28, 31–33, 37, 39–44, 46–50, 52, 57, 61f., 65f., 68–70, 74–78, 80–83, 85–87, 90, 97f., 100, 102, 110, 112f., 120–122, 127, 130, 136, 138, 143–151, 158, 161–163, 165, 170–178, 182–185, 188f., 191–200, 203, 210, 215–218, 223, 229, 239, 247–251
– future-making 5, 15, 25, 27, 40f., 147, 151, 174, 221, 224, 235f.
– future sense 2–4, 22, 25f., 28f., 57, 63, 105, 108f., 111, 113, 120, 125, 128, 143, 146–148, 151, 164f., 171, 173, 178, 181, 184f., 187, 191, 196f., 199, 205, 210, 212f., 216–231, 233, 235, 237f., 240, 242f., 245f.

galaxies 46, 122, 154, 200, 205, 207
gap aesthetics 57, 69–86, 90, 92, 110, 185, 233, 241
gender 24, 95, 102, 143f.
genocide 2, 20, 30, 51, 66, 93, 141, 148, 198, 218, 231–236
geopolitics 11, 14–16, 46, 157, 167, 177
German Democratic Republic 45
Germany 1f., 7, 9, 33, 42, 45, 50f., 53, 63, 82, 112, 141, 144, 149, 155, 175, 178, 183, 191f., 203, 211–214, 216, 225, 231f., 236f., 244f.
globalization 8, 11f., 14, 29f., 37f., 40f., 67, 91, 113, 132, 149, 155, 162, 168–172, 175–177, 179–182, 188f., 191f., 195f., 206, 218, 220, 242
gravity 31, 45, 75, 154, 158, 186, 215
grief 141, 221, 242

Halberstadt 1–4, 31, 45, 199
happiness 4, 18, 28f., 56, 63f., 78, 86f., 97f., 106, 112, 120, 126, 129f., 135, 137f., 152, 174, 194
heliotrope, heliotropism 3, 5, 13, 32, 35, 37, 47, 49f., 70, 88, 91, 95–98, 100–103, 105f., 108f., 126, 139, 143, 146, 173, 183f., 213, 218, 230
– secret heliotropism 36, 49, 97f., 100, 109, 183
history 3, 8, 11, 17, 20–24, 26, 28, 31–33, 36f., 40, 43–46, 48, 56, 59, 63, 66–70, 72–74, 76f., 83, 85, 93, 97f., 109, 111, 113, 120, 143, 145, 150, 152–154, 162, 165, 167, 172, 174f., 178–180, 183, 185, 190f., 194, 198, 209, 211, 225, 229, 231f., 238f., 243
Holocaust 2f., 29, 91, 141, 198, 200f., 212, 224, 229, 231–246
hope 1–5, 10, 20–22, 29, 32f., 36–43, 45, 47, 49, 57f., 60, 63–69, 76, 80, 85, 87–89, 91f., 97–102, 109, 111, 113, 119, 129, 141, 144, 146, 149, 153, 155, 159, 175, 177, 184, 188, 191, 200f., 213f., 216, 218, 230, 233, 237, 240f., 243, 246
– anti-realist hope 26, 197
– counterfactual hope 4, 28f., 50–71, 73, 76–79, 84f., 87, 91f., 95, 99, 109f., 112f.,

120, 123, 126, 143, 145, 166, 178, 185, 193, 196, 202, 218, 230, 233, 237 f.
– hopeless, hopelessness   64, 66, 102, 230
– ironic hopefulness (see also Eshel)   37
– stock of hope   18, 43, 155
horizon   4 f., 10, 12 f., 16, 21, 29, 32 f., 36 f., 45–47, 57, 61, 63, 73 f., 76, 78–80, 82, 85, 87, 96–99, 103 f., 107 f., 112, 117, 119 f., 123, 125 f., 128, 130, 134, 140, 142, 145, 165, 169, 175–178, 182, 184, 186, 189–191, 195 f., 198, 200, 204–206, 212, 216, 218, 220, 244
Hubble Space Telescope   205, 213

inclusions   119, 174, 179
index, indexicality   26 f., 36 f., 65, 73, 75, 77, 79, 92, 99, 134, 169, 171, 178, 192, 199, 239
– secret index (see also Benjamin)   37, 141, 174
indifference   135, 138, 141 f.
intelligence   7 f., 16, 20, 156, 158
– military intelligence (see also *Nachricht*)   4, 218, 225, 240
intensification   3 f., 6, 38, 81, 139
intensity   6, 85, 111, 196, 200, 235
interlocutor, interlocution   1, 10, 26, 112, 115, 117–123, 127, 130 f., 139–142, 158 f., 162, 176, 179, 181, 183 f., 187, 190 f., 195, 204, 213–216, 226, 228–230
intimacy   96, 102, 108, 129, 199 f., 214, 243, 245
invisible, invisibility   5 f., 10, 15 f., 46, 48, 90, 112, 147, 151, 153 f., 156–158, 165, 178, 233, 237, 240
Iran   168

Jews   51, 66, 103, 112, 201, 218 f., 222, 224, 229, 231–233, 235–237, 239 f., 242

Kleist Prize   7, 9, 189

labor   5, 9, 20 f., 24, 40, 42, 50, 54, 67–69, 74, 93, 112 f., 119, 125, 134–136, 144, 151, 160–162, 167 f., 181, 185, 189, 192 f., 195, 198, 227, 238
– labor power   23, 111, 120

Lagrangian point   45
legible, legibility   36, 47, 52, 80, 83, 90, 171, 199, 220
life   4–6, 10 f., 13 f., 16–18, 20 f., 26, 30, 32, 35, 38 f., 41, 43, 45 f., 54, 58–60, 66, 69, 71 f., 74, 76, 79, 84, 87 f., 91, 94, 96 f., 99, 104, 106–109, 111–114, 120–125, 128, 134, 138, 142–145, 147, 149, 163–165, 176 f., 188 f., 198 f., 201, 203, 209, 214, 216–218, 220, 222, 224, 226, 228–230, 233, 235, 237, 241 f., 245
– life force   16, 122, 155, 164
– life writing   199 f., 217–231
– liveness   36, 201, 204, 218, 221–224, 226, 228–230
– other life   15, 20, 22, 32, 37, 60 f., 107 f., 113, 125, 143, 155, 162 f., 165, 184, 191, 199, 215, 228, 237, 241
locomotives   40, 52, 175, 179–181, 185 f., 191, 236
– locomotives of history (see also Marx)   178–180, 185
– trains   131, 137, 139, 178 f., 181 f., 185 f., 236 f.
  – toy trains   178, 184, 186
  – train of History   178

Mangelmutante   43, 54
Märchen   5, 59, 194 f.
Mars   10, 44, 62, 148, 151
Marxism   8, 22, 24, 28, 34, 42, 54, 59 f., 67–69, 72–74, 83, 90, 110, 137, 147, 151, 153, 166, 169 f., 173–178, 180–182, 195 f., 218 f., 223, 228
materialism   32, 36, 40, 42 f., 45, 47, 53 f., 66–68, 72, 98
mathematics   6, 68, 94, 112, 115, 122, 129, 143, 240
– mathematical equations   114 f., 122, 133, 135
memory   2, 4, 22, 36, 43, 83, 93, 95, 100 f., 108, 112, 141, 198 f., 203, 211 f., 233, 236, 238 f., 242, 244
– postmemory   238 f.
Menetekel (see also writing on the wall)   196

message in a bottle (see also *Flaschenpost*) 1f., 87, 91
metaphor 5, 19, 31, 45, 52, 72, 78, 92, 98, 102, 160, 176, 179–182, 187, 208, 216, 220
metaphysics 20, 41, 52, 55, 73, 79, 88, 114, 126, 136, 141, 143, 167, 177, 240
– metaphysical experience (see also Adorno) 52, 57, 59, 79, 110, 112, 126, 172, 177
metonymy 180f., 183
Mexico 229
micropolitics 23, 177
Milky Way 205, 207, 213
miniature
– cosmic miniature 4, 10, 18, 27, 29, 31f., 37, 39–41, 43–50, 52, 56, 60, 68–71, 75–77, 79–82, 84f., 88–90, 92, 94, 109f., 113, 116, 118, 120f., 125–127, 144–148, 161, 165f., 170–173, 178, 183, 197, 200f., 205f., 208, 212, 215, 217f., 235, 239
– German miniature 4, 29, 46, 200–202, 205f., 212, 216, 218, 230–236, 239, 246
– global miniature 4, 29, 49, 52, 90, 167f., 170–176, 178–182, 184–188, 190f., 193–197, 200, 217f., 222, 230, 236
– *kleine Prosa* 44, 47f.
– metropolitan miniature (see also Huyssen) 3, 48, 71, 89–93, 97, 100, 191
– micro-histories 16, 45
– micro-text (digital) 44
– micronarrative 48
– modernist miniature 3, 32, 47f., 71, 89–92, 99, 101, 143
mit Haut und Haaren 132, 136
modernism 31, 47, 53, 89, 100, 103, 118, 207
monads 41f., 129, 201
montage 1, 3, 15, 30–32, 43, 57, 77, 81–85, 87, 126, 149f., 156, 164, 179, 187, 194, 205, 211, 221
moon 5, 10, 14f., 45, 205–208, 213
moral law 16f., 19, 21, 198f.
murder 104, 218, 224, 232, 236

Nachricht (see also news, see also intelligence) 1–5, 174, 194, 225
narration, narrative, narratology
– anecdotal narration (see also Fleming) 70
– biographical narration 199, 218, 220, 222, 224, 245
– counter-histories 30, 37, 65, 77, 81, 84, 149f., 164, 198
– experimental literature 104, 168, 181, 193
– factual narration 159
– first-person narration 101–103, 119, 234, 240f., 244
– future fictions (see also Koschorke) 26, 144
– future narratives (see also Bode and Dietrich) 26f., 65f., 145f.
– heliotropic narrative 70, 88, 91, 95, 108, 146, 230
– Holocaust stories 3, 29, 232f., 239, 245f.
– incommensurate narration 118
– linear narration 32, 53, 200, 206, 208, 210, 235
– micronarrative 48
– non-linearity, non-linear narration 22, 36, 49, 69, 81, 173, 185f.
– progression 97, 115f.
– red-thread narration 221, 235
– second-person narration 119
– third-person narration 103f., 106, 115–117, 119–121, 123, 130, 132, 137, 139, 143, 159, 162, 201f., 234, 239f.
– unnatural narrative 29, 104f., 109–125, 130, 168, 173, 194, 204, 215
National Socialism, Nazism, Nazi 1–4, 9, 51, 53, 66, 93, 160f., 176, 201, 210f., 213f., 216, 218f., 222, 224–226, 230f., 233, 236f., 239, 242
New York University 160, 162
news 2–4, 66f., 192
non-identity 23, 35, 72, 87f., 99, 130, 133f., 138, 143
nostalgia 60, 189

obstinacy (see also *Eigensinn*) 3, 23f., 26, 67, 95, 122, 175, 179, 194
– "The Obstinate Child" 24, 26, 113, 194

off-planet, off-worldly   4 f., 8, 22, 29, 69, 73 f., 79, 82, 84, 91 f., 97, 99, 110, 113, 117, 120, 126 f., 134, 147, 163, 166, 168, 171, 174, 176, 184 f., 187, 190, 194, 196, 200, 208, 215–217, 242
ontology   19, 28, 42, 52, 79, 105, 114, 119, 121, 124, 140, 176 f., 181
opera   93, 187, 229
orality   1, 190
orientation   1, 5, 8, 11, 14, 22, 24 f., 29 f., 34, 41 f., 50, 60–63, 69 f., 73, 76, 83, 85, 88, 90, 98, 100, 102, 105, 108, 112, 116, 126, 134, 140, 143, 146, 155, 163, 166, 172, 177, 183 f., 186 f., 189, 191, 194, 196 f., 199 f., 204 f., 213 f., 217, 223, 228–230
oscillation   64, 67, 69, 73, 75 f., 78 f., 91, 100, 111 f., 119 f., 122, 126, 128, 130, 139, 141–143, 145, 183–185, 191, 193, 195 f., 200, 202, 204 f., 208, 223 f., 226, 229, 239 f.

Pangea   169, 173 f., 179
parallel societies   149, 155
parallel universes   149, 153
pedagogy   111–113, 165
Peking University   192, 219, 223, 227, 229
perception   4, 21 f., 25, 29, 35 f., 42, 44, 48 f., 69, 76, 81 f., 86, 89 f., 104, 113 f., 116, 139 f., 147 f., 151, 153, 159, 172, 178, 180, 191, 197, 200, 203, 210, 221, 223, 231, 242, 244
person, persons   1, 29, 83, 100, 102, 104, 109, 117, 120, 133 f., 137, 181, 199 f., 203, 208, 219 f., 226–230, 245
perspective   2–5, 12–16, 20, 25, 28 f., 35, 37, 43, 48, 58, 62, 80, 82 f., 86, 88 f., 100, 102, 104–109, 113, 123, 126 f., 130, 132–134, 137, 139 f., 142 f., 146, 149, 157, 159, 162–164, 166, 171, 176 f., 181, 184, 186 f., 189 f., 195, 197, 199 f., 202 f., 205 f., 208, 210 f., 213, 216–218, 220–227, 230, 235 f., 238–243, 245
philology   160 f.
philosofiction (see also Szendy)   10, 13–16, 125, 128, 143, 145
philosophical anthropology   53 f., 60, 67 f.

philosophy   10 f., 13, 19 f., 36, 39, 42, 46, 54 f., 58 f., 61 f., 67 f., 73, 86 f., 93 f., 97 f., 101, 112, 123 f., 148, 151, 172, 176 f., 179, 181, 209, 213
phoenix   18, 216
planets, planetary   6, 8, 10, 16, 32, 34, 38, 46, 49, 78, 84, 87, 90, 94, 97, 126, 132, 148, 152, 155, 158, 168, 170–173, 197, 200, 205 f., 215
portal (see also door logic)   32, 44, 69, 78, 127, 147, 149, 154, 156 f., 163 f., 170, 210, 213, 218, 239, 245
possibility   1, 12–14, 19, 23, 26 f., 29, 31, 33, 37, 45, 55, 57, 60 f., 64–67, 73, 77–80, 85, 91, 99, 105–107, 109 f., 117, 120–122, 134, 141, 145, 148, 156, 170 f., 174, 178, 184, 198 f., 205, 209, 230, 243
practice   1, 3, 5, 8, 22, 26, 29 f., 41, 47, 49 f., 68, 81–83, 85, 103, 124, 147 f., 169, 171, 173, 175, 177, 179 f., 190, 195, 197, 202, 221, 228
presentism   170
print literature   44, 71, 82 f.
prizes   1, 4, 7, 9, 86, 150, 189
progress   6, 20, 22, 45 f., 52 f., 63, 66 f., 70, 107, 150, 179, 181 f., 196, 209 f., 236
pronouns   102, 187, 202, 207, 212–214, 234, 240
– pronominal deixis   187
public sphere   83, 153, 166 f.
– bourgeois public sphere   166 f.
– global public spheres   231
– proletarian public sphere   166, 184
punctuation   214

quantum physics   6, 38, 149, 153 f., 159, 168
queer theory   63

Radio Leipzig   213 f., 216
realism   3, 22, 31, 53, 76, 80, 110, 120, 140 f., 150, 207
– anti-realist realism   27, 80, 140 f., 159, 171–173, 198, 208
– doubling of reality   87, 181, 189 f., 194, 228, 237
red thread   220–222, 228 f., 235

redemption   20, 22, 34, 37, 58, 73, 79, 101, 108, 123, 143, 150, 154 f., 199, 239
reification   59, 68 f., 72, 79, 112, 117, 133, 141
relationality (see also *Zusammenhang*)   23, 41, 71, 73, 80, 83, 85, 142, 166, 185, 190, 221
revolution   15, 48, 55, 72, 114, 153, 168, 172 f., 175 f., 178–182, 185 f., 191, 200, 218, 220, 222, 227 f., 244
– permanent revolution   75, 166–179, 181, 195, 222, 244

Saturn   56, 126
scale   3, 71, 81, 97, 149, 153, 159 f., 164, 167, 172 f., 187, 194, 209, 232
science fiction   5, 8, 14 f., 59, 147–152, 163, 237 f.
sensation, sense perception   4, 20 f., 25, 69, 81, 114, 151
– long-distance senses   4, 22, 40 f., 57, 69, 86, 151, 197, 200, 231
– short-distance senses   40
September 11 (see also 9/11)   86 f.
sequentiality   92, 113, 185, 188, 228
sex   96, 128 f., 132–135
Shanghai   91, 191–193, 230
simultaneity   16, 29, 32, 124, 126, 135 f., 138, 154, 163, 166, 180, 189, 196, 203, 214, 218, 226, 228, 230
Skype   180, 192, 228
sleep, sleeplessness   60, 142, 194
social fiction   5, 22, 26, 65, 69, 144 f., 150, 163, 173
something missing, lack   5, 35, 37, 41, 43, 50–74, 82 f., 85 f., 89, 98, 112, 164, 173, 193, 213, 233, 242
Soviet Union   33, 82, 93, 158, 176, 178, 188, 236
space   3, 8 f., 12, 15 f., 18, 27, 41, 46–48, 53, 71, 76, 79, 83, 90, 99, 109, 120, 126, 130, 140 f., 143, 146, 151, 153, 169–171, 176, 182 f., 191, 193, 202
– outer space   8, 11 f., 32, 34, 46, 48, 95, 158, 174
Stalingrad   2–4, 9, 44, 53

standpoint   13, 20, 73, 79, 88 f., 101, 123, 163, 199, 201
stars, starry heavens, starry sky   8–11, 16 f., 19–21, 30, 32, 34 f., 40, 46, 49 f., 56, 70, 100, 152, 169, 172, 180, 198, 200 f., 203–205, 207–210, 212–216
– sidereal motifs   34 f., 56, 98, 174
– sidereal relations   35, 43
sun, suns   10, 13, 30, 32, 34, 36 f., 39 f., 50, 98, 126, 160, 175, 177, 183 f., 205 f., 212–216, 230
supplement (see also *Zusatz*)   4, 133, 135–143, 158, 178, 184, 194
survival   4 f., 16, 20–22, 33, 39, 43, 45, 49, 53, 56, 78, 86 f., 94, 141, 154, 163 f., 187, 218, 231
syntax   181, 190
Syria   186, 204

taboo   51, 242
The Promise (see also Chen Kaige)   193 f.
thin characters   188
Third Reich   2, 44, 66, 100, 141, 198, 213, 216, 231, 235, 237, 243
Tiananmen Square   175, 192, 221, 228, 242
time, temporality   1, 3–6, 8 f., 16, 18, 20–22, 24–34, 37–42, 44 f., 47–52, 57 f., 62 f., 65, 67, 69–72, 76, 78 f., 81, 86 f., 90 f., 94, 96, 99–101, 105 f., 108 f., 112 f., 125 f., 130, 133–140, 145–151, 153–162, 164–167, 169–171, 173, 175–178, 181–183, 185 f., 189–191, 193 f., 197, 199–207, 209–218, 221, 227–230, 239, 241–243, 245
– clockwork universe   213
– differential temporalities   7, 9, 22, 33, 57, 60, 62, 66, 78, 84 f., 108, 119, 135, 143, 164, 234, 239, 245
– grammar of time   9, 189
– need for time   242
– Newtonian time   217
– temporal conversion   27, 45, 239
– temporal core (see also *Zeitkern*)   57, 68, 91, 134, 142, 174
– temporal imperialism (see also Pavsek)   9, 33

– temporal perception 4, 22, 29, 148, 178, 197, 200, 210, 223, 231, 242
– time-space compression (see also Harvey) 169, 176, 182, 193
– time travel 8f., 27, 148–151, 154, 164f., 179, 204, 213f., 240
– *Zeit-Zeugen* 231–246
totality 3, 47, 60, 69–74, 88, 148f., 178
transcendental homelessness (see also Lukács) 8, 34, 173
translation 2, 5–8, 11f., 16f., 23–25, 34, 36f., 41, 50–53, 56f., 61, 71, 73, 75, 80, 85, 88f., 91, 93–95, 97, 100, 102f., 105f., 111f., 131, 136, 141f., 158, 167, 175, 185, 191, 195, 199, 226f.
trial 231
tunneling 154, 162–164

unification, German (see also 1989) 33, 175
United States, USA 1, 91, 160, 168, 178, 191, 200, 230
University of Oxford 240
utopia 28, 32f., 41, 50–52, 56–60, 62f., 68, 72, 87, 90, 93, 99, 107, 125–144, 148, 175, 184, 197, 219, 222
– anti-utopian utopianism (see also Lukes) 59
– concrete utopia (see also Bloch) 42, 59f., 68
– temporalization of utopia (see also Koselleck) 22, 41, 52, 61–63, 126
– utopian dimension 5, 58, 61, 63, 70, 76, 79, 86, 96, 99, 101, 106, 108, 127, 143, 146, 166, 173, 184, 186f., 194, 199f., 212, 216f., 239, 244f.
– utopian impulse (see also Bloch) 59, 147
– utopian longing 63, 86–95, 99, 117, 126, 133f.
– utopian socialism 59, 182
– utopian tradition 28, 52, 62f., 90, 143
– utopianism 57, 59f., 62, 83, 149f.

value 6, 27, 81, 84, 94, 111, 114, 116, 124, 129, 135–137, 146, 196, 198, 209, 238
Vergangenheitsbewältigung 4, 200, 210, 212, 235

vision, optics 2, 13–16, 48, 58, 62, 73, 121, 150, 163, 174
voice 5f., 10, 21, 25, 28f., 39, 41f., 44, 102–110, 112f., 116–128, 130–135, 137–144, 156–160, 162–164, 166, 183f., 187f., 192f., 195f., 200–204, 208, 210–218, 220–226, 229f., 233f., 236f., 239–241, 243–245
– co-operative voice 231–246
– collective voice 200f., 214, 234–236, 243
– first-person voice 101f., 105, 134, 157, 240f., 243f.
– heliotropic voice 230
– loss of voice 187f.
– unnatural voice 103–106, 109, 118, 120, 123, 130, 133, 139, 183, 205, 211, 215

war 2–5, 9, 11f., 20, 30, 74, 79, 93f., 122, 152, 162, 174, 178, 198, 217, 230, 237, 242f.
– cold war 7, 11, 54, 152f., 162, 173, 175, 188
– Iraq war 153, 168, 173
– star wars 9, 11
– World War I 8, 47, 97, 185, 223, 226, 239
– World War II 1–3, 11, 45, 53, 150, 162, 198, 223
way out, ways out (see also *Ausweg*) 7, 52, 70–76, 78–87, 99, 111, 127, 141, 185, 190, 197, 214, 219, 231f.
weather 18, 185
White House, Oval Office 5, 7–10, 16f., 22, 155–157, 235
witness 2, 24, 60, 172, 201, 234, 236–243
– cowitnessing (see also Kacandes) 238
– eyewitness 236f., 242
– secondary witness (see also Assmann) 238
writing on the wall 75, 116, 196

YouTube 60

Zeitkern (see also temporal core) 57, 68
Zusammenhang (see also relationality) 71, 73–75, 83–85, 116, 166, 185, 221
Zusatz (see also supplement) 135f., 158, 194

www.ingramcontent.com/pod-product-compliance
Lightning Source LLC
Chambersburg PA
CBHW031723230426
43669CB00007B/223